Charles Henry Pope

**A History of the Dorchester Pope Family, 1634-1888**

With Sketches of Other Popes in England and America

Charles Henry Pope

**A History of the Dorchester Pope Family, 1634-1888**
*With Sketches of Other Popes in England and America*

ISBN/EAN: 9783337064129

Printed in Europe, USA, Canada, Australia, Japan

Cover: Foto ©ninafisch / pixelio.de

More available books at **www.hansebooks.com**

# A HISTORY

OF THE

# Dorchester Pope Family.

## 1634-1888.

WITH SKETCHES OF OTHER POPES IN ENGLAND AND AMERICA,
AND NOTES UPON SEVERAL INTERMARRYING FAMILIES.

---

CHARLES HENRY POPE,
MEMBER N. E. HISTORIC GENEALOGICAL SOCIETY.

---

BOSTON, MASS.:
PUBLISHED BY THE AUTHOR, AT 70 FRANKLIN ST.
1888.

PRESS OF L. BARTA & CO., BOSTON.

# PREFACE.

It was predicted of the Great Philanthropist, "He shall turn the hearts of the fathers to the children, and the hearts of children to their fathers." The writer seeks to contribute something toward the development of such mutual affection between the members of the Pope Family. He has found his own heart tenderly drawn toward all whose names he has registered and whose biographies he has attempted to write. The dead are his own, whose graves he has sought to strew with the tributes of love ; the living are his own, every one of whose careers he now watches with strong interest.

He has given a large part of his recreation hours and vacation time for eight years to the gathering of materials for the work ; written hundreds of letters ; examined a great many deeds and wills, town journals, church registers, and family records ; visited numerous persons and places, and pored over a large number of histories of towns and families ; and has gathered here the items and entries thus discovered. He has traced out each branch of the family as far and as completely as possible, endeavoring to be impartial in the chronicles of each, counting every member of the family worthy of honor.

He has made a journey to England during the past summer, and brought home an extensive array of facts concerning the Pope Family, from the time of the Crusades down to the settlement of New England ; the chapter containing these records being the first connected account of the Pope Family throughout England ever compiled. Articles in the Appendix, upon the individuals of our name who were enrolled among the first settlers of America, will be found valuable, not only to persons who are of our Dorchester line, but to those descended from Joseph of Salem, Thomas of Plymouth, Thomas of Elizabeth, N. J., George of South Carolina, and Thomas of Virginia.

In the Appendix there are also notes upon several pioneers of other names,— settlers in Dorchester, Braintree, etc.,— the ancestors of some of those who have blended their stock with our own.

iii

In 1862, " The Genealogy of a Portion of the Pope Family" was published, being an autobiography of Col. William Pope, of Boston, an honored member of our family (see p. 200), and a sketch of " His Ancestors and Descendants." Although we have gone back to original sources, instead of quoting from that volume (except with reference to its author and a part of his family), yet we desire to pay a tribute of gratitude to Col. Pope for his creditable pioneering in the field in which we have the honor to follow.

This work aims to furnish a complete genealogy of the Dorchester Popes, and such particulars of the Plymouth and Salem groups as will make this a good "Pope Book" for them, until some more extended genealogies of their branches may be composed.

With deep consciousness of the imperfectness of his work, he commits it to the patient, forbearing consideration of the kindred.

Thanks are hereby extended to all who have answered our letters of inquiry, giving names, dates, and other particulars ; to the N. E. Historic-Genealogical Society, for access to its books and manuscripts ; to the registrars of deeds and wills in Suffolk, Middlesex, Essex, Norfolk, Bristol and Worcester Counties, Mass., and York County, Maine ; to the clerks in the manuscript room, at the Massachusetts State House ; to the clerks of many towns and cities ; to the authors of numerous town and family histories ; to the officials at the Probate office in Exeter, England, and the librarian of the Albert Museum there ; to Mr. W. H. K. Wright, editor "Western Antiquary," Plymouth, Eng., and Mr. R. N. Worth, F. R. S., historian of that city ; to Mr. Edward Windeatte, of Tottness ; to the officials of the British Museum and Somerset House, London ; to Mr. Henry George, Bristol ; to Alfred Pope, Esq., the mayor of Dorchester ; to Rev. C. S. Taylor, St. Thomas, Bristol ; to Mr. Franklin Leonard Pope, of New York, and Dr. Henry Wheatland, president of the Essex Institute, Salem, whose valuable articles appear in our Appendix ; and to numerous other persons. And deep sense of indebtedness is felt toward many faithful recorders and annalists of the past.

But especially ought this page to record the great aid received from two individuals, viz. : Mr. William Blake Trask, of Dorchester, who has brought the treasures of his experience in genealogical research to aid our gropings and correct our blunders in many instances ; and Col. Albert A. Pope, of Boston, who generously furnished the means for our English researches, advanced funds for publication, and permits us to date and distribute the book from his place of business.

# CONTENTS.

v

# APPENDIX.

# EXPLANATORY.

## THE FRONTISPIECE

### IS A HISTORICAL PICTURE OF GREAT IMPORTANCE.

It represents the " New Hospital in Plymouth," England, where Captain Roger Clap says he and his associates of the Dorchester church colony " kept a solemn Day of Fasting, spending it in Preaching and Praying; where that worthy Man of God, Mr. John White of Dorchester in Dorset was present, and Preached unto us the Word of God, in the fore part of the Day; and in the latter part of the Day, as the People did solemnly make Choice of and call those godly Ministers the Revd. Mr. John Warham and Mr. John Maverick to be their Officers, so also they did accept thereof, and expressed the same."

This took place *before* March 20, 1629, on which the company set sail in " The Mary and John." It was the real organization of the body which, six weeks later, begun the first permanent settlement on Boston bay.

This cut has been made for this volume from a photograph taken some years ago for Mr. R. N. Worth's "History of Plymouth" (now out of print). The building was taken down in 1859. It was just about completed, but not occupied when the " Mary and John " passengers assembled in it. Two months later it was formally accepted by the town authorities. It was " The Hospital of Poor's Portion," i. e., a work-house. The shadow of St. Andrew's steeple fell upon it, but God's smile shone on the enterprise there inaugurated, fulfilling the pious motto chiselled over the main doorway of the building, " By God's helpe, through Christ."

In the Pedigree Table, page 8, each *Pope father* is named, and his lineage and relationship shown, the attached figure marking his generation. The story of himself and his family — so far as it has been made known to us — is given in the chapter devoted to that generation, which may be found by reference to the Table of Contents, pages 3 and 4, where also the names of sons-in-law are noted. All the genealogies are arranged according to the order of descent, so that by observing the sections and letters, every case may be located, and its connections traced.

The Indexes should also be consulted in the study of each individual.

Notice Table of Errata, page 339.

# HEADS OF FAMILIES FOR EIGHT GENERATIONS.

Those in italics left no sons who perpetuated the name.

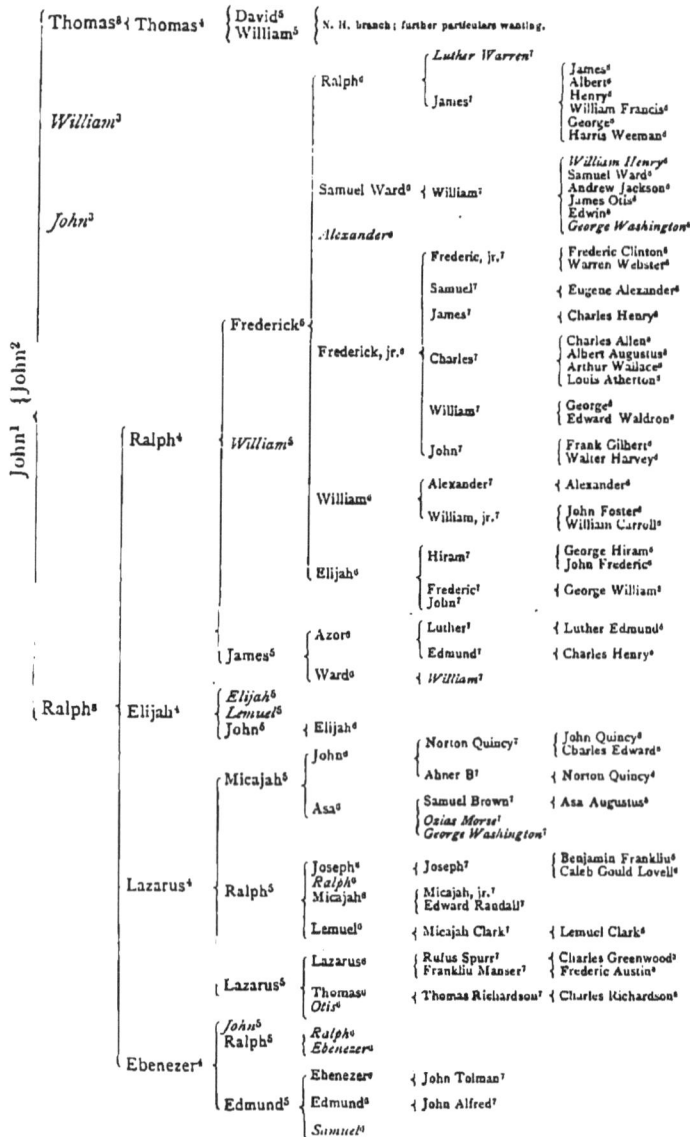

Thomas[8] { Thomas[4] { David[5] } { N. H. branch; further particulars wanting.
William[5]

*William*[3]

*John*[3]

John[1] { John[2]

Ralph[4]

{ Ralph[8] } Elijah[4]

*William*[5]

Luther Warren[7]

Ralph[6] {
Luther Warren[7]
James[7]
}

James[4]
Albert[8]
Henry[4]
William Francis[8]
George[8]
Harris Weeman[8]

Samuel Ward[6] { William[7]

*William Henry*[8]
Samuel Ward[8]
Andrew Jackson[8]
James Otis[8]
Edwin[8]
George Washington[8]

*Alexander*[6]

Frederick[6] {

Frederic, jr.[7] {
Frederic Clinton[8]
Warren Webster[8]
}

Samuel[7] {
Eugene Alexander[8]
}

James[7] { Charles Henry[8]

Frederick, jr.[6] {

Charles[7] {
Charles Allen[8]
Albert Augustus[8]
Arthur Wallace[8]
Louis Atherton[8]
}

William[7] {
George[8]
Edward Waldron[8]
}

John[7] {
Frank Gilbert[8]
Walter Harvey[8]
}

William[6] {

Alexander[7] { Alexander[8]

William, jr.[7] {
John Foster[8]
William Carroll[8]
}

Elijah[6] {

Hiram[7] {
George Hiram[8]
John Frederic[8]
}

Frederic[7] { George William[8]
John[7]

James[5] {

Azor[6] {
Luther[7] { Luther Edmund[8]
Edmund[7] { Charles Henry[8]
}

Ward[6] { *William*[7]

*Elijah*[5]
*Lemuel*[5]
*John*[5]

Micajah[5] {

Elijah[6] {

John[6] {
Norton Quincy[7] {
John Quincy[8]
Charles Edward[8]
}

Abner B[7] { Norton Quincy[8]
}

Asa[6] {
Samuel Brown[7] { Asa Augustus[8]
*Osias Morse*[7]
*George Washington*[7]
}

Lazarus[4]

Ralph[5] {

Joseph[6] {
Joseph[7] {
Benjamin Franklin[8]
Caleb Gould Lovell[8]
}
*Ralph*[6]
Micajah[6] {
Micajah, jr.[7]
Edward Randall[7]
}

Lemuel[6] { Micajah Clark[7] { Lemuel Clark[8]

Lazarus[5] {

Lazarus[6] {
Rufus Spurr[7] {
Charles Greenwood[8]
Frederic Austin[8]
}
*Franklin Manser*[7]
}

Thomas[6]
*Otis*[6]
{ Thomas Richardson[7] { Charles Richardson[8]

*Ebenezer*[4]

*John*[5]
Ralph[5]
{
*Ralph*[6]
*Ebenezer*[6]
}

Edmund[5] {

Ebenezer[6] { John Tolman[7]
Edmund[6] { John Alfred[7]
*Samuel*[6]
}

# CHAPTER I.

## CONCERNING THE TOWN.

Dorchester is now a district in the southern part of Boston, Mass., but was originally settled as a separate "plantation," and maintained its town existence 240 years. It seems fitting that a short sketch of its history be prefixed to this story of one of its oldest families, identified with its best life from colonial days until now.

The settlement at Dorchester was the third on Massachusetts soil, leaving out of view temporary and individual locations. The "Mayflower" pilgrims, in 1620, at Plymouth, were the foremost; the Cape Ann and Salem settlers were second, 1624–1629; and the Mattapan or Dorchester colony, in the spring of 1630, came next. The Tremont or Boston colony did not arrive until a month later.

Two motives led these English people to the founding of a new country. One was the *adventurous spirit* of their race, which had moved westward from the Asiatic cradle of humanity, centuries before the Christian era ; then swept onward from the shores of the Baltic and the North Sea in the Danish and Anglo-Saxon expeditions of the fourth to the eleventh centuries of our era ; then pushed still further in transatlantic explorations and fishing voyages, through the fifteenth and sixteenth centuries. The spirit of the West of England had been rising with its Cabots, Drakes, and Raleighs ; and the "Merchant Adventurers" of Bristol, the "Plymouth" (England) "Council," and the "Dorchester" (England) "Company" were organized expressions of this adventurous spirit.

9

The commencement in Virginia had been somewhat encouraging. Fishing-vessels were coming to the Bay of Maine and the Gulf of St. Lawrence every year by hundreds; and the New Plymouth colony was doing fairly well; Pemaquid and Popham in Maine were advancing. The rival nations, Spain and France, had been still more prosperous in their New World ventures. No wonder that we find that

"1623, Dec. 8, the king" [James I.] "addressed a note to the Lords Lieutenant of Cornwall, Somerset, and Devon, and to the cities of Bristol and Exeter, urging them to persuade persons of quality to adventure their private estates and fortunes for planting a colony in New England," because he believed it would prove advantageous to England. [State Papers.]

But the second and deeper motive, impelling the persons who came over here to live, was

"*That they might worship God according to the light of their own consciences.*"

Persecuted and hindered from the study and practice of simple Bible religion by the mistaken zeal of the rulers of the established Church of England, they sought religious liberty; and they believed that the country they should found would be a means of helping forward the cause of God and humanity. Of this motive Rev. John White of Dorchester, England [see Appendix], was the most efficient expounder, a man who has been well called the "Father of New England"; and the church colony, which came to Dorchester, *New* England, was the finest embodiment, — excepting only the Plymouth Pilgrims.

Let us read what was written by one of the ancestors of the Pierce-Pope branch of our family, the historian, James Blake (born 1688, died 1750), in "*The Annals of Dorchester.*"

"When many most Godly and Religious People that Dissented from the way of Worship then Established by Law in the Realm of England, in the Reign of King Charles the first, being denied the free exercise of Religion after the manner they professed, according to the light of God's word and their own consciences, did under the Incouragement of a Charter, Granted by the said King Charles, in the Fourth Year of his Reign, A. D. 1628, Remove themselves and their families into the colony of Massachusetts Bay in New England, that they might Worship God according to the light of their own Conscience, without any burthensome Impositions, which was the very motive and cause of their coming;

Then it was that the First Inhabitants of Dorchester came over, and were the first Company or Church Society that arrived here, next to the Town of Salem who was one year before them.

In the year of our Lord 1629, Divers Godly Persons in Devonshire, Somersetshire, Dorcetshire and other places, proposed a Remove to New England, among whom were two Famous Ministers, viz., Mr. John Maverick* (who, I suppose, was somewhat advanced in Age) and Mr. John Warham† (I suppose a Younger Man), then a preacher in the city of Exon or Exeter, in the county of Devon.

These good People met together at Plymouth, a Sea-port Town in the county of Devon, in order to ship themselves and Families for New England, and because they designed to live together after they should arrive here, they met together in the New Hospital in Plymouth [see frontispiece] and Associated into Church Fellowship and Chose the said Mr. Maverick and Mr. Warham to be their Ministers and Officers, keeping the Day as a Day of Solemn Fasting and Prayer, and the said Ministers accepted of the Call and Expressed the same ; the Revd. Mr. John White, of Dorchester in Dorcet, (who was an active Instrument to promote the Settlement of New England and, I think, a means of procuring the Charter) being present and Preaching the fore part of the Day, and in the latter part of the Day they performed the work aforesaid.

This people being too many in number to come in one Vessel, they hired one Captain Squeb to bring them in a large ship of 400 Tons ; they set Sail from Plymouth the 20th of March, 1629–30,‡ and arrived at Nantasket (now Hull) the 30th of May, 1630, having a Comfortable tho' long Passage, and having Preaching or Expounding of the Scriptures every Day of their Passage, performed by their ministers.

---

* The registers of the Bishop of Exeter give us evidence of the "apostolical succession" of these two pastors of the Dorchester Church. "Jobannes Maverick, literatus," John Maverick, an educated person (not a University graduate), was ordained deacon and presbyter by the Bishop at Exeter, July 26, 1597.

† John Warham, in artibus mags," i. e., John Warham, master of arts, was ordained by the Bishop at Silterton, May 23, 1019. Silierton is near Cullompton ; and we may naturally connect the following. Marriage license granted John Warham, of Witheridg, gen., and Cecilia Hacca, of Cullompton, gen., June 17, 1619.

‡ There is no list of these passengers extant. Only a few persons are *certainly known* to have been of the number, though a large number have been *guessed* to be.

They found out a neck of Land Joyning to a place called by the Indians Mattapan (now Dorchester) that was a fit place to turn their Cattle upon to prevent their straying.

They began their Settlement here at Mattapan the beginning of June, I suppose, or thereabouts, A. D., 1630, and changed the name into Dorchester, calling it Dorchester Plantation.

Why they called it Dorchester I never heard, but there was some of Dorcet Shire and some of the Town of Dorchester that settled here ; and it is very likely it might be in honour of the aforesaid Rev. Mr. White of Dorchester.*

Our People were Settled here a Month or two before Governor Winthrop and the Ships that came with him arrived at Charlestown, so Dorchester Plantation was settled next to the town of Salem in the Massachusetts Colony, being before Charlestown or Boston.

And the Church of Dorchester the oldest in the Colony Except Salem ; and I suppose the only Church that came over in Church Fellowship, the other churches being gathered here. . . .

These first Settlers took up every one his spot to set down upon, pretty thick together at the northerly end of the Town next to the aforesaid neck of Land and on the Easterly side next to the Sea."†

Early in July, 1630, the ship "Lyon," Captain Pierce, was chartered by Governor Winthrop to return to the mother country for provisions. She arrived on her return "from Bristol," England, Feb. 8, 1631, says the "History of Dorchester," bringing some new colonists to Dorchester. A larger accession came a year and a half later, according to Winthrop.

"July 24, 1633. A ship arrived from Weymouth with about 80 passengers and 12 kine, who sate down at Dorchester. They were 12 weeks coming, being forced into the Western Islands by a leak, where they stayed 3 weeks and were very courteously used by the Portugals ; but the extremity of the heat there, and the continual rain, brought sickness upon them. So as — died."

---

* Sept. 7, 1630, the "Court of Assistants," the real government of Massachusetts Colony, passed this now famous order : "Trimountaine shalbe called Boston ; Mattapan, Dorchester ; and the town upon Charles Ryver, Watertown." It would thus appear that the central board of management of the company, whose seat of deliberations had been the English City of Dorchester, bestowed that name on this plantation, the settlers, no doubt, favoring the course.

† The region of this earliest settlement is roughly stated as lying between Dudley Street Railway Station and the Old Burying Ground at Upham's Corner, and eastward of that section. The " Five Corners " is an ancient land-mark. Willow Court, running west from Boston Street, is pretty well established by tradition and calculation, as the spot where Roger and Edward Clapp and John Pope first lived.

Neither the name of this ship, nor any list of her passengers, has come to light. We shall see, below, presumptive evidence that Aquila Purchase and Bernard Capen were among them. There is, in the British Museum, a manuscript diary which Mr. James Phinney Baxter, of Portland, Maine, had copied, and has kindly permitted us to examine and make extracts from.

The author is William Whiteway, of Dorchester, England, and the entries date from November, 1618, to April, 1634. The following passages will help one to realize the "making of New England," and bring our ancestors vividly before our minds : —

" 1624, March 31st met the committee chosen for the New England busyness at the free school.

| | |
|---|---|
| S<sup>r</sup> Walter Erle, | Govno<sup>r.</sup> |
| M<sup>r.</sup> Humphreys Esq. | Tres<sup>r.</sup> |
| S<sup>r</sup> Richard Strode. | M<sup>r.</sup> John Hill. |
| S<sup>r</sup> Arthur Smithyes. | M<sup>r.</sup> Wm. Derby. |
| M<sup>r.</sup> John Browne. | M<sup>r.</sup> James Gould. |
| Doctor Bradish. | W<sup>m</sup> Whiteway, jun<sup>r.</sup> |
| M<sup>r.</sup> John Keate. | M<sup>r.</sup> Henry Maniford. |
| M<sup>r.</sup> Giles Greene. | * * * |
| M<sup>r.</sup> Edw Clarke. | * * * |

" Aprill, 1630. The beginning of this moneth, many of the towne went to plant in New England, and among the rest Mr. Sandford.

" Feb. 26, 1632. This day Christopher Gould married with Rachell Beake & shortly after when Aquila Purcess,* Bernard Capes† & others went for New England, he was by Mr. White chosen clarke of Trinity parish & by the towne made schoolmaister of Trinity school.

" February 1633. This moneth Sr Richard Sutton started with John Humphrey & others of the chiefest of the New England Planters were sent for to the consell tabell and were required 1 to take the oath. 2 the oath of supremacy. 3 to suscribe to the discipline of the Church of England. The two oaths they took but refused to subject unto our discipline, saying they went unto New England principally to

---

* " Purcess " is doubtless **Purchase.** " The Widow Purchase " is mentioned in Dorches-ter Records, Aug. 5, 1633 ; " Oliver Purchase," later, apparently her son. This " Aquila " is likely to have been the " widow's " husband, and companion on the voyage.

† " Capes," combined with " Bernard," points pretty certainly to Bernard Capen, ancestor of all the Dorchester Capens. Capin, Gapin, and Gapen, are ancient styles of the spelling of the name. " Shortly after " Feb. 20 is the date when the Weymouth ship mentioned above sailed for Dorchester, and it seems altogether probable that this company were of her pas-sengers.

decline that. Whereupon after some consultation they were dismissed.

"Mr. Pope of Mannton died 12 Feb 1634.*

"April 17, 1634, Mr. Newburgh of Marthwoodvale and many others set saile from Waimouth towards New England & the 27th of the same Mr. John Humfreys with his wife, the lady Susan Fries, set saile likewise for the same place. This somer there went over to that plantation at the least 20 saile of ships and in them 2000 planters."

These jottings of Mr. Whiteway appear to be worthy of confidence, though some statements, like the concluding one, must be regarded not as historical records, but as the current talk of the day.

Wood, in his "New England Prospect," said, in 1631 : —

"Dorchester is the greatest towne in New England; well wooded and watered ; very good arable grounds and Hay ground, faire Cornefields and pleasant Gardens. In this Plantation is a great many Cattle, as Kine, Goats and Swine. This Plantation hath a reasonable Harbour for ships."

Capt. John Jocelyn, who visited the New England settlements in 1670, states that there were *then* "two hundred and more houses " in the town, and speaks of it in a complimentary style.

The General Court assessed taxes upon the towns of Massachusetts Colony, October, 1633, rating Dorchester at £80, while Boston, Roxbury, Newton, and Watertown were taxed but £48 apiece, and Salem only £28. This shows the relative rank of Dorchester in those days.

We may properly make another extract from "Blake's Annals " : —

"1635. This year arrived here on Aug. 16th, the Revd. Mr. Richard Mather that was a long time after Pastor of this Church, and with him a great Number of Godly people that Settled here with him. There came with him 100 Passengers & 23 Seamen, 23 Cows & Heifers, 3 Sucking Calves, & 8 Mares, & none Died by the way, though they met with as terrible a Storm as was almost ever heard of."

---

* Perhaps this record may pertain to George Pope, Esq., of Manston, whose epitaph in the church there states that he died Feb. 11, 1633.

About the time of the coming of these Lancashire immi-
grants, many of the original Dorchester settlers joined in a new
settlement at Windsor, Conn. In fact, they went a second time
as a church-colony, taking along one of the pastors, both of the
deacons, and the clerk, Matthew Grant (ancestor of General
and President U. S. Grant).

Yet so many of the "first-comers" remained in Dorchester,
and continued religious and civil life on the original location,
that the town and church never lost their right to date from the
organization in the New Hospital at Plymouth, in March, 1630,
and the inauguration of work and worship in Mattapan, in June
following.

Dorchester the first *town* in the American sense.

Here is one of the acts in which we may presume our
ancestor had a part.

"An agreement made by the whole consent and vote of the Plantation, Mooneday, 8th of October, 1633.

*Imprimus* it is ordered that for the generall good and well-ordering
of the affayres of the Plantation their shall be every Mooneday before the Court by eight of the clocke in the morning, and presently
upon the beating of the drum, a generall meeting of the inhabitants
of the Plantation att the meeteing house, there to settle (and sett
down) such orders as may tend to the generall good as aforesaid ; and
every man to be bound thereby without gaynesaying or resistance." *

Four months later Charlestown organized in a similar way,
and others followed.

Our Dorchester pioneers are also celebrated for devising and
establishing the Town School System, since the first vote on
record, laying a direct tax on the property of the people of a

---

* Our pilgrims, in this action, reproduced ideas of their mother-town in England. "1414.
At a Law Court held at Dorchester before Thomas Wyke and William Forde, bailiffs of the
same, twenty-four good and lawful men of the aforesaid borough did say and ordain " various
matters relating to the public good; and some twenty years before the migration, the merchants and tradesmen were enrolled into a company entitled " The Governor, Assistants and
Freemen of the Borough of Dorchester." Thus our ancestors did not originate the idea of
"town-meeting government," but the " Dorchester Company," which received the Massachusetts Bay grant of land and became its "General Court," incorporated ideas in vogue at
their home ; and the citizens of the namesake made early application of the same principles
in a fashion which was the prophecy of our democratic government.

town for the support of a school free to all its children, was passed by the Dorchester town-meeting, May 20, 1639. It set apart the revenues arising from Thompson's Island (a portion of the territory of the town), for school purposes.

Two years later the inhabitants, jointly and severally, presented the Island to the town as such, the better to secure this object. And the deed or "Petition" wherein this was done is recorded on the town book, with its priceless autographs. Our John Pope, Senior, is one of the signers, his trembling hand only allowing him to make the initial P, while some friend wrote the name; but he had before signed his name in full to the church covenant, as we are glad to find.

The old town extended from "Dorchester Point" (now called South Boston Point) to within 160 rods of the line of Rhode Island; about 35 miles "as the road goeth." It was subdivided from time to time, setting off Milton in 1662; part of Wrentham, 1724; Stoughton, 1726; Sharon, 1765; Foxborough, 1778; Canton, 1779. A strip was also set off to Dedham in 1739, one to Boston in 1804, and another in 1855. Quincy, the northernmost of the towns which grew up in the territory of ancient Braintree, received a strip in 1820 and another in 1855; so that all of old Squantum now falls within her lines. In 1870, after 240 years independent existence, Dorchester united with and was merged into Boston, being ward 24 of the city.

It is still a post-office and a "place," and should never cease to be definitely and particularly recognized, honored and loved.

While its settlers were Puritans in doctrine and character, they were notably free from harshness or bigotry. They burned no witches, harried no Quakers, antagonized nobody; but stood by their faith and did their duty. "With malice toward none, with charity toward all."

For at least two hundred and twenty years a farm on the Squantum peninsula remained in the possession of one branch of our family.

From a very early date our name has rested on one of its fair knobs, "*Pope's Hill*," at whose base the Old Colony Railroad has now a station of that name. It was in the great lot originally laid out to Christopher Gibson, but conveyed by him to

John Pope in an "exchange of land," in 1642, as we shall see more fully in a later chapter.

In a deed of Joseph Leeds to his son Samuel, in 1714, the locality is stated to be "commonly called Pope's Hill," although the land had passed out of the ownership of persons of the name half a century before.

On account of our direct ancestor, then, and of those other pioneers to whom we are related through maternal lines, we all have a right to feel great interest and some family pride in the history of the "good old town of Dorchester."

## CHAPTER II.

## CONCERNING ENGLISH POPES.

WE trace our ancestry back to England, although our "pilgrim-father" left us no scrap of writing to show whence he came, because (1) the colony, of which he was an early and honored member, was clearly English ; because (2) his connections with church and state, the trade he followed, the articles mentioned in the inventory of his estate, and many other circumstances *incidentally prove* that he was a Briton ; and because (3) his own name and those of his family are so often found in English records.

As we have not yet been able to fix with certainty on the very spot which gave him birth, it is proper for us to consider the history of all the families bearing our name throughout England, before and in his day. This chapter contains an abstract of all that we have found upon the subject ; and it is here presented as a nucleus for a history of the Pope Family or Families in England.

No such work has heretofore been printed—or attempted, so far as can be learned. English genealogists, in general, have sought to trace the pedigree of celebrated or ambitious individuals, and have purposely omitted to follow out the untitled or inconspicuous members of a family. The so-called "Visitations" of the several counties are all thus limited, defective ; for the persons who make them copy out items concerning those they suppose to belong to the "upper families," and coolly pass by other records which relate to persons of whose standing they happen to be ignorant, or whom they believe to belong to

the poor or working classes.  Thus *flagrant omissions* charac-
terize all such books.

Our American theory of genealogy is broad, comprehensive,
regarding every brother as a BROTHER, and follows St.
Paul's charge, "Mind not high things, but condescend to men
of low estate.  Be of the same mind one toward another."

In England and in America the children of rich and noble
families have often been reduced to poverty, and compelled to
get a living by menial servitude, while the children of obscure
parents have often gained wealth and rank.  Genuine family
affection clasps every relative's hand.

## THE ORIGIN OF OUR NAME.

The word appears at first sight to be the same as the title of
the head of the Church of Rome, and many writers have stated
that it was originally given as a nickname, referring to "the
Pope."  This title, *pope*, is the French *pape*, the German *papst*,
the Latin *papa*, the Greek *pappas* (vocative, *pappa*), the "baby-
word" for father.  The title was applied at an early period to
all Christian ministers or priests, because of their fatherly relation to the churches.  It was then restricted by certain departments of the church to the bishops or patriarchs of leading
dioceses, then claimed exclusively by the bishop of Rome, when
that official assumed to be father of the whole Christian family.
It is, however, still used by the heads of the Greek and Syrian
churches.

The common people of Russia (belonging to the Greek
Church) call a parish priest "pope."

But there is another word from which our name is far more
naturally derived, the Greek and Latin word *pōpa*, meaning
"the priest who slays the victim."  This term was applied in
Italy before the introduction of Christianity, before the birth of
Christ, and is certain to have gone with Roman colonists wherever they carried their "household gods."  Of course, they
took priests with them into France, Germany and England.
The name *Poppe* (which is still common in Germany) may have
been derived from that Latin word for a priest, in days when
"Germania" was a Roman province.  The Danish (Norse)
name *Bopp* seems to be akin.

All these appear to be completely distinct from the term by which the head of the Church of Rome was called. The conclusion seems to me reasonable that our family name has nothing to do with the title, "Pope of Rome"; that it is an older word than that office; and that it was *either* coined in Britain, in the days of Roman occupation, *i. e.*, before the year 465, and handed down through all subsequent revolutions, *or* brought across the North Sea by Saxons, who had themselves derived it from the same Italian source, or from a still older Aryan word.

## POPEHAM.

In the "Domesday Book," a survey of England made under the orders of William the Conquerer, completed A.D. 1086, we find a passage which is of foremost importance to us, relating to a parish in Hampshire, a dozen miles or so north of Winchester.

"*In Miceldevre Hundred, Abbatia Sancti Petri de Wincestre in dominio, quataor liberi homines tenuerunt de abbatia, Tempore Regis Edwardi pro quatuor maneriis, Granborue, Draitune, Straitune, Popeham; et nequiverunt recedere cum terra; sicut testantur homines ejusdem hundred.*"

"In Micheldever Hundred,"—township,—"in possession of the Abbey of St. Peter of Winchester, *four free* men held from the abbey in the time of King Edward four manors of Granborue, Draitune, Straitune, Popeham; and they are unable to remove with the land," — cannot retain ownership if they remove,— "so testify the men of that hundred."

According to the laws of the formation of English words, "Popeham" is derived from the surname of a family, *Pope* and the Saxon word *ham*, equivalent of the German *heim* and our *home;* it must signify, the home of the Pope family. So we notice Clapham, Fordham, etc., of similar composition. The word "ham" or "the hams" is used by farmers in the county of Southampton, where Micheldever is situated, to describe the field containing or adjoining the house.*

The manor has been called "Popham" for many centuries, and a family of that name has long lived there. Gilbert Pop-

---

*The other manors became respectively, Granborough, Drayton and Stratton.

ham was there in 1251. But this is evidently a surname taken from the family residence, as so many have been,— John de lane, Henry de forest, William Lake, etc., etc. ; so that it is fair to say that the Popham * family must have sprung from the ground of the Pope family. The word, with the record quoted in " Domesday Book," prove that a *free man*, of our name, occupied that farm and manor-house before the year 1066, or more than eight hundred years ago, and altogether before the Norman Conquest ; that he was prominent enough to have the place called by his name.

The oldest Hampshire records show the name of Pope at Whitchurch, Christchurch, Newport (on the Isle of Wight), Portsmouth, and Fording-bridge, and Ringwood in the New Forest. Mr. T. S. Pope, architect, of Bristol, in the West of England, is of the Fording-bridge family ; says that " some of his ancestors were head foresters ; that a member of the family was a secretary of the Royal Society ; that they were related to Sir Christopher Wren."

## RALPH POPE OF BENETLYE.

In the British Museum's collection of manuscripts [additional charters, 9576] there is a little piece of parchment, some nine inches by five or six, with a round cake of dark green wax attached by a parchment tape, which is the oldest relic and memorial of any individual of our name that we have discovered. Under its beautiful penmanship and hard Latin words, we find a deed of land made, signed and sealed by a Pope, five hundred and seventy-one years ago.

### "RADULPHUS POPE DE BENETLYE."

Ralph Pope of Benetlye [Bentley], in the county of Suffolk, conveyed lands in Bentley near lands of Geofrey Ovilkyne and adjoining other lands of his own, " in fee forever," warranting the title, to " Pauline, daughter of Thomas of Frestone." The deed bears the names of the following witnesses : " John de ffreston, Thomas de

---

* Another parish called Popham exists in North Devonshire, and may have been a colony from that we have been considering. In the vicinity of each there have been Popes living, from time immemorial.

Wolferton, Ryngild, Haman de ffreston, Hugo Talemasch, Edmund de Chatesham, William the priest, son of Ralph, Stephen Michaeleboy, Roger Underwood, John le Scherrend, William del Waldenne, Alexander de ffrestone."

It is dated " at Benetlye, Monday, the morrow after the day of St. Mark the Evangelist, in the ninth year of the reign of Edward the son of Edward" [Edward II., A. D. 1316].

The seal is interesting, because, at that period, coats of arms were little known or used, while seals were often heirlooms, greatly prized, the motto and device frequently expressing a memorial of some important event in the family history, or some deep purpose or strong characteristic of the owner.

THE SEAL OF RALPH POPE OF BENTLEY, SUFFOLK, A. D. 1316.

The name, Ralph, is particularly attractive to us, because it was given by our second sire, John[2] of Squantum, to that son who perpetuated the line in Massachusetts, who in turn gave it to one of his sons ; and it has been a favorite name in several subsequent generations.

Yet this *does not prove* that Ralph of Bentley, in 1316, was our ancestor!

We note " William the priest, son of Ralph." We find mention of one who seems to be the same in other documents. In papers of Queen's College, Oxford, there is

"The account of Sir William Pope, priest, and Brother Reginald de Cottesdone, serjeants of God's House at Southampton, for Michaelmas, 9, Edward II," the same year, 1316, as the deed just described. The title, "Sir," is important, showing the rank of the family. "W. Pope" is a witness to the payment of rental in Southampton, in the year 1325 ; doubtless the same.

Bentley is five and one-half miles south of Ipswich, and Freston is one and one-half miles west.

Another MS. [9,641], at the British Museum, is a deed of "John Pope, capellanus," who, with Margaret his wife, and John his son, deeded a "messuage "[homestead], "in Freston, in the county of Suffolk, in the year 1367. It would not be strange if the elder of these Johns were that "John de ffreston," one of the witnesses in the former document ; it was so common in those days for a man to write his Christian name and that of his residence without giving his surname.

MS. 8,564 contains the name of "Robert Pope" at Mildenhall, Suffolk, as one of the witnesses to a deed, July 8, 1422.

Passing into the county immediately north of Suffolk, we find, by means of another Br. Museum document [14,009], that "Thomas Pope and Margaret, his wife, of Shortesham in the county of Norfolk," bought houses and lands in Fordamhytte and Helgley, May 10, 1381.

It is but a step beyond these parishes to Paston, in the adjoining county of Lincolnshire, where "William Pope" was vicar, in the year 1447, as we learn from his witnessing MS. 17,235.

About as far westward, in Northamptonshire, is Higham Ferrers, which may be supposed to be the "High Ferris," near which was "Newton," where "James Pope" subscribed as a witness, in 1462 [MS. 223].

Speaking of Northamptonshire, there was a Walter Pope, M.D., in Fawsley in that county, who published, June 22, 1666, a book entitled, "The Eclipse of the Sun," and later "The Life of Seth Ward, Bishop of Salisbury," and "The Old Man's Wish," in 1697. He was half brother to Dr. Wilkins, Bishop of Chester ; was educated at Trinity College, Cambridge, and Wadham, Oxford.

"Hockington" was the home of one "Anthony Pope" who sold land to Queen's College, Cambridge, Dec., 1560.

## THOMAS POPE OF OXFORD.

The *earliest* person of our name I have found *mentioned by name* is "Thomas Pope," one of the witnesses to a deed convey-ing a tract of land in the parish of St. Mildred, in the county of Oxford, "in the 13th year of King Edward I," 1287. The tract afterward became the property of Exeter College, at Ox-ford, in whose history this bit of our genealogy (?) occurs.

In the parish church at Dedington, in the county of Oxford-shire, and near this city of Oxford, there is a memorial window to John Pope, Margaret his wife, and Gabriel and Anne, their children. The mother died in 1401. Locally, they seem to be-long to Thomas of Oxford, the witness of 1287; but the names remind us of the Freston couple, who bought property thirty-four years before : a mere conjecture, of course.

In the records of the Ewelme Almshouse, in Oxfordshire, for the 12th year of King Henry IV. (1411), there is a "Court Roll of the Manor of Connok," of which Sir Thomas de la Pole was said to be the lord.

It is stated that "Thomas Pope, the lord's naif by blood, has eloigned himself from the demesne," —which means, I suppose, that Thomas Pope's mother was a sister of Sir Thomas de la Pole, and that he had not taken possession of the manor, for some reason of which we are ignorant, "though it was his law-ful right, and so his nearest relatives are ordered to bring him into court." The memorandum follows that "John Pope and Phillip Pope" were fined for failing to produce the missing youth. Seventy-five years later, "3 Ric. III." [1485], Connok Manor was leased to "W. Pope and Joan, his wife," at a yearly price of £22.

We may note that the Pole family figures prominently in the history of those times. Michael de la Pole, son of a wealthy merchant of Hull, became chancellor in 1382, and was created Earl of Suffolk. Reginald Pole was a kinsman of Henry VIII., who educated him ; but when he wrote a book against the king's divorce, and stayed on the continent to escape the royal wrath, Henry executed his mother and brother for correspond-ing with him. What the relationship was we do not know, but we shall see that Henry gave an important trust to one of the Oxford Popes, and perhaps the relationship extended to them as well.

The History of Dedington gives a pedigree which includes

1. JOHN, who married Grace Simpson.
2. WILLIAM, their son, who married 1, Julian Edmonds, 2, Margaret Yate ; he possessed land in D., and died in 1523, leaving his estate to his widow for her widowhood, then to his youngest son, Thomas, at that time fourteen years of age. An older son was
3. JOHN, who married successively Anne Stavely, Elizabeth Brockett and Jane Wyndham, whose home was at Wroxton [Rockston]. He died in 1583. [See pp. 30, 31, 32.]
4. WILLIAM, his son, was knighted and afterward created Earl of Downe and Baron of Beltirbet, in Ireland. His arms were " Topaz, two chevronels Ruby ; on a canton of the second a mullet of the first," which we shall discover to be the coat of the Kent and Sussex Popes, in effect, differing only in the terms used to describe the colors ; and nearly the same as that of the Dorset branch.
5. THOMAS, one of his sons, succeeded to the earldom, and was followed by the son of his brother *William*, who had died during their father's lifetime.
6. THOMAS, third Earl of Downe, married the daughter of John Dutts, of Sherborne in Co. Gloucester. Their only child,
7. ELIZABETH, who married 1, Sir Francis Henry Lee, 2, Robert Bertie, Earl of Lindsay.

Thomas, second Earl of Downe, brought a large force of troops over from Ireland to assist King Charles I. in his conflict with the Parliamentary troops, in 1643. But later he was on such terms with the Cromwell party as to have a pass for foreign travel, June 3, 1651.

Nothing has come to our sight concerning other branches of the family of John,[3] though there were probably many in the successive generations. John Pope, LL. B., was named for warden of All Soul's College, Oxford, by Cardinal Pole, in 1558, but died before entering on the office.

But we must return to that youngest son of William,[2] Thomas, who became one of the foremost men of his day. He was educated at Banbury and Eton, became a lawyer of good repute, a member of Gray's Inn, London. When King Henry VIII. resolved to check the power of the priests and monks, by sweeping their wealth into his coffers, he chose this "Thomas Pope, Esquire," to "have charge of the relics of the suppressed monasteries," giving him the title of "Treasurer of the Augmentations." This appointment was made July 6, 1536.

He was knighted and received the following grant of arms:

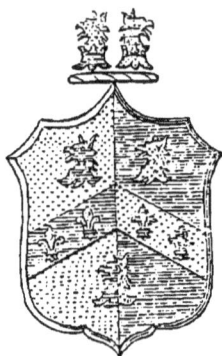

THE ARMS OF SIR THOMAS POPE OF OXFORD.

"Party per pale, or and azure, on a chevron between three gryphons' heads erased, four fleurs de lis, all countercharged." The crest is "two gryphons' heads erased."

He retained the favor of Henry's successors, Edward VI., Mary and Elizabeth; was the "keeper" of the princess Elizabeth for a number of years before Mary's death, residing with her at Hatfield House. There he received "the answer of the Lady Elizabeth, given at Hatfield to Sir Thomas Pope, as to the proposal of marriage made by the King of Sweden"; which proposal she authorized her guardian to decline in her name.

His greatest deed was the endowment of Trinity College, one of the collateral institutions of Oxford University, in 1555.

He died at Clerkenwell, Jan. 29, 1558-9, was buried at Walbrook by the side of his second wife, Margaret, and his only child, Alice, but removed later to the chapel of Trinity College, where a large tomb was erected with this inscription:

*Hic jacent corpora Thomæ Pope militis, fundatoris hujusce collegii Trinitatis et dominae Elizabethæ et Margaretæ uxoris ejus; qui quidem Thomas obiit xxix die Januarii MDLVIII.*
" *Quod tacitum velis nemini dixeris.*"

This motto, " Whate'er you wish untold to no one tell," was probably a favorite one with the statesman; and such prudent keeping of his own counsel, joined with fidelity to the trusts reposed in him, doubtless made him the successful man he was.

He left no child.

## THE POET, ALEXANDER POPE,

is said to have stated that his father was of a gentleman's family in Oxfordshire, the head of which was the Earl of Down, whose sole heir married the Earl of Lindsay. The exact relationship has not been traced. He was born May 21, 1688, at his father's house in Plough Court, Lombard Street, London. This building was demolished in 1860, and a small piece of its wainscoting is in the possession of the N. E. Historic-Genealogical Society, No. 18 Somerset Street, Boston, the gift of G. A. Somerby, Esquire. His father was born in 1643, and died in 1717, being thus contemporaneous with the first generation of our family born in this country.

The poet lived and died at Twickenham, London, on the Middlesex bank of the Thames; there the grotto he constructed remains, and an obelisk he erected to the memory of his mother. She was the daughter of Rev. Mr. Turner, a minister of the Established Church, whose sons were martyrs to the Royalist cause. Of his services to Literature, to Ethics, in his poems, nothing need be said here, further than to call attention to the fact that we may cherish the hope that he was a scion of the very stock from which we have sprung; and we may feel a family interest in his life and works. He died May 30, 1774.

## KENT POPES.

Hasted, in his History of Kent, says that there was a family of Popes at High Halden, a younger branch of the same at Hockeridge, in the parish of Hawkhurst, and at Maidstone, in Kent. Their arms are described as,

THE ARMS OF THE POPES OF KENT.

" Or, two cheverons gu., a canton of the last charged with a mullet ar. Crest, an heraldic tiger, statant, ppr., ducally gorged and chain reflexed over the back, or."

## THE POPES OF SUSSEX.

At Rye, one of the "Cinque Ports," "Thomas Pope was a bailiff in the 10th year of Henry II," [1422,] as we find by his signature to a document, June 10th of that year; the same name occurs in 1431 and 1435 in Rye documents, and as buyer of Thomas Dobyll's property there in 1455.

Thomas Pope of Little Horsted, said by Berry to have been a member of the Privy Council of Henry VI., married Jane Weston, a descendant of Ralph of Wistoneston, Wiston, or Weston, who received a grant of that manor from William de Braose, in the 20th year of William the Conqueror. She brought him Hendal in Buxtead. The Weston arms are, " Ermine on a bend, Azure, three lions' heads erased, or."

The arms of the Hendal family are :

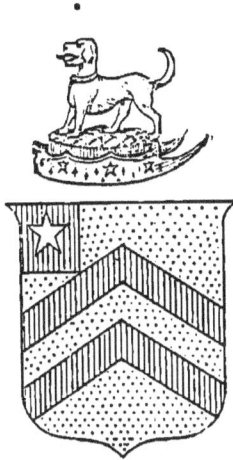

THE ARMS OF THE SUSSEX POPES,

" Or, two cheverons gu., on a canton of the last a mullet of the field. Crest, On a chapeau gu., turned up erm, a talbot, statant, ar., collared sa., ringed and studded or."

The line of this family runs thus :

Thomas,[1] and Jane Weston.

John[2].

Edmund,[3] died in 1530.

Nicholas[4].

Thomas[5]; and John,[5] who married Barbara Onley.

Rafe[6] [Ralph].

Sackville[7].

The will of this Ralph is on file at Somerset House, London. Sons, Sackville and Nicholas ; daughters, Susan and Cicilia ; son-in-law, John Foster of Eastborne, and brother, Thomas Pope, of Staple Inn. Enumerates "the manors of Hendall and Francklin," and property in "Buckstead, Mayfield, Wevelsfield, Lynfield, Cuckfield, and Ditchinge, in the County of Sussex." The will was probated Aug. 21, 1621.

The following year his brother Thomas died, and his will is also at Somerset House, leaving his estate to his brother's children. One of the witnesses is "Jo : Pope" (an abbreviation for *Johannes*, the Latin for John, often seen in ancient writings).

"John Pope was buried Aug. 31st, 1641." (Staple parish register.)

John Pope, one of the owners of a vessel against which a suit was brought at Rye, June 8, 1558, may, very likely, belong to this family.

## LONDON POPES.

"John Pope of London, gentleman," and "Anthony Foster of the same, gentleman," sold a messuage in the parish of St. Margaret, London, to Thomas Archer of the same, 27 Sept. 36 Henry viii [1544]. Two seals are attached to the deed [Ad. Ch. 5317], that over against John Pope's signature a medallion likeness of a head.

After the foregoing was in type, our kinsman, John Tolman Pope, mentioned "an old Pope deed" he had seen, in the possession of Mr. David Pulsifer, of Boston, an eminent antiquary. On examination, the writer found it to be one made by the very persons mentioned above. Mr. Pulsifer bought it several years since, along with other literary curiosities.

By the great kindness of Mr. Pulsifer we have been permitted to have a photo-engraving made of this ancient piece of vellum, so that all may be able, by the aid of magnifying glasses, to read its Latin words, and observe the elaborate work of the scrivener. We fail to show the two dangling cakes of wax, each bearing the impression of the seal of one of the grantors. We translate the opening phrases of the deed, and give an abstract of the remainder :

"*To all the Faithful of Christ* to whom this present writing may come, *John Pope*, gentleman, and *Anthony Foster*, gentleman, send Greeting in Lord Everlasting; Whereas our sovereign lord, King Henry the Eighth, by the grace of God, of England, France and Ireland, King, defender of the faith, and of the church in England and Ireland, Supreme head, by his letters patent, under the great seal of England, made and given at Westminster the

twenty-sixth day of September, in the thirty-sixth year of the said present lord the King, did, for a certain sum of money paid to him by me the said John Pope, grant and release to us the aforesaid John Pope and Anthony Foster a certain enclosure or precinct lately the *Priory of the Preaching Brethren* in the town of Beverly, in the county of York,"—lands, buildings, orchards, gardens, etc., described ;—all that estate they sell to *Richard Faircliff, gentleman*, for the sum of sixteen pounds sterling, and authorize James Cransmore and Anthony Ferrour, as their attorneys, to give possession of the premises. On the back of the deed is the memorandum that the transfer was made, Oct. 2, 36, Henry VIII. [1544]; witnesses noted, "William Brakenbury, gentleman, John Kychen, clerk, Roger Taylor, Richard Stamp, Richard Watson, Robert Carter, William Harrison, Hugh Kyrfott, and William Statord, with many others."

Was it the same "John Pope" who bought a large quantity of land in and about the city of Dorchester, in 1544? "36 Henry VIII; six messuages in All Saints and St. Peter's parish, parcel of Bindon, and other messuages, parcel of Cerne, Abbotsbury, and Dorchester monasteries, were granted unto John Pope for £996, 14s., 4d." We have the bare mention in Hutchins that lands in Stalbridge, Dorset, "belonged to Mr. Pope after the time of Henry VIII." Was there any connection between the "Treasurer of the Augmentations" and this buyer of property lately owned by monasteries?

*Paul Pope*, of London, notary, and his son, *Edmund*, bought property in Northamptonshire, Bedford, Huntington, Devon, and Somerset, July 12, 1570. [Ad. ch. 6136.]

## DORSET POPES.

John and Joanna Pope, residence not given, sold, in 1523, certain lands in Tyneham, Dorsetshire, inherited by Joanna from the Russel–Chyke family, to John Williams; and their son, "Thomas Pope, citizen and merchant taylor of London, dwelling at a house called the Sign of the White Lion, in Watling Street, near Paul's gate, in the city of London," sold to Henry Williams, son of John Williams, the reversion of the same lands, May 22, 1563.

"At Marnhull was formerly an ancient and respectable family named Pope who had a considerable estate here, but are now extinct. They have a pedigree of three generations in the Visitation book of

1627, commencing with John Pope of Southampton, father of Robert Pope, who, by Joan, daughter of Thomas Polden of Marnhull, was father of George and John Pope; the latter married Catherine, daughter of —— Buckler of Woolcombe in the county of Dorset. Their arms were Argent, two chevronels within a bordure gules, on a Canton an escallop." "In 1608 Robert Pope, of Marnhull, died, seized of a capital messuage and lands there; Robert, his grandson and heir, aet. 16." Robert Pope, baptized 1559. John, son of Mr. John and Elizabeth Pope, baptized 1683. Robert, son of the same, baptized 1685. Edward, son of Robert Pope and Margaret his wife, baptized 1683; Robert, do., 1685. John Pope, gentleman, buried 1653. Mr. John Pope, buried 1693." [Hutchins' Hist. Dorset.]

The will of "George Pope the elder, of Stowerton Cawndell in the county of Dorset, yeoman," is at Somerset House, admitted July 31, 1620. Wife, Elizabeth; sons, George and James; daughters, Dorothy Remye and Christian Davidge.

At Manston, Dorset, is this epitaph:

".Here lieth the body of George Pope counsellor in the lawe who died the 11 day of February 1633, being of the age of 70 years."

Hutchins' statement that this family "is now extinct," means only that no representatives of it were living in the vicinity, claiming the estates, titles, etc. If some members of the family had emigrated to America, they would have been likely to drop correspondence, or to have been forgotten, and counted as if deceased.

At Corsecombe, Toller, and Kingcombe (Kentcomb), Dorset, a family of Popes has had good standing for two centuries and a third. Alfred Pope, Esq., at present Mayor of Dorchester, is of this branch, as are Revs. William John Pitfield Pope and Edward J. Pope, of the neighborhood. The earliest parish registries of the family extant are the marriage of William Pope, Jan. 15, 1654, at Bristol, to Ann Phillips; and baptisms of their children at Corsecombe, in 1665, et seq. William, John, and Thomas were favorite names in the family. They may have descended from the wealthy proprietor at Dorchester, in 1544, or from some other progenitor.

In the museum at Dorchester (Dorset) there is a manuscript "Visitation Book of Dorsetshire," completed in 1623.

Here is a copy of page 215 (the shield being *fac-simile*):

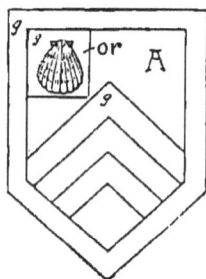

*Pope*

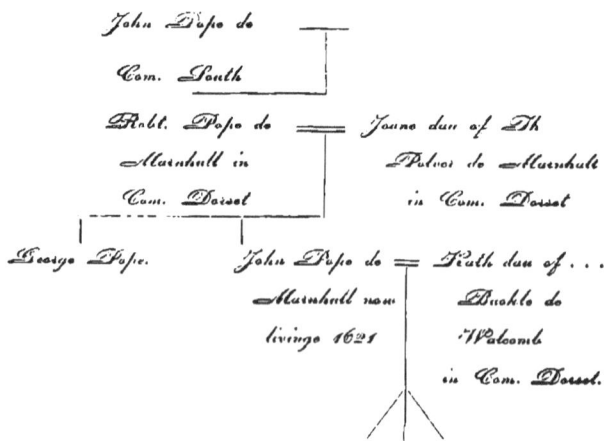

John Pope de
Com. South

Robt. Pope de ═══ Joane dau of Th
Marnhull in    Pulvor de Marnhull
Com. Dorset   in Com. Dorset

George Pope.  John Pope de ═ Ruth dau of . . .
      Marnhull now  Buckle de
      livinge 1621  Walcomb
         in Com. Dorset.

In Wiltshire there have been numerous Popes. At Salisbury, in 1650, there was a "William Pope" living, as appears from a deposition of William Palmer and others in Massachusetts General Court, Oct. 16th of that year.

## SOMERSETSHIRE POPES.

The Probate files of Taunton contain several wills of persons of this name, as the indexes show; but the documents are too *passé* to admit of examination. A recent article in the "Western Antiquary," of Plymouth, gives an account of an enterprising man we may be glad to reckon a relative. James Hurley Pring, M.D., quotes from Hakluyt, vol. iii, p. 7.

"A brief extract of a patent to M. Thomas Gregory, of Taunton, and others for traffic between the river Nonnia and the rivers Madradumba and Sierra Leona, on the coast of Guinea, An. 1592.

In May, the thirty-four yeere of our gracious soveraigne, Queene Elizabeth, a patent of speciall license was granted to Thomas Gregory of Taunton in the county of Somerset, and to Thomas Pope and certaine other marchants, to traffique into Guinea from the Northernmost part of the river Nonnia to the Southernmost parts of the rivers Madradumba and Sierra Leona, and to other parts, as well to the Southeast as to the Northwest, for a certain number of leagues therein specified, which amount to an hundred leagues or thereabout."

Mr. Pring goes on to say, that, in his opinion, there can be no doubt but that this Thomas Pope founded the almshouses in Taunton, on whose gate this inscription stands:

" POPE'S
ALMSHOUSES,
1591.
REBUILT
1637."

The Taunton Popes were strongly in favor of the Puritan cause, and "Humphrey Pope" was one of the supporters of Lord Monmouth's Rebellion in 1685, who were transported for their part in that struggle against religious tyranny.

"Christopher Pope of Combe St. Nicholas, Somerset, husbandman"; his will was probated April 6, 1627, at Somerset

House, London. Wife, "Kathereen"; son, John ; son, Leonard, and his two gr.-, sons John and Stephen. Winifred Pope, widow, one of the witnesses. This couple's license to marry is on the bishop's register, at Exeter : "Christopher Pope, of Combe in Co. Somerset, and Katherine Bevis of Culliton in Co. Devon," Aug. 17, 1626.

At Norton Small Reward (or Malreward), in the northern part of the county, and close by the city of Bristol, there lived a John Pope, whose daughter Sarah married Clement Miner about 1620. The author of the "Miner Family" Genealogy gives as his arms the shield of Sir Thomas Pope of Oxford ; whether from the family's actual use, or from his own belief that there was some relationship between the families, one cannot tell.

## AT BRISTOL

and vicinity there were numerous persons of our name, at the period of American settlement. St. Thomas' parish had a large number. Michael married in 1603 ; Richard m. in 1630, to Ann Deane; " John Pope, pinmaker," buried in 1637, and many others ; but none who "fit in" to our pioneer's history. "Mr. James Pope," of this parish, was a distinguished citizen ; his son James, born Aug. 30, 1682, went to Madeira, it is said, and acquired a large fortune, which he left, in 1747, in trust, to his nephew, James Barrett, to pay legacies to his widow and to his sister, Barrett's mother, and for Barrett's use; after his death, if he left no children, "to the family of the Popes, his relatives." Rumor estimates this property, still in "Chancery" (Probate Court), at £800,000. But none of the English Pope families have been able to establish claim thereto. It is not worth while for American wearers of the name to entertain the remotest expectation of succeeding in any suit for it. There are many of our name now living in Bristol and vicinity; one of the most prominent of these is Mr. George H. Pope, treasurer of the ancient and honorable society of Merchant Adventurers.

" Robert Pope of the hundred of Barclay," 1599, bequeathed property to William, Giles and Thomas, his sons, Elenor his daughter, and Elizabeth his wife. No other wills there seem significant, unless one of the Isaacs may prove to have been a connection, as that name appears in the early generations of the Plymouth (America) Popes. " Isaac Pope, mariner," will 1703 ; no clue to home or relatives in the document. " Isaac Pope," 1722. No examination made.

At Leigh, *Gloucestershire*, the parish registers give the burial of "John Pope, Feb. 19, 1560;" the baptism of "John, the son Richard Pope, Jan. 26, 1613," and the marriage of "John Pope and Margerie Bro——, April 8, 1616."

*Herefordshire* and *Shropshire* have had families of our name within the past century, but perhaps not anciently. The crest of the Salop (Shropshire) family is given, as " In hand ppr. a pair of scales, or. Motto, *Mihi, tibi*." In some delineations the scales are held by "a cubit arm vested, gu., cuffed ar." Two forms of their shield are given by Burke : " 1. Or, two chevrons, the uppermost gu., the under one az." " 2. Or, two chevrons gu., a canton az."

### VARIOUS PERSONS OF THE NAME.

"Francis Pope" sought to collect a bill from "the lady Cecilia," April 6, 1566.

"Henry Pope's " invention of a process of roasting ores was recommended by the council of the Royal Mines Company for Cumberland, 1572.

"Nov. 26, 1653, John Pope, of Clifford's Inn, attorney, was buried." This was in London.

John Pope was prebendary of S. Decumen in the See of Bath and Wells, in 1497.

In 1607, John Pope, of Plymouth, refers to his son John as "of London"; whether he returned to Plymouth or continued to live in London until his death, or removed elsewhere, deponent saith not.

Mary Pope, residence not stated, was the author of two quartos published in London : ".Treatise of Magistracy," 1647, and "Behold, here is a Word," 1649.

James Pope, London, 1646, composed "The unveiling of Antichrist."

We wish more might come to light concerning these two Puritan writers, who *may* have been related to those of our name that came to America.

John Pope of Ribchester, 1641 ; John Pope of Whittingham, 1562 ; R. Pope of W., 1589 ; wills in Arch-Deaconry of Richmond files, now removed to London. Not seen. At Somerset House further wills not reached in our inspection. Richard, 1597 ; Thomas, 1604, 1605, 1612, 1614 ; Robert, 1605, 1608 ; John, 1612, 1614, 1617, 1630 ; Guinne, 1609 ; Arthur, 1614 ; Cecilia, 1614 ; Thomasyne, 1617 ; Walrom, 1617 ; Axicicia, 1617 ; Roger, 1621, 1629 ; James, 1623 ; Louis, 1623 ; Matthew, 1624 ; Margaret, 1625 ; Peter, 1626 ; Alexander, 1627 ; Israel, 1627.

## THE DEVONSHIRE GROUP.

In Exeter, Devon, and in its vicinity there have been very many Popes from a remote antiquity.

Walter Pope, bailiff, Exeter, 1430 ; sheriff 1432, mayor 1452.

Hugh, bailiff, Exeter, 1544 ; sheriff 1561, was chosen mayor in 1562, but declined and paid his fine.

John, sheriff 1566 ; receiver 1574 ; sheriff 1575. William, sheriff 1597. This same William was Master of the Guild, or, as it was technically called, " The Company of Weavers, Fullers, Tuckers and Shearmen," an association of clothmakers. The society is very ancient, and its records, though imperfect, are full of value to the student of history. By the payment of a fee to the lawyer who chances to be secretary of the Guild—not now at all connected with manufactures, but the holder of considerable property—the writer was allowed to search these records : but no other person of our name appeared there, save William referred to above, and there was no statement of the residence of any of the members ; probably some of them, like this "Master," lived in the city, but others carried on their business in neighboring towns, such as Crediton.

> " Crediton was a market town,
> When Exeter was a furzy down,"

says an old rhyme, and was the home of many Popes, as we shall presently show. It was the seat of the bishop during Saxon days ; and in its parish church one may see remnants of the stone " stall-work " of the ancient cathedral, which was erected a thousand years ago, probably.

One of the Dorchester pioneers, Captain Roger Clap, left a brief autobiography, in which he states that he was born in Salcombe [ Regis ], twelve miles from Exeter ; and describes his experience, while living at Exeter, and the interest taken by him-self and others, who were parishioners of Rev. John Warham, of Exeter, in the scheme of a New England colony. There were so many parishes in the city at that time, and the people who remained took so little interest in those that emigrated, that no evidence has yet been found of the particular parish in which Mr. Warham and these people lived. I entered on no search after this matter, but turned, rather, to the files of the Probate Office. In these there are wills and administrations of more than one hundred Popes, from the middle of the sixteenth to the middle of the seventeenth century. Twenty-six of these persons bore the name of *John;* twelve that of *Thomas;* four, of *William;* then there were Robert, Bartholomew, Stephen, Mary, Henry, Peter, Margaret, Christian, Thomasine, Elizabeth, Nicholas, Joane, Edward, Christopher, Alice, Matthew, James, Agnes, Richard, Elinor, Margerie, Methusael, Michael, Gregory, Edissa, Wilmote, Samuel, Gilbert, some of the names repeated. Several wills indexed are lost, nearly all before 1600. Careful examination of many of these was made. Below the chief points of these are noted :

1. Bartholomew of Ashcombe, wife, Margery. July 10, 1548.
2. Robert, Cheriton Bishop, mentions John, Robert, Richard, and Christian Pope. Dec. 26, 1586.
3. John, Cheriton Bishop ; wife, Mary ; children, Robert, Steven, Beth ; brother of foregoing. Feb. 6, 1595.
4. John, Sandford ; wife, Elizabeth ; children, Matthew and Anne Cox. June 22, 1671.
5. Thomas, Exeter, merchant ; wife, Marie ; son, Thomas ; dau., Marie Battishill. Gave bequest to " the poore of the city that work." Dec. 20, 1619.
6. Thomas, Exeter, merchant ; wife, Wilmote ; dau., Mary. Dec. 7, 1627. [This will at Somerset House.]
7. John, Mamhead ; bequest to Thomas Pope. 1608.

8.  Thomas, Dawlish; "All to Thomas Pope, the younger of Daw-
    lish, being his brother." Dec. 14, 1617.
9.  Peter, Kenton; wife, Mary; Thomas P., co-bondsman. October,
    1622.
10. Thomas, Kenton; wife, Joane; children, Peter, Joane, Wilmont.
    April 17, 1624.
11. Johan, widow, Powderham; children, Hugh, Susan, Margaret.
    April 17, 1639.
12. John, Plymouth; wife, Dorothie; children, "John Pope of Lon-
    don," Thomasyne, Dorothy, wife of John Stone, Alice, wife of
    Nicholas Tuchill. June 26, 1607.
13. Jane, widow, Kingscarswill; child, Richard; mentions Thomas
    and John Pope. March 20, 1591.
14. John, the elder, Torbrian; "wife"; children, John, Samuel,
    Joan. Oct. 7, 1606.
15. John, the elder, Torbrian; son, John; sons-in-law, Roger Codner
    and Richard Bully. Refers to John Pope, of Denbury. April
    5, 1623.
16. John, Denbury; wife, Elizabeth; children, Jacob, Marie Bonne,
    and Agnes Longe. July 16, 1632.
17. John, Buckfastleigh; brothers, Symon and Peter. Jan. 12, 1609.
18. John, batchelder, Ashburton; mentions Matthew, son of Gilbert
    P. Aug. 3, 1619.
19. Thomas, yeoman, Staverton; wife, Mary; children, Thomas, Hugh
    (minor), Thomasyn; grandchildren, John, Elizabeth, Thomas,
    and Mary Pope; mentions Thomas Pope. June 13, 1639.
20. Nicholas, Bratton Fleming; wife, "Garthrude"; daus., Helene
    and Mabby. June 22, 1612.
21. Alice, widow, Highbray; son, "Henry Pope, of Bratton Flem-
    ing, husbandman." Nov. 28, 1621.
22. John, yeoman, Barnstaple; wife, Thomasyn. July 16, 1623.
23. Margery, Shebbear; granddaus., Prudence Pope and Grace
    Buse; mentions Richard Pope. July 27, 1636.
    Later than the emigration considerably is the following, but
    of interest from the business of the testator and the persistence
    there of those family names so much used before, and also
    employed by our family in this country:
24. William, clothier, Revelstock; wife, Mary; "kinsman, John, son
    of John Pope, deceased, and William, son of Thomas Pope,
    deceased." May 9, 1743.
    Highbray, mentioned in the list, is close by the Devonshire
    Popham.

The "search clerk" of the Probate office remarked, when the examination of these wills was completed and the student longed to see more: "*I* think you have seen a *goodish few* already!"

From the registers in the office of the bishop's secretary, at Exeter, several items may be added to this section.

William Pope of Uplyme was ordained at Exeter, by the bishop, Sept. 29, 1601. (Uplyme is near the border of Dorsetshire, not far from Axminster.) This is, presumably, the rector of Bundleigh, whose will has just been noted.

Leonard Pope, of Axminster, and Mary Poor, of the same, were licensed to marry, without banns, Leonard Pope and John Pope his brother, of Wambrook, in Co. of Dorset, giving surety, Nov. 29, 1611.

Nicholas Pope, of Crediton, and Arminella Canesbye, of the same, licensed Jan. 13, 1624. Philip Pope, of Morehard Bishop, and Thomasine Gover, of Sandford, May 27, 1626.

Henry Pope, of East Bundleigh, and Martha Rabyant, of the same, Jan. 6, 1611. Banns to be declared in St. Nicholas' church, Exon.

John Pope, of Dow St. Mary, and Arminella Hill, of Clanaboroughe, Dec. 29, 1617.

The Popes of ancient Crediton and vicinity have for three centuries kept a steady existence, as a "good, old, country family." Relationship is known to exist between some branches, others do not know of any; but none are reported to possess family registers of great date, or any wide knowledge of the Popes·in general. There is no collection of items, names or facts, of which I could learn, touching the connection as a whole. They are exceedingly intelligent, worthy, respectable, so far as known. For example, John Pope, Esq., a retired lawyer in Exeter, with sons rising in the professions of law and medicine, is a gentleman of excellent standing in society, and of extensive property. Rev. Henry Pope, of Sandford,·is a Congregational minister, well approved. Many large estates are held by others of the clan.

No coat of arms is *reported*, nor any theory as to the origin of the family. One suggestive point in the local history is this: "Mr. John Pope preached at Crediton, after having been

silenced elsewhere, and became pastor of a Presbyterian congregation there when King James II. gave liberty to Dissen-
ters. He removed to Exeter in 1668, and died there the next
year." [Nonconformist Ministers, vol. 1, p. 425.]

Was he of the Crediton connection? and was there such a
feeling among the Popes of Devonshire in 1630? Would not
such a spirit take deep and practical interest in the planting of
a Christian colony in a new country, where free worship might
prevail?

All is left to conjecture. Our ancestor may have been of
this Devonshire group, though no particular place appears to
show good enough evidence to claim him as a native.

Plymouth and its suburbs have had representatives of our
"folks" from remote antiquity. A recent branch is that de-
scended from Charles and Thisbe (Kirby), married in Plymstock,
March 2, 1776. She was daughter of Richard Kirby, and baptized
July 25, 1749. Their son Charles, born Dec. 18, 1781, married
Mary Chown, in Plymouth, Jan. 13, 1805, and, in 1818, came to
New York with five children. One of these is Dea. Thomas
Pope, a prosperous and honored citizen of Quincy, Illinois.

Several eminent divines, also, have graced the list of our
Plymouth "cousins," besides manufacturers, ship-builders, and
at least one musical professor, very clever and successful in
spite of the affliction of blindness.

Altogether the name *Pope* has excellent representatives in
England, both in the annals of former centuries, and in the lists
of the present day. And we of America, legitimate successors
of the same ancient stock, count ourselves most happy in recog-
nizing and fraternizing with our "English Cousins," whom it
will give us great pleasure to know more fully hereafter.

There yet remains a large field to be explored; for instance,
in the parish registers of the towns and cities where these
persons lived; in the wills on file at Blandford in Dorsetshire,
Salisbury in Wilts, and Wells in Somerset, with parishes which
will be suggested in them.

At any point the inquirer may suddenly discover birth-rec-
ords, or allusions in a will, or some other definite proof of
identity; or long search may be necessary before any clue is
gained; or there may not be any documents extant which will

settle the question. The writer hopes, however, that the quest will be pursued by somebody, and believes it will prove success-ful, his own experience in the discovery of important facts regarding the Clapp family [see Appendix, Clapp] having greatly encouraged him in this hope.

The problem of the inter-relationship of the various families of Popes in England is not easy of solution, although the prevalence of the Christian names, Thomas, John and Wil-liam, *strongly suggests* that all are branches of one ancient stock. The writer believes that there are data extant for the ascertaining of this point, and that it will yet be made clear.

## RESUMÉ.

To sum up what has been gleaned as to English Popes.

1st. We find evidence in "Domesday Book," in the descrip-tion of *Popeham*, that a freeman, named Pope, had his home in Hampshire before the Norman conquest.

2d. We have a Thomas Pope, in Oxfordshire, in 1287 ; Ralph and William, in Suffolk, in 1316 ; John and Margaret, in the same, a little later ; Thomas, in Sussex, a bit further on ; and by 1450 we see persons of the name in several other counties, as far west as Devonshire.

3d. Thenceforward, definite family groups are found in all the coast counties, from the Wash to the Plym, and inland from Northamptonshire to Shropshire, and southward.

4th. The families have been highly respectable, as a rule,—merchants, yeomanry, tradesmen, in the majority of cases ; frequent instances of wealth, learning, statesmanship, enter-prise, being on record.

# CHAPTER III.

## THE DORCHESTER PIONEER.

THE earliest official document in which our forefather's name has yet been found, is the Records of the governing body of the Massachusetts Colony, in the list of "*Freemen\* made att the Gen'all Court September* 3, 1634." Fifty-four persons were so honored, their names being given, but not their residences. Among them we read

*"John Pope."*

"Tho: Newbury," "Thomas Thorneton" and "Matthias Sension," are the only other Dorchester names given.

This record of freemanship is valuable as showing that one was a man of good standing in the community, a member of the

---

\* WHAT WAS A "FREEMAN?"

The charter which King Charles gave in 1628 to the Massachusetts Bay Company, provided that the patentees (incorporators) "and all such others as shall hereafter be admitted and made *free of the Company and Society*," should constitute "one body corporate and politique in fact and name";—"should pass lawes not contrarie to the lawes of this our realme of England"; and in other respects should maintain the government of the province.

WHO SHOULD BE "FREE" OF THE COMPANY?

It was enacted by the General Court, (that is, the representatives of the Massachusetts Bay Company in New England,) at the session in May, 1631,

"In order that the body of the commons may be preserved of good and honest men," . . . "that, for the time to come, none should be admitted to the freedom of the body politic, but such as were church members." Application must be made by an individual, accompanied with his minister's certificate of good standing in the church; and then permission being given by the Court, the freeman's oath must be taken before a magistrate.

The "freeman" had a right to vote in elections of governor, deputy and assistants; and, before the representative system commenced, was a member of the General Court. He might become a magistrate, officer, juryman, etc., etc., and he had peculiar rights in the distribution of lands.

44

church, a brother in that band which had organized four years and a half before in Plymouth, England. Whether he had come at the first or within a few months before his application for freemanship, nothing here shows; as we know that some were here several years before applying.

Here is the obligation which was assumed at the day mentioned :

### "THE OATH OF A FREEMAN."

[Adopted as a " newe oath," May 14, 1634.]

" I. A. B. being, by God's providence, an inhabitant and ffreeman within the jurisdiccion of this conōnweale, doe freely acknowledge my selfe to be subject to the govermt thereof, and therefore doe heere sweare, by the greate and dreadfull name of the everlyveing God, that I wilbe true and faithfull to the same, and will accordingly yeilde assistance and support thereunto, with my *p*son and estate, as in equity I am bound, and will also truely indeavr to maintaine and preserve all the libertyes and privilidges thereof, submitting my selfe to the wholesome lawes and orders made and established by the same ; and furthr that I will not plott nor practise any evill against it, nor consent to any that shall soe doe, but will timely discover and reveale the same to lawfull aucthority nowe here established, for the speedy preventing thereof.

Moreover, I doe solemnly bynde myselfe, in the sight of God, that when I shalbe called to give my voice touchiug any matter of this state, wherein ffreemen are to deale, I will give my vote and suffrage, as I shall judge, in my owne conscience may best conduce and tend to the publique weale of the body, without respect of p[er]sons, or favor of any man.

Soe helpe mee God, in the Lord Jesus Christ."

*The Dorchester Town Records* are the principal source of our information concerning the first, second, and third generations of the Pope family in Dorchester. By the liberality of the Boston city government, these chronicles of its oldest suburb were printed in 1880, from the original MS. book. Many a chimera of a former period gives way, now, to clear, connected history.

We find in this book eighty-nine persons mentioned, before anything like our surname appears. Then, on the 12th page of the old journal, we read thus :

" November 3d, 1634. It is ordered . . . . . . that the common gates shall be forthwith made and set up sufficiently with the pales belonging to the same one at M.ʳ Woolcotts one at Walther Filers one at Goodman* Poapes, one at Goodman Grenwayes, and to be palled betwixt Horsefords lott and the Creeke."

" November 22ᵗʰ· 1634.

It is ordered that John Poape and Thom: Swift shall have each of them five acres of ground adjoyning to the lotts of Witchfeild, John Newton † etc : "

" The 4th of January 1635. It is ordered the p'tyes here under written shall have great lotts at the bounds betwixt Roxbury and Dorchester at the great hill betwixt the sayd bounds and above the marsh as foll not to inclose medowe."

Seventy names are given, among them

" John Pope " ——— " 20 acres." This " great lott " was afterward exchanged for another in 1642.

The colony of Dorchester now passed through a peculiar experience, in the removal of a large part of its earliest members to form a new settlement. But one of those who staid by the original plantation, and helped to reorganize the town and church, was our ancestor. Let me quote the account given by the annalist, James Blake :

" This year (1636), made great alteration in the Town of Dorchester, for Mr. Mather & the Godly people that came with him from Lancashire, wanting a place to settle in, some of the People of Dorchester were willing to remove and make room for them, & so Mr. Warham and about half the Church removed to Winsor in Connecticut Colony, and Mr. Mather & his people came & joined with Mr. Maverick and that half of the Church that were left, and from these people so united are the greatest part of the present Inhabitants descended. When these two Companies of people were thus united,

---

*The Puritans, strictly speaking, gave the title, " Goodman," to a specially prominent church-member, of mature years. Only four persons had been so entitled in these records before this entry. Frequently, however, it became a mere easy handle to a name otherwise undistinguished.

† " 5 Aug : 1633. It is consented unto, that John Witchfeild, and John Newton shall have all that plott of Marish ground, that lyeth betweene Nicholas Denslowe and the brooke next to Rockesbury equally to be devided betweene them."

they made one Church, having the said Revd. Mr. John Maverick, & the said Revd. Mr. Richard Mather for their pastors, and entered into the .following Covenant, viz :

### 'DORCHESTER CHURCH COVENANT
#### MADE THE 23ᵈ DAY OF THE 6 MONTH 1636.

We whose names are subscribed being called of God to Join our-selves together in Church Communion; from our Hearts acknowledge-ing our own unworthiness of such a privilege, or of the least of Gods mercies ; and likewise acknowledgeing our disability to keep Cove-nant with God, or to perform any Spiritual Duty which he calleth us unto, unless the Lord Jesus do enable us thereunto by his Spirit dwell-ing in us ; Do in the name of Christ Jesus our Lord, & in trust and Confidence of his free Grace assisting us, freely covenant & Bind ourselves, Solemnly in the presence of God himself, his Holy Angels, and all his Servants here present ; That we will by his Grace Assist-ing, endeavour constantly to walk together as a Right Ordered Con-gregation of Christ, according to all the Holy Rules of a Church Body rightly established, so far as we do already know it to be our duty, or shall further understand out of God's Holy Word : Prom-ising first & above all to cleave unto him as our Chief and only Good, and to our Lord Jesus Christ as our only Spiritual Husband & Lord, & our only High Priest & Prophet & King.

And for the furthering of us to keep this blessed Communion with God & his Son Jesus Christ, & to grow up more fully herein ; we do likewise promise by his Grace assisting us, to endeavour the Estab-lishing amongst ourselves all his Holy Ordinances which he hath ap-pointed for his Church here on Earth, and to observe all & every of them in such sort as shall be most agreable to his Will, opposing to the utmost of our power whatsoever is contrary thereunto, and be-wailing from our Hearts our own neglect hereof in former times, and our poluting ourselves therein with any Sinful Invention of men.

And lastly, we do hereby Covenant & promise to further to our utmost power, the best Spiritual good of each other, & of all and every one that may become members of this Congregation, by mutual In-struction, Reprehension, Exhortation, Consolation & Spiritual watch-fulness, over one another for good. And to be subject in and for the Lord to all the Administrations & Censures of the Congregation, so far as the same shall be guided according to the Rules of God's most holy word. Of the Integrity of our Hearts herein, we call God the Searcher of all Hearts to Witness ; Beseeching him so to bless us in this & all our Enterprises, as we shall sincerely endeavour by the assistance of his Grace to observe his Holy Covenant in all the branches of it inviolable for ever; and where we shall fail, there to wait upon the Lord Jesus for Pardon and acceptance & healing for his Name's sake.

<table>
<tr><td>*Richard Mather,*</td><td>*Natha'l Duncan,*</td></tr>
<tr><td>*George Minot,*</td><td>*Henry Withington,*</td></tr>
<tr><td>*Thomas Jones,*</td><td>*John Pope.'* "</td></tr>
<tr><td>*John Kinsley,*</td><td></td></tr>
</table>

These seven are spoken of by contemporary writers as "the seven pillars of the Church." A council called in April did not feel ready to recognize the persons who *then* offered themselves. It is not known who they were, but the second council, in August, wholly approved of these seven.

The church records do not give the original autographs, but a copy of them; yet there is no doubt that each man's signature is copied correctly.

There is no list of the other members who "entered into covenant" at this reorganization, nor any orderly history of church proceedings for several years. But previous to June, 1639, the following entry was made:

"The names of such as since the constituting or gathering of the church at Dorchester have been added to the church and joyned thereto as members of the same body, by profession of faith and Repentance and taking hould of the Coven't before the Congregation."

.  .  .  .  "Jane Capin, Radigan Capin, *Jane Pope,*" etc., etc.

No other person of the name of Pope is mentioned in the church records after this couple, John and Jane, until more than fifty years have passed.

Returning now to the town records, we read:

"January 16, 1636.  .  .  .  "Ordered that all the hoame* lotts shall be sufficiently paled by the first of March."

Individuals were designated to examine fences in specified localities, among them:

---

* "*Hoame*" — *home.*

"William Sumner, Goodman Hawes to vew the feild where they dwell"; and next following comes this:
"John Poape* and Edward Clap to vew their feild."

Does this imply a relationship of the Pope and Clap families, or simply a friendly combination?

"The 2d of January, 1637," a large amount of business was transacted "By a meeteing of 20 men Chosen to order all the affayres of the Plantation."

The list of this board of Selectmen (much larger than usual, for reasons connected with the departure of the Windsor colony) contains the name, "*John Pope.*"

In a special committee named in the report of this meeting, we find the name, *John Poape*, associated with three others who have been mentioned in the list of the "20"; this fact, together with others, shows that this was actually a sub-committee of the Selectmen, and therefore proves *the identity* of *this man, John Poape*, with the person named in the list of selectmen as *John Pope.*

In a subsequent part of the record of this meeting, we read:

"It is ordered that John Poape have an acre of land behind Good: Sampford to one veud by Goo: Gaylor and Good: Dyer.
It is ordered that he have more 2 akers of meddow p' Goo: Munnings."

The next entry (containing this name) gives a list of the portion of land each man was to have, in certain tracts which had been "Commons" up to this date. Among the 104 named with their proportions comes "*John Pope*, 4 akers, 18 rodes."

A map of the "Meddows beyond the Naponset river," made about the year 1637, is given in the Town Book. One lot is marked "Pope, 4 a."

"October 31ᵗʰ, 1639." "It is ordered that John Pope shall have 2 akers of marsh towards foxe poynt in lew of some land taken frō him for making the way to the neck."

* "*Poape*" —Pope. Similar variations in these records are "*Foard*," "*fford*," "*Ford*"; "*Warham*," "*Warum*"; "*Grenway*," "*Greenway*," "*Grinway*."

At the town meeting held the

"12 of 1 mo. 1641."

"Jo Pope, Jo Holman," were elected overseers for a piece of
fence-building. This abbreviation was not an uncommon one
for *John* in these records.

One of the signatures to the celebrated Thompson's Island
Petition, "the seventh day of the 12th month 1641," in a
style of signature very frequent at that day, shows that through
dimness of vision, or because somehow out of the habit of
writing at that time, our ancestor only made his *initial*, and
another person, at his request, wrote the full name. It was
counted quite a different thing from "making one's mark,"
and considered a legal "signature." In 1636 John Pope had
subscribed his name to the Church Covenant, as we have seen,
and showed his ability to write.

Another year reveals an interesting document on the *Town
Records*, "24 of 3 mo 1642."

"Agreemente maide betwine John Pope and Christopher Gibson
Aboute the Exchange of land, John Pope is to have the great lott of
Christofer Gibson with in the pale containeing ten acors more or lese:
which lyes on the south side of the saide John Pope, with the house
wood and timber; except some wood that is Cut out and some wood that
lies in the boundes for the feyor. And the said Christofer Gibson is to
have all John Popes propriety without the peale excepte Fourty Roods
Ajoyneinge to the fence Containeing nineteene Acores and three quarters bee it more or lese, which 40 roods hee is to have forever; and the
parsell of meddow at the est end of Mr. Israell Stoughtons Lott, containeing one Acore more or les dueering life of Christofer Gibson, the
saide John Pope is to have the old wood that is downe, or may be
blowne downe Twenty Roodes from the fence and hee is to have
six years to take it Away in and he is to have the goeinge of Six
swine for six yeares after the 29ᵗʰ Septemb next 1642: for the aforesaid land." *

[No signatures.]

---

* Deeds and similar agreements between citizens were often thus entered on the records
of the town ; transfers of property must have been made, however, in numerous cases
without any writings ; possession alone, in an orderly community, being sufficient evidence
of lawful ownership.

A period of three years and eight months now passes, during which the town clerk does not favor us with a single item. But he makes up for his deficiencies when that time has passed. Here is a common-place statement about the appointment of fence-viewers,— an office of considerable importance in a farming community, where cattle and crops were both so precious,— but in this conventional chronicle of a town election, the clerk gives *us* a golden link for the two first generations of our line in America, an *evidence* that the "Goodman," "Freeman," and "Pillar of the Church" we have been following, was the father of one universally admitted to be our ancestor.

"27$^{th}$ of the 11 mo : 45."

"Of the great lotes and captines neck Jo : Phillips John Smyth Henrie Way and John Pope senior."

The meaning of this phrase is, in my opinion, this :

*The John Pope of whom we have been learning had a son John, now at least twenty-one years old, living at this time in Dorchester*, and therefore it had become necessary for the clerk to specify which of the two he meant.

We note this the more eagerly, because some historians, who had not read this statement of the clerk, have doubted whether John Pope, the first, of Dorchester, was the father of John Pope, the second. But this word " senior " is very strong. To be sure, some cases have been observed in records of that half century in England and America, where the word senior was applied to the elder of two *brothers* of the same Christian name; but these were so rare, and usually explained by those who mentioned them, that they need hardly be brought into the account. And, after examining the Dorchester journal carefully, referring to the known history of the persons called senior therein, we cannot find any case ( unless this be one ) where it does not signify *the father of a namesake.* So we consider this a definite proof of such relationship.

But the clerk did not have to use the title again, for " Father Pope " was near the close of his life. It was an unhealthy season, as the pastor of the church at Roxbury, close by ( Rev. John Elliot, the saintly missionary to the Indians ), wrote in his church record : —

"This winter we had much sickness in Roxbury & greater mortality than ever we had before in so short a time, 5 dyed in 8 days &
more followed as appeareth in the record."

Whatever the disease was which cut off the "Goodman," he
had a Puritan's faith to buoy up his soul in the last struggles,
and a bright glow of hope over the western sky through which
he passed.  He had been a pilgrim from Old England to New
England, and had helped to lay the foundations of a coming
republic which was to become "The land of the free and the
home of the brave."  But now he passed trustfully over a wider
sea, to a land still less known than America had been, a land,
however, seen through "the telescope of faith," and longed
for as the perfect home.

All that was mortal of the pilgrim was laid, we may be sure,
in that "decent burying place bounden in upon the knapp"
[knob] "by Goodman Grenwayes," which had been set apart by
the town, Nov. 3, 1633, which is the upper corner of the "Old
Burying-ground" at the junction of Boston and Stoughton
Streets.

No stone remains to mark the spot (although in that ground
one bears the date of 1644).  Perhaps our family affection
may some day rise to the point of erecting a suitable monument
to his memory.  Surely we owe a large debt of respect and
gratitude to him for being so good and faithful a man, and for
transplanting our stock from the repressing conditions of the
old England he left to the delightful and uplifting conditions of
the New England he helped to found.

The only evidence of his death we have exists in the documents which describe and devise his property.

We are exceedingly fortunate in having on file, in Boston, the
following document.  It is in Docket, No. 82 ; is not recorded.

### THE PIONEER'S WILL.

" The Last Will and Testament of John Pope }
        who deſſeſed the 12 of the second month. }  1646

*Item   I give unto my wif all my Land and  my howse in the great
Lots: 35 Ackers  in the great Lots:  and  Two  Ackers of  Meadow in the
Calves pasture, And  nine Ackers by the mill: And nine Ackers by the* 20

*Acker Lots : more my 20 Acker Lote more also 12 Ackers of Land I bought of Mr Borne: And my Right in all the Common of the meadow : also own Acker at Mr. Stoughton's great Lots end of meadow : Item I give unto my Daughter my dwelling howse and ground belonging to it : provided that she be willinge that hir mother should Abide in It As long as hir mother doth se Cause : if she be not Willing : hir mother shall have the disposing of it as she do se Cause and all my goods Item I give unto my sarvant mayd Ane Wellmoton 15 shillings and unto my sarvant Hannah Janson 5 shillings at the end of hir time Also unto William' Smead,\* my Littell boye my Lomes and such Taklinge as do belong unto them which is to the vallew of three pound : provided that he be willing to dwell with my wife after his time is out also provided that he be willing to Learn my Trad : and that their be A comfortable Agrement mad betwene the Afterward : Also I do Consider Stephen Hoppen, in Regard of his meannes† and also in regard of his Willingness tow the Trade to set him in A way of worke I do give unto him a Lome that I have that is half mad and like-wise a Reed that I have which I do vallew in 5 shillings : And to my Bro-ther Thomas my new stufe sut of Azell : And to my Brother Joshua my sister's husband I give tow uper Coats, and som other Azell.*

Witnes HENRY KIBBE ...................................
JOHN PEIRCE ...................................

*Taken uppon oath 5 (4) 49 before the Court by the aforesaid Henry Kibby and John Pierce.*

William Aspinwall, Recorder.

*The above sd Henry Keeby & John Pierce further witnes that the testator did declare to them that it was absolutely his will that his wife should have his goods and dispose of the same, whether his daughter be willing that her mother abide in the house or no :*
*Testifyed uppon their former oathes in presence of*

Increase Nowell Secret."

There was a custom in the south and west of England, known as "Borough English," in accordance with which a father gave wild or "assert" lands to his eldest son (at his majority, often), but gave the homestead to his youngest. We

---

\* We find in Suffolk Probate files an Inventory of the estate of the "Widow Smead," of Dorchester, dated " 18 ; 3d : 1639 "; it contains this item. " Payd to John Pope, of Dorchester, w^th William Smeed, w^ch is repayed into y^e Deacons hands, £32." This undoubtedly relates to the apprentice mentioned in the will.

† Poverty.

shall be informed in a court order regarding the division of the estate of the second John Pope, that he had given "a quantity of land" to his eldest son, Thomas, before his death, and the home place went to the youngest, Ralph. So this Ralph gave his eldest and third sons their portions in the "New Grant" (Stoughton), while he bequeathed his "homestall" to the second and youngest sons. From these facts it may be fairly judged that the Pope family habit was to give the eldest son a portion in outlying lands, and to let the home estate pass to the younger child or children. The "Goodman" had undoubtedly drawn a share of land at Squantum, as other of the earliest settlers did, although there is not any record of the grant.

And John, junior, who must have been of age before the clerk felt constrained to note the father as "senior," had, *in all probability*, received a generous farm and means; so that he had neither claim nor desire to be mentioned in his father's will. If there were other sons, they do not appear at Dorchester, nor do we have a hint of other daughters, though there may have been. No will proves the non-existence of persons not named in it; but there is evidence in the added statement of the witnesses, about the widow's *having the goods and disposing of them*, whether the daughter was dutiful or not, that there were other heirs to whom the widow would give the property if Patience was not kind to her!

We note that the trade of "John Pope, senior," was that of a *weaver*, and that one kind of cloth he wove was "azell," or hazel-colored cloth, a term found by us in only one other place, namely, in the will of "William Clapp, the younger," brother of Roger and Edward Clapp of Dorchester, who lived at Salcombe, near Exeter, Devonshire.

A straw, this, suggesting that region as our forefather's old home. Then the fact that William Pope, of Exeter, was master of the Weaver's Guild in that city only a generation earlier, and that trades generally descended in families, give further hints in the same general direction.

Another matter exceedingly interesting, is the mention of a brother, Thomas, carefully distinguished from a brother-in-law. Thomas Pope, of Plymouth, is undoubtedly the person referred to. [See Appendix B.]

This is a "nuncupative" will, not signed by the testator, and naturally incomplete. To illustrate how *such* wills were often made, we will give an *abstract* of the endorsement made, at its probating, on the nuncupative will of that near neighbor, Edward Clap,* with whom our ancestor's name was early associated.

Two sets of appraisers labored on this work, for some unexplained cause. Notice here the word "senior" again applied to the deceased.

The will was not taken to court until three years had passed; perhaps then only because of the daughter's claiming more than her mother thought best to allow, — as the final testimony of the witnesses would seem to indicate. But the property was duly appraised, as we learn from the following inventory.

## THE PIONEER'S ESTATE.

"An Inventory of all the goods and chattels of John Pope senior (of Dorchester) defeaffed. Taken upon the first off June: 1649: by us whose names are hereunder written:

| | | £. | s. | d. |
|---|---|---|---|---|
| *Item:* | His wearing apparell of all sorts | 04 | 10 | 00 |
| *Item* | In the room called the parlor one Bedstead 2 hassock beds, 1 bolster 3 pillows 1 payr sheets 1 rug greene with 1 payre of greene curtains | 04 | 05 | 00 |
| | 2 greene cushions | 00 | 04 | 00 |
| | A trundle bedstead a table a form a stoole a table a chayre 1 payr boad/es one bedstead 2 tubbs | 00 | 10 | 00 |
| *Item* | In the chamber over the parlor 1 trunk 2 tubs 1 box 1 bucket the lanterne | 00 | 07 | 06 |

* [Abstract.] The testimony of Roger Clap, Jno Capen and Nicholas Clap. We, every one of us, being present at the house of " Edward Clappe " on the 3d. day of January 1664, did hear the writing now presented read unto the said Edward Clap, now deceased, he approved of it to be his will and he caused it to be read again in the hearing of his wife to see if she had any exception to make; and appointed it to be writ fairly out again, which accordingly was done. And we coming, to the intent to have it perfected, were informed that he was asleep; and, it being late in the night, — went away and forbore at that time. And afterward it was neglected to be presented; "so nothing else was done concerning settling his estate that we know of."

|  |  | £. | s. | d. |
|---|---|---|---|---|
| *It.* | a litle flok bed and 4 bags | 00 | 11 | 00 |
|  | 1 payer of blanketts | 00 | 05 | 00 |
|  | 2 payer sheetes at 10ˢ and 6ˢ | 00 | 16 | 00 |
|  | 4 payer of pillow byes att | 01 | 00 | 00 |
|  | 1 table-cloth 2 napkins | 00 | 12 | 00 |
|  | 2 baggs and 2 small winow sheets | 00 | 10 | 00 |
|  | Old Iron in the chamber | 00 | 08 | 00 |
|  | skales & waights at | 00 | 07 | 06 |
|  | 1 furne att | 00 | 03 | 00 |
|  | 1 trunk 1 boxe 2 tubs 1 churne 2 bere barels 2 keelers 1 paile 3 trays 2 linen wheels | 00 | 15 | 00 |
|  | In the chitchen 1 bed one bolster one coverlidd | 02 | 00 | 00 |
| *Item* | 3 brasse kettles 14ˢ 3 brassepans 11ˢ | 01 | 06 | 00 |
|  | 2 brasse skillits 1 warming-pan and one candlesticke | 00 | 09 | 00 |
|  | 2 brasse pots | 00 | 12 | 00 |
|  | a morter and pestle | 00 | 04 | 00 |
|  | Pewter of all sorts | 01 | 06 | 00 |
|  | 1 frying pan att | 00 | 03 | 06 |
|  | 2 seins 2 stools | 00 | 02 | 06 |
|  | 1 grt Copper kettle | 01 | 15 | 00 |
|  | 1 coverlidd sold att : | 00 | 19 | 00 |
| *Item* | In tools of all sorts | 02 | 11 | 06 |
|  | muskett sword bandelies vest | 01 | 04 | 00 |
|  | ffor loombes and Tacklinge with it | 03 | 10 | 00 |
|  | 1 yoke of oxen | 14 | 00 | 00 |
|  | 2 steers exchanged for 2 cows | 10 | 00 | 00 |
|  | Cart plow and wheels | 01 | 11 | 00 |
|  | 1 yoke 2 chains | 00 | 11 | 00 |
|  | 1 plow sold | 00 | 04 | 00 |
|  | a fanne att | 00 | 02 | 06 |
|  | depts owing to him | 08 | 00 | 00 |

HUMPHREY ATHERTON
WALTER HARRIS
HOPESTILL FFOSTER

|  | £. | s. | d. |
|---|---|---|---|
| ffor the corne on the ground | 04 | 00 | 00 |
| 2 piggs | 01 | 10 | 00 |
| ffor other small things unseene | 00 | 12 | 06 |

| | | £. | s. | d. |
|---|---|---|---|---|
| *Item* | 35 Ackers of Land within great lotes & the house | 45 | 00 | 00 |
| *It.* | 18 Ackers of commons and a 20 acker lote | 14 | 00 | 00 |
| *It.* | 12 Ackrs the land bought Mr. burne | 08 | 00 | 00 |
| *It.* | 2 acres of meadow in Calves pasture one acre at mr. Stoughtons lotes end & 3 acres at Commons meadow | 05 | 00 | 00 |
| *It.* | His dwellinge house given to his daughter & orchard & acr of land | 40 | 00 | 00 |
| | Sumᵃ totalis of the goods & land is | 184 | 12 | 06 |

GEO : WEEKES
RICHARD BAKER

A bill of the debts owing to John Pope as by the perticulars appere.

| | £. | s. | d. |
|---|---|---|---|
| | 32 | 10 | 06 |
| paid more in legasyes to the some of | 04 | 00 | 00 |
| More for debts as by the p'ticulars | 30 | 00 | 02 |
| •       *       *       *       •       • | — | — | — |
| | 66 | 10 | 06 |

In *Edward Bullock's* will, dated the 25th of the fifth month, 1649, there is a list of his debts; one line reads thus : —

"To Jane Pope vidzt 20 shills.  15s in Rye & 5 pecks of peas."

At the close of the list one of those named "overseers" of the will adds this minute : —

"The five shillings Widdow Pope was to receive of the sume above said, she doth owe Hannah Johnson 5s she says yt it shall pay hir more, she says yt I, George Weekes shall have 2ˢ 6ᵈ in Corne Rye, of what is due to her above said 9 shill: 8ᵈ."

The Inventory of the estate of Henry Sandyes, which is on file in Suffolk Probate Office, dated "7: 11: 1651," stated that the estate was indebted, among others, to "Goodm Pope, Dorchester"; most likely a reference to John, senior.

AFTER THE DEATH OF JOHN POPE, SENIOR, we find in the town records references to his widow and to the property he had owned.

"2 of the 12 mth 1646:" the proprietors of the "grett lotts, the capttens neck, the 6 aker lotts and other proporsions of land now within the same fence" found it necessary to appoint "arbitrators" to settle some "matters in controversy." One of the fifty-five names subscribed to the paper which these proprietors left on record is "Jane pope."

The report of the referees, recorded the 23d of the same month, gives a list of the same fifty-five persons, but varies titles, abbreviations, spelling, etc., somewhat; and here we read "widow pope," with specification of the length of fence for which her property was assessed, viz., "14 rod — 3 foot."

Another extract from the Town Records will show the locality of one piece of the real estate of the family.

Fence-viewers were yearly appointed for the various districts of the town.

The description of one of these districts for the years 1651, 1652, and 1653, runs thus :

"That part of the great lotes called Captayne's Neck, and so round about Rocky Hill untill you com to the West end of widow Popes lote." And the two following descriptions in succeeding years point to the same, at least in part :

"From Mrs. Holland's and so Round Westward and end so far as Widow Popes Lott," and "From Daniel Prestons and soe round Westward and end so farre as the Widow Pope's lot."

"11 (1) 1660 or 1661." "Appointed to view the fence in the common corne feilds for this year 1661.          *          *          *

The great lotts from Daniel Prestons soe round westward soe farr as the widow Pope's lott. } Edward Brecke. Richard Hall.

The rest of the great lotts } Thomas Tolman. Thomas Trott."

"10: 1: 166½.

Great lotts from Daniel Prestons unto popes lot. } Richard Leads. John Smith."

The rest to the River } Abraham How. William Robinson."

Now notice the omission of the family name in the following entry, made a few weeks after the widow's death.

"9 (12) 1662."

Great lot from Daniel Prestons unto Thomas { Steven Minott.
   Tolmans house                 { Samuel Rigbey.

From Thomas Tolmans unto the River { Thomas Tolman.
                                    { Thomas Tilstone."

We have still more definite location of this "great lot," in "Suffolk Deeds, Liber II. p. 274." Joseph Twitchell of Dorchester sells to Stephen Minott of the same place, "24th (3d), 1656."

"A parcell of land in Dorchest', being twelve acres more or lesse, with all the fruit trees thereon and appur*rees* thereof, Lyeing within the feild commonly called the great Lotts: being bounded p'tly with the lands of George Proctor, and p'tly with the land of Jane Pope on the North p'te, and the land of m'. George Minott in p'te & the Marsh of Abraham How in p'te on the South p'te, one end butts upon the Land of Thomas Tollman on the East p'te the other end butts upon the highway leading to Naponsett mill on the West p'te."

This inquiry into the localities of John Pope, senior's, broad acres will be aided by one other extract from the Town Book.

William Stoughton purchased individual "rights in the land yet undivided commonly called the New Grant," and on the 8th of March, 1663¾, made a report of them to the selectmen, in order that the town might confirm to him a general title to the entire tract. Among the names he gives of those whose "proporsion" he had bought, he names two together.

| | acres. | qrers. | Pole. |
|---|---|---|---|
| "John Pope's & Whetcome's | 8 | 3 | 28 " |

At a later time Mrs. Stoughton, reporting the same lands, specifies, on the south side of Neponset river, "4 acres, 18 rods" as having originally belonged to "John Pope."

And now the well-thumbed volume, whose first entries were made in 1658, gives us this brief record :

" Jane Pope deceſsed the 12 (11) 1662."

We turn again to the Probate archives to a file marked, evidently, by the recorder on its first folding, " *The Widow Pope's Will.*"

" *The Laſt will and Teſtament of Jane Pope of Dorchester.*

I, Jane Pope, of Dorchester, widdow, in good health, make my will, 18 April, 1662.

First, I give and bequeath my soul into the hand of the Lord and my body to a decent buryall in the earth.

And for this world's goods which God have given me, my will is first, that all debts dew from me to any p'son shalbe faithfully paid and my funerall discharged. Secondly my will is (that my whole Estate being justly and equally prized) that my Daughter Patience Blake shall have £40 at her own disposing, Unto her children, when it shall please God to take her away by death ; if she dye before they Com to Age and make no disposall thereof, then my will is that it be equally divided amongst her children as they com to the age of 16 years, each child.

But if my dau. Patience Live Longer and at Last make a disposall of it, then it shall be in her power to dispose of it to her Children as she shall Judge meete. For the other part of my Estate over and above this forty pound, my will is that it be equally divided amongst the children of my dau. Patience, only Jane Blake, her Daughter shall have five pounds more than any one of the other Children.

My will is, that Mary Blake have my feather Bed and bolster and Bible as pt. of her portion, and my pewter shall be divided between Sarah and Jane as part of their portion. If any of the children dye, them that survive shall have it equally divided between them, and at the age of 16 years each child shall have the benefit of their portion for their own Advantage, and in the meantime he or they in whose hands this Estate shall remain, shall give good security for the p'formance of the premises.

And that this my will may be p'formed and my eſtate justly and truley prized I doe desier and appointe my loveing friends John Capen & John Gornell to be overſeers heerof, and I doe appoint my son-in-law, Edward Blake, to be executor of my whole estate in witnes whereof I have hereunto set my hand and seal the day and year above said.

JANE POPE. { SEAL. }

*Signed Sealed and dl*
*in presence of us  w*

JOHN CAPEN
JOHN GORNELL
MARY CAPEN

the marke of INCREASE CLAP."*

#### Endorsed on the Margin.

"Jno Capen & John Gurney have subscribed their names as witnesses to this paper were present & did both hear & see on the day of the date hereof the aforesaid Jane Pope to signe seale & publish it for the same as hir last will & Testament and that when she so Did she was of a disposing minde.

EDW. RAWSON RECORD.

#### INVENTORY.

"An Inventory of the goods & Estate of Jane Pope of Dorchester widdow who dyed the 12th day of January 1662.

Taken & apprized by us whose names are under written the 16th day of January 1662.

|  |  | £. | s. | d. |
|---|---|---|---|---|
| *Impr* | In money in the house | 1 | 14 | 03 |
| *It* | one feather-bed & bolster | 05 | 00 | 00 |
| *It* | on flock bed on feather pillow & 4 other pillows & pillow bys, on pair plankits 3 Curtains on rugg | 03 | 18 | 04 |
| *It* | on bedsteed & cord seven sheets on blankit 2 table cloths a pa of pillow bys 5 napkins 1 trugle-bedsted & cord & other small things | 04 | 06 | 10 |

---

*Increase Clap was a son of Thomas, a son of Richard, of Dorchester, England. Edward Clap's first wife, Prudence, was a sister of Thomas. John Capen, another of the witnesses, had married Redigon Clap, daughter of a brother of Thomas and Prudence, for his first wife; Mary, who signed above, was his second wife.

|  |  | £. | s. | d. |
|---|---|---|---|---|
| *It* | fouer pewter platters 1 flagon five frute dishes two drinkeing bowles 1 salt & other small things of pewter | 00 | 19 | 06 |
| *It* | on worming pan: 3 brass-pans 2 kittles on pot on Candlestick all of brass | 01 | 12 | 06 |
| *It* | on yron pott & kittle | 00 | 09 | 00 |
| *It* | of white earthen ware, spoons, trenchers, some butter and other small things | 00 | 13 | 02 |
| *It* | 4 chayres on Chest on smalle table | 00 | 12 | 00 |
| *It* | on cubberd 1 Trunk two bonds 1 Carpitt & a pa of cards | 01 | 05 | 00 |
| *It* | on small hogg, pease malt, salt, meale & Indiane Corne bags & other things | 03 | 09 | ·00 |
| *It* | on fry-ing pan, pot-hooks & hangers, Cobb-yrons, Spit, scales & weights, on bible & other household implements | 01 | 06 | 10 |
| *It* | more wheate, pease & Indian | 00 | 16 | 00 |
| *It* | land broken up & unbroken within fence & in Common | 70 | 06 | 08 |
| *It* | meddow Ground | 10 | 00 | 00 |
| *It* | several depts dew to the Estate | 56 | 17 | 00 |
|  | The total summe is | 163 | 08 | 04 |
|  | beside wearing apparell prized at | 7 | 18 | 00 |

which some say that the widdow said should be for her daughter.

|  | Severall depts dew to be paid out of the Estate | 09 | 09 | 07 |
|---|---|---|---|---|

EDWARD CLAP
The marke of
THOMAS LAKE

| *It* | more dew to the Estate | 00 | ·06 | 06 |
|---|---|---|---|---|

At a meeting of the magists the 2ᵈ April 1663 Edward Blake deposed that this is A true Inventory of the Estate of the late Jane Pope of Dorchester widdow to the best of his knowledge that when he knows more he will deliver the same.

EDW. RAWSON RECORD."

NOTE. Those who have studied wills need not be told that they are usually very incomplete documents. They do not always mention all the relatives of the testator; no list of one's children can be made from such a document with safety; they do not always show the entire property one had possessed, nor all that remained in possession at the time the will was made. Property might be willed to certain heirs, and the Inventory show other property not designated or devised; as the "wearing apparell," "which some say that the widow said should be for her daughter." The fact that no mention is made by Jane Pope of John, junior, is no evidence, therefore, that he was not her child, or that he was not living at the time she made her will. It may be she was his step-mother. Of course there may be another explanation. But at all events he lived in "that field" ten years afterward, according to Elder Topliff's "Information," and very likely he was entirely satisfied with matters.

Traditions respecting the location of Captain Roger Clapp's first house have remained in Dorchester from time immemorial, and have been carefully verified. As John Pope, senior, lived in the same field with Edward and Roger Clapp, we may join with the Clapp family in the veneration of that spot. It is on Willow Court, which runs westerly from Boston Street, a little way north of the "Five Corners." All about there the first settlers "took up each one his spot to set down upon, at the northerly end of yᵉ town, next to yᵉ aforesaid neck of Land."

The Inventory of the estate of Thomas Swift, of Dorchester, June 18, 1675, mentions "4 acres of land called pops lott."

In an agreement made between the heirs of Thomas Swift, recorded in the second volume of the town records, April 8, 1679, it was stipulated that

"William Grenow and John Whit together is to have pops lot at the price of forty pounds."

Joseph Leeds conveys to his son Samuel, Jan. 4, 1714, several parcels of land, among them one described thus: "A Lott of upland and some salt meadow the whole Seven Acres more or less, at a place commonly called Popes hill, being butted and bounded Easterly upon a Salt Creek, Westerly upon the land of Joseph Leeds junr, Northerly upon the land of Timothy Tilstone and Southerly upon the Land of Ebenezer Paul." [Lib. 29, p. 70.]

*Whence and When did John Pope, senior, come to Dorchester?*
We do not find any record which answers either of these questions; in an absolute sense, it must be admitted that we do not know.

*But we have reason to believe,*

1st, That he came from England; because the colony was composed of Englishmen, from the counties of Dorset, Somerset and Devon, chiefly, as we have testimony. The movement was one which included very few others at the first, and when persons of Scotch, Irish or other nationalities were spoken of in the town or church records of Massachusetts towns, during the first half-century, it was customary to specify their origin. The surname, too, was a well-known one in England, at that time, but has not been found in the annals of either Scotland, Wales or Ireland of the period. Further, his prominence in the church and town, the articles of property inventoried, and the contents of his will, all involve the same. We have *full reason* to believe he was a native of England.

2d. We have testimony that he was living in Dorchester, Massachusetts, November 3, 1634. Then, identifying "Goodman Poape" with the "John Pope" made freeman September 3, 1634, (as no other person appears to compete for the honor, in any other plantation,) we are certain that he had been some time in the colony and had been admitted to the church. We cannot limit this period. Roger Clap, who came, it is certain, with the first company, was only made freeman the 14th of May of that very year, 1634; and other persons are known to have been here several years before applying for the privilege. So that all that can fairly be deduced from this is the general statement,

" *He lived in Dorchester in the autumn of* 1634."

Referring to the chapter on the town of Dorchester, it will be noticed that a ship from Weymouth, Dorsetshire, had arrived there July 24, 1633, with a large number of passengers; an earlier re-enforcement had come in the "Lyon," which arrived from Bristol, Feb. 8, 1631; and earliest of all was the "Mary and John," the ship which brought the church-colony to land, May 30, 1630. He may have been a passenger in either of these; certainly he was in Dorchester before the colony was three years and a quarter old; *it may be he was one of the very first company.*

We know that he was one of the selectmen and one of the "pillars" of the church, in the reorganization of the colony after the Lancashire contingent arrived, in 1636 and 1637; which gives most gratifying proof that he was considered by his fellow-citizens a man of ability and virtue : and we need not be concerned at the lack of particulars on other points.

As to the part of England from which our ancestor came, we have no knowledge.  The writer has found *some* facts which look as though Exeter, in Devonshire, or its vicinity was the former home of the " Goodman " ; while other considerations seem to point to Dorchester, in Dorsetshire.  But as, in the matter of time, we are narrowed down to the limit of about three years, so, in the *locality* of our ancient English family home, there is no wide range, for all the probabilities shut us into a region easily spanned in an afternoon's railway ride.

*How Many Children Had John Pope, senior?*

We answer,

*First,* JOHN, junior, who must have been born in England, whence he may have come with his father, or at a later time.

*Second,* PATIENCE, also born in England, very likely.  Yet the date of her marriage might not require this, and she may have been born after the family arrived in America.

These two, were they both children of Jane?  Evidence is wanting.

*Had They Other Children?*

The Court Record of births, marriages, and deaths "from the year 1630 until the fifth of the first month, 1644," a summary of reports from all the towns, contains these three entries.  Like the others in the book, the latest relating to a *surname* is given first, then the earliest, and so down.

"Thomas the son of John Pope & Alice his wife was Born 27$^{th}$ ( 10$^{th}$ ) 1643.

"John the son of John Pope & Jane his wife was born 30th ( 4$^{th}$ ) 1635.

"Nathan the son of John Pope & Jane his wife born and dyed ( 5$^{th}$ ) 1641."

Were John and Nathan children of John, senior, and Jane, his wife?  Or was this " Jane" the first wife of John, *junior,* and this " Alice " his second wife?

If the former, then we have John, senior, naming two sons " John " — a rare, but not unknown thing.

But we know that this Thomas was the son of the younger John, for we can trace his history clearly. And it would seem very strange, if one of these entries referred to one and the other to another "John Pope," that the clerk should give no distinguishing mark to their names, as by calling the one "senior" or the other "junior."

But if the *father* were one and the same person, and the mother, only, different, then the clerk would feel no necessity for adding any other token than the simple change of maternal name. Is not this the probable explanation?

It is not to be forgotten that the ambiguity of this record has led more than one student of Dorchester history to conclude that the two John Popes were not father and son; but the word "senior," in town records and probate papers, cannot be neglected; a word which former writers on this subject had not seen, I am persuaded.

While admitting the difficulties of the case, I have been led to adopt the second theory, "as a working hypothesis": viz, *that the three entries all refer to John, junior's, children.*

Perhaps the "Goodman" had other children beside John and Patience. Several other persons of our name were in the colonies at the time of his death, whose age and other circumstances make it easy to adjust them to this family.

Thomas, the Plymouth pioneer, may be believed to have been his brother, from a number of particulars in the history of the families.

Several items suggest that the Salem pioneer, Joseph, *may* have been either a brother or a son.

Thomas, of Stamford, Conn., who named his son John, who was associated with a colony, members of which went from Watertown, *may* have been a son, also. Yet these are guesses, only. Documents may yet come to light which will give us *facts* on these points. At present we will be thankful for what we have.

# CHAPTER IV.

## RELATING TO THE
## FAMILY OF PATIENCE[2] (POPE) BLAKE.

PATIENCE,[2] daughter of *John Pope, senior*, and probably of *Jane*, his wife, was mentioned in the wills of both parents, as we have seen; her husband being named as the executor of the second document.

It is proper that we should give what has come to light in authentic documents concerning this couple.

*Edward[2] Blake*, husband of Patience[2] (Pope), was a son of the immigrant, William Blake, who, with his wife, Agnes, and his children, came from England to Massachusetts at a very early date, and was one of the most valuable citizens of Dorchester.

The exact time of the family's arrival in New England is not absolutely determined at present, nor are the dates of the children's birth, within our reach. Neither have we the time of the wedding of Edward and Patience. His name first appears in the town records in 1656, on the occasion of his being chosen one of the "fence-viewers," which proves him to have been at least twenty-one years of age then. But he was probably married before that date, since three of his children are mentioned in the will of their grandmother Pope, in 1662, the youngest of whom we know to have been born in 1658.

In 1657 the Dorchester Register of Births, Marriages, and Deaths was burned in the house of Thomas Millett; so we have only a few facts in this line concerning the pioneers before 1658. But the book then opened is extant, and from that date forward a majority of these items are recorded.

In 1657, Edward and his family removed to the adjoining town of Boston ; a fact which we learn from the record of his " bond " on the Boston Town Book. The colonists believed it was indispensable for them to receive persons to their settlements with extreme care, and even when all probabilities were in favor of a new comer, they insisted on his giving some guaranty that he would not become a burden to them !

"The 27th of the 2d month, 1657."

" Edward Blake is admitted an Inhabitant, and John Blake is heerby bound in the sum of twenty pounds sterll to save the town from any charge either from the sayd Edward or his family. And this attested by his hand.

John Blake."

*Edward Blake* was elected in Boston, a "constable" and a "culler of staves," at various subsequent times. His cooper-shop was spoken of in the reports of the inspectors. He was a member of the "2d church," and was thought worthy to be entrusted with a license to "keepe a house of publique entertainment," the 25th of April, 1670.

The following birth registers are found in the Boston Book :

" Jane, of Edward and Patience Blake, born Sept. 29, 1658."
" Susanna, of Edward and Patience Blake, born July 20, 1661."
" Abigail, of Edward and Patience Blake, born Nov. 10, 1663."
" Edward, of Edward and Patience Blake, born Oct. 16, 1666."
" Mercy, of Edward and Patience Blake, born March 26, 1670."
Dorchester Records now give the following :

" Jonathan, sone of Edward Blake (baptized) 7. 5. 72, his father being formerly a member of this church, & after joyned to y* second church in Boston, & now dwelling in Melton."

" Edward, the son of Edward Blake, died September 30th, '76."

In 1678, we find the name of Edward Blake in the list of the seven persons who united in forming the church at Milton, with this memorandum, "Member of the 2d church in Boston."

The will of "Edward Blake of Milton," dated August 31, 1692, is on file, Suff. Prob. lib. 13, fol. 59, from which we learn of his "son Jonathan," his "son Solomon," and his daughters, "Mary Picher," "Sarah Talley," "Jane Kelton," "Susanna

Wales," and "Abigail Blake." He constitutes his "two sons-in-law, viz., Richard Talley & Nathaniel Wales," the executors of his will. The inventory was taken ."3d of November, 1692."

No mention is made, it will be noticed, of either the wife, Patience, or the daughter, Mercy, and it is *not improbable* that they had died before this date.

We learn from a deed (below) that Patience was living in 1684 ; further no record showeth. An interesting token of her home feeling for old Dorchester, appears on the church book there :

"24, 4, 83. Patience, yᵉ wife of Ed. Blake, owned yᵉ Covenant in oʳ Church, though her husband a member at Melton."

Boston records attest that

"Jonathan Blake and Elizabeth Candage were married by Mr. Cotton Mather, Feb. 16, 1699"; and

"Solomon Blake and Abigail Arnold were married Aug. 24, 1704."

We may do well to construct the following family register, although it must necessarily be very incomplete.

PATIENCE,² daughter of John¹ Pope, senior, and [probably] Jane, his wife, born [it is likely] in England, married *Edward*,² son of William¹ and Agnes *Blake*, born in England, died in Milton, in September or October, 1692. She died ~~some time after~~ August & ~~1684~~

### CHILDREN OF EDWARD AND PATIENCE (POPE) BLAKE.

1. MARY BLAKE, b. ——; m. —— Pitcher.
2. SARAH BLAKE, b. ——; m. Richard Talley.
3. JANE BLAKE, b. Sept. 29, 1658 ; m. —— Kelton.
4. SUSANNA BLAKE, b. July 20, 1661; m. Nathaniel Wales.
5. ABIGAIL BLAKE, b. Nov. 10, 1663 ; single in 1692.
6. EDWARD BLAKE, b. Oct. 16, 1666; d. Sept. 30, 1676.
7. MERCY BLAKE, b. March 26, 1670.
8. JONATHAN BLAKE, baptized Sept. 5, 1672; m. Elizabeth Candage, Feb. 16, 1699. Was a shoemaker; lived in Boston, in 1722.

In the *Bangor Historical Magazine* for July, 1886, there is a very readable article upon the descendants of this man, by Rev. Chas. M. Blake, M. D., of San Francisco, Cal. It has been brought to our notice too late to be quoted from satisfactorily here. Suffice it to say, that a large and honorable posterity descended from this child of our *aunt* Patience.

9. SOLOMON BLAKE, b. ———; m. Abigail Arnold, Aug. 24, 1704. Was a cooper, living in Boston in 1720. His will is on file, dated Sept. 26, 1740, proved Aug. 25, 1741. Bequeaths to his wife Abigail, sons Joseph and William, daughters Abigail Holden and Elizabeth Russell, and grandson Solomon Russell, son of Skinner Russell.

A beautiful little volume entitled, "A Record of the Blakes of Somersetshire," etc., "Boston, 1881, Privately Printed," a work edited by W. H. Whitmore, Esq., from matter collected by the late celebrated genealogist, Mr. Somerby, contains an account of the descendants of *Solomon³ Blake* through his son Joseph⁴ down to the present time. A number of names very favorably known in Boston, Worcester, and elsewhere appear, and several of national reputation; the most distinguished among them being the late Commodore Blake, eminent for valuable coast survey services, and for his able superintendency of the Naval Academy. The English matter in Mr. Whitmore's book will be referred to in our Appendix under the title, BLAKE.

Incidental interest attaches to the deed, on record in Boston, wherein "Jonathan Blake, cordwainer, and Solomon Blake, cooper, of Boston," with their wives, Elizabeth and Abigail, convey "lands inherited from their grandfather, William Blake, late of Dorchester, deceased," under date of Dec. 6, 1720.

The following deeds are also important here:

"Edward Blake of Boston Cooper" conveys to "John Minott of Dorchester yeoman," "Patience Blake ux" [or], also signing, "ten acres of upland Bec it more or less in Dorchester bounded with the lands of the aforesaid Edward Blake and Thomas Trott on the North pt. of the same and the land of the said John Minott on the South pt. of the same, one End Butts on the lands of Mr. George Minott

and Sam'l Humphrey on the East, the other End Butts upon a highway leading to Naponsett Mill toward the West," etc., etc. "And
the said Edward Blake the day of the date hereof is and standeth
lawfully seized to his own use of land in the said Bargained premiſses
and Every part thereof in a good, perfect and Absolute Estate of
*Inheritance.*"

"The eight day of June in the year of our lord one thousand Six
hundred sixty and three."

[Both *names signed* in full.]

"Edward Blake of Boston in Suffolke in the Mattathusets collony
of New England Cooper, & patience his wife," convey to John
Minot "eight Acres of plantingl and more or leſse lying & being
in a certain field commonly called yᵉ great lotts in Dorchester aforesaid Bounded with yᵉ land of Thomas Trott on yᵉ north pte. of yᵉ
same yᵉ land of yᵉ said John minot on yᵉ south pte. of yᵉ same one
end buts upon a piece of Land formerly sold by yᵉ said Edward
Blake unto yᵉ said John Minot toward the west, the other End Butts
upon yᵉ land of James Humphrey toward yᵉ East." "A good, perfect
and absolute estate of Inheritance in fee simple" is alleged on the
part of the sellers, and the wife's "right of dower" is also pledged.

Jan. 5, 1663.

"Edward Blake of Boston Cooper and Patience his wife" convey
to "Thomas Pearse of Dorchester, Husbandman" "a parcell of
upland lying & being in a feild commonly called the great Lotts in
Dorchester aforesaid, & Containeth by estimation seven Acres &
an half Acre, bee it more or leſs and is bounded by the land of
Thomas Tolman Southerly and by the Land of Thomas Trott Northerly and butteth on the highway leading from the Towne aforesaid
toward neponsit mill Easterly and on the Lands formerly in the ten-
nor and occupation of Thomas Birch Westerly and foure rods of
fence lying at the weft End of the Land formerly in the Tennure of
mr. John Glover, deceased."

The same "estate of inheritance" is affirmed, and Patience gave
up her "right to the thirds" in the property.

July 14, 1667.

Patience Blake also joins her husband in a deed to Robert Bad-
cock, of "his now dwelling-house and out-houses ; Together with
sixty acres of land," etc., in Milton. In similar terms it is stated
that he held the land as an inheritance.

Aug. 6, 1684.

"Jonathan Blake of Boston, cordwainer," conveys to John King, of Taunton, his right in lands in the divisions of Dorchester, "once the property of John Pope, deceased (the Grandfather of the sd Jona. Blake)." Acknowledged before Samuel Thaxter, Justice of the Peace, Jan. 9, 1722.

Here is a token that the estate of the "widow Pope" had been duly set off to the grandchildren, according to her will.

N. B. In the study of this family great care needs to be exercised, because the Blakes of Dorchester, Boston and Milton had so many children bearing the same Christian names.

# CHAPTER V.

## JOHN[2] POPE, JUNIOR.

THE earliest record concerning this man, which we *absolutely know* applies to him, is that in the Court Book of Marriages and Births, which has been quoted near the close of the chapter on John Pope, senior :

"*Thomas the son of John Pope & Alice his wife was Born 27th (10th) 1643.*"

This son's life is easily traced, and he is altogether certified as a son of John of Squantum. It was not *common* in those days for a man to call his oldest son by any other name than his own : we naturally look for an older child than this, to whom the father gave his own name, John. And, as we have seen in the passage referred to, there was a "John, son of John Pope & Jane, his wife, born 30th (4th), 1635," and a "Nathan, son of John & Jane, born and died (5th), 1641." These things look to me like tokens that our second John Pope had been married to a wife named Jane, who bore him two boys, and then died soon after the birth and death of the younger ; that he had then married a second wife, the "Alice" of the entry at the head of this chapter, who was the mother of Thomas, and possibly of oth   hildren.

But perhaps this supposition is not correct, and that John and Nathan were the children of John, senior, and the Jane who survived him. If that be the case, we may presume that they called their boy in 1635 for his father, although the name had been given long years before to another son! But the only way that could come to pass would be, that the older namesake

had remained in England when his father came to Massachusetts, and was not expected to come over here.* Supposing
thus, we might be justified in guessing that they were surprised
a few months later by the arrival of John, No. 1!

In a list of passengers for "Virginia"—indefinitely used,
sometimes, for some American port not specified—we read:

"*21st August*, 1635, *in the George, Jo: Severne master*, ...
*Jo: Pope*."

This is the precise abbreviation for *John* which we have
noticed in Dorchester Town Records and in the signature of a
witness to the will of Thomas Pope of Sussex.

We find no mention of any John Pope in Virginia in those
times, although Popes of other cognomens were there, and it is
*possible* that this passenger was our John[2] Pope, jr.

At whatever time he came, he was surely born in England,
at least seven or eight years before the founding of Dorchester
Colony, or as early as 1622. It may be he was considerably
older, and that he married before coming. The Dorchester
Birth, Marriage, and Death book, destroyed in 1657, undoubtedly
contained the evidence which we want on these points..

There is much likelihood that he is the person alluded to
in the following passage we copy from the Dedham Town
Records:

"At a meeting of Inhabitants in 1639, the 25th of yᵉ Month comōn-
only Called March," among the votes passed is the following:

"John Pope entertayned unto a twelve acre Lott p'vided yᵗ he sub-
scribeth to our orders & assureth us of comeing to inhabit wᵗʰ us
before."

Was this after the death of his first wife, Jane (if he had
one!), and did he contemplate making his home in some new
region? And did he fail to comply with the conditions given
above, because his father deeded him a handsome estate on the
sunny slope of the Squantum hill?

Enough of conundrums.

Again we turn to entries which belong to this man beyond
all question.

---

* Such a double-naming took place in the Littlefield family in Wells, about this period.

The first item in the *Town Journal* relating to any Pope beside John, senior, and his widow, is the following :

"Account of the Rates gathered in the yeare 1651," . . . Disbursed as followeth." . . . "It. to Alce pope for laks child, 3ˡⁱ· 14ˢ, and for cloths 10ˢ. 4ˡⁱ· 4ˢ, 0ᵈ·"

The next year's account gives :

"Itm̄. to John Popes wife about Ales Lakes childeren, 0ˡⁱ 10ˢ 8ᵈ·"

Many families of the town thus took care of poor children (or adults), and were paid out of the town treasury.

In the list of "Divisions in the Cow walke," or shares in the pasture lands (in the second town book), a list made in the year 1651, you may see the lines :

"No 67. John Pope, 8*a*, 3*q*, 28*r*," and among the holders of lots in the "Second Division," "No. 54. John Pope, 8*a*, 3*qr*, 28*r*."

One of the earliest lines in the town book opened immediately after the Millet fire, is this :

"John Pope the sonne of John Pope was borne the 1 : 5 : 1658."

This babe lived, grew to manhood, married, begot three daughters, and died in 1698.

Other children must have been born soon after, who come into the annals later ; and it was not easy to feed all and find cash for taxes.

"The 12 of the (12 Mo) 1665," "There was a warrant granted to the Constable Thomas Trot to levie upon John Pope, and Thomas Wilkinson, for what they are behind to the Rate of the Ministery for severall years. John Pope is behind for 3 years 1 — 18 — 11 Thomas Wilkison for 4 yeers. 1 — 17 — "

The son does not seem to have followed in the footsteps of his father in zeal for religion ; we have reason to believe he was not a member of the church, and not a "freeman." Let us hope he was not trying to evade the payment of his lawful taxes, but that some good excuse for his delinquency existed, either in his family expenses or otherwise.

There is evidence that he owned his Squantum estate at this time, though no proof that he lived there, although that may be the case.

*From the Town Records, Second Volume.*

" We whose names are underwritten, being appointed by the Selectmen in Dorchester to view the highway which goes over the land of John Pope at Squantum's Neck, upon his desire of removing the highway, upon condition that he may have the land that lies betweene Goodman Leeds his medow and the said highway; we judge meet that he have the sayd land home to the common-land southward ; always allowing passage unto Goodman Leeds and his successors to his medow, as his or their occasions shall require from time to time.

In witness whereof we have set our hands and seals this on and twenty of March, 1665.

> WILLIAM SUMNER,
> JOHN MINOTT,
> ROGER BILLING.

By order of the Selectmen entred & examined
> by me,      .
> William Pole, Recorder."

The next chronicle shows our ancestor suffering annoyance from the application of a rigid rule which all Massachusetts towns had adopted. We will first note the order adopted by the town in 1658.

" Wheras the generall Court hath taken care what strangers shall Reside in this jurisdiction and how lisenced as by the law title strangers it doth appeare, but have taken noe order for families ore p'sons that remove from one towne in this Jurisdiction to another : now to p'vent such inconvenience as may come if every one be at liberty to receive into this towne whom they please. It is ordered therfore by the select men of this towne that if any maner of p'son ore p'sons in this towne shall intertaine any sojorour ore inmate into his or ther house ore habitation above one weeke, without lisence from the selectmen ore the major parte of them first had and obtained, shall forfeit five shillings, and for every weekes Continuance three shillings foure pence."*

---

*In 1666 William Chaplin was rebuked for entertaining his *brother*, and finally gave bonds in the sum of twenty pounds to secure the town from charges.

Now comes practical application.

"It was agreed upon—13. 10. 1669—that ther should be an order sent to John Pope (the Select men understanding that a daughter of his is come from Boston into his famely) that he doe forthwith come to the Select men and give Security to save the Towne harmles from Damedg or els to expect the penalty which the towne order lays upon such as entertain Inmats."[*]

John Pope, jr's, eldest daughter Margaret, who some-time married —— Peirce, may have been by this time in her teens, and an inmate of some family, — Edward Blake's, naturally, or, possibly, a home of her own, — in Boston ; and now, visiting her father's house, gave oppor-tunity for the town authorities to levy a small bill upon him, — at least to enforce, impartially, the General Court's edict.

In 1674 another of the strict laws of the period was brought to bear on the family.

It was ordered that "John Pope himself and such of his chilldren as are of Capaccetie for learning doe appeare before the Select men at their next meeting."

Six weeks later he was again "warned to Come before the Select men with such of his children as are of Capacetie to be Cattechised."

And in order that he might not feel lonely, they added, "And John plum is then to appeare alsoe."

The town officers were enforcing a recent edict of the general government, and must be vigorous and impartial.

So " 12. 2. 75 " we are relieved to learn that

" John Pope appeared before the Select men to give an acct of the Education of his Children by way of Cattechizing who p'mised to Endeavor for time to come to be more dillegent that way to attaine instruction for them."

---

[*] Boston Records, "The 25th 7th mo. 54.— Farnham is fined five shillings for Receiving goodman Wales into his house as an inmate." Yet this was a "freeman " who had been an honored citizen of Dorchester twenty years, and was now in process of removing with his family to a town only four miles away !

To add to the size of the class to be catechized, another birth occurred a little later, as the town record shows.

"Jane the Daughter of John Pope, Born May 23 : 77."

Then, two years later, a son came, who staid long enough to receive a name, perhaps a token of kinship with the Salem pioneer, Joseph Pope, and passed up to a higher school :

"Joseph the son of John Pope was Born October 17ᵗʰ· & Died the 24ᵗʰ day of the same month, 1679."

Now a passage in the town book points to the building of a house. In order to get *clear-logs* which might be split into *clove-boards*, our ancestor sought permission to cut on the town lands ; for large, fine timber was now growing scarce in private tracts. So we find that,

"The 10. 3. 80 It is granted to John Pope libertie to git 1400 Clobords out of the Common Swamps belonging unto Dorchester."

A quantity, by the by, sufficient to "weatherboard" quite a respectable mansion. Very likely a primitive house on the Squantum hillside now gave place to the "home-stall," which sheltered the family for long years afterward.

We look in vain for other items regarding this father's life. He was probably a hard-working husbandman, full of care and toil to supply the wants of his large family. He brought his farm to a good state, and left a large property. We do not find his name among town officers or notables. He seems less religious, less efficient than his father had been. But who knows what his inner life was ?

Presently comes the record :

"John Pope died October: 18 : 1686."

With no delay the following documents were duly filed in the Probate Office.

### ADMINISTRATION GRANTED.

"By the honᵇˡᵉ Joseph Dudly Esqʳ· Presidᵗ of his Majestys Territory & Dominion of New Engᵈ in America. Full Power and Authority to administer all and Singular the Goods Estate and

Credits of John Pope late of Dorchester Decease^d· is Graunted unto Margaret Pope his relict Widdow, she having given Bond and Security to administer the Same according to Law, Boston 11 Novemb^r 1686.        Attest^r

DANIEL ALLIN, CLER."

"Mrs. Margaret Pope Relict Widdow of John Pope late of Dorchester Decs^d· William Sumner, and Preserved Capen of Dorchester" gave bonds Nov. 11^th· 1686, for her performance of the duties of administratrix of the estate of her late husband.

"Margaret Pope Administratrix personally appearing made Oath that the within ac^co contains a just & true Inventory of the estate [of which] her late husband J^no· Pope Dyed Seized & is yet come to her hands & that when more appears she will cause it to be added.

Boston, 11 Novemb^r 1686.        Jurat coram preside

Attest^r DANIEL ALLIN, CLER."

In the following Inventory notice "on" for one; "to" for two; and other peculiarities. Observe, too, that the date of his death is written " 19," while it stands " 18 " in the town record; which probably shows that he died during the night, when the 18^th was passing into the 19^th·

"November the 3 1686
Inventore of the eſtat of John Pope Senior deſeſſed
October 19 1686.

Taken by us whos names are under written.

|  | £ | s. | d. |
|---|---|---|---|
| Three fether beds on rug | 2 | 0 | 0 |
| fower blankets on sheet & three bedsteds | 7 | 0 | 0 |
| On musket on sword & belt | 1 | 4 | 0 |
| on table on form & chest | 0 | 15 | 0 |
| on tabell cloth & three napkins | 0 | 3 | 6 |
| on great chest old cupboard on mixing trough | 1 | 9 | 0 |
| to spinning whells three chaiers | 0 | 11 | 0 |
| on churn to payls & on tub milkinge | 0 | 8 | 0 |
| fower pewter platers three glass bottles | 0 | 10 | 6 |
| on warming pan on chamber pote with other t'ming waer | 0 | 6 | 0 |
| to iron pots on trowell to andierns fier shovell and tongs on'payer of belos | 1 | 8 | 0 |

| | £. | s. | d. |
|---|---|---|---|
| on brasse Ketall earthen drinking cups, dishes and spouns & trenchers to jars | 0 | 8 | 0 |
| in miln Corn | 7 | 0 | 0 |
| in ry and barly | 1 | 0 | 0 |
| in wheat and oats | 2 | 0 | 0 |
| on Cart and whels plow irons other takling | 3 | 0 | 0 |
| on panell and on ladell | 1 | 0 | 0 |
| to Cows and fower yong Cattell | 8 | 0 | 0 |
| on hors to maers and on Colt | 7 | 0 | 0 |
| in swin | 4 | 0 | 0 |
| land in tilladg 43 acres | 129 | 0 | 0 |
| on hous and barn with fower acers land Joyning to the hous | 50 | 0 | 0 |
| sixteen acers of pastuer land | 32 | 0 | 0 |
| on cannen with other things | 2 | 0 | 0 |
| the sum totall | 260 | 0 | 0 |
| depts from the estate with several charges the sum totall | 14 | 13 | 3 |

THOMAS PEARS
HENRY LEADBETTER
ROGER BILLENG."

Somehow the business of settling the estate did not prosper to the satisfaction of all. After thirteen years new appraisers were appointed and went over the estate, and the Probate Court issued a detailed order by means of which all points were covered well, and all parties satisfied, it would appear.

### THE INVENTORY OF 1699.

" Wee whose names are hereunto subscribed, being nominated and appointed by the Hon^ble William Stoughton Esq: Jugg of Probate for and in the County of Suffolke

To apprise the housing & Lands of John Pope of Dorchester Deceased Intestate accordingly we have mett this 18 of feb^r 1699 & have Apprised as followeth.

| | £ | s. | d. |
|---|---|---|---|
| House & Barne | 50 | 00 | 00 |
| Six Acres of Land lying about the house | 24 | 00 | 00 |
| Twenty acres of Land Lying on the North side of the Paralell Line | 60 | 00 | 00 |

| | £. | s. | d. |
|---|---|---|---|
| Twelve Acres of Land Bounded with Daniel preston's Land on the north and south | 40 | 00 | 00 |
| Twelve Acres of Land lying near to a place called the Chappell * | 36 | 00 | 00 |
| fourteen acres of Pasture Land on the south side of the paralell line | 28 | 00 | 00 |
| The whole Two hundred thirty eight pounds | £238 | | |

> HENRY LEADBEATTER
> SAMUEL TOPLIFF
> SAML ROBINSON."

### ENDORSEMENT.

" Boston Feb⁷ 29 1699

The above written Apprismt was then exhibited by Henry Leadbetter Samuel Topliff and Saml Robinson the three Subscribers as their apprisemt of the housing and land of John Pope late of Dorchester deced.

at<sup>lr</sup>  JAS ADDINGTON.

And now we come to a document of remarkable value, better than a will, because it necessarily alludes to matters a will might have omitted.

"Order for Settling the Houses and Lands of John Pope of Dorchester dece'd upon his son Ralph Pope.

SUFFOLK ss. By the Hon<sup>ble</sup> William Stoughton Esq<sup>r</sup> : Judge of Probate &c.

Whereas, It having been represented and made to appear unto me that the Estate in Houses and Lands of John Pope, late of Dorchester, in the County of Suffolk, aforesaid deceased Intestate, could not be divided among all the children of said deceased without great prejudice to or spoiling of the whole : the same by virtue of an order from me hath been apprized by Samuel Topliffe, Henry Leadbetter and Samuel Robinson three sufficient Freeholders by me appointed and sworne for that purpose, at the sum of two hundred and thirty-eight pounds, as by the return of the apprizers and the records thereof doth and may appear. And whereas there hath been produced and shewn forth unto me a writing under the hand and seal of

---

* Pattee, in " Old Braintree and Quincy " says that an " Abrupt pile of rocks, known by the name of ' the Chapel,' at the northeast extremity of the peninsula of Squantum," was the mark referred to in Mr. Roger Ludlow's grant, in 1634, as " Musquantum Chapell."

In the early part of the present century the Dorchester fishermen used to offer for sale what they called " Chapel Eels," caught near this rock."

Thomas Pope deceased, eldest son of the s⁴ Intestate, wherein he
doth acknowledge to have had and received a certain quantity or
parcel of Land therein mentioned, in full of his part and share and
portion of his Father's Estate, and in consideration thereof doth release
and quit all further claim to any part of the same. So that the children
of the s'd Intestate and their legal representatives who now have a
right and interest in his Estate are as hereafter named, *That is to say,*
The Children of his sonn John Pope deceased, his sons William Pope
and Ralph Pope, Margaret Peirce only child of his Daughter Margaret
Peirce dece'd ; and his Daughters, Susanna Cox wife of John Cox ;
Mary Cox widow, Thankful Woodward wife of Smith Woodward ; and
Jane Munney wife of John Munney: To each of whom an equal part
or portion of the s'd Intestates Estate doth belong.

*And whereas* it hath also been represented unto me That the s⁴
John Pope Second Son of the s⁴ Intestate is deceased without having
left any male heirs; and that the s⁴ William Pope the third Son of
the Intestate hath sold his Interest in his s⁴ Father's Estate, and is
gone beyond Sea, and hath not been heard of for several years.

*Pursuant* therefore to the Act of the General Aſsembly Intitled An
Act for the Settlement and Distribution of the Estates of Intestates, and
by virtue of the power and authority to me thereby granted, I do by
these presents order and assign the whole Estate of the s⁴ John
Pope first above named, in houses and Lands, mentioned in the
Return of the before named Apprizers, To wit, The s⁴ Intestates
house and Barne ; Six acres of Land lying about the Same ; Twenty
acres of Land lying on the North side of the Paralel Line ; Twelve
acres of Land bounded with Daniel Prestons Land on the North and
South ; Twelve acres of Land lying near to a place called the Chappel ;
and Fourteen acres of Pasture Land on the South Side of the Paralel
Line ; Together with the rights, members and appurtenances to the s⁴
Housing and Lands belonging unto the beforenamed Ralph Pope, fourth
Son of the said Intestate, and to his heirs and assignes forever (*Saving*
unto Margaret Pope late Wife of the s⁴ Intestate her Dower or Thirds
in the s⁴ Houses and Lands during the terme of her natural life).

The s⁴ Ralph Pope paying unto his Brothers and Sisters and the
Legal Representatives of such of them as are deceased the respective
sum and sums of money herein after mentioned and expressed. That is
to say — To the Children of his s⁴ Brother John Pope dece'd or
their lawful Guardian the sum of £19, 16s., 8d., being the single
share of two-third parts of the value of s⁴ Estate, accrueing unto
them in right of their s⁴ Father ; To his s⁴ Brother William Pope
or his legal Representative or assignes, the like Sum of £19, 16s.,

8d., being the Single Share of two third parts of the value of the sd Estate belonging to the s[d] William: To Margaret Peirce only child of his s[d] Sister Margaret Peirce dece'd or her lawful Guardian, the like sum of £19, 16s., 8d., being the Single Share of two Third parts of the value of s[d] Estate accrueing unto her in right of her s[d] Mother; and to his s[d] Sisters Susanna Cox, Mary Cox, Thankful Woodward and Jane Munney the like Sum of £19, 16s., 8d., each; being their respective Single Shares of two third parts of the value of the s[d] Estate in Houses & Lands of their before named Father: Or giving good Security to pay the s[d] respective Sums unto his beforenamed Brothers and Sisters, Children of the sd Intestate, or their respective Guardians, legal Representatives or assignes as aforesa[d] within the Space of two years next ensueing, Together with allowance for the same in the interim after the rate of six pounds per cent per annum, as by the afore recited Act is provided.

The said Ralph Pope also giving good Security to pay further at and upon the decease of the s[d] Margaret late Wife of the s[d] Intestate, as follows Vi[z]. To the Children of his s[d] Brother John Pope or their lawful Guardian the Sum of £9, 18s., 4d., being the Single Share of the remaining third part of the value of said Houses and Lands, accrueing unto them in right of their s[d] Father; To his s[d] Brother William Pope; To the s[d] Margaret Peirce only Child of his s[d] Sister Margaret Peirce; And to his s[d] Sisters, Susanna Cox, Mary Cox, Thankful Woodward and Jane Munney, or to the legal Representatives of such of them as may then be deceased, or the Guardians duly appointed for any of them that may be under age; the like Sum of £9, 18s., 4d. each, being the Single Share or portion of the remaining third part of the value of the Houses and Lands of the sd Intestate, of right accrueing unto his s[d] Children respectively or their respective legal Representatives as afores[d] at the decease of the s[d] Wife of the Intestate. (The part of his s[d] houses and Lands belonging to her for her Dower or Thirds therein during her natural life, then also falling to the s[d] Ralph Pope by virtue of the before written Settlement of the whole of the same upon him.)

*In Testimony* whereof I have hereunto set my hand and the Seal of the Court of Probate for the County aforesaid the fourth day of April Anno Domini 1700.                         WM. STOUGHTON."

" Entered and Security taken for the within named Ralph Pope paying unto his Brothers and Sisters or their legal Representatives their respective portions out of the houses and Lands settled upon him by the before written Order, according to the true intent and meaning thereof.

                              Ja. ADDINGTON *Reg*."

As to the children here mentioned, we note first, *Thomas*, whose birth has been chronicled; the next chapter is devoted to his life and his family.

Second, *John ;* Lancaster chronicles his marriage, September 20, 1683, to Beatrix Houghton, a native of Lancaster, born in 1665, daughter of John and Beatrix Houghton.

Three daughters are registered as having been born there, though the dates of their births are not given ; they were living, we see, in 1700, and one we discover considerably later, when she received some property as an heir of her father. He was a corporal in the company of Capt. John Withington, in the French and Indian war, from 1690 onward. He seems to have come to Dorchester to live, after his discharge, and to have died there. At least, this is the natural inference from the Probate papers, which were filed in Boston.

"Beatrix Pope of Lancaster, in the County of Midd[x.] Widow & John Houghton of Lancaster yeoman & Smith Woodward of Dorchester in the county of Suffolke yeoman," gave bonds in the sum of fifty pounds, June 16, 1698, for her administration of the estate of "her husband John Pope late of Dorchester above s[d] husbandman."

"An Inventory of the lands and Estate of John Pope sumtime of Lancaster, late of Dorchester Deceased June 14th, 1698.

Apprized by JOHN HOUGHTON
JONAS HOUGHTON."

On the back this is endorsed, "Exhibited by Beatrix Pope Relict widow & admin[x] of the Estate of John Pope, late of Dorchester."

The township of Ashburnham, or "Dorchester Canada," as it was first called, was granted by Massachusetts to the members of Captain Withington's Company, after the war. In the year 1736, "Susanna, the wife of Thomas Wilder, of Lancaster," received a tract of land there "in the right of her father, the late John Pope." We have no further account of the family.

The third son has left several memorials.

On the tax-list of Marlborough for the year 1688, his name is found, taxed for "1s., 8d." "May 21, 1692 Mary daughter of William and Mary Pope was born," is the solitary item of family history we have been able to glean.

In Suffolk deeds there is confirmation of the statement made in the Court Order:

" William Pope of Marlborough, in his Majesty's Province in New England," deeded to " Smith Woodward of Dorchester," for the sum of eighteen pounds, " All that right which I have in any part of that estate which was formerly the Estate of my father John Pope late of Dorchester desc'd, both of housing, Lands and moveables, all that part of his Estate that belongeth unto me, the said housing and Lands lying and being within the township of Dorchester at a certain place commonly called and known by the name of Squantum neck.

" Acknowledged Nov. 27, 1695, in presence of John Blake, Hannah Blake and Jonathan Pitcher, by William Pope."

The deed was entered and recorded, April 24, 1717, doubtless by some member of the Woodward family.

Having the note in the Court Order above that William had "gone beyond the sea and hath not been heard of for several years," the writer made search in England for probate papers which might give further information of him. Here was one noted :

"William Pope of Stockly English, yeoman"; wife, Mary; children, William and Mary, minors at date of will. Brother-in-law John Bradford, and Edward and William Pope mentioned. Feb. 6, 1698. No hint of the relationship of Edward and William.

Another William came to light in " Barton Regis, in the co. of Gloucester," also a "yeoman." Date, Jan. 19, 1699. Wife not mentioned. Children, Abraham, William, John, Ann Barrows, Mary, and Elizabeth; brother-in-law, Richard Jeffries. Presented for probate by Elizabeth Granger, Jan. 28, 1715.

I contribute this material to any other inquirer who may feel like pursuing this member of the Squantum family :

*Ralph*, the fourth son, will have suitable notice in a chapter devoted to himself and family.

*Margaret*, eldest daughter, evades all our investigations ; not a clue is found as to herself, her husband, or her child, beyond those given in the order above.

As to the other daughters of *John Pope, junior*, we have a number of facts.

After the death of her husband, the widow, Margaret, joined
the church.   The entries in the church book from that time
forward furnish us numerous pieces of information upon the
family,—children and grandchildren as well.

" May 15, 92, Widow Pope admitted."
" Susannah pope, mary pope, thankfull pope, Jane pope, thes four
owned the covenant : and were Baptised 29, May 92."

N. B.  It is noteworthy that the three elder of these sisters
were already married, and yet the clerk here recorded them by
their maiden names.   The next entry plainly shows this ; and
we know that Thankful had been the wife of Smith Woodward
nearly a year.

" 5 March 169⅔.   Margratt, Mary, Sarah, John, thankfulll, thes 5
wer the children of susannah Cocks the dau of goody pope she having owned the Covenant."
" Ebenezer son of Goodman Cock whose wife is daughter to sistᵣ
pope baptized May 10 96."
" James son of John Cock Grandchild of oᵣ sister the widow Pope
—baptized 18ᵗʰ 4ᵗʰ ᵐᵒ 1696, being thanksgiving-day for our King's
deliverance."
" Elizabeth Cocks, sistᵣ Popes Grand child 26. 7. 97."

☞ " Ralph Pope son of sister Pope Nov. 28. 97." ☜

" Thomas Cocks Grandchild of sister Pope 9. 3. 98."
" The Double Seat át yᵉ right hand of yᵉ Pulpit" was the place
where ten old ladies regularly sat, in " the new seating," " 5 (10) 98."
Among them was " Widow Pope."

We find, further on, record of the baptism of " Susanna Cock"
April 9, 1699 ; of "Submit," March 28, 1703, and of " Benjamin,"
April 1, 1705.   The town Birth Register tells us that a child
"Joseph," was also born to John and Susanna,  April 8, 1700 ;
and a second " Susanna," Sept. 20, 1702, testifies to the death
of the child baptized three years before.   The historian of the
Cox family,— the modern spelling of this name,— must wrestle
with the problem, whether any of these " grandchildren of Sister
Pope " were Thomas and Mary's offspring, or whether all filled
the " quiver " of John and Susanna,— a baker's dozen of them !

The incomplete statements of the registrars leave me in doubt, but with an inclination to the latter theory.

The fourth daughter, *Thankful*, became the wife of Smith Woodward, July 29, 1691, and sixteen children blessed their union.   Like her older sisters, she had a home adjoining the old farm, and there she died.   Her will, dated May 24, 1738, is on file in Boston, as are the administration papers of her husband's estate, a year earlier.

Of *Jane*, fifth daughter, we have only these two facts ; that she was born May 23, 1677, and was married to John Munnings, April 2, 1698.

Did they live at the " Moon," a crescent-shaped island, in Boston Harbor, which John's grandfather first owned?

Of the mother, Margaret's, parentage we are totally ignorant. Her marriage to John Pope, jr., must have been, of course, some time after 1651, when Alice is noted as his wife.   We *believe* she was the mother of all the children whose names have come down to us, later than Thomas.

The clerk of the church alludes to her in a way that makes her seem an honored member of that body.

She survived her husband sixteen years, during which, as we have seen, she joined the church and saw a large number of her children and grandchildren also gathered into the fold.   With a son for a "right hand man " at the old home, and married daughters with their families all about her, she may be supposed to have had a serene old age.

We find her joining her son Ralph in a deed to Nathaniel Butt, March 22, 1700, conveying

"Twelve acres of land lying in that place called and known by the name of Squantum Neck, bounded Easterly and Westerly by the sea, Northerly with the land of Nathaniel and Hezekiah Butt."

March 22, 1701, Ralph bought of Daniel Preston (and Abigail his wife), for "forty-eight pounds current of New England," "two pieces or parcels of land situated within the township of Dorchester, at a place commonly called Squantum's Neck, one of said pieces containing ten acres more or less, and is butted and bounded as followeth, viz : Northerly with the meadow of Smith Woodward, southerly with the mount-bay, easterly with the land of Roger Billings, westerly with the meadow of Nichols and Pratt.   The other piece of land mentioned is bounded

northerly with the parallell line, southerly with Mount bay, easterly
and Westerly with the land of Ralph Pope and is in quantity one
acre three quarters and twenty rods, more or less." . . .

" Memorandum that before the signing and sealing of the within instrument it is mutually agreed by and between all the parties concerned that Margaret Pope widow and relict of John Pope shall have
and retain her third in the land bought of Daniel Preston in lieu of
her third in that land which is sold to Nathaniel Butt during the time
and term of her natural life." Nathaniel Butt with his wife Sherebiah,
witnesses.

The document was not "acknowledged," until Oct. 17, 1718. Long
before that date the widow ceased to need what her thoughtful son
secured to her in this document.

In the Old Burying Ground in Dorchester there remained,
until a few years ago, a stone which bore the following inscription (copied, with others, by that worthy genealogist, Mr.
William Blake Trask, for the "Genealogical Register," Vol. I.).

*"Here lyes yᵉ Body of*
*Margaret Pope wife to*
*John Pope Aged about*
*74 years died October*
*yᵉ 20ᵗʰ 1702 "*

In addition to the names given in the Court Order there is
another, a son, to be added. When Ralph³ made his will in 1744
he bequeathed to *his son Ebenezer* all his " right in the new
Township granted by the Government to the Officers and
Soldiers that served in the expedition against Canada, under the
command of Captain John Withington ; he fulfilling the conditions of said grant."

This would seem to indicate that Ralph³ had been a soldier
in that expedition, which set out when he was about seventeen
years of age: not impossible in the nature of the case, but
unlikely.

*Au contraire,* we discover in the Massachusetts Archives,
Book 114, p. 193, a list of "Persons admitted as Settlers
or Grantees into a New Township, Granted by yᵉ Great

and General Court of Massachusetts Province in New England on Petition of Thomas Tilston Esq. in behalf of y* Officers and Soldiers who served in y* Expedition to Canada, under y* Command of Capt. John Withington of Dorchester."

Among the persons mentioned there is, "Pope, Ralph, in the right of His Brother Ebenezer Pope of Dorchester."

In a list of the company published in the History of Dorchester, the name of Ebenezer Pope is found. Putting this fact along with Ralph's bequest, we can do no other than give this additional son a place in the list of John[2] Pope, jr.'s, children. He may have been only a little older than Ralph, and not yet married when he enlisted ; he may have fallen in battle or camp. He cannot have left heirs, or they would have been noticed in the settlement of the estate of his father. His name is one which was a favorite in the Salem Pope family, and passed down along that line, as well as in ours. It also occurred among the early generations of the Plymouth family.

The Register of this second family of Dorchester Popes is a very imperfect one truly ; but we will put it into due form.

N. B. Where birth dates are wanting, the order of the children is conjectural in part ; that is to say, the Order of Court gives the sons and daughters separately.

JOHN[2] POPE, JUNIOR, son of John[1] Pope, senior, born in England, married (1st) [?] Jane ——.

### CHILDREN OF JOHN[2] AND JANE.

I. JOHN,[3] b. June 30, 1635 ; d. ——.

II. NATHAN,[3] b. July ——, 1641 ; d. July, 1641.

He married (2[d]) *Alice* ——.

### CHILD OF JOHN[2] AND ALICE.

III. THOMAS,[3] b. Nov. 27, 1643 ; d. before 1700. [See following chapter.]

JOHN[2] married (3[d]) *Margaret* —— ; b. in England in 1628 ; d. Oct. 20, 1702.

CHILDREN OF JOHN[2] AND MARGARET.

IV.   MARGARET,[3] b.———— ; m.——Peirce ; *Child*, Margaret Peirce.

V.   JOHN,[3] b. March 5, 1658 ; m. Beatrix Houghton, Sept. 20, 1683 ; d. in 1698. *Children*, 1. Susanna,[4] m. Thomas Wilder ; 2, Beatrix[4] ; 3, Margaret[4].

VI.   SUSANNA,[3] m. John Cock [Cox].

VII.   WILLIAM,[3] m. Mary ————. *Child*, Mary,[4] b. May 21, 1692.

VIII.   MARY,[3] m. Thomas Cock [Cox].

IX.   EBENEZER,[3] d. before 1700.

X.   THANKFUL,[3] m. July 29, 1691, Smith Woodward ; d. in 1738.

XI.   RALPH,[3] b. in 1673 ; d. Feb. 2, 1744-5. [See following Chapter.]

XII.   JANE,[3] b. May 23, 1677 ; m. April 2, 1692, John Munnings.

XIII.   JOSEPH,[3] b. Oct. 17, 1679 ; d. Oct. 24, 1679.

# CHAPTER VI.

## THE THIRD GENERATION.

*1, THOMAS³. 2, RALPH³.*

### SECTION 1.

#### THOMAS³ AND HIS FAMILY.

ONLY two sons of John² Pope, jr., had sons, and perpetuated the family name (unless William,³ of whom all trace was
lost by his mother and brethren, left such heirs).

The oldest of these, Thomas,² had but one son of whose marriage we have evidence, and this son became a resident of New
Hampshire, where his descendants have lived. By some means
they failed to report or to be sought out; and there has never
been any communication between them and the posterity of
Ralph³. By assiduous search the writer has learned a number
of facts about these "cousins," and will give, in this section,
what he has gathered, not placing them in the following chap-
ters, along with our own representatives of succeeding generations, because so little is known about them.

THOMAS,³ son of John,² junior, and Alice ——, born in Dorchester, Nov. 27, 1643, married (1ˢᵗ) in 1669 – 70, *Elizabeth*,
dau. of Henry Merrifield, baptized 16ᵗʰ of April, 1649.

Deprived of his mother at an early age, and not properly
"catechized" by his father, as the "town's husbands" felt, this
boy had much to keep him back, little to develop his best qualities,
it may be conjectured. When he was twenty-four years old the
selectmen were minded to admonish certain "young men not
under the Government of famyles according as the law en-
joins"; and though not called to the lecture-room for a warn-

ing, Thomas was "privately" cautioned that he must have a place as an obedient child under his father's roof, or find some other home.   The result was, he found a bride in the daughter of the farmer who cultivated part of the Clapp lands.

When on the threshold of majority he put his name to a petition of the inhabitants of the town, addressed to King Charles the Second.   New Englanders had been strong sympathizers with the Cromwell party during the Revolution and Commonwealth ; now they feared that the son of a beheaded monarch would revenge himself on them by taking away some of their liberties and privileges.   So the colonists sent over humble, submissive words to the Restored Stuart.   The document is given in the " Genealogical Register," Vol. v. p. 393.

He was chosen "fence-viewer" at about the time of his marriage.

In 1675 the town

"granted to Thomas Pope libertie to git about 2 or 300 of railes out of the 500 acrs " ; and four years later they gave him permission to cut and haul from the same town lands " soe much timber as to build a hous of 18 foot long and 16 wide."

His father had furnished ground for the home to rest upon, and to cultivate, as we have learned.

He was not rich ; and when the legacy of Jane Burges to the needy people of the town was distributed, he received a share, as did also his father-in-law.

Meanwhile several children had been born, of whom we shall presently speak ; and while they were all very young, their mother passed away.   Exactly when, we do not discover, but the town clerk tells us of a second marriage, which involves the parting of the first by death.

(2d.) " Thomas Pope & Margaret Long were married by the Worshipfull Humphrey Davy Es⁴ November 18ᵗʰ 81." ,

We next learn of arrangements for emigration to another colony ; and though it is poor policy for a man to get into debt to many neighbors, it certainly reflects credit on one who is about to remove, that he arranges to pay all his creditors.   He bonded or sold his property to Increase Sumner, and gave him a list of the debts he was to pay out of the proceeds. We will print this list of names, because it has historical value, by reason of the location of so many individuals at that date.

Of course the spelling is no better than that of the town clerks of that day!

"An Account of my due Debts to be paid by increase Sumner upon the account of a bond Due unto me Thomas Pope of 23 pounds to be paid on or before the last of october 1683," etc.

[We omit the respective sums.]

"Left Caipin,                    Mr. Cowile sign[or.]
Samuel Topliffe,                 John Bull,
Samuell Caipin,                  wido george,
John pason,                      Mr. Miriam, sign[r.]
Mrs. poole,                      Samuell Sumner,
Roger Billing,                   Richard baker,
wido Smith,                      Thomas Tolman,
phillip Withington,              israell How,
obadiah Swift,                   Ezra Clapp,
Joseph Crosbe,                   Daniell preston, sign[r.]
georg minot,                     Edward pason,
Charles Danford,                 incres Sumner,
David Jones,                     John Tolman."

John Breck witnessed, and apparently wrote the paper ; and it was preserved among Breck Family documents.

Freed from debt, — altogether, it is to be devoutly hoped, — Thomas set out for the Connecticut valley, where he spent a number of years. Suffield records give the death of a "John Pope, Aug. 20, 1683," who, not being otherwise accounted for, may be believed to have been the first babe of the second wife.

At all events, we *know* of one child of this marriage, born in that town.

"Mindwell, dau. of Thomas Pope and Margaret his wife was born Sept. 12, 1687."

But the family found their way up the valley a year later; and Springfield records tell us that

"Margaret, wife of Thomas Pope was sicke and died Dec. 28, 1688."

Further travel brought further trouble; for in Northampton

"Experience Pope died Sept. 20, 1689."

Whether the widower betook himself to Lancaster, the home of his brother John, we know not; but there, years afterward, his youngest daughter, Alice, was living, the wife of John Harris.

But she was in Dorchester, "Jan. 17, 96," when she joined the church, in company with "Eliz. Maudsley dau. of Eben[r] Mosely."

And the father. was there two years later, when he had a "right" laid out to him, July 29, 1698, in "the 12 divisions of land in the New Grant beyond the Blew Hills," — that is, in Stoughton. His name is coupled in the town list with that of Samuel Rigbee ; why, we cannot understand.

| " Lott | Name | Acres |
|---|---|---|
| 66 | { SAMUELL RIGBEE | 39 |
|  | { THOMAS POPE | 18 " |

Where and when he died we do not find ; but the Court Order in 1700 attests that he had "deceased" before that date.

After many years, public documents resume the thread of this family's history. In Suffolk Deeds, under date of Oct. 3, 1739, we find a conveyance by

"Thomas Pope of Haverhill yeoman" to "Smith Woodward of Dorchester," of "The one Fourth part of the Land laid out by the proprietors of Dorchester and Stoughton unto the right of his late Father Thomas Pope deceased in the Sixty Sixth Lot in the Twelve Divisions of Land so called, . . . laid out in common with the rights of Samuel Rigbee" ; also, one-fourth of the fifty-third lot ; also one fourth of the twenty fifth lot in the Ced-  - Swamps ; also one-fourth of the forty-first lot in the Division of Meadow Bottom ; also one-twelfth of the land that was laid out to "Henry Merrifield deceased (grandfather by the Mother's side unto the said Thomas Pope)."

Oct. 9, 1739, "John Harris of Lancaster in the county of Worcester, . . and Alice his wife (who is daughter to Elizabeth Pope deceased and grandaughter to Henry Merrifield late of Dorchester, deceased)," sold her one-twelfth part of the Merrifield property referred to above, to Thomas Bird.

Smith Woodward seems to have been a man of excellent business qualities; and if other heirs survived, their deeds should have been obtained and recorded in that same county. In default of such we infer that Thomas was the only surviving son.

The Register of this family has serious gaps, but we must systematically arrange what we have.

### CHILDREN OF THOMAS[3] AND ELIZABETH MERRIFIELD.

I.   THOMAS,[4] b. in Dorchester, Nov. 26, 1670.   (See below.)
II.  WILMONTON,[4] b. do., May 21, 1672.
III. HENRY,[4] b. do., Dec. 20, 1673.
IV.  EXPERIENCE,[4] b. do., June 21, 1675; d. Sept. 20,1689.
V.   ALICE,[4] b. do., Dec. 23, 1676; married John Harris, of Lancaster.
VI.  JOHN[4] [supposed child of Thomas[3] and Margaret (Long)], d. Aug. 20, 1683.

### CHILD OF THOMAS[3] AND MARGARET LONG.

VII. MINDWELL,[4] b. in Suffield, Conn., Sept. 12, 1689.

The only one of these whom we can follow into the next generation is

THOMAS,[4] son of Thomas[3] and Elizabeth (Merrifield), b. Nov. 26, 1670; m. in Roxbury, Jan. 2, 1705-6, *Margaret Downing.*

"Thomas Pope, adult, was baptized and owned y[e] Covenant, Oct[or] 28, 1705."

Among the adult persons baptized at the New South Church, Boston, Oct. 30, 1719, "Margaret Pope."

But somewhere Thomas[4] married a wife "Mercy," of whom we have information in a town on Cape Ann.

"1727-8, Received to full communion, Feb. 25th, Mercy Pope," 2d Church, Gloucester; children of the family, too, join this Church:

" 1737, July 10th   { ELIZ[A] POPE
                    { HANNAH MILLETT."

" August 7th        { ANN STEELE [wife of Wm.]
                    { MARGARET POPE."

In 1740 part of the family removed again.

"Dismissed March 15th 1740–1 Mercy Pope to Haverhill 2ᵈ Chʰ·"

But one daughter, certainly, remained behind.

"Married by Rev. Richard Jaques, Gloucestʳ· Jan: 15th. 1740–1, David Haskell & Elizᵃ Pope, of Gloucestʳ·"

The boundary line between Massachusetts and New Hampshire was finally established in 1741, and was found to pass through Haverhill. Thomas Pope was mentioned in the Haverhill records as one of those inhabitants whose homes were on the north side of that line, and, consequently, the family made a transfer from one State to another — without actually travelling.

The records of the Second Church of Haverhill (afterward Plaistow, N. H.) note, "Nov: 1: 1741.

"Mercy, the wife of Thos: Pope, Received by a Letter of Dismission from 2ᵈ Chh of Gloucester."

Now, over in the adjoining town of Methuen, we learn that

"Thomas Pope of Haverhill, and Hannah Austin of Methuen were married by the Rev. Mr. Christopher Sargent, Pastor of the first church in Methuen, October 14, 1742."

This bride seems, from comparison of persons mentioned in the records, to have been

"Hannah Austin, the daughter of Thomas Austin and Sarah, his wife, born April 8, in the year 1722."

Returning to Plaistow, we find Thomas and Hannah "owned the covenant, Feb. 26, 1743," and among the children baptized :

"June 3, 1743, Hannah, d. of Thomas Pope jͬ."
"1746, Apr. 20, David, s. of Thomas Pope, jr."
"1750, Nov. 4, Betty, d. of Thomas Pope."

The father had become aged, but was alive a little later than this, as we know from his bill for a pair of stockings and shoes, costing the startling sum of "3 pounds fifteen shillings."

"Thomas Pope, junr., of Plastow, yeoman," with "Hanah Pope his wife" sold land in Plastow — " 40 Acres be it more or less " — to Daniel Poor, the 14th of April, 1750.

And now this enterprising, efficient, God-fearing man becomes one of the pioneers of a new town.

"Thomas Pope jun$^r$ of Plasto" bought Lot number 53 in Goffstown, New Hampshire, of Thomas Hall of G., May 2d, 1753.

"Thomas Pope of *Goffestown* so-called, in the province of New Hampshire, yeoman " sold to Thomas Karr of the same place, Lot No. 54, in this same new town, April 25, 1757.

The leaving off the word junior may indicate that his father had meantime died.

"Thomas Pope" and "David Pope" signed a "Petition of the Inhabitants of the Place called Number Six of the Line of Towns ; or New Marlborough in the Province of New Hampshire," March 14th, 1768 : [N. H. Town Papers].

"David Pope is entered in the Roll of Capt. Aaron Adams' Company, 1776," while "Thomas Pope " is upon "A Larm List for Henniker" of the same date.

In a Petition for the location of a new meeting-house in Henniker, Sept. 11, 1786, these two also joined, together with " Simion Pope."

*Hopkinton* people petitioned the legislature in favor of a certain justice of the peace . . . . and one of the petitioners is " simeon pope."

*Weare* soldiers, mustered by Col. Moses Kelley July 20, 1779, had among them "Simeon Pope," whom the editor of the N. H. Town Papers marks, " lived in Henniker."

From the History of Henniker we learn that Thomas[5] died there Nov. 12, 1806, and we learn of another child of his, Jesse,[6] beside those we have already discovered. A few notes on the descendants of this New Hampshire pioneer are added.

David[6] married Lucy Saltmarsh, who died Jan. 20, 1858, having resided on the homestead.

William[7] and David,[7] their sons, married sisters by the name of Emerson, of Hillsborough. David removed to Bradford, where he died, leaving several daughters.

John[3] Pope, a grandson of David,[6] a blacksmith, lived in Henniker until a few years since, but moved West, so making it impracticable for the historian to obtain further details of the family history.

We trust, however, that the publication of this book, with its account of the history of the Pope family prior to the founding of Henniker, — details entirely unknown heretofore to the family there, — may be a means of bringing to light much more information respecting the descendants of Thomas[6].

[The author will be gratified to correspond with any of the family who may chance to read these lines.]

[The following, received soon after publication, corrects the closing statements of pages 97 and 98, and is additional thereto. Welcome to our newly-found cousins!]

DAVID POPE, son of Thomas[5] and Hannah (Austin), b. in Plaistow, N. H., March 13, 1746, m. (probably in Henniker) ———— Clark. He lived on the old homestead, which his father had originally located, on the south side of "Craney Hill," Henniker's highest eminence. He died about 1820. Children :

    I.   HANNAH,[7] b. Sept. 4, 1774 ; m. Elisha Brown.
    II.   THOMAS,[7] b. Jan. 18, 1776. [See below.]
    III.   BETTY,[7] b. Feb. 7, 1777 ; m. Jonathan Kimball, of Weare ; d. Sept. 11, 1865. Children : Jesse, Susanna, William, Miriam, and Sarah *Kimball.*
    IV.   SARAH[7] [SALLY], b. April 16, 1780 ; d. about 1865.
    V.   DAVID,[7] Jr., b. April 5, 1782 ; d. May 31, 1861. [See below.]
    VI.   SUSANNA,[7] b. Aug. 2, 1784 ; m. ———— Stoning.
    VII.   ADA[7] [EDITH], b. April 24, 1786 ; d. about 1865.
    VIII.   MEHITABLE,[7] b. Feb. 25, 1789 ; m. Jonathan Collins, of Weare.
    IX.   WILLIAM,[7] b. March 17, 1791. [See below.]
    X.   JOHN,[7] b. 1793 ; d. young.

THOMAS[7] [see above, II.] removed to Weare, N. H., and later to Washington, Vt., where he bought land, Sept. 5, 1799, and spent the remainder of his life. Children, recorded in Washington, Vt. :

    1.   JOHN[8], b. Nov. 5, 1797 ; m. Lucy Saltmarsh [correction of error on page 98]. He d. Jan. 20, 1858.
    2.   HANNAH,[8] b. Dec. 9, 1799.
    3.   RALPH,[8] b. May 14, 1802.
    4.   LUCINA,[8] b. Sept. 25, 1806.
    5.   ELISHA BROWN,[8] b. Feb. 13, 1809.
    6.   MARIA,[8] b. Sept. 23, 1814.
    7.   SALLY,[8] b. May 14, 1820.

# THE THIRD GENERATION.

## SECTION 2.

### RALPH,[3] SENIOR, AND HIS FAMILY.

RALPH,[3] SENIOR, born in the year 1673, was but thirteen years old when his father died. Remaining at home, under the care of his mother, until he reached maturity, he became a very capable and successful farmer, or "yeoman" as he calls himself in the bond we have examined, the word that probably expressed the position in society which his ancestors had generally held in England,— owners and cultivators of the soil.

The name *Ralph* is worthy of particular notice. It does not appear in any other of the American families of Popes, in the early generations, to my knowledge ; nor did I discover it in any list of English Popes save two cases, — Ralph of Bentley, Suffolk, 1316 ; and Ralph of Buxtead, Sussex, 1621. It may have come down as one of the *secondary* family names, in that line ; or it may have been given for altogether separate reasons in each case. The Latin form of the name is *Radulphus* or Ranulphus, from which we have Rudolph, Rodolph, Ralphe, Rollo, Ralph, Raphe and Raph.

Our Ralph found a bride in the neighboring town of Braintree, and the parson, Rev. Moses Fiske, tells us *within a day* when he married them.

" Ralph Pope of Dorch' & Rachel Neale of Brantry, 24 or 5. 1. 169⅞."

Likely enough the second of the two days, which was " Lady Day," or Annunciation Day, March 25th, the New Year's Day of that period, was the time of their nuptials.

Rachel was the second child of the name (the former having died early) in the large family of Henry Neale, whose gravestone chronicles him the "father of 21 children," and whose will gave portions to fifteen surviving sons and daughters. Her mother was Mr. Neale's second wife, Hannah Pray, believed to have been a daughter of Quinton Pray, who, like Henry Neale, was one of Braintree's earliest settlers.

Perhaps it was when this bride was brought home to the Squantum farm, that there seemed to be need of a revised settlement of the father's estate. But she and "mother Margaret" got on together well, we trust, and enjoyed one another for the few years that remained to the widow.

There came a goodly following of little ones, now ; nine within twenty years. Before the wedding-day Ralph had "owned the covenant," on the 28th of November, 1697 ; and Rachel had similarly united with the Braintree church, I suppose. So each babe was promptly taken to church to be committed to the care of a " covenant-keeping God," and to receive on its brow the sign of the cleansing procured through the "blood of the everlasting covenant."

One of these infants was taken to church on the very day of its arrival, by the nurse and the father, as the custom was. And a good family they were, too ; four sons grew up to become efficient men, fathers of families, and three of the daughters worthily presiding over homes of their own.

A slate-stone in the old burying-ground sums up one brief career.

*" John Son to*
*Ralph & Rachel*
*Pope Aged 5 Wek,*
*& 5 Dayes Died*
*Febuᵒʸ yᵉ 21 1708."*

It is matter of rejoicing that our ancestor has left so many waymarks along the line of his life, as a citizen of Dorchester.

When business requiring good judgment and sagacity was in hand, he was frequently called to act on the town's behalf.

" Maj. Thomas Tilstone, Deacon Jonathan Clap and mr. Ralph Pope " were chosen a committee of the town of Dorchester to " receive of the treasurer the sum of Fifty Thousand pounds last granted to be left in the Tresury for the Town, and let it out at six per sent " to suitable persons, in sums of not more than £30 each.

Another trust laid upon him at about the same period is here indicated :

" Mr. Ralph Pope " was one of a committee of " proprietors of the undivided lands in the town of Dorchester," who conveyed certain lands to " Ebenezer Maudsley of Dorchester, Weaver," July 25, 1723.

In the tax list of Dorchester for 1727, Ralph Pope is taxed for 33 acres mowing land, 24 a. pasture, 12 a. tillage land, 3 oxen, 9 cows, 2 horses and 4 swine : total, the slight sum of 18 shillings, 7 pence.

March 2, 1729, Ralph Pope was chosen one of the surveyors of highways.

May 12, 1729,

" Upon the request of Mr. Ralph Pope it was voted that he have liberty to build a pew in the meeting-house, wher y$^e$ short Seats for y$^e$ Women now are, so as to contain about half that Room ; and y$^e$ Building there to be under y$^e$ inspection & Regulation of y$^e$ Selectmen."

In a list of qualified jurors, April 25, 1737, we find " Ralph Pope," with the memorandum added, " Excused by the town March 6th, 1737."

The town clerk may in some cases refer to Ralph, senior, and in others to Ralph, junior ; but he does not so designate either. During the later years of the father's life, his namesake was residing in the adjoining town of Stoughton.

It is exceedingly interesting to get into the personal matters of this father and his family, as we do in the elaborate will he left ; and there is not a little of interest in the document which follows, which tells how the home place was divided between the two sons to whom it was bequeathed.

The mother, Rachel, survived her husband a good many years, " falling asleep," at length, in the spring following her eighty-fourth winter.

How great the contrast between the course of the two branches of our family in that third generation ! Thomas, with a succession of misfortunes, on devious ways, his children and grandchildren also bearing hardships : Ralph happily settled, an honored citizen, the happy father of a prosperous family.

### THE WILL OF RALPH POPE.

[Suffolk Probate, Book 37, page 454, etc.]

"In the name of God, Amen. This 4th day of October, in the year of Our Lord 1744, and in the 18th year of the Reign of our Sovereign Lord George the Second, King of Great Britain, I, Ralph Pope, of Dorchester, in the County of Suffolk, within his Majesty's Province of Massachusetts Bay in New England, yeoman, being weak in body, but perfect in mind and memory, Blessed be God : But therefor calling to mind the mortality of my body, and knowing that it is appointed unto all men once to die, do make and ordain this my last Will and Testament; that is to say, principally and first, I give and recommend my soul into the Hands of God, who gave it, trusting alone for salvation in the merits and righteousness of Jesus Christ my only Saviour and Redeemer. And my body I recommend to the Earth, to be buried in decent Christian burial, at the discretion of my Executors hereinafter named ; nothing doubting, but at the General Resurrection of the dead, I shall receive the same again, by the mighty power of God.

"And touching such worldly Goods and Estate wherewith it hath pleased God to bless me in this life, I give and dispose of the same in the manner and form following.

"*Imprimis*, I give and bequeath unto Rachel my well-beloved wife, the use and improvement of one half of my Dwelling House and Cellar, which end thereof she shall choose ; and likewise the use and improvement of one third part of all the rest of my Real Estate, lying in the Towns of Dorchester, Braintree and Milton. And I give her all my Household or indoor Goods and moveables forever. And I also give her the use of one of my Cows, which she shall choose, and oblige my Executors hereafter named, to find her with a Horse for her to ride to meeting and where else she shall find occasion, and also to keep the said Horse and Cow well, Summer and Winter; and likewise to find their Mother with sufficient firewood—brought home to her house, and cut up fit for the fire. And, also to carry her Bread Corn to the Mill and bring the meal home to her house, from time to time, as she may have occasion. And all this to be performed and done for her so long as she shall remain my Widow and no longer. And, also, I give her as much pork and beef, as she shall see cause to lay in for her own store, for the space of one year after my decease.

"*Item*, I give and bequeath unto my son, Ralph Pope, and to his heirs and assigns forever, (besides what I have heretofore given him,) my Lot of Land in Stoughton which I purchased of Benjamin Billing, with the one half part of my Saw-Mill in Stoughton, and the one half part of my Meadow called Ironmine Meadow; he allowing my son Lazarus to take as much pine timber as shall be necessary for the building and finishing his house, out of the Ring Swamp called Little Quanticut, lying in the Lot above mentioned: provided always, and I give unto my said son Ralph Pope, the lands abov sd upon condition, that he do discharge a debt, for which I am bound for him unto Edward Winslow, Esq., late High Sheriff of the County of Suffolk, so as that my Estate is thereby saved harmless; which if he do not, then I hereby give my Executors of this my last Will, full power and authority to make sale of so much of the Land I have given him in this my Last Will, as to pay the said debt and charges, the bequest aforesaid notwithstanding.

"*Item*, I give and bequeathe to my son Lazarus Pope and to his heirs and assigns forever, my Lot in Stoughton whereon my Saw-Mill stands, with the Dwelling House and Barn thereon, and the other half of the said Saw-Mill. He allowing convenient yard room about the said Mill for the space of Fifteen Years, after my decease, and, also he paying my said son Ralph, for one half of the charge, he the said Ralph has been at in providing Saws and other utensils for the said Saw-Mill, to be paid within one year after my decease. Also I give him all the Land in the 20th Lot in the Twenty-five divisions of Land in Stoughton, which I purchased of Robert Royal and others; and likewise the one third part of my Meadow called Ironmine Meadow, all of which I give him besides what I have done for him heretofore.

"*Item*, I give and bequeath unto my two sons, Elijah Pope and Ebenezer Pope, their heirs and assigns forever, all my Lands in Dorchester, Braintree, and Milton, with my Dwelling House, Barn, Orchard and all the appurtenances thereunto belonging, to be equally divided between them for Quantity and Quality, and to come into possession thereof, the one half of the House and two thirds of the Lands Immediately after my decease; (excepting that part of the House which I have assigned to my daughter Rachel, as hereafter mentioned). And the other half of my House and one third of my Land after the decease of my wife and the expiration of the term I have given to my daughter Rachel in my House as is hereafter named.

" And also, I give them all the remainder of my Personal Estate, Cash and Husbandry tools not here particularly mentioned and disposed of, by this my Last Will. They my said two sons Elijah and Ebenezer paying all my just debts and funeral charges out of their own proper portions, and likewise out of their own proper portions to pay all the Sums of Money which I give to my children and others, in this my Last Will and Testament, and also do and perform all that for their mother which I have ordered in this my Will during the term of her Widowhood ; and at her decease to give her a decent burial : and find my daughter Rachel with firewood, &c. as is hereafter expressed.

" *Item.* — I give and bequeath to my said son Ebenezer,* and to his heirs and assigns forever, all my Right in the new Township granted by the General Court to the Officers and Soldiers that served in the Expedition to Canada, in year 1690, under the command of Captn. John Withington ; he fulfilling the Condition of the said Grant.

" *Item.* — I give and bequeathe unto my daughter Rachel Pope, her heirs and assigns forever, besides what I have done for her already, all the Land that was laid out to the Right of Nicholas Allen, in the 21st Lot in the Twenty-five Divisions of Land in Stoughton, which is the 4th Lot in the Subdivision of the 21st Lot among the Proprietors thereof : also half the Land I have in the 5th Lot in Subdivision aforesaid, that was laid out to the Right of Samuel Rigbee. It being about Twelve Acres and a half ; and also the remaining Third part of Ironmine Meadow. I also give her the sum of One Hundred Pounds Old Tenor to be paid her by my said sons Elijah and Ebenezer, within one year after my decease, at the value that Bills of Credit of the Old Tenor now pass at. Also the use and improvement of the Westerly Chamber in my Dwelling House, that hath a chimney in it, so long as she shall remain single and will dwell in the said Chamber, and the said Chamber to be kept in repair and sufficient firewood to be provided and brought home to her during the said term. The said repairation and firewood to be done and found by my said two sons Elijah and Ebenezer.

" *Item.* — I give and bequeath to my daughter Jerusha Pimer, besides what she already hath had, one hundred Pounds in Province Bills of Old Tenor ; to be paid within two years after my decease,

---

*See list of children of John2. jr.

and in case she shall live three years longer, after the first Payment, then the like sum of One Hundred Pounds more. And in case she live three years longer after the second payment, then the like sum of One Hundred Pounds more. All to be paid her by my two sons Elijah and Ebenezer, to the value that Province Bills now pass at.

"*Item.*— I give and bequeathe unto my daughter Jemima Vinal, besides what she hath already had, one hundred Pounds in Province Bills of Old Tenor, to be paid her within four years after my decease, in case she live so long ; but in case she die before the said four years are expired, the said sum never to be paid ; and in case she should have one or more children, then I give to them all the like sum of One Hundred Pounds in Bills of Credit of the old Tenor ; provided one or more of them arrive at the age of five years. To be paid by my said two sons Elijah and Ebenezer according to the value that Province Bills now pass at.

"*Item.*— I give and bequeathe unto my daughter Hannah Wardwell, besides what I have heretofore given her, the Sum of One Hundred Pounds in Bills of Credit of Old Tenor, to be paid her within three years after my decease. And in case she live three years longer after the said first payment, then I give her the like sum of One Hundred Pounds more, in like Bills of Credit ; but in case she shall decease before the time appointed for the second payment, then I give the last mentioned sum to so many of her children as shall arrive at the age of Twenty-one years, to be equally divided among them. Provided that if any of her children she shall so leave be female, and marry under the said age of twenty-one years, then her or their portion of the said sum, to be paid at marriage. And all to be paid by my said two sons Elijah and Ebenezer, according to the value the Province Bills now pass.

"*Item.*—I give unto my sons Ralph and Lazarus, and to my daughter Jemima Vinal, each of them a Cow.

"*Item.*— My Will is that my two sons Elijah and Ebenezer, have liberty at any time or times within the space of two years after my decease, to cut and take out of my Lands in Stoughton, pine or chesnut for Boards and Rails to the quantity of two thousand feet of Boards and of one thousand Rails.

"*Item.* — I give and bequeathe unto my grandson Ralph Pope, son of my said son Lazarus Pope, and to his heirs and assigns forever, the remaining half of the Land I have in the 5th Lot in Stoughton, laid out to the Right of Samuel Rigbee, containing about Twelve Acres and a half ; but in case he die before he arrive at the age of Twenty-One Years, then my Will is, that it go in like manner to my grandson Frederick Pope, son of my said son Ralph Pope.

"*Item.*—I give and bequeathe unto the Church of Christ in Dorchester. The Sum of Twenty Pounds in Province Bills of Old Tenor, to be laid out in Plate for the Communion Table, in such a manner as the Church shall order; and to be paid by my said two sons Elijah and Ebenezer Pope, within the space of six years after my decease, according to the value that Province Bills now pass.

"And I do constitute and appoint my said two sons Elijah Pope and Ebenezer Pope, Co-Executors of this my Last Will and Testament. And I do hereby revoke and utterly disallow and disannul all and every other former Testaments, Wills and Legacies and Bequests, and Executors by me in anywise named heretofore, satisfying and confirming this and no other to be my Last Will and Testament. In witness whereof I have hereunto set my hand and seale, this Day and Year first above written.

*Ralph Pope*

"Signed, Sealed, delivered, and declared in the presence of the said Ralph Pope, the Testator, to be his Last Will and Testament, in presence of us the Subscribers.

REMEMBER PRESTON,
THOMAS BIRD,
EBENEZER MOSELEY,
JAMES BLAKE.                     Examined by A. BELCHER."

" SUFFOLK *ss.*    By the Hon. JOSIAH WILLARD, Esq., Judge of Probate.

" The within written Will having been presented to me for Probate on the 14th of February last by the Executors therein named, on the 12th of March last Remember Preston, Thomas Bird and James Blake made oath that they saw Ralph Pope the subscriber to this Instrument sign, &c., and heard him publish and declare this to be his last Will and Testament. And that when he did so he was of sound disposing mind and memory, according to the deponents best discerning, and that they together with Ebenezer Moseley set their hands as witnesses thereof in the said Testator's presence. And having considered the Objections made to the said Will, together with the Answers to said Objections, I do allow and approve thereof as the last Will and Testament of the said Ralph Pope Deceased.

J. WILLARD, *Judge of Probate.*

"*Boston, March* 26, 1745.

A. BELCHER, *Register.*"

The bequest of so large a sum as twenty pounds to the church, was the occasion of an attempt to break the will.

March 4, 1744, Thomas Pimer, husband of Jerusha,[1] and Nathaniel Wardell [Wardwell], husband of Hannah,[1] through their attorney, Benjamin Kent, filed their objections to the probate of the will of him they affectionately term " Father Pope." Their complaint took this ·form : that the witnesses to the will, being church-members, were not competent to act as witnesses to a will which conferred a gift upon their society ; and that the will was therefore null and void. Elijah and Ebenezer replied, through their attorney, that the case had no precedent ; that witnesses were not to be doubted without strong cause ; that the share of each of these men, if the whole legacy were divided up by the church to its members, would be but trifling ; and, finally, that the church would no doubt prefer to forego the bequest rather than that the will of their deceased brother should not be fulfilled.

After duly weighing the objections and answer Judge Willard admitted the will March 26th, and the estate was accordingly distributed as the good yeoman had wished. There was formal division of lands and buildings, both of the homestead and the Stoughton property, and many details of an interesting sort came out in the order respecting the shares of Mother Rachel, daughter Rachel, Elijah and Ebenezer in the Squantum estate. We quote the first section of this order, that relating to Elijah, as a sample of the very particular care taken in such matters in those days.

*Extract from the Order of Partition concerning the Squan-tum estate.*

"*To Elijah Pope* we have sett off the whole of the dwelling house of the deceased & the Northerly part of the Barn, although a small part of it stands upon the land hereafter assigned to.the said Ebenezer

Pope, and the little Building and the Corn Crib, standing near the dwelling house : the piece of mowing & tillage land lying on the Northerly part of the Homestead of the said Ralph Pope, deceased, next to the land of Mr. Remember Preston, containing Sixteen acres & twenty-six rods, be it more or less, extending as far south as the line we have now made and the fence as it formerly stood, which is the southern bounds of the said piece of land, and separates it from the pasture land lying on the southeasterly side of the said Homestall, commonly called yᵉ Commons Pasture ; & it extends as far west as the wall on the west side of the way, that is used to pass from the said Remember Preston's House to yᵉ said Dwelling House, as far as that extends southward, and at the end of the said wall, a little to the Northward of the well of water, it turns to the Westward, about two or three rods, to the corner of a fence, and from thence on a straight line to a stake on the westerly side of the Barn, and then through the Barn to ' a stake on the easterly side of it, and then to the corner of the wall on the westerly side of the little Orchard, and so down that line on the westerly side of the Orchard, about eight or nine rods to a heap of stones, and then across the said orchard to a heap of stones on the easterly side thereof, and so by the line of the sd Orchard until it comes to a heap of stones, the corner of the said Commons Pasture being the westerly end of the said line made by us to be the partition between the peice now describing and the said Commons Pasture. The said Elijah Pope to make and maintain at his own cost & charge the westerly half of the division fence between yᵉ sᵈ Ebenezer Pope's part of the said Commons Pasture and the above described peice set off to Elijah, and the said Ebenezer Pope the easterly half thereof ; and Easterly it extends to another peice of yᵉ sᵈ Homestall fenced in by itself.

"He, the said Elijah Pope always allowing unto his sd. brother Ebenezer Pope, his heirs and assigns forever, the Liberty of passing and repassing at all times of the year, with Horse or Team, or otherwise, as he or they shall have Occasion, to & from the Dwelling House of the said Ebenezer Pope, over the above described piece of Land, where he conveniently can, unto the way that he himself useth to go off Squantum Neck and then, in that way, to the Land of the said Remember Preston ; and also he the sd. Elijah Pope to allow the said Ebenezer Pope Liberty to take away all the stones of an Old wall lying within the limits of the above said piece that is not made use of, at such a time of the year as may do his Land the least Damage by going over it. And a piece of Tillage and Mowing Land adjoining to the above described piece, on the Easterly side thereof, and reaching to the Sea on the Easterly side of the said Squantom Neck, containing eight acres one quarter of an acre & seventeen rods, be it more or less. And eleven acres, be it more or less, on the Easterly side of the said piece of Pasture Land called the Commons-pasture, as it is divided and set off by a Line beginning at the Northerly side of the said pasture next to the first described piece, and turning South three degrees East, (variation of the needle excepted) down toward the Sea, until it comes to a heap of stones about two rods from the Bank, and then turns westerly keeping about two rods from the Bank until it comes between the Springs at the Bottom of the Bank, and then leaving two of those springs to the Eastward and one to the Westward the line runs down into the Sea on the said South side of the Neck. The said Elijah Pope to enjoy all the Rockweed that grows against the Land set off to him to the Eastward of the above described Line that runs into the Sea between the Springs, except that Rockweed that grows on the said South side of the Neck, between the line aforesaid by the Springs' & the land of Mr. Jonathan Davis, which is to belong to the said Ebenezer Pope, his heirs and assigns forever: and the said Elijah Pope to allow to the sd. Ebenezer Pope the Liberty of Carting said Rockweed over his part of the said Commons Pasture if there be occasion ; and the said Elijah Pope also to have and enjoy all the stons and slate lying upon the Beach against any part of the sd. land set off to him, and also one Block of slate lying against the Land set off to the said Ebenezer Pope at a place called hard point, upon which the said Elijah hath already dug some slate. And three Acres and one half, be it more or less, of the piece of Land at little neck so called, lying near the said Squantum-neck, at the Southerly end thereof, next to the Salt marsh of the said Jonathan Davis, with the priviledge of passing over the other part thereof to the Beach as he shall have occasion. And the whole of a piece of Salt marsh lying at a little distance from the Homestall, containing fourteen acres, be the same more or less, and is parted from the Salt marsh adjoining to the said Homestall by a little Creek, and the southerly half of a piece of woodland lying in Milton, the said half containing ten acres and one half acre, be the same more or less. And the one half part of the Pew in the meeting house in Dorchester, aforesaid ; in full of his, the said Elijah Popes half part of the Real Estate of the said Ralph Pope, deceased."

Four sons are thus pointed out, who lived to perpetuate the family, and who will form the subjects of the next chapter.

For the daughters, a few lines will suffice to record all that has come down to us.

RACHEL,[4] the eldest child, passed through fifty-eight years of life's joys and trials, without the experience of matrimony.

JERUSHA[4] married Thomas Pimer, of Dorchester, Nov. 30, 1759, was a widow after eighteen years; then lived on, almost a third of a century longer.

JEMIMAH[4] married a Mr. Vinal, of whom no reliable account has come to the writer's knowledge.

HANNAH[4] married Nathaniel Wardwell, Sept. 25, 1740, and removed to Bristol, R. I.

### CHILDREN OF RALPH[3] AND RACHEL (NEALE).

 I.  RACHEL,[4] born Dec. 8, 1699; d. April 21, 1757.

 II.  JERUSHA,[4] b. Oct. 23, 1701; m. Nov. 30, 1739, Thomas Pimer of Dorchester; d. Jan. 4, 1789.

 III.  JEMIMAH,[4] b. Nov. 3, 1703; m. —— Vinal; d. ——.

 IV.  RALPH,[4] b. Nov. 10, 1705. [See next chapter, 1.]

 V.  JOHN,[4] b. Jan. 12, 1707; d. Feb. 21, 1707.

 VI.  ELIJAH,[4] b. April 1, 1711. [See next chapter, 2.]

 VII.  HANNAH,[4] b. June 9, 1713; m. Sept. 25, 1740, Nathaniel Wardwell; d. ——.

 VIII.  LAZARUS,[4] b. Oct. 31, 1715. [See next chapter, 3.]

 IX.  EBENEZER,[4] b. May 27, 1718. [See next chapter, 4.]

# CHAPTER VII.

## THE FOURTH GENERATION.

### SECTION I.

#### THE FAMILY OF DOCTOR RALPH[4].

RALPH,[4] son of Ralph[3] and Rachel (Neale), born Nov. 10, 1705. Married Nov. 27, 1729, Rebecca, dau. of Richard and Rebecca (Lobdell) Stubbs, of Hull, Rev. Ezra Carpenter officiating. She was born in Hull March 18, 1707, not far from ·Nantasket Beach, now so renowned.

Her father was a substantial farmer of that place, the son of Richard Stubbs, senior, one of the pioneers of the town. ·Isaac Lobdell, Rebecca's father, was an associate there. His wife, Martha, was a child of Samuel Ward, a wealthy citizen, first of Charlestown, then of Hingham ; proprietor of large tracts of land at those towns, and at Hull, "Alderton Hill, Strawberry Hill, Whitehead, Sagamore Hill, Petty's Island, Bumkin Island," (bequeathed to Harvard College, and since called " Ward's Island,") and other points.

Rebecca (Stubbs) Pope named one of her sons for this grandfather of hers, and several other descendants have borne the name.

Dr. Ralph Pope lived on what was originally called "The Road to Dorchester Swamp," or rather on a continuation of that road, near the Bridgewater line. It is now·called Sumner Street. His brother Lazarus lived on an adjoining tract ; his house faced in the opposite direction, on the " Bristol Turnpike," a parallel road. This tract their father had bequeathed them, as we have learned from his will, leaving the mill he had built for their joint use. . . .

These places passed to their sons, and remained long in their families.

The first tax-list in Stoughton which bears Ralph Pope's name is that for the year 1731. July 15th of that year he and his wife united with the church (now Canton) and on the same day he brought for baptism his daughter, Rebecca. In due time each child was taken over all the seven miles of bad road to be christened; usually when several months old, so permitting the mother to participate in the ceremonies. The family were "constant worshippers," tradition says, making their way to the "meeting-house" on horseback or afoot.

In a town record of 1747 we read of " Dr. Ralph Pope " ; and the name of "Capt. Ralph Pope" occurs on the Stoughton Tax List, Aug. 25. 1748.

The former title indicates his profession, that of physician. He may have pursued some studies at Harvard College, but was not a graduate ; *tradition* points to Compton, Rhode Island, as the place, and Rev. Richard Billings as the instructor of his medical training. Nothing has come down concerning his practice of medicine, except that " he always refused fees for services on the Sabbath."

His character left its impress ; his name has stood through four generations as " a kind and benevolent man, greatly beloved by those who knew him."

He carried on a farm, and was a partner in the lumber business with his brother. He owned at least one slave. But the estimate he placed on him was humane ; as is seen from the circumstance that he had the man baptized at the same church and on the same day as his own first-born child ! the register so proving. It is also on record that "Scipio, a negro slave to Dr. Ralph Pope, and Mary Sloame, an Indian, were married Dec. 22, 1747." They lived in a house near the mill, whose cellar-ruin was known until a recent day as "Scip's cellar."

The origin of the title "Captain" does not come to light. The "War of the Spanish Succession" or " King George's War" had been involving our English colonies in strife with those of France in Canada. Perhaps the Doctor had been, like his uncle, half a century before, on a campaign thither ; or, like his son, thirty years afterward, he may have served in the defence of the coast.   But there's history under that word "captain."

Whether military service had anything to do with shortening his days, we cannot tell ; but he died in middle life " of nervous fever, Jan. 1, 1749–50."

The gravestone erected to his memory soon after, is still standing in the cemetery at Stoughton village, an interesting memorial of a good man.

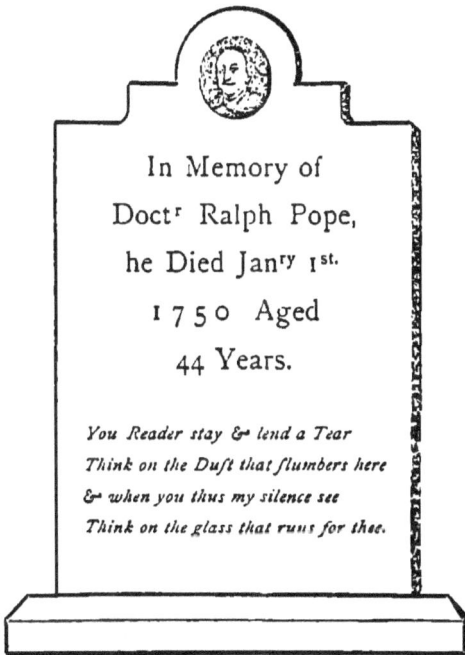

In Memory of
Doct$^r$ Ralph Pope,
he Died Jan$^{ry}$ 1$^{st.}$
1 7 5 0   Aged
44 Years.

*You Reader stay & lend a Tear*
*Think on the Dust that slumbers here*
*& when you thus my silence see*
*Think on the glass that runs for thee.*

The widow, Rebecca, lived to the age of 84, passing through many trying scenes, but lovingly cared for by her son Frederick, in her declining years.   In the feebleness of her last days she used to slip out of the house at dusk, saying, "I must go home."

Otherwise she retained her faculties well till her death, July 1, 1791.[*]

Of the children of this couple, one, Samuel Ward, died at sixteen; another, Alexander, (named, very likely, in honor of the poet who had but recently died,) born a few weeks after his father's death, breathed out his little life at the end of but nine months.

But there were three sons and four daughters who survived their parents, married, had children and lived as their father and mother had taught them, usefully, honorably. In the next chapter those of the male line will be noted in particular. We subjoin a few facts concerning the others. We come now to another valuable document.

### THE WILL OF DR. RALPH POPE, OF STOUGHTON.

" In the name of God Amen. This Twenty-fourth day of December, A.D., 1749, and in the Twenty-Third year of His Majesty's Reign, Our Sovereign Lord, George the 2d, King of Great Britain, etc.

" I, Ralph Pope, of Stoughton, in the County of Suffolk, and within His Majesty's Province of the Massachusetts Bay, in New England; Gentleman. Being weak in Body but of perfect mind and Memory, Blessed be God, But calling to mind the mortality of my body; and that it is appointed unto all men once to die ; do make and ordain this my Last Will and Testament. That is to say, first and principally of all, I give and recommend my Soul into the hands of God who gave it. Trusting alone for salvation, in the merits and Righteousness of Christ my only Saviour and Redeemer. ' And my body I recommend to the Earth to be buried by a decent Christian burial, at the discretion of my Executors, hereinafter named. Nothing doubting but at the General Resurrection of the Dead, I shall receive the same again by the Mighty Power of God.

"And as touching such worldly Estate as it has pleased God to bless me with in this Life; I give and dispose in manner and form following.

" *Imprimis*, I give and bequeathe unto my Well Beloved Wife Rebecca, the use and improvement of my whole Estate so long as she remains my widow. But if she should marry, then I give her one half my Dwelling House and privilege in the Cellar, with Ten Acres of my Land. And I empower my Executrix to sell so much of my Land

---

out of the Eighth Range as shall be necessary to pay all my Just debts and Funeral Expenses.

" *Item*, I give and bequeathe unto my two sons Frederick Pope and Samuel Ward Pope, and to their Heirs and Assigns forever.  The remaining part of my Land in the Eighth Range, and also another piece of Land lying in the Town of Easton, which I lately bought of Peter Sallard, with a Dwelling House and Orchard thereon, containing about Eight Acres.  Also,

" I give to my two sons  Frederick and Samuel Ward Pope,  my whole Right and Interest in the Meadow, called Iron Mine Meadow. And also, One half my Saw Mill, with all my Right and privilege thereunto belonging.  Also I give unto my two sons Frederick Pope and Samuel Ward Pope, Fifteen Acres of Land out of the Seventh Range, at the South West part of the said Range ; and I also give them Pine Timber enough to make Three Thousand feet of Boards apiece, to build their Houses with.

" *Item*, I give and bequeathe unto my two sons William Pope and James Pope, and to their Heirs and Assigns forever, All the remaining part of my land with my Dwelling House and other Buildings thereon.

" *Item*, I give and bequeathe unto my daughter Rebecca Pope, and to her Heirs and Assigns forever.  One Hundred and Fifty Pounds in Bills of Old Tenor, to be paid on her Marriage day out of my personal Estate.   But if she should not marry, the above sum not to be paid her until she arrive at the age of Twenty-four years.   Also, I give her One Hundred and Sixty Pounds in Bills of Old Tenor to be paid her by my son Frederick Pope, in Three Years after he comes of age.

" *Item*, I give and bequeathe unto my daughter Lucretia Pope, the Sum of One Hundred Pounds in Bills of Old Tenor, to be paid her by my son Samuel Ward Pope, after he arrives at the age of Twenty-One Years ; and in One Year after, the sum of One Hundred Pounds more in like Bills of Old Tenor.

" *Item*, I give and bequeathe unto my daughter Rachel Pope, the sum of One Hundred Pounds in Bills of Old Tenor, to be paid her by my son William Pope, in one year after he arrive at the age of Twenty-One Years, and One Hundred Pounds more in One year after, in like Bills of Old Tenor.   And in One year after, One Hundred and Ten Pounds.

" *Item*, I give and bequeathe unto my daughter Hannah Pope, the sum of One Hundred Pounds in Bills of Old Tenor ; to be paid her by my son James Pope, after he arrive at the age of Twenty-One years ; And in One year after One Hundred Pounds more in like Bills of Old Tenor.   And in One year after to pay her the sum of One Hundred and Ten Pounds in like Bills of Old Tenor. Provided my Four sons Frederick Pope, Samuel Ward Pope, William and James Pope, or either of them, should refuse to pay either of their sisters, what I have ordered them to pay unto them, I hereby give my Executrix of this my Last Will and Testament, full Power and authority, to make sale of so much of the Land I have given them.

"*Item*, I give and bequeathe unto my two sons Frederick Pope and Samuel Ward Pope, all my Personal Estate and Husbandry Tools.

"*Item*, I give and bequeathe unto my two daughters, Rebecca Pope and Lucretia Pope, all my indoor movables that are not yet disposed of. And I do hereby constitute and appoint my Well Beloved Wife to be sole Executrix, of this my last Will and Testament.

In witness whereof, I have hereunto set my hand and seal, this day and year first above written.

*Ralph Pope*

Signed, sealed and delivered in the Presence of us,
     ELIAS MONK,
     WILLIAM GLOVER,

*Lazarus Pope*

"The above written Will being presented by Rebecca Pope, the Executrix above named, to the Probate, Elias Monk, William Glover and Lazarus Pope made Oath that they saw Ralph sign the above named Will, and heard him declare it to be his Last Will and Testament. And that they set their Hands and seals as witnesses thereof."
*January* . . , 1750.

Concerning the daughters of Dr. Ralph, we take the following from the work of Col. William Pope :

"REBECCA, the eldest, married Mr. Thomas Glover, of Dorchester, Feb. 20, 1752, and lived in Stoughton, about one mile from the first-built meeting house, on the road leading to Easton. She had eleven children, all but one of whom married and had families. At the time of her death, in 1812, she had seventy-five grandchildren. She was a useful and industrious woman, a good wife, and a kind mother. Mr. Thomas Glover died in Stoughton, Jan. 5, 1811 aged 88 years. She survived him, and died Aug. 11, 1812, aged 84 years.

" LUCRETIA, the second daughter, married James Pike, of Boston, Jan. 16, 1772, and went there to live. He died in Boston, leaving two children, viz., James, born about 1774, married Mary Whitney, of Newton, Aug. 23, 1802, died in Boston, Sept. 17, 1835, aged 63 ; and Lucretia, born in Boston about 1777, who married Elisha Tolman, of Concord, and went there to live. She had six children, born in Concord, viz., Elisha, Albert, James, Lucretia (who married Lysander Bascom), Abby, and Benjamin Tolman.

· " RACHEL, third daughter, married Daniel Littlefield, of North Bridgewater, Aug. 31, 1758, and went there to live. They had one son, Ralph Pope Littlefield, born 1760, died young. She died in North Bridgewater, ——, 1760, aged 19 years ; and Daniel Littlefield married, 2d, Catharine Cole, daughter of Joseph and Mary Cole, and sister of Mary, who married Frederick Pope.

" HANNAH, fourth daughter, married Alexander Glover,* Dec. 28, 1769, and went to Dorchester to live. They had six children — three sons and three daughters. She died in Dorchester, Sept. 28, 1825, aged 81 years. She was a woman of superior abilities."

CHILDREN OF RALPH,[4] JUNIOR, AND REBECCA (STUBBS).

I.   REBECCA,[5] b. Dec. 29, 1730 ; m. Feb. 20, 1752, Thomas Glover ; d. Aug 1, 1812.

II.   FREDERICK,[5] b. May 15, 1733. [See next chapter, A, 1.]

III.   SAMUEL WARD,[5] b. Jan. 5, 1734 ; d. Jan. 31, 1750.

IV.   LUCRETIA,[5] b. Nov. 11, 1736 ; m. Jan. 16, 1772, James Pike ; d. ——.

V.   WILLIAM,[6] b. Feb. 5, 1738–9. [See next chapter, A, 2.]

VI.   RACHEL,[6] b. May 1, 1741 ; m. Daniel Littlefield ; d. ——, 1760.

VII.   HANNAH,[5] b. June 1, 1744 ; m. Alexander Glover ; d. Sept. 28, 1825.

VIII.   JAMES,[5] b. Jan. 28, 1749–50. [See next chapter, A, 3.]

---

* Son of Alexander and Sarah (White) Glover.

THE older of the two sons who remained on the Squantum estate was Elijah, born April 1, 1711.

As there is no one of his descendants in Dorchester, and none elsewhere with whom the writer has been able to communicate; and as references to himself and his family in public documents are very few, the sketch of this branch of the family must be brief. Yet, what we know of them, first and last, is honorable, and entitles them to a good place in our regard.

April 19, 1775, the day the battle of Lexington was taking place, "Elijah Pope" and "Elijah Pope, junior," were among the "minute men" who gathered in Dorchester, and entered into the service of their country. The father was sixty-four years old. He was twice married, and had fourteen children. He made good improvement of his estate, and left a respectable fortune.

His first wife was Jemima Vose, of Milton; they were married in Boston, Oct. 7, 1730, by Samuel Checkley, Esq.

She died March 24, 1760. Going to the town where his brother Ralph had found his bride, he married, Jan. 2, 1761, a second wife, Ann Stubbs, a relative of Rebecca. His residence is given in Boston, by the parson who performed the ceremony, Rev. Samuel Veazie. He died Oct. 4, 1777. His estate was administered on by his widow and son Elijah.

The Court Order for division assigned one-third to the widow, "Anna"; a double portion of the remainder to Elijah, Jr.; and equal shares of the balance to "John, Chloe, Salome, Jerusha, Jemima, Hannah, Mary, Anna, Rachel and Lemuel, or their legal representatives."

The widow died in Boston, in December, 1785, and Anna, "spinster," also "of Boston," became administratrix of her estate, Feb. 21, 1786. Samuel Belcher (the husband of a daughter of Ebenezer[4]), having bought the rights of "Elijah, John, Mima and Solima" in their mother's estate, had her portion "set off" to him, Anna and Rachel afterward ceding their shares, also, to him.

Respecting the children little can be said.

*Elijah,*[5] *jr.*, left no son, nor any grandson by the name of Pope ; yet quite a posterity through his daughters.

The following is *conjectured* to be the subsequent history of the widow of Lemuel[6] :

"Married in Boston, at the New South Church, Oct. 30, 1803, Ebenezer Phillips and Betsey Pope."

*John*[5] is supposed to be the person to whom the following entry in the town records of Lunenburg refers:

"Elijah Pope, son of John Pope and Frances his wife, was born at Lunenburg, Sept. 3d, 1783."

William,[5] son of Ralph,[4] resided in L. some years, we have seen. It would be natural that his cousin should follow him there. Did he also remove to Vermont, and leave posterity in some fair vale among the Green Mountains? Not a note of the man, woman or child yet discovered, after this Lunenburg record. Thus we have no evidence of any person living now to bear the Pope name after *Elijah*[4] of Squantum.

*Hannah*[5] was married, Sept. 29, 1768, in the New South Church, Boston, to "Robert Molton."

He was afterward a resident of Bristol, Maine ; whence "James Morton" came, Aug. 25, 1798, to receive £13, 13s., 6d., of Samuel Belcher, for a share in the estate of Elijah Pope ; acting as attorney for Thomas Morton of Bristol, carpenter, being the sole heir of "Hannah Pope."

Concerning the others who married, we know little beyond the names of their husbands and date of marriage, as is shown in the following list:

CHILDREN OF ELIJAH[4] AND JEMIMA (VOSE).

I. ELIJAH,[5] JR., born April 22, 1732; married Jan. 1, 1778, Martha White, of Weymouth, who was born April 2, 1732. He died Dec. 11, 1800.

*Children:*

1. Sally Loring,[6] born Nov. 9, 1778.
2. Patty[6] [Martha], b. Dec. 12, 1780; m. Feb. 23, 1806, *Elijah Glover;* had *children,* (a) Louisa *Glover,* b. Aug. 5, 1808, who m. Joseph Parshlee, of Braintree; (b) Martha Harriet *Glover,* b. May 22, 1810; m. Isaac T. Dyer, of Braintree; (c) Mary Smith *Glover,* b. May 25, 1813. *Patty[6] (Pope) Glover* d. July 16, 1813.
3. Polly,[6] b. July 1, 1782; m. *Cyrus Balkum,* of Dorchester, Jan. 23, 1803; had *children,* (a) Martha White *Balkum,* b. April 25, 1804; (b) Mary Pope *Balkum,* b. July 31, 1805; (c) Elijah Pope *Balkum,* b. Dec. 27, 1808; (d) Cyrus *Balkum,* baptized June 2, 1811; (e) Sarah Howe *Balkum,* b. Sept. 25, 1820. Mrs. *Polly[6] (Pope) Balkum* died Sept. 9, 1824.

Capt. Cyrus Balkum married (2) Rebecca Preston, April 25, 1826, and had other children.

II. CHLOE,[5] b. March 12, 1733 – 4; m. 1765, Rev. Jonathan Vinal; d. ——.

III. JOHN,[5] b. Dec. 19, 1735; d. Oct. 14, 1750.

IV. LEMUEL,[5] b. Sept. 15, 1737; m. Oct. 22, 1773, Elizabeth White; d. —— 1778. *Child:* Betsey, b. April 1, 1774; m. Thomas Shed, Nov. 26, 1795.

V. SALOME,[5] b. July 11, 1739; d. ——.

VI. JERUSHA,[5] b. Feb. 12, 1741 – 2; m. Feb. 20, 1766, Col. Ebenezer Williams; d. ——.

VII. JEMIMA,[5] b. Oct. 28, 1744; m. Dec. 10, 1767, Thomas Collyer; d. ——.

VIII. HANNAH,[5] b. May 4, 1747; m. Sept. 29, 1768, Robert Molton [Morton]; d. ——.

IX. MARY,[5] b. Sept. 10, 1749; appears to be the person who was "married in Boston, Dec. 30, 1790, by Samuel Stillman," to William Jeffrey.

X. RACHEL,[5] b. Jan. 5, 1750; d. Sept. 25, 1762.

CHILDREN OF ELIJAH[4] AND ANN (STUBBS).

XI.   (1.) JOHN,[5] b. July 22, 1762 ; m. Frances —— ; d. ——.
XII.  (2.) ANNA,[5] b. Dec. 7, 1763 ; d. ——.
XIII. (3.) SHEREBIAH,[5] b. July 11, 1765 ; d. Sept. 5, 1765.
XIV.  (4.) RACHEL,[5] b. July 8, 1768.

I append to this list an account of a person who *seems* to have belonged to this family, although the fact that she was not mentioned among the heirs in the distribution of Elijah,[4] senior's, estate appears to bar the possibility of her being his child. Yet why should she name her eldest son "Elijah Pope"? Possibly she was an adopted child ; or it may be Elijah,[5] junior, had married a wife before Martha White, and that Catharine [Katy] was the child of that marriage.

"KATY POPE," b. 1771, m. Nov. 27, 1788, Mr. William Vose of Dorchester, son of William and Hannah Vose, b. Sept. 14, 1757. "William Vose, cordwainer, and Catharine Vose his Wife," join in a deed with other children of Hannah Vose, April 11, 1803.

*Children:* 1. Stephen Vose, b. Nov. 3, 1789. 2. Sarah Williams Vose, b. Nov. 7, 1791. 3. Elijah Pope Vose, b. Nov., 1802. 4. Albert Vose, b. Jan., 1805. 5. Pamelia Vose, b. April, 1807. 6. Hannah Davis Vose, b. Aug. 20, 1809. 7. William Vose, ——.

The estate of William Vose, blacksmith, was administered upon Feb. 4, 1844, and distribution made to "Stephen Vose, brother, Sarah Sweet, niece, Pamelia V. Reed, sister, and Hannah D. Baker, sister of the deceased." "Eleaner Vose, George W. Vose, and Charles J. Reed" signing the receipts with them.

"Mrs. Katy Vose died July 5, 1817, aged 46."

# SECTION 3.

### THE FAMILY OF LAZARUS[4].

LAZARUS,[4] son of Ralph[3] and Rachel (Neale), was born Oct. 31, 1715.

Of his youth we know nothing. He married, Jan. 19, 1740, Susanna, dau. of John and Susannah (Ellison) Glover, of Dorchester, who was born Jan. 8, 1715. Quite likely their home was in Dorchester until the death of his father, judging from the directions in Ralph's[4] will respecting the mill property at Stoughton. His name is on the tax list in Stoughton, Aug. 25, 1748. He was one of the assessors at the time, so we see was a man of affairs, public matters claiming his attention somewhat. He seems to have been successful in business, and to have trained up his children in habits of industry and efficiency. But, like his brother Ralph, he was cut down early, dying of fever, April 4, 1750.

As one of the witnesses to his brother Ralph's will he has left us his beautiful signature. [See page 116.]

He had made no will ; letters of administration were granted, March 26, 1751, to his "widow, Susanna," and his brother, "Ebenezer Pope of Dorchester."

Whether his and his wife's names were placed on the roll of the church or not, I have not learned. But Jan. 17, 1768, a good deputation of their children with one of their grandchildren made public confession of their faith, namely :

"Micajah Pope, Ralf Pope, and Lazarus Pope and Jerusha Pope, Martha Fletcher, daughter of Micajah Pope."

The widow saw her children's children and their children, having attained the remarkable age of 89 years. She went to her rest Nov. 3, 1803.

Each of the five children of this family married, and each of the sons had children who will be enumerated in the next chapter.

Susanna⁵ married, first, Capt. Joseph Farrington, and, second, Peter St. Medard, M.D. The latter is said to have been connected with the U. S. Navy.

Jerusha⁵ married, first, "Philip Marchant of Boston," and second, Samuel Bisbee of Stoughton.

This second husband was born in West Bridgewater, March 29, 1757, and died in Canton, May 2, 1845. He served in the Revolutionary War.

We regret the meagreness of our information respecting these families.

### CHILDREN OF LAZARUS⁴ AND SUSANNA (GLOVER).

I.    MICAJAH,⁶ b. June 6, 1741. [See next chapter, B, 1.]

II.   RALPH,⁵ b. Oct. 1, 1742. [See next chapter, B, 2].

III.  SUSANNA,⁵ b. Dec. 27, 1744; m. (1) Oct. 5, 1767, Capt. Joseph Farrington; (2) April 12, 1781, Peter St. Medard, M.D.; d. ——, 1840.

IV.   LAZARUS,⁵ b. Jan. 19, 1746. [See next chapter, B, 3.]

V.    JERUSHA,⁶ b. April 18, 1749; m. (1) Dec. 11, 1773, Phillip Marchant; (2) in 1783, Samuel Bisbee.

# SECTION IV.

## THE FAMILY OF EBENEZER[4].

LIKE his father, this youngest son was a "home boy." Receiving a half of the old place, he held it through life, and his son, Edmund,[5] and that son's son, Edmund,[6] also spent their lives there. It has not often happened that *five men in line* have thus lived and died on one farm, in America.

To be sure, he might have gone elsewhere. When the General Court gave the township of "Dorchester Canada" (Ashburnham) to the veterans of the expedition of 1690 and their heirs, his father passed over to him the share which fell to the lot of the deceased uncle whose name he bore; and he became proprietor of "the 32d right or share," or the owner of one sixty-third part of the township, which was located in "Lot 28, 1st Division, 57, 2d Division, 11, 4th Division and 46, Equivalent lot." On these he paid taxes in 1759.

He might have gone, like many a young man of the day, to make a home for himself in this "new country," where he had so good an outlook. But, four years after his father's death, he married Abigail Billings, whom we believe to have been a daughter of a son of the pioneer Roger Billings, one of the nearest neighbors.

A Dorchester farm, in good state of cultivation, with market near, and neighbors and relatives at hand, had more charms for the young man than a hillside or marsh in the northern part of Worcester County; and he brought up his family on the old spot and let the wild land remain untrodden. Three sons and three daughters married; two became "old bachelors"; only one child, the first Samuel,[5] died in childhood.

Death came to the father the first day of winter, 1787. But he was not unprepared. Let us read his well-conceived will, kindly copied from the original, for this work, by his descendant, John Tolman Pope[7].

## THE WILL OF EBENEZER[4] POPE.

IN the Name of God Amen This First Day of February Anno Domini One Thousand Seven hundred Eighty & Four, I Ebenezer Pope of Dorchester in the County of Suffolk within the Commonwealth of Massachusetts, Gentleman being in a good meafure of Health & Strength of Body & of Sound & of Disposing Mind and Memory thanks be given unto God Calling to Mind the Mortality of my Body & knowing that it is Appointed unto all Men to Die, do make & ordain this my last Will and Testament, that is to say Principally and first of all, I give & recommend my Soul into the hands of God that gave it, trusting in the Merits of a Glorious Savior for Salvation, and my Body I recomend to the Earth, to be Buried at the discretion of my Executors hereafter named nothing doubting but at the general Resurrection, I shall receive the Same again by the mighty Powers of God.

And touching such Worldly Estate wherewith it hath pleased God to Blefs me in this Life, I give Devise & Dispose of the Same in the following manner & form. Imprimis I give Bequeath unto Abigail my Beloved Wife a Horse & my Chaise to her own Dispose alfo a Cow & so much of my In Door Moveables as to make up one third part of my Perfonal Eftate including the Cow & the Improvement of one Third part of my Real Estate so long as she remains my Widow, but if she Marray then to be paid Sixty Dollars a Year in Specie by my Sons in equal Proportion and to quit my Real Estate. Item I Give & Bequeath to my Sons Ebenezer Pope, John Pope, Ralph Pope Edmund Pope & Samuel Pope their Heirs and Affigns my Real Estate lying in Dorchester, Braintree Milton & Afhburnham also my Creaturs excepting two Cows and my out Door Moveables referving to my Wife the improvement of one third part of my Real Estate so long so she remains my Widow, and reserving to my Daughters Abigail Pope & Mary Houghton the Widow of Jofeph Houghton improvement of the Eafterly Chamber in my Dwelling House Cellar Room & as long as theay or either of them remain unmarried. My Real Estate my out Door moveables &c. I give & Bequeath to my Sons before named in equal Proportions theay paying my Funeral Charges and Just Debts & to theire Mother if she marries again & their Sisters the Sum of Money hereafter given them in equal Proportions.

I give & Bequeath to my Daughter Abigail Pope a Cow a Bed & Beding the improvement of the one half of the Easterly Chamber in my Dwelling House Convenient Room in my Cellar Convenient yard Room & passing & repasing to & from my house as she may have occafion & one Cord of Wood yearley to provided for her by her Brothers, so long as my Wood shall Laft. The Improvement of the whole of the Easterly Chamber in my Dwelling house if her Sifter Mary Houghton be Married again or Shall Die before her. The Improvement of my Easterly Chamber &c. granted her so long as She remains unmarried & no longer. I Give & bequeath to my said Daughter Abigail Pope her Heirs & Assigns the Sum of Three hundred and forty Dollars in Specie to be paid her by her Brothers in equal Proportion within one Year After my Decease.

*Item* I Give & Bequeath to my Daughter Mary Houghton the Widow of Joseph Houghton besides what I have already given her a Bed The Improvement of the one half of the Easterly Chamber in my Dwelling House, convenient room in my Cellar & Convenient Yard Room & liberty of pafsing & repafsing at all times to and from my House, as She may have Occafion, & one Cord of Wood to be provided for her Yearly so long as my Wood Shall last by her Brothers in equal proportion. The Improvement of the whole of the Easterly Chamber in my Dwelling House if Sister Abigail Pope be married or Die before her. The improvement of my Easterly Chamber &c granted her so long as She remained unmarried & no longer. I Give & Bequeath to my said Daughter Mary Houghton, her Heirs & Afsigns, the sum of two Hundred & Eighty Dollars in Specie to be paid by Her Brothers in Equal proportion within two years After my Decease : — My Will is that if my Daughter Abigail Pope out live her Sister Mary Houghton or her Sister be married, that She have two Cords of Wood provided for her Yearly by her Brothers in equal Proportion & on the other hand if she out live her Sister Abigail Pope or her Sister be married, that she have two Cords of Wood provided for her Yearly by her Brothers in equal Proportion so long as my Wood Shall Last.

*Item*, I Give & Bequeath to my Daughter Rachel Belcher the Wife of Samuel Belcher her Heirs & Assigns the Sum of Two Hundred & Eighty Dollars in Specie besides what I have already given her to be paid her by her Brothers in equal Proportion within Three Years After my Decease.

I Give & Bequeath my In Door Moveables, not heretofore Disposed off to all my Children in equall Proportions. I Constitute make & ordain my Sons Ebenezer Pope & John Pope Sole Executors of my last Will & Testament and I do hereby utterly disallow revoke & disannull all & every other former Testaments, Wills, Legacies, Bequeasts, & Executors by me in any ways before named Willed & Bequeathed Ratifying & Confirming this & no other to be my Last Will & Testament.    In Witne/s whereof I have hereunto set my Hand and Seal the Day & Year first Above written.

EBENEZER POPE & seal.

Signed, sealed Published Pronounced & Declared by the said Ebenezer Pope as his Last Will and Testament in the Presence of us the Subscribers.                                NOAH CLAP.
                                         NATHANIEL CLAP.
                                         SARAH CLAP.

Suffolk, ss.   The above Writing being presented by the Executors named, Noar Clap, and Nathaniel Clap made Oath that they saw Ebenezer Pope the Subscriber to this Instrument sign and seal and also heard him publish and declare the same to be his last Will and Testament and that when he so did he was of sound disposing Mind and Memory acording to these Deponents best Discerning & that they together with Sarah Clap now p'sent set to their Names as Witnefs thereof in the said Testator's presence.

*Dorchester, August 7, 1788.*

The widow was alive when her son Ebenezer[5] made his will (proved Mar. 6, 1798).

The dates of her birth and death are, thus far, wanting ; her will, dated Dec. 1, 1802, proved March 1, 1803, limits the time of her demise, however.   John, Edmund, Mary, and Abigail were her heirs.

The Ashburnham lands were sold by the sons, Ebenezer[5] and John,[5] in accordance with the father's wish (as stated in the deeds), as follows : one tract to Samuel Foster, of Ashburnham, Feb. 12, 1790 ; Lot 57, 2d Division, to Hezekiah Cony, jr., of Ashburnham, March 24, 1791 ; the " Equivalent lot " and 75 acres more, to E. Williams, of Dorchester, Dec. 18, 1797.

When the battle of Lexington was reported in Dorchester, the Popes responded quickly to the gun "heard round the world," and either Ebenezer,[4] then fifty-two years old, or his son, Ebenezer,[5] twenty-three, was one of the men who instantly enlisted for defence of home and rights.

We have failed in efforts made to obtain full details of the families of the daughters, Abigail,[5] wife of —— *Rawson*, of Milton ; Rachel,[5] wife of Samuel *Belcher;* and Mary,[5] who was the wife, first, of Joseph Houghton, and, second, of Jonathan Rawson, save the following notes upon the children of the latter marriage.

### CHILDREN OF EBENEZER[4] AND ABIGAIL (BILLINGS).

I.   ABIGAIL,[5] b. Nov. 16, 1748–9 ; m. David Rawson ; d. Sept. 30, 1806.

II.  RACHEL,[5] Jan. 5, 1751 ; m. Sept. 27, 1772, Samuel Belcher ; d. ——.

Rachel, daughter of Samuel and Rachel (Pope) Belcher, married James Lucas, of Boston, afterward of Manchester, Mass.

III. EBENEZER,[5] b. Dec. 14, 1752 ; d. Oct. 1, 1798.
IV.  JOHN,[5] b. Jan. 14, 1755.   [See next chapter, C, 1.]
V.   MARY,[5] b. Jan. 18, 1757 ; m. (1) March 29, 1775, Joseph Houghton ; (2) Feb. 25, 1787, Jonathan Rawson, of Braintree ; d. March 28, 1831.

*Children of Jonathan and Mary[5] (Pope [Houghton]) Rawson.*

Ebenezer, b. July 6, 1787.   Settled at Townsend, Mass.
Jonathan, b. Nov. 1, 1789.   Settled in Boston.
Mary, b. Sept. 12, 1791 ; m. Beza Soule.   Settled in Quincy.
Abigail, b. Jan. 12, 1793.
Samuel, b. Feb. 22, 1794.   Resided in the homestead in Quincy.
William, b. Aug. 22, 1796.
Henry, b. Jan. 7, 1798.
Clarissa, b. July 7, 1800.
Mrs. Mary (Pope) Rawson died March 28, 1831.

VI.   RALPH,[5] b. March 14, 1759. [See next chapter, C, 2.]
VII.  SAMUEL,[5] b. Jan. 14, 1761 ; d. Sept. 21, 1770.
VIII. EDMUND,[5] b. May 6, 1765. [See next chapter, C, 3.]
IX.   SAMUEL,[5] b. May 27, 1768 ; d. Aug. 6, 1801.

He grew to manhood and became a capable business man, but died single, Aug. 6, 1801.

# CHAPTER VIII

## THE FIFTH GENERATION.

### SECTION A.

THE GRANDCHILDREN OF RALPH[4] IN THE MALE LINE.

*1. FREDERICK[5] AND HIS FAMILY.*
*2. WILLIAM[5] AND HIS FAMILY.*
*3. JAMES[5] AND HIS FAMILY.*

### I.

### THE FAMILY OF FREDERICK[5].

THE oldest son in a country home, he had peculiar burdens when his father died. Less than seventeen years old, he had a great test made of his manliness, and loyalty to his remaining parent. We are told that he stood the test finely, and bore his new burdens like a hero. The business of the farm was on his hands, and as his Uncle Lazarus's death quickly followed his father's, the mill, too, came under his care, naturally.

But he grew up tall, lithe, and strong, unusually composed and calm under excitement, able, alike, to command himself and others. Not greatly given to speech-making, he was called into prominent positions because he knew well how to *listen*, and was a keen reader of human nature. But when he spoke, it was to the point. It was said of him, as of his brother William, that he was inclined to be sarcastic.

An instance of this was told us by "Aunt Susanna," widow of his son Elijah[6].

At one of the town meetings in Stoughton, political feeling had run high, and quite a contest had risen over the electing of a representative to the "General Court," the legislative assem-

bly of Massachusetts, in spite of which Colonel Pope had been
re-elected by a strong majority.    As people were coming out of
the voting-place, one ignorant fellow, grumbling at the result,
said,

"I don't believe, Colonel Pope, you are the greatest man in
town.    I think *I* can see through a millstone as far as you can."
The good-natured colonel, as he strode out, quietly answered,
"Well, very likely ; and I think *you* can see as far through a
*millstone* as you can through anything."

He married a Bridgewater girl, Mary, or "Molly," as that
sweet name came then to be twisted, daughter of one of the old
Plymouth families.    Here is the official record :

"Married in North Bridgewater, June 8, 1758, by Rev. John Porter, Frederick Pope of Dorchester to Mary, dau. of Joseph and Mary
Cole."

Plymouth registers give us the information that Joseph Cole's
wife was the daughter of Edward² Stephens of that place,
granddaughter of Edward,¹ who was an early resident of Marshfield.    Her mother was Mary, daughter of Eleazer² Churchill,
son of John,¹ who came to Plymouth in 1643, and married Hannah, daughter of William Pontus, an earlier settler.    The Cole
line is not fully traced ; enough is known, however, to place
Joseph among the descendants of that family whose name is
memorialized in the widely celebrated "Cole's Hill," in Plymouth ; and the writer feels certain that the earliest of this line
in the "old colony " did *not* come in the "Mayflower ".!

The bride of Frederick⁵ Pope proved to be a wide-awake,
capable woman, a worthy companion for her spouse.

One or both of them must have been members of the church,
for their children were duly baptized, and their home had daily
worship in it, like those of the former generations.

The military record of a grandsire is often magnified by tradition.    We have documents to measure that of this hero — in
a few points only.    At the Massachusetts State House there
exists a precious parchment, entitled,

"A Muster Roll of the Company in the Colony Service ; Which
Marched from Stoughton on the alarm on the 19th of April 1775 under
the command of Capt. Peter Talbot."

Among the eighty-five names on the Roll, we find James Pope, Ralph Pope, and Frederick Pope.

They were mustered out after less than two weeks' service, and received their pay in accordance with a resolve of the Council, passed Feb. 20, 1776.

James Pope was the second lieutenant of the company, Ralph Pope one of the corporals, and Frederick Pope is in the list of privates.

The following extracts from this pay-roll are presented in their original form :

| Name. | rank | Miles traviled | Amount of Travil | Days in Service | Amount of Service | Amount of Travil & Service |
|---|---|---|---|---|---|---|
| | | | *s. d.* | | *s. d. qr.* | *s. d. qr.* |
| James Pope | 2d Lieut. | 38 | 3 2 | 6 | 15 0 0 | 13 2 0 |
| Ralph Pope | Corp'l | 38 | 3 2 | 6 | 9 5 0 | 12 7 0 |
| Frederick Pope | private | 38 | 3 2 | 4 . | 5 8 3 | 8 10 3 |

"In June (1775,) Capt. Frederick Pope enlisted a company of fifty-eight men for one month and nine days' service." [Hist. of Norfolk County.]

In the Massachusetts Military Documents, Vol. 28, Book of Militia Officers, p. 64, we find the following :

" SEA COAST OFFICERS COMMISSIONATED.

1777

May 8ᵗʰ  John Robinson Colᵒ: ) of a Battalion to be raised
John Jacobs Lt: Colᵒ: } for the defence of yᵉ
Fredᵏ Pope—Major ) Harbor of Boston."

The family tradition that he was commander of a regiment during the Revolutionary War, has not complete verification ; yet, with the foregoing voucher for his appointment as Major, and the fact that the war continued five years thereafter, we may reasonably believe that he rose to higher rank and did larger service before its close. His uniform title from that time was " Colonel."

The name of Col. Frederick Pope first appears on the roll of the House of Representatives as the colleague of Elijah Dunbar, Esq., May 30, 1787, representing the town of Stoughton.

The journal of the House does not report any of his speeches, but chronicles several of his votes. He voted nay upon the

question of repealing " The Disqualifying Act, &c., for raising
troops to be employed in the Western counties, and for pardoning all persons concerned in the late rebellion, excepting as
mentioned therein." In short, he was not disposed to pass
lightly over the conduct of those who had participated in
" Shay's Rebellion."

He voted yea on the adoption of a " Bill for the continuance
of and in addition to an act entitled, An Act for suspending
the laws for the collection of private debts under certain limita-
tions." — Nov. 13, 1787.

Oct. 25, 1787, the house considered the Proposition for as-
sembling a State convention for the consideration of the proposed Federal constitution ; and although he was not a member of that convention, yet he was one of those who considered
in the Legislature the great problems of the infant Republic,
and aided in shaping " the Massachusetts idea," which entered as
a strong factor into the composition of the general government.

He was sole representative in 1788, and continued in 1789.
He voted against the constitutional right of persons to seats in
the Legislature when holding such Federal offices as were a
disqualification for the Legislature by State statute.    It was
decided as he believed right, by a strong vote, Jan. 22, 1790.

In March, 1790, James Endicott, Esq., succeeded him ; but
he was returned again in 1791, and re-elected in 1792.    In 1793
Elijah Dunbar, Esq., was returned.

" In 1794 a novel experiment was tried for supplying the
town treasury, by voting that the person who should be chosen
representative should serve for 6s. 7d. per day, and if the General Court should fix a higher rate, 'y* over-plus is to be returned to the town.'    Col. Frederick Pope was chosen, and accepted the condition prescribed."    At the next election the
plan was dropped.

In 1795, Mr. Elijah Crane was the representative ; but in
1796 Col. Pope held the office again, making seven terms in all
that he thus served his native town.

His death occurred Aug. 20, 1812, in the midst of the
stirring events of the " Second War with Great Britain," and
no obituary notice has come to light, though it is well known
that he was highly esteemed as a citizen of Stoughton.

He was buried in S., but afterwards re-interred in the tomb of his sons, Frederick[6] and William,[6] in Dorchester, where also his wife's dust reposes. She followed her husband "into the silent land," Dec. 24, 1823.

All of their eight children mentioned in church and town records, reached maturity. Five of the six sons left families of which particular account will be given in the next chapter.

CHILDREN OF COLONEL FREDERICK[5] AND MARY (COLE).

I. · RALPH,[6] b. 1760. [See next chapter, A, 1.]

II. RACHEL,[6] b. 1761 ; m. Feb. 2, 1786, *George Lyon Farrington*, son of Joseph and Eva (Thorp) Farrington, of Roxbury, b. April 14, 1764.

III. SAMUEL WARD,[6] b. Feb., 1763. [See next chapter, A, 2.]

IV. ALEXANDER,[6] bapt. May 1, 1764, has left but few memorials. When, after the Revolutionary War, Charleston, South Carolina, was thriving prosperously, he went thither, in company with his two older brothers, and entered upon the business of house-building. There he is said to have married and had a daughter, and there his death is reported as taking place, April 7, 1797. But the attempts made by his nephew, Col. Wm. Pope, to gather further points in the matter, proved unsuccessful. It appears to be certain that he left no issue in the male line.

V. FREDERICK,[6] born Aug. 20, 1772. [See next chapter, A, 3.]

VI. WILLIAM,[6] b. Nov. 12, 1774. [See next chapter, A, 4.]

VII. MARY,[6] bapt. May 17, 1778 ; m. Feb. 24, 1800, *Stoughton Morse*, son of Joshua Morse, of Clinton, N..Y., born April 3, 1776. They resided some time in Massachusetts, then removed to Manlius, N. Y., where Mr. Morse died, April 20, 1822. [See Morse Genealogy.] *Children :* Charles *Morse*, was clerk for his father's brother, Samuel Adams Morse, of Machias, Me., a few years ; but went to New York to the family home. Mary *Morse*, married, ——. Resided at some place in N. Y. State.

VIII. ELIJAH,[6] born June 10, 1780. [See next chapter, A, 5.]

## II.

## THE FAMILY OF WILLIAM[5].

WILLIAM,[5] son of Ralph[4] and Rebecca Stubbs, was born in Stoughton, Feb. 5, 1738–9. Married Mary Kingman of Easton, born about 1743.

We have few traces of their early married life. Their home was in Stoughton for several years. Their daughter, Mary, was born June 3, 1768, and we learn of the baptism of another daughter : "1776, March 17, Rebecca, Daughter of William Pope," [Stoughton Church records,] who appears to have died young. But he had already bought a piece of land in a "border" settlement, we discover, and thither he soon after removed.

"William Pope of Lunenburg," bought land in L. of Peter Page and Amos Kendall, Nov. 2[d], 1770.

Philip Goodridge and Daniel Steward of Lunenburg, deed land in L. to William Pope of L., Oct. 3, 1777.

"William Pope of Lunenburg in the county of Worcester and state of Mafsachusetts, gentleman," and "Molly Pope his wife," deed land in L. to Amos and Asa Nelson and David Mighill of Rowley, May 3, 1780.

"William Pope of Jaffrey in the county of Cheshire in the State of New Hampshire, Gentleman," and "Molley Pope" sign another deed, Feb. 15, 1783, conveying land in Lunenburg, Mass., to Silas Snow of L.

But while living in Lunenburg, he was reaching farther north for a home ; we trace him along by public documents and deeds, and fully identify the man.

Among the petitioners for the incorporation of Hillsborough, N. H., Feb. 15, 1770, we find the name of "William Pope."

"Will[m] Pope" was credited with ten pounds for service in the "Experdishon to Proverdance or Rodisland," Aug. 8, 1778, in the roll of Hillsborough soldiers.

In 1780 he signed a petition for authority to tax non-resident property owners, and was also a signer to a petition concerning the Drawing of Town Lots, which the New Hampshire Legislature acted upon Feb. 17, 1785. A little later Jaffrey had become his home, for we find his name on a protest of the citizens of this place, May 24, 1787, against setting off a portion of the town.

¹ We are grateful for the information in the "History of Jaffrey, N. H.," by Dr. Daniel B. Cutter, of Peterboro, N. H.

"William Pope (Captain) came to Jaffrey at an early date, and settled on Lot 20, Range 6, now owned by Joseph Davis. He was in service during the Revolution, and on committees to procure provisions for the army; member of the board of selectmen, and held other offices of honor and trust. Of his origin we have no knowledge. He married Mary ——, who died May 7, 1821, aged 78. He died Nov. 16, 1820, aged 80. One child, Polly, married Nathan Cutter, of New Ipswich.

"Nathan Cutter came from New Ipswich, where his father, Nathan, a grandson of Ephraim, died March 6, 1778, aged 42, and settled on Lot 20, Range 6, now owned by Addison Pierce. The time of his settlement in Jaffrey is not precisely known, but some time previous to 1785. About 1812 he removed to Shoreham, Vt., and died about 1818.

"His children were:

I.   Polly *Cutter*, d. in Jaffrey, Dec. 29, 1798.
II.  William Pope *Cutter*, b. in Jaffrey, June 13, 1785; graduated at Dartmouth College in 1805; studied medicine, and settled in Shoreham, Vt.; m. Prudence Evans, March 24, 1808; d. at Shoreham, Vt., July 8, 1815.
III. Rhoana *Cutter*, b. in Jaffrey; m. Nicanor Needham, of Shoreham, Vt., physician; d. ——.
IV.  Orinda *Cutter*, m. Darius Cooper, farmer.
V.   Abdilla *Cutter*.
VI.  Rosina, m. Leander Cass; had a son and daughter.
VII. Nathan *Cutter*.

William Pope Cutter (Dr.) had children:

I.   Dorothy *Cutter*, b. Sept. 20, 1809; m. Daniel Abbott; d. Nov. 19, 1862; had one daughter.
II.  William Pope *Cutter*, b. Nov. 23, 1811; d. 1822.
III. Rhoana N. *Cutter*, b. in Hartford, N. Y., Dec. 21, 1814; m. Walter Robbins, of Leicester, Vt., Dec. 31, 1838; had children:

1.  Milo N. *Robbins*, b. Dec. 9, 1840 ; m. Annie P. Whittier,
    Sept. 17, 1866 ; real-estate dealer, in Boston, resides at
    Melrose ; one son, b. May 19, 1869.
2.  Hannah M. *Robbins*, b. April 15, 1843.
3.  Emma R. *Robbins*, b. Sept. 4, 1845 ; m. Edwin H. Hub-
    bard, Feb. 24, 1864.
4.  Thirza L. *Robbins*, b. 1849.
5.  Mary J. *Robbins*, b. Sept. 19, 1852.
6.  Julia A. *Robbins*, b. May 22, 1855."

"Captain Pope," as he was called, was often in office in Jaffrey, and was spoken of by one who knew him, as "a man of fair
talents, considerable acquirements, strict integrity, sound
judgment," and original in his ideas.   He was a Free Mason.

---

III.

## THE FAMILY OF JAMES[5].

JAMES,[5] son of Ralph[4] and Rebecca (Stubbs), b. July 31,
1746; m. May 19, 1772, Sarah, dau. of David and Relief
Capen, who was b. Oct. 22, 1753.

A very active, intelligent, faithful man, often called to the
lead in public matters in Stoughton, and much respected by his
neighbors,— such is the report which has come down to us
regarding this third son of "Dr. Ralph" Pope.   How he passed
his youth, and what the details of his life were, we should be
glad to learn ; but the burning of a chestful of old papers has
robbed us of private mementos and records, while public documents have yielded but few particulars.

We have already given in full the record of his beginning of
military service, in the foregoing section.   He took rank as
lieutenant, while his older brother, Frederick, was enrolled as
private.   Perhaps this was a sign of his greater personal popu-
larity among the young men of his acquaintance ; it *may be*
that both he and his brother had previously seen service in
some of the campaigns of the long French and Indian War.
Tradition cannot be followed here.

After the war the brother passed as colonel and he as captain, memorials, I suppose, of the rank each had reached before the long contest had come to an end.

He and his wife were also faithful in religion, and the baptisms of several of their children are recorded.

The first four little ones died in early childhood. Then came a daughter, Milly,[6] who lived to the age of twenty-two, but died without having fulfilled the hopes of fond love, whose plan was thus written on the town book :

"Marriage is intended between Jonathan Belcher and Milly Pope of Stoughton.   May 31, 1801."

She "faded away" Sept. 20, 1801.   The next child to Milly was a fourth boy, Luther,[6] who lived but three and a half years.

Azor,[6] Relief,[6] Anna,[6] and Ward,[6] the children next in order, passed safely through the diseases incident to childhood, and came to maturity and parent life : but meantime one other boy, Rufus,[6] had been born only to die "of canker," as the "Bill of Mortality" reported, at the age of two years.   Thus four only of the ten children furnish materials for memoirs here. Yet who does not look hopefully for the *future* biography of those who have been early taken from the poor chances of earth's school to the magnificent advantages of the School Supreme !

Each child born is worthy of our registration, and recognition and *hope*.

Another "Bill of Mortality" has a paragraph for us.

"1798, September 26, Capt. James Pope, Æ. 52.   By a fall from a loaded wagon."

So there was another shock of grief for one often afflicted, and another "light in the window."

Administration on the estate was granted, at her request, to Samuel Talbot, and Lemuel Gay became the guardian of the children, Nov. 6, 1798.   The division of the property was announced Aug. 7, 1804.

The widow died Jan. 18, 1816.

CHILDREN OF CAPTAIN JAMES⁵ AND SARAH (CAPEN).

 I. JAMES,⁶ b. March 23, 1773 ; d. Oct. 8, 1778.
 II. OLIVER,⁶ b. Nov. 2, 1774 ; d. Dec. 30, 1777.
 III. REBECCA,⁶ b. March 2, 1776 ; d. Oct. 21, 1778.
 IV. ELIJAH,⁶ b. Dec. 20, 1777 ; d. Oct. 25, 1778.
 V. MILLY,⁶ b. Aug. 24, 1779 ; d. Sept. 20, 1801.
 VI. LUTHER,⁶ b. April 8, 1781 ; d. Oct. 20, 1801.
 VII. AZOR,⁶ b. May 6, 1783.  [See next chapter, A, 6.]
 VIII. RELIEF,⁶ b. April 21, 1785 ; m. March 27, 1804, Capt. Thomas Pownal Richards, of Sharon ; d. Jan. 23, 1821.  The children of this couple were :

  1. Milly Pownal Richards, b. 1804 ; became the wife of Capt. James Hill, son of John and Susanna Hill ; d. March, 1883.
  2. Relief Richards, m. April 20, 1840, Nathaniel Smith, of Easton.
  3. Thomas Richards, m. Anna Kepley ; *children :* Mary *Richards,* Benjamin *Richards,* Augusta *Richards,* Elizabeth *Richards.*   One of these daughters is the wife of Charles Bartlett, and lives in California.
  4. Pownal Richards, m. Sally Beals.
  5. Benjamin Richards, d. in early manhood.
  6. William Richards.
  7. Nathaniel Richards, m. Mary Hayden.

 IX. ANNA,⁶ b. May 3, 1787 ; m. Jan. 7, 1807, Barney Richards, of Sharon, brother of Thomas P. Richards, who d. June 5, 1857. ˙ He was b. May 11, 1776, and d. March 31, 1837.  Their children :

  1. Sarah Ann Richards, b. July 8, 1809 ; m. Luther Southworth ; she d. July 3, 1874.
  2. Barney Richards, b. Dec. 18, 1810 ; d. Feb. 3, 1811.
  3. Mary Richards, b. Nov. 23, 1812 ; m. Henry Drake, of Sharon, Nov. 28, 1833.  They (Henry Drake and Mary) removed to Sharon soon after.  He d., after great suffering from rheumatism, in May, 1885.  Mrs. Drake is full of vigor in mind and body, as

these lines are penned, and has taken great interest in the preparation of these annals of her mother's family. *Children of Henry and Mary (Richards) Drake:* (1.) Margaret *Drake,* m. July 6, 1856, Charles, son of Daniel and Elizabeth Hill, of Boston. They have a son, Charles Webster Hill, b. July 9, 1857, residing in Stoughton. (2.) Henry Albert *Drake.* (3.) Herbert *Drake.*

4. Barney Richards, b. Nov. 14, 1814; d. Feb. 16, 1815.
5. Nelson Richards, b. Jan. 13, 1816; died May 5, 1880.
6. Martha Richards, b. July 26, 1818; d. Oct. 5, 1822.
7. Albert Richards, b. March 25, 1824; m. Sarah Bucklin, of Marlboro, Oct. 19, 1853; d. Nov. 8, 1853. Just three weeks of wedded life.

X.  WARD,[6] b. April 4, 1789. [See next chapter, A, 7.]
XI. RUFUS,[6] bapt. Nov. 16, 1794; d. July 28, 1796.

## SECTION B.

---

I.

## THE FAMILY OF MICAJAH[5].

MICAJAH,[5] eldest son of Lazarus[4] and Susanna (Glover), was born June 6, 1741. At twenty-five years of age he gave his heart and hand to Sarah Whitney, of the neighboring town of Braintree. The date of their marriage is not given, but, Jan. 17, 1768, he was admitted to the Stoughton church, in company with several others of the family, and brought his babe, "Martha Fletcher," for baptism.

This child, *Martha Fletcher*,[6] was "married to Anthony Hunt, of Braintree, by Rev. Ezra Weld, Nov. 13, 1786," or when a few days more than eighteen years of age.

The life he lived passed rapidly away, with what special successes we do not know; nor are we certain on what day it closed. Probate files reveal to us his will, dated Dec. 2, 1773, bequeathing his property to his wife, "Sarah," and to his "two beloved children, John Pope and Martha Fletcher." The will was presented in court March 10, 1774; so his death fell between these two dates.

About that time another child was born, whom the widow presented for baptism, April 21, 1776.

In 1789 she removed to Braintree, where her sons grew up to be a comfort to her old age; and where she closed her eyes in the sleep that knows no waking, Dec. 19, 1800.

CHILDREN OF MICAJAH[5] AND SARAH (WHITNEY).

I.   MARTHA FLETCHER,[6] b. Nov. 1, 1767 ; m. Nov. 13, 1786, Anthony Hunt.

II.   JOHN,[6] bapt. April 23, 1769. [See next chapter, B, 1.]

III.   ASA,[6] bapt. April 21, 1776. [See next chapter, B, 2.]

B, 2.

RALPH,[5] the second son of Lazarus,[4] senior, and Susanna (Glover), was a man of considerable force, judging from three circumstances.   First, he took the stand of a church-member, Jan. 17, 1768 ; second, he was chosen corporal in the company of volunteer infantry, which organized under the captaincy of Peter Talbot, on the day of the Lexington alarm ; and, third, he was chosen " tything-man," (or meeting-house policeman,) in Braintree, March 7, 1785.

His wife was Hannah, daughter of David and Hannah (Talbot) Gay ; and Jan. 1, 1771, was their wedding day.   Five children cheered their hearts, all spared to adult and family life.

Of these one, only, was a daughter, NANCY[6] ; who married, June 12, 1796, Joshua Wild of Randolph.   A son, George, and a daughter, Sarah, survive them.

CHILDREN OF RALPH[6] AND HANNAH (GAY).

I.   JOSEPH,[6] born Oct. 4, 1771.   [See next chapter, B, 3.]

II.   MICAJAH,[6] b. May 5, 1774.   [——— B, 4.]

III.   NANCY,[6] b. June 12, 1776; m. June 12, 1796, Joshua Wild ; d. ———.

IV.   RALPH,[6] b. Feb. 18, 1779.   [See next chapter, B, 5.]

V.   LEMUEL,[6] b. Oct. 12, 1781.   [——— B, 6.]

B, 3.

LAZARUS,[6] third son of Lazarus[4] and Susanna (Glover), was born on the 19th of January, 1746.

He seems to have been a person of refined sensibilities and of good "capacitie for learning"; for in the list of scholars at " William Billing's Sacred Music School at Stoughton," in the year 1774, his name is enrolled as "one of the singers of tenor."

Four years earlier he had taken his place as a Christian; and we may imagine him a person well esteemed in the community, when he was able to win in marriage the hand of Mrs. Mary (Swan) Spurr, whose husband, Thomas Spurr, jr., had some time before passed away.

The date of the marriage is missing; so are those of the births of the nine children who graced the union of the tenor singer and the young widow.

Perhaps the climate of that region was malarial. The chronicles of Stoughton tell us that "Lazarus Pope died March 16, 1802, of fever," as his father and uncle had done before him. Like them he was still at an age where force and vigor should naturally be in full tide; but the "husbandman," as Probate records designate him, was done with earthly sowing and reaping.

The widow survived him not many years; "consumption," says the record, was the name the doctors gave to the merciless messenger of death which touched her beyond their curative skill, Sept. 28, 1807; and May 9, 1809, public documents furnish their latest mention of her name, when her eldest son, Lazarus, made report as administrator of her estate.

#### CHILDREN OF LAZARUS[6] AND MARY (SWAN) (SPURR).

I.   MARY (*Polly*, *Patty*),[6] b. 1778; d. Dec. 25, 1846.
II.  SUSANNA,[6] b. 1780; d. ——.
III. LAZARUS,[6] b. April, 1782. [See next chapter, B, 7.]
IV.  EBENEZER,[6] b. 1784; d. ——.
V.   SARAH,[6] b. 1787; d. ——. ·
VI.  ABIGAIL,[6] b. 1789; married, first, Dec. 9, 1807, Isaac Washburn, of Kingston, Mass. He died March 27, 1828, a. 53 yrs. She m., second, Samuel Wales, of Stoughton, Nov. 23, 1836. She died Nov. 9, 1861.

#### CHILDREN OF ISAAC AND ABIGAIL[6] (POPE) WASHBURN.

1. Susan St. Medard *Washburn*, b. March 23, 1809; m., Jan. ——, 1829, Sumner I. Ruggles, of Dorchester. She died June 27, 1858, a. 49 yrs·

Children : Cynthia Maria *Ruggles*, b. ——, 1831 ;
m. G. V. Nordstrom, of Boston.  Frank Sumner
*Ruggles*, b. ——, 1833 ; m. Emmeline Summer-
hayes.  Mary Emma *Ruggles*, b. ——, 1845 ; m.
Granville M. Fiske, of Dorchester.

2.  Cynthia Bradford *Washburn*, b. June 6, 1811 ; m.
Nov. 27, 1834, Sumner A. Hayward, of North
Bridgewater (now Brockton).  He died June 20,
1883.  Children :

(1.)  Sarah Washburn *Hayward*, b. Nov. 24, 1839 ;
m. Aug. 5, 1860, *Portus B. Hancock* of Coven-
try, Vt. ; *child*, Sumner Hayward *Hancock*, b.
Sept. 17, 1876.

(2.)  Abbie Wales *Hayward*, b. May 14, 1842 ; d.
Sept. 16, 1864.

(3.)  Maria Chilton *Hayward*, b. April 27, 1845 ; d.
Oct. 27, 1858.

(4.)  Lora Standish *Hayward*, b. July 10, 1848 ; m.
May 21, 1876, *Charles W. Sumner*, of Fox-
boro ; *child*, Warren Ellis *Sumner*, b. May 8,
1880.

(5.)  Julia Bradford *Hayward*, b. Oct. 5, 1850 ; m.
April 23, 1873, *William M. Thompson*, of
Brockton ; *child*, Edgar Hayward *Thompson*,
b. June 10, 1879.

3.  George Hiram *Washburn*, b. March 7, 1815 ; d. June
28, 1843.

4.  Sarah *Washburn*, b. March 5, 1817 ; d. April 17,
1864.

VII.  JERUSHA,[5] b.1790 ; m. May 11, 1809, Ichabod Holbrook,
jr. ; d. ——.

VIII.  THOMAS,[5] b. 1792.  [See next chapter, B, 8.]

IX.  OTIS,[5] b. Oct., 1795.  [See next chapter, B, 9.]

# SECTION C.

I.

## THE FAMILY OF JOHN[5].

JOHN,[5] son of Ebenezer and Abigail (Billings), born Jan. 22, 1755, married, June 17, 1799, Sarah, dau. of Elijah and Lydia Davis, born Jan. 12, 1764.

Colonel John Pope was a very prominent man in his day, of whom many facts of interest ought to be told here. But efforts to secure them, in any definite form, have proved unsuccessful.

### CHILDREN OF COLONEL JOHN[5] AND SARAH (DAVIS).

I. ABIGAIL,[6] b. July 19, 1799, m. Feb. 5,1826, Mr. Robert Vose, son of Reuben and Polly Vose, b. March 28, 1798, who has left a famous name as a schoolmaster in Dorchester ; a man skilled in business affairs, and an honored citizen. Children :

    1. Robert *Vose*, jr., b. Jan. 26, 1827 ; m. Abbie Ann, dau. of Wilder and Sarah Harding, of Dorchester, June 28, 1853. Resides in Washington, D. C. *Child*, Mary Wilder *Vose*, b. July 19, 1854.

    2. John Pope *Vose*, b. June 15, 1829 ; d. March 24, 1872.

    3. Sarah Pope *Vose*, b. Sept. 3, 1831 ; d. June 2, 1836.

    4. Andrew Jackson *Vose*, b. July 6, 1833 ; m. Dec. 29, 1870, Abbie Tibbets, dau. of Jacob and Catherine (Rogers) Buzzell, of West Newfield, Maine. Resides on the old place in Dorchester. *Child*, Sadie Lizzie *Vose*, b. March 26, 1873.

    5. Reuben *Vose*, b. July 7, 1837 ; d. Nov. 30, 1843.

II. CAROLINE,[6] b.———; d. March 22,1847.

III. SARAH,[6] b. Dec., 1805.

## C, 2.

## THE FAMILY OF RALPH.[5]

RALPH,[5] son of Ebenezer[4] and Abigail (Billings), was born March 15, 1759.

"Ralph Pope of Dorchester and Elizabeth Nash of this town were married by Rev. Anthony Wibird, Oct. 25, 1786." [Braintree records.]

"Ralph Pope" was one of the company of Capt. Oliver Billings, organized in Dorchester, April 19, 1775, to hasten to the relief of the militia who had been attacked at Lexington and Concord. He probably engaged in service subsequently, during the war. He became a very sagacious and adventurous merchant. Associated with his brothers at Dorchester, and opening a store in company with a brother and brother-in-law, at Petersburg, Va., he carried on a large business. After his death in 1798, and that of his brother Samuel, Aug. 6, 1801, his sons and Mr. George H. Jones, also of Petersburg, Va., continued the business under the style of "Popes & Jones," the brother Ralph managing the business in Boston, while Ebenezer and Jones attended to matters in Virginia.

"Ralph Pope of Boston" made will, dated at Quincy, Sept. 9, 1798. Bequeaths to sons Ebenezer and Ralph the estate inherited from his father Eben[r]. Pope; to wife Elizabeth a third of the remainder; to Mrs. Sarah Hill, widow of Edward Hill, a suit of mourning; to "my three children, viz.: Ebn[r]., Ralph, and Elizabeth," the remainder of the estate. Desires his brother Samuel Pope appointed guardian to his two sons, and Dea. Jona. Webb, guardian to his daughter. Speaks of his brother Samuel as "of Petersburg in Virginia," whom he appoints executor jointly with Jona. Webb of Quincy, and Paul Nash of Richmond, Virginia.

> AMOS STETSON
> JOHN POPE and } witnesses.
> SARAH HILL.

The Inventory calls him "Merchant," the business carried on by him and his brother Samuel being the shoe business and grocery combined. "The real and personal estate at Dorchester left by will to the two sons" is one of the items.

" Moses Hall of Boston, Distiller, and John Pope of Dorchester,"
were bondsmen with the executors, Paul Nash and Samuel Pope,
Oct. 9, 1798.

Feb. 15, 1847, "Thomas B. Bond" sells to "Thomas H. Bond,
Maria A. Bond, Ada Bond and Atrobus Bond, all of Petersburg, in
Virginia," all his title to a tract of land in Quincy; and immediately
afterward "Thomas H. Bond, merchant," sold to Wm. R. Belzer, of
Quincy, one fourth part of the same land, "being the estate which
descended to me from my mother, Elizabeth Bond, as one of her
heirs at law."

Elizabeth[d] Pope, it thus appears, married Thomas B. Bond
of Petersburg, Va., and had children, as the foregoing document
testifies.

Mrs. Bond visited the relatives of her father and mother in
Dorchester and Quincy, within the memory of some now living,
and was highly esteemed by them.

The "cruel war" destroyed many records in Virginia, and
perhaps obliterated registers which would have greatly helped
the details of this sketch.   But family affection is unchanged ;
and we should be glad to renew the ancestral bond with any
who may survive in this branch of our Dorchester Pope family.

### CHILDREN OF RALPH[6] AND ELIZABETH (NASH).

I.   EBENEZER[6].
II.  RALPH[6].
III. ELIZABETH[6] ; m. Thomas B. Bond ; d. before 1847.

---

## C, 3.

## THE FAMILY OF EDMUND[5].

EDMUND,[5] son of Ebenezer[4] and Abigail (Billings), born
May 27, 1765 ; married, March 20, 1808, Susanna (Suky),
daughter of Dyer and Suky (Webb) Rawson, born Feb. 4,
1781.

He was a diligent, faithful man, a worthy successor to his
forefathers' estate, and left a good name.   As he did not marry
until nearly forty, his children saw comparatively little of

him after they reached years of understanding, and have brought down but little knowledge of his peculiarities and experiences.

Being almost the youngest child of a large family, and the son of one who was the youngest, and *he* the son of one who was next to the youngest, he furnishes, so to speak, a bridge across the generations; for his daughter, Mrs. Abigail⁸ (Pope) Glover, now living, is only the great-granddaughter of the first Ralph,³ whose father was born in England. Only five steps back from our contemporary, Mrs. Glover, to the English cradle! The average length of a generation in that branch of our family has been forty-six years; while the average length in another branch, now represented in its tenth generation, has been but twenty-six years.

Edmund⁵ Pope lived in a house built by his father, a little way from the site of the first house of which we know as the family home, the cellar of that most ancient one, dug above two centuries ago, being still visible in the field hard by. The old spring, too, has been re-opened since the place passed into other hands, and its water, forced by a windmill through many feet of pipe, has supplied a mansion on the hill beyond.

*The Squantum Estate now in the Town of Quincy.*

When Quincy was enlarged, in 1820, by the establishment of the Neponset River as the boundary line between that town and Dorchester, this clause was inserted in the legislative enactment:

" Provided, nevertheless, that John Pope, Edmund Pope, Moses Billings, and Oliver Billings, with their respective families, and all their lands and estates lying in said Squantum and the Farms . . . shall remain annexed to the town of Dorchester."

But in 1855 "so much of the town of Dorchester . . . near to and at the place called Squantum, and including the estates now owned and occupied by George B. Billings, Edmund Pope, and George W.· Billings " was annexed to Quincy.

Here we see "instead of the fathers — the children."

Feb. 27, 1840, Edmund,⁵ sen., passed away. His widow lived until Aug. 31, 1851, when three adult children and the widow and two daughters of the fourth child were her heirs. Their only daughter was

ABIGAIL,[6] born May 21, 1810, who married, March 27, 1832, *John Glover*, son of Alexander and Jemima (Tolman) Glover, grandson of Alexander and Hannah[4] (Pope) Glover, who was born in Dorchester, Sept. 28, 1804, and died April 14, 1868, in the city of San Francisco, Cal.

He succeeded to his father's business, saw-mill and wharf and wood, etc., etc. Built a house next his father's, and lived there until fire destroyed the mill. Then he bought an estate in Quincy, where he resided for a while, till, in 1852, he went to California. For a number of years their home was in a lot they owned on Market Street, opposite the present site of the " Palace Hotel." In spite of poor.health, the loss of an arm, through accident, and many other misfortunes, Mr. Glover kept resolute and diligent, and " conquered fortune." He returned to Massachusetts, only to long for the climate of California; yet there he yielded up his life too soon for her who had spent so many eventful years as his helpmeet.

Mrs. Glover resides at Atlantic, in Quincy.

CHILDREN OF EDMUND[5] AND SUSANNA (RAWSON).

I.   EBENEZER,[6] b. Aug. 5, 1808.   [See next chapter, C, 1.]
II.  ABIGAIL,[6] b. May 21, 1810; m. John Glover.
III. EDMUND,[6] b. Sept. 3, 1813.   [See next chapter, C, 2.]
IV.  SAMUEL,[6] b. March 30, 1817.   [See next chapter, C, 3.]

# CHAPTER IX

# THE SIXTH GENERATION.

## SECTION A.

1. RALPH[6] ; 2. SAMUEL WARD[6] ; 3. FREDERICK,[6] JR. ; 4. WIL-
LIAM[6] ; 5. ELIJAH[6] ; 6. AZOR[6] ; 7. WARD[6].

I.

## RALPH[6] AND HIS FAMILY.

RALPH,[6] eldest son of Col. Frederick[5] and Mary (Cole), was
born in the year 1760, the statement of his age at the time
of his death being our only clue to this date.

He was spoken of in town as "Ralph Pope, 2[d]," his father's
cousin, the son of Lazarus,[4] being "Ralph Pope, 1st," who
also gave the name to *his* son, Ralph,[6] jr.

Over in Dorchester there was still another Ralph, who was
the son of Ebenezer[4]; and it will not be strange if some facts
relating to one of these four should be transferred to the account of some other.

The subject of the present article, Ralph,[6] son of Col. Frederick, is pretty certainly known to have served in the Revolutionary War, on the staff of his father, and also in some other
capacity; but his rank is not known.

It is altogether probable that he was the "Ralph Pope" who
was enrolled as a member of the company of which Eliphalet
Sawen was captain, in the regiment commanded by Col. William
McIntosh, "for guard in Massachusetts Bay, Aug. 24th, 1778."

He had learned the trade of carpenter, and "went to Charlestown, S. C., to engage in house-building, soon after the close of

the War ; he remained there but a short time. The climate in-
jured his health, and he returned to his family in Stoughton."
He had married, while the war was still in progress, viz :
Aug. 17, 1780. His bride was Abigail Swan, born Nov. 19,
1761, whose father, Major Robert Swan, with Rachel (Draper),
his wife, had come from Dedham to Stoughton some years previous, and made a home there.

The strain of business in a Southern climate, with habits óf
activity acquired in the North, told upon him ; and he fell a
victim to the disease which has laid low so many sons of New
England.

The " Mortality " record is this :  " 1797, April 25, Ralph
Pope, 2[d], æ. 37. Consumption."

The widow had no slight care, with six children, the eldest a
daughter of but sixteen years, to bring up. But a mother and
children working together can accomplish wonders ; and the
family did well.

ABIGAIL,[7] born Dec. 5, 1786 : married, Feb. 28, 1811, Mr.
Samuel Atherton, of Stoughton, born Sept. 9, 1784. He died
Feb. 11, 1877. She died, March 19, 1868.  Children :

1. Mary *Atherton*, b. Aug. 21, 1811 ; m. W. S. Belcher, of
   Stoughton ; d. Aug. 25, 1849.

2. Vesta *Atherton*, b. June 17, ·1813 ; m. James Swan, of
   Stoughton ; d. Dec. 10, 1882.

3. Samuel *Atherton*, b. Jan. 26, 1815 ; m. Susan M. Hotten
   of Boston, where he resides. Is president of the
   New England National Bank.

4. Abigail *Atherton*, b. Nov. 13, 1817 ; m. Joseph T. Swan,
   of Dorchester ; d. May 7, 1859.

5. James *Atherton*, b. May 6, 1819 ; m. Mary Marshall, of
   Boston ; d. March 4, 1879.

6. William *Atherton*, b. Jan. 20, 1821 ; m. Mary B. Dwight,
   of Brooklyn, N. Y.   Resides in Boston.

TYLA,[7] dau. of Ralph[6] and Abigail (Swan), b. June 4, 1787,
was married in Stoughton, July 19, 1812, to Jesse Weeman,
who was born in Durham, Me., in 1786. They settled in Harmony, Me., where their numerous children were brought up,
and where they "entered into rest" after long and worthy lives.

He d. Jan. 8, 1855, aged 69 years.  She d. March, 1877, a.
90 years.  Children :

1.  Mary R. *Weeman*, b. June 4, 1813 ; m. March 11, 1840,
    Ira Hurd ; d. July 8, 1874.
2.  Harris *Weeman*, b. Sept. 29, 1815 ; d. Apr. 19, 1864.
3.  Abigail *Weeman*, b. March 9, 1817 ; d. May 25,
    1817.
4.  James Pope *Weeman*, b. March 18, 1818 ; m. Jan. 11,
    1843, Elizabeth True.  James Pope Weeman resided
    many years in Freeport, Me., carrying on the hard-
    ware business.  In 1865 he removed to Brunswick,
    Me., where he still resides.  *Children :* (1) Harriet
    Elizabeth *Weeman*, b. 1845 ; (2) Annie Bell *Wee-
    man*, b. 1847 ; (3) Abbie Caroline *Weeman*, b.
    1849.
5.  Harriet Newell *Weeman*, b. March 9, 1820 ; m. June
    19, 1838, Thomas S. Mitchell ; d. Sept. 29, 1844.
6.  Jesse *Weeman*, b. Apr. 5, 1822 ; m. Oct. 27, 1860,
    Fannie Hurd.
7.  Abigail Swan *Weeman*, b. Nov. 18, 1824 ; m. Sept. 28,
    1852, Rev. John B. Newell.
8.  Luther Warren *Weeman*, b. Nov. 2, 1826 ; m. June 2,
    1851, Mary Elizabeth Bailey ; d. April —, 1880.
9.  Joseph *Weeman*, b. Nov. 2, 1829 ; m. Sept. 22, 1851,
    Elizabeth Newell ; d. April, 1881, a. 52.

After her children were grown, the widow of RALPH[7] married
a second time, giving her hand to Mr. Lemuel Bird, of Stoughton, March 5, 1812.  She died " Nov. 19, 1852," aged 91 years.

CHILDREN OF RALPH[6] AND ABIGAIL (SWAN).

  I.  VESTA,[7] b. 1781 ; d. Oct. 6, 1801.
 II.  LUTHER WARREN,[7] b. 1783.  [See next chapter, A, 1.]
III.  ABIGAIL,[7] b. Dec. 5, 1786 ; m. Feb. 28, 1811, Samuel
      Atherton ; d. March 19, 1868.  [See above.]
 IV.  TYLA,[7] b. 1787 ; m. July 19, 1812, Jesse Weeman ; d.
      March, 1877.  [See above.]
  V.  SAMUEL,[7] b. 1790 ; d. Jan. 13, 1796.
 VI.  JAMES,[7] b. Aug. 29, 1792.  [See next chapter, A, 2.]

A, 2.

## SAMUEL WARD⁶ AND HIS FAMILY.

SAMUEL WARD,⁶ second son of Colonel Frederick⁵ and Mary (Cole), was born in Stoughton, in February, 1763.

Being a dozen years old when the Revolutionary War broke out, he was probably a valuable "aid" to his mother, at home, while his father and older brother took part in the battles for Independence.  It seems likely that before the war closed his youthful ardor prompted him to enter the army ; but there are no records to verify the family tradition.

Soon after the war was over he went to South Carolina with his brothers, to engage in house-building.  He found a fair bride there, Mary Wood, accomplished and well educated, who used to come to Stoughton sometimes with her husband and children, but never lost her deep love for her native State and city, though she won many friends among her husband's relatives and acquaintances.

But a fever, epidemic in Charleston, seized upon the husband, then upon the wife ; and in April, 1797, their three children were orphans.

Good homes were opened at once to the children, at the houses of their grandfather in Stoughton and their Uncle Frederick in Dorchester, with plenty of love and care : though no *other* affection can ever take the place of father-love and mother-love, especially to children of such fine organization as were these.  They grew up, however, developing well ; one to have his light quenched at manhood's dawn, but the others to live long and useful lives, leaving children who have also proved "life worth living."

CHILDREN OF SAMUEL WARD⁶ AND MARY (WOOD).

I.   WILLIAM,⁷ b. March 30, 1787.  [See next chapter, A, 3.]

II.  ELIZABETH,⁷ b. 1790; m. Aug. 4, 1811, Jeremiah O'Brien; d. June 11, 1848.

III. JOHN,⁷ b. May 29, 1792 ; d. in 1813.

Of the eldest son, "Colonel" William,⁷ due notice will be given in the next chapter.  The youngest son, JOHN,⁷ born in Stoughton, May 29, 1792, a young man of promise, was the sub-

ject of a melancholy fate.  He sailed from Eastport, Me., in
1813, in a vessel bound for Lisbon, Portugal.  They arrived there
duly and set sail for Cadiz,—but no further tidings were ever received of vessel, crew or passengers.

ELIZABETH, dau. of *Samuel Ward*[6] and Mary (Wood), was
born in 1790 in Charleston, S. C.   She was educated there and
at Dorchester ; taught a private school in a room of her Uncle
.Frederick's[6] house in Dorchester, instructing some of his and her
Uncle William's[6] children with other pupils.  She went on a visit
with her uncle to Machias, Maine, where she was wooed and
won.    She was married Aug. 4, 1811, in Dorchester,  by Rev.
Thaddeus M. Harris, to Jeremiah O'Brien, of Machias.  He was
a grandson of Maurice and Mary (Kane) O'Brien, who removed
from Scarboro to Machias, Me., not far from 1770, and a son of
Captain Gideon and Abigail (Tupper) O'Brien, a prominent citizen of M.  Another of the sons of Maurice was Jeremiah, who
commanded the little lumber schooner which .captured the British sloop of war, Margarita, off the mouth of the Machias River,
in the summer of 1775,—the first naval battle of the Revolution.
Gideon O'Brien was the first man to step on board the sloop
when the grappling irons were over the rails.

Hon. Jeremiah O'Brien was a prominent and worthy citizen,
called to represent his native district in State legislature and
national Congress.   Amassed a fortune in commercial pursuits.

Mrs. Elizabeth[7] (Pope) O'Brien was a woman of mark.
Stately in person, handsome in face, brilliant in conversation,
faithful in her family, an ardent Christian, an ornament to the
society in which she moved.   She died very suddenly,  June
11, 1848.   Children :

1.   John Gideon *O'Brien*, b. Sept. 21, 1812 ; graduated at
     Bowdoin College in 1831; read law at Reading, Pa. ;
     was shipwrecked at Seal Islands, on his way to visit
     his home, Oct. 21, 1834.

2.   William *O'Brien*, b. Sept. 5, 1814 ; preparing for the
     ministry, and giving great promise of usefulness, he
     entered Bowdoin College.  But consumption smote
     him down, and he died at Brunswick, Jan. 25, 1836.

3.   Joanna *O'Brien*, b. Sept. 9, 1820; died December, 1826.

4.  Jeremiah *O'Brien*, b. Sept. 5, 1818; also became a
    student at Bowdoin, but died before completing the
    course, April 21, 1838.
5.  Mary Elizabeth *O'Brien*, b. Sept. 1, 1822. Married,
    Sept. 20, 1856, Rev. Henry Fiske Harding, a native
    of Union, Me.

Mr. Harding is a graduate of Bowdoin College, class of 1850,
and Bangor Theological Seminary, 1854. Was pastor at Machias
eighteen years; took the leading part in the establishment of
Hallowell Classical School; spent some years in business, in
the manufacture of wire, at H.; resumed ministerial labors,
and is now minister of the Congregational church at East
Machias, Me.  Children:

(1.)  Elizabeth Pope *Harding*, born Aug. 29, 1857.
      Married, July 29, 1884, John Washburn, eldest
      son of Algernon Sidney Washburn of Liver-
      more Falls. He is a member of the firm of
      Washburn, Crosby & Co., Minneapolis, Minn.

(2.)  Henry O'Brien *Harding*, b. March 22, 1859;
      resides in Minneapolis; is connected with the
      above-named house.

(3.)  Carroll Everett *Harding*, b. Aug. 23, 1860;
      graduated at Bowdoin College, 1881; graduated
      at the General Theological Seminary, New
      York, May, 1885; married, in Portland, Nov.
      4, 1885, Alice Miriam, dau. of Hon. John H.
      and Isabella G. Philbrick, of Standish, Me.;
      ordained deacon June 10, priest Sept. 2, 1885,
      by Bishop Neely, of Maine. Is in charge of
      the Chapel of the Holy Evangelists, Baltimore.
      *Child:* Weston O'Brien *Harding*, b. Jan. 1,
      1887.

(4.)  Mary O'Brien *Harding*, b. Mar. 26, 1862; d.
      May 8, 1862.

(5.)  Harriet Walker *Harding*, b. Nov., 1863; gradu-
      ated from Hallowell Classical School, June,
      1883. Jan. 1, 1885, she entered the "New
      Haven Training-School for Nurses." After a

year there she went to a hospital in New York City for special training.  Returning to New Haven, she entered upon the six months' outside work required of pupils before graduation. While caring for one of her patients she contracted typhoid fever, and died at the Nurse's Home, after a few weeks' illness, Aug. 14, 1886.

"Added to a pleasing exterior, she possessed to a great degree the power of winning affection. To a remarkable degree she gained the confidence of teachers, physicians and nurses with whom she was associated, but most of all she won grateful regard from her patients.  For her chosen profession she showed great aptitude ; she felt its responsibilities deeply, giving up only when her strength failed, and dying at the post of duty."

    (6.)   Florence *Harding*, born Nov. 18, 1865.

6.   Harriet Jones Chase *O'Brien*, b. May 15, 1825 ; m., May 29, 1851, George Walker, Esq., a native of Fryeburg, Me., a distinguished lawyer; resided many years at Machias ; removed to Portland, Me., in October, 1875, where he still resides ; has been mayor of the city.   Children :

    (1.)   Harriet O'Brien · *Walker*, b. Aug. 17, 1852 ; d. Sept. 2, 1854.

    (2.)   William O'Brien *Walker*, b. Jan. 16, 1856 ; graduated at Amherst College, in 1878 ; is in New York with James E. Ward & Co., ship commissioners.

    (3.)   George Pope *Walker*, b. July 27, 1857 ; d. Oct. 26, 1858.

    (4.)   Annetta O'Brien *Walker*, b. July 7, 1858 ; resides with her parents.

    (5.)   Robert Wyman *Walker*, b. Oct. 23, 1861; is with Claflin, Larrabee & Co., dry-goods dealers, Boston.

    (6.)   Harold *Walker*, d. in infancy.

7.  Joseph *O'Brien*, graduated at Bowdoin College in 1847;
    read law, and was admitted to the Washington
    County bar; practiced at Machias; m., March 19,
    1855, Mary Elizabeth, daughter of Thomas Adams
    and Ardelia Louisa (Lawrence) Staples, of Machias,
    b. in Groton, Mass., July 3, 1833. He died Oct. 16,
    1869. After the death of Mr. O'Brien his widow
    m. (2), Sept. 22, 1874, Mr. John Fisher Harmon,
    son of Samuel and Mercy (Fisher) Harmon, of
    Marshfield, Me. They reside in Machias, on the
    ancient O'Brien homestead.  Children :

    (1.)  Josephine *O'Brien*, b. Sept. 25, 1856; m. Frederic
          I. Campbell, of Cherryfield, Me., son of Hon.
          Alexander and Caroline (Ricker) Campbell.
          *Children :* Maurice O'Brien *Campbell*, b. May
          10, 1883; Mary Elizabeth *Campbell*, b. Decem-
          ber, 1884; Colin *Campbell*, b. July 16, 1886.
    (2.)  Frances Lawrence *O'Brien*, b. May 11, 1860; d.
          July 5, 1864.
    (3.)  Maurice *O'Brien*, b. May 26, 1862; d. Sept. 30,
          1864.

---

A, 3.

## THE FAMILY OF FREDERICK,[6] JR.

FREDERICK,[6] jr., born in Stoughton, Aug. 20, 1772, came
with his brother, William,[6] to Dorchester, soon after attaining
his majority. They went into the wood and lumber trade, acquir-
ing by industry and economy, wharves, store, and yard at Commercial Point, and building several vessels for coast trade. The
names of some of these are remembered by his daughter
Hannah[7] (Mellish) ; the "Sally Ann," the "Frederick and William," the "Humming Bird," and the "Dorchester." One of
these, a good-sized brig, was wrecked on one of the outer islets
of Boston harbor, since called "Pope's Rock." The firm continued in business more than thirty years, under the style of
" F. and W. Pope."

At the junction of Adams and East Streets, Frederick built two houses alike, about 1804; the corner house became the residence and school of the Misses Sanders and Beach. The next was his home for a long time, where all his sons were born; it was burned about 1826.

The firm had the sagacity to see, at an early stage of their business, the advantage of securing a hold on the lumber supply; so the senior partner, Frederick,[6] went to Washington county, in the District of Maine, somewhere about the year 1799, and purchased cargoes of lumber of those who cut and sawed the logs. In a few years they established a store at the eastern village of Machias, and one at Lubec; having for clerks their nephew, Luther Warren[7] Pope, son of their deceased eldest brother, Ralph,[6] and their brother-in-law, Jonas Pierce, of Dorchester. After a while they also took to Machias another nephew, who had been some time in their Dorchester office, William[7] Pope, son of their second brother, Samuel Ward,[6] who had died in the South. Frederick divided his time, henceforward, between Dorchester, where his family was growing and being educated, and the scene of his business in Maine. The books of the firm, which would have thrown light on the history of these years, have, unfortunately, gone to ashes or paper stock. But the children of the brother partners are able to establish the facts stated in this article.

"The Embargo," as it was called, greatly crippled commercial operations, and affected F. & W. Pope seriously. Then the "War of 1812" followed, making still further trouble; but there were compensations to be found in the way of private risks, exchange of commodities with parties "over the line" in New Brunswick, and so on, which kept up excitement for those who engaged in them, — whether this firm did or not. Gradually the business altered its character; Frederick[6] had separate store-interests in Maine, William matters of his own in Dorchester.

Here is a yellow document written in a hand well remembered by the children now living, — one of the few tokens of the man, possessed by his descendants; let us transcribe it:

"I Frederick Pope of the Town of Lubec, in the County of Washington, in the State of Mafs. Retailer of Merchandise including Wines & Spirits : hereby make application for a License to retail

Merchandize including Wines & Spirits, for one year following the 10ᵗʰ day of April, 1815, at my store in the township afore said.

To Gideon O'Brien Collʳ.
of the Rev. for 1ˢᵗ Collⁿ.
Dist. of Mass."

And with this there was found the collector's receipt for the following year's license, the clerk's name coming in as a shred of circumstantial evidence.

"Machias October 7 1816 then receved of Frederick pope by hand of Capt. pall Crockʳ Eleven dollars & twentey five Cents for Jones Perses Lishens.

GIDEON O'BRIEN COLL."

Many Massachusetts officials of that and earlier days, spelled in as free a style as this hero* did.

Lumbering operations carried on in the woods, shipments by vessels, frequent journeys from home to business, retailing — and growing portly over — the articles specified in the application ; so the years went by.

He saw his nephew embark on the sea of business and sail prosperously ; his brother-in-law settle on a farm; his niece and eldest daughter become wives of two of the most enterprising young men of the town ; and his third son domiciled in the family of the latter.  But he reached premature old age, exchanging the fire and vigor which had thrilled his majestic form so many years for the good-natured, bland, easy-going spirit which delighted all who met him, but brought a paralysis upon his business.  It was a natural reaction from an intensely busy and wearing life.

And one morning, when the friends at whose house he was boarding, in East Machias, went up to his chamber, they found him sitting upright in his chair, fully dressed ; peace was written on his face, and his eyes were closed in the sleep that knows no waking.  This was the 16th of December, 1826.  His body was taken to Dorchester, and laid in the tomb which the firm had provided.

---

*The hand that so overpowered English orthography struck the first blow in the first ocean contest of the Revolution.

He was above six feet in height, of remarkable strength, and, up to fifty years of age, an uncommonly efficient business man. He was full of good cheer, a delightful friend, trustful and well-disposed toward all about him.

His son, Samuel,[7] was said to resemble him in appearance.

He married a little before he was twenty-four, *Mary* ["Molly"], daughter of John and Sarah (Blake) *Pierce* of Dorchester, born Dec. 29, 1776.

(As Mary Pierce was a sister of Sarah, the wife of William,[8] and as a very large number of descendants have sprung from the two pairs, the writer has thought wise to give quite an extended account of the pedigree of these sisters; which will be found in the Appendix, under the title, " Pierce Ancestry.")

She was a sweet woman, by all accounts ; a judicious adviser, and kind in repairing troubles which arose from neglect of good advice. Her children found great comfort and stimulus in her *gentle strength ;* and they have given much credit to her for their training, being left the more to her care because the father, who greatly endeared himself to them, was very much absorbed in business.

Of their twelve children, two died in infancy : *Charles,*[7] b. Sept. 29, 1799, d. Sept. 30, 1800 ; and *William,*[7] b. June 23, 1808, d. July 30, 1808. All the others lived to help history.

CHILDREN OF FREDERICK,[6] JR., AND MARY (PIERCE).

I.   SALLY PIERCE,[7] born Oct. 24, 1797, was married, May
      16, 1820, to *Obadiah Hill*, son of Obadiah and Sarah
      (Harris) Hill, born in Machias, Me., where he lived
      an active and prosperous business life, and died Aug.
      14, 1860.

      Mrs. Hill was a rare woman ; so quiet and peaceful as
      to make those who saw her entirely ignore *her* diffi-
      culties and burdens, and bring her theirs, to get help
      from her faith and philosophy.  To the little brother,
      James, whom she borrowed from the Dorchester hive,
      and who grew up under her tutelage, to her children,
      and to her neighbors, she was a refining, ennobling
      presence.  The waves of business and the cankering

cares of life swept many a burden upon her, and many
a trying experience came to her home and heart ; but
the Lord's peace was within her soul. She "went
home " Oct. 9, 1850.   Children :

1.  Mary *Hill*, born July 6, 1821, died July 29, 1851.   Was
    very talented ; showed rare gift in literary lines·
    Ill health and other circumstances prevented her
    fulfilling what, evidently, was within reach of her
    powers.   But her life made a good mark on her
    acquaintances.

2.  Warren *Hill*, b. Jan. 10, 1823.   M. Maria Bucknam
    Shaw, of Gouldsboro, Me., Mar. 13, 1857.   She was
    born in Gouldsboro, Feb. 17, 1830, dau. of Capt.
    Nathan and Eunice Bradish (Smith) Shaw, of
    Taunton, Mass.   *Children :*  (1.) Samuel Warren
    *Hill*, b. Feb. 8, 1858, m. Jan. 1, 1883, Addie Anne,
    dau. of Martin and Melissa Holmes, of East Machias.
    *Children :* (*a*) Charles Frye *Hill*, b. Dec. 15, 1883.
    (*b*) Carrie Elizabeth *Hill*, b. Aug. 2, 1885.   (*c*)
    Jeanette *Hill*, b. July 1, 1887.   (2.) Walter John
    *Hill*, b. Jan. 4, 1860.   (3.) Sarah Pope *Hill*, b.
    Oct. 31, 1862.   (4.) Edwin Shaw *Hill*, b. March 5,
    1865.

3.  Sarah *Hill*, b. Nov. 25, 1824, died July 8, 1875.   A
    woman of calm, dignified character, who filled her
    place in both homes most admirably.   M., Nov. 8,
    1854, *William Thaxter*, son of Marshall and Su-
    sannah (Gardner) Thaxter, of Machias, Me., b.
    Oct. 20, 1816.   Lived in Faribault, Minn., and Iowa
    Falls, Ia.   He died March 20, 1871.   [Appendix,
    Thaxter.]

4.  Lucy *Hill*, b. March 14, 1827, d. Oct. 11, 1833.

5.  Caroline *Hill*, b. Jan. 21, 1829.

6.  Samuel *Hill*, b. Feb. 22, 1831.   A person of large en-
    dowments, devoted to the highest life-work.   Fitted
    for college at Phillips Academy, Andover, but the
    failure of his health obliged him to give up his
    course of study.   He went to Faribault, Minn., but
    died there, of consumption, Nov. 21, 1857.

7. ⎰ John *Hill*, b. June 11, 1832; m. in 1858, Mrs. Maria
⎹ (Bagley) Mills, b. at Fort Edward, N. Y., in 1830.
⎹ *Children:* Charles Harris *Hill*, Nathan Henry *Hill*.
8. ⎱ Sophia *Hill*, b. June 11, 1832. Was a very ardent
⎹ soul, cordial, hopeful, generous, — a happy Christian.
⎹ After long struggling against consumption, she "fell
⎹ asleep" Dec. 3, 1882, in Vineland, N. J., where she
⎲ and Carrie had made their home.

II.   CHARLES,⁷ b. Sept. 29, 1799; d. Sept. 30, 1800.

'III.  MARY,⁷ b. Feb. 25, 1801 ; m. Feb. 27, 1825, *Thomas
Beals*, of Dorchester, b. May 19, 1800, son of Jacob
and Hannah (Bird) Beals.  She died April 28, 1843.
He married, second, Sept. 5, 1844, a cousin of his first
wife, Sarah Blake Ford, dau. of Charles and Lois
(Pierce) Ford, b. Sept. 15, 1805, d. July 1, 1884.  He
died Jan. 10, 1881.

Thomas Beals, born May 19, 1800, died Jan. 10, 1881.  He
was son of Hannah (Bird) and Jacob Beals.  Of his family on
the Beals side no record has been preserved.  Hannah Bird
was born Nov. 30, 1770, married Jacob Beals, Nov. 24, 1791,
died Nov. 3, 1825.  He died April 22, 1812, aged 48.  She was
daughter of Thomas and Mary (Clap) Bird.  Thomas Bird was
born Sept. 14, 1722, married Mary Clap, daughter of Ebenezer
and Hannah, Dec. 14, 1749, died Aug. 28, 1772.  She died
May 16, 1808, aged 82.  He was son of Thomas Bird, who was
born Jan. 1, 1692-3, married Mary Clap, Dec. 18, 1718.  She
died April 6, 1761, in the 62d year of her age.  He died May
3, 1770.  He was son of James Bird, who was born about 1647,
and married for his second wife Ann Withington, Nov. 13,
1673.  She died Sept. 21, 1723.  He died Sept. 1, 1723.
James was son of Thomas Bird, the immigrant, who was born
in England about the year 1613, in the reign of James the First.

Mr. Beals was a music engraver and printer, the first to do
very extensive work in this department in the city of Boston.
He was in business by himself some years, then had full charge
of the publishing department of the widely celebrated firm of
Oliver Ditson & Co.  Was a member of one of the first bands

organized in Boston for the playing of classic music. He had critical taste, especially in regard to instrumental music.

Mrs. Beals won the hearts of a wide circle of friends, and her early death was much deplored.

CHILDREN OF THOMAS AND MARY (POPE) BEALS.

1. Mary *Beals*, b. Dec. 13, 1825, resides in Dorchester.
2. Thomas Henry *Beals*, b. Aug. 16, 1827. Resides at Sequoia, Cal.
3. John Pierce *Beals*, b. Dec. 14, 1828, m. Dec. 14, 1852, Harriet Rebecca Hawes, of Dorchester, dau. of Benjamin and Mary Hawes. *Children:* (1.) Mary Elizabeth *Beals*, b. Dec. 1, 1853, m. Edward Hanson, of Redwood, Cal., son of Peter and Catharine Hanson, b. in Boston, July 5, 1855. *Child:* Frank *Hanson*. (2.) Charles Henry *Beals*, b. Sept. 11, 1855. (3.) George Edward *Beals*, b. Aug. 26, 1857.
4. Elizabeth Pope *Beals*, b. Dec. 17, 1831, d. Sept. 10, 1833.
5. Amelia *Beals*, b. Sept. 5, 1834, m. June 12, 1856, Edward R. Hemmenway, son of Benjamin Hemmenway, of Boston, b. in Boston, March 14, 1836, d. June 21, 1856. He was a young man of fine qualities and large promise, but came to an untimely death by falling from the roof of a building where business had called him. Mrs. Amelia (Beals) Hemmenway, with her sister, Mary Beals, resides in the house their father occupied in Dorchester. *Child:* (1.) Edward Augustus *Hemmenway*, b. Feb. 4, 1857, m. Alice Henry Todd, dau. of Benj. and Sarah A. G. Todd, b. in Bath, Me., Aug. 2, 1853. He is a mechanical engineer and draughtsman in Boston. Resides in Dorchester. *Child:* Helen Louise *Hemmenway*, b. Jan. 25, 1884.
6. Eliza *Beals*, b. Sept. 29, 1837, d. Sept. 3, 1838.
7. Sarah Elizabeth *Beals*, b. July 19, 1839, m. Richard Clapp Humphreys, March 5, 1863. He was son of Henry and Sarah Blake (Clapp) Humphreys, b. in Dorchester, June 10, 1836. *Child:* Clarence Blake *Humphreys*, b. March 25, 1873. Mr. Humphreys is a descendant of Jonas Humphreys, of Wendover,

Buckinghamshire, England, who came to Dorchester at an early day and bought the homestead of William Hannum [Hammond], Sept. 10, 1637, — on which lineal descendants of the pioneer have continued to live, down to the present time. It is at the corner of Humphreys and Dudley Streets. Mr. Humphreys is an administrator of estates.

#### CHILD OF THOMAS AND SARAH BLAKE (FORD) BEALS.

Frederic *Beals*, b. Sept. 11, 1845, d. April 20, 1869. He became a winning young man, an efficient person in the store with his father, and gave promise of great usefulness. His early death was much lamented.

IV. ELIZA,[7] b. Dec. 1, 1802; d. May 31, 1885; never married. She loved all true and beautiful things, and had many a helpful word for those about her, especially the young. She was an invalid many years. One of the earliest members of the Baptist church in Dorchester, she maintained an ardent Christian life. She went to find the reality of her hopes, May 31, 1885.

V. HANNAH,[7] b. April 13, 1804; m. Sept. 1, 1828, William Eaton Mellish, son of Stephen and Roxalina Mellish, born in Walpole, N. H., June 16, 1799, died May 1, 1858. When her older sister was married and went to Machias to live, Hannah[7] went to visit her, and remained in the town, for a while, teaching a little school of which Col. William's[7] older children were members. Since the death of her husband she has resided in Dorchester, and now has her home with her daughter, Mrs. Bird.

William Eaton Mellish was a cabinet-maker. Learned his trade at Walpole, N. H., and came to Dorchester, Mass., to work, where he found his wife. Afterward he was a dealer in furniture in Boston. He returned in 1849 to Walpole, N. H., and died there May 1, 1858. He was a person of medium size and vigorous temperament. He inclined to liberality in theology, and was well-famed for fidelity and strict honesty. Children:

1.  Oscar *Mellish*, b. Nov. 24, 1831, in Boston, m.
    March 18, 1855, Helen Augusta, dau. of Increase
    Sumner and Esther Guild, b. Feb. 14, 1832, in
    Walpole, N. H. He learned the trade of carver,
    at which he wrought some years very successfully.
    Later he entered upon the making of the finer
    sorts of frame chairs for parlor, office, and dining-
    room use, particularly antique styles. The firm,
    Mellish, Byfield & Co., are extensive manufacturers
    and exporters, with factory on Albany Street, and
    office opposite the Boston & Maine R. R. station.
    His residence is on the hill above Faneuil station,
    Newton.

2.  Orianna *Mellish*, b. Oct. 29, 1833, m. Sept. 17, 1860, to
    Charles Henry Smith, of South Boston. He died
    April 30, 1862. *Child:* Walter Bradlee *Smith*, b.
    Oct. 20, 1861.

3.  Olivia *Mellish*, b. Oct. 18, 1837, m. Nov. 17, 1869,
    John Hosea Bird, b. Aug. 14, 1827, son of
    Isaac and Lydia Bird, died June 8, 1883. *Child:*
    Florence *Bird*, b. July 2, 1873. Resides in Dor-
    chester.

4.  Walter Eaton *Mellish*, b. June 16, 1841, m. Jan. 8,
    1867, Lizzie Ella Ball, b. July 3, 1846. Lived some
    time in Mechanicville, N. H. Resides in Cambridge.
    He served in the Third N. H. Vol. Infantry during
    the war of the Rebellion; was commissioned succes-
    sively 2d and 1st Lieutenant. *Children:* (1.) Walter
    Edward *Mellish*, b. May 22, 1869. (2.) Annie Laurie
    *Mellish*, b. May 30, 1878.

VI.   FREDERICK,⁷ JR., b. March 28, 1806. [See next chapter,
      A, 4.]
VII.  WILLIAM,⁷ b. June 23, 1808; d. July 30, 1808.
VIII. SAMUEL,⁷ b. Sept. 11, 1809. [See next chapter, A, 5.]
IX.   JAMES,⁷ b. Nov. 23, 1811. [See next chapter, A, 6.]
X.    CHARLES,⁷ } b. Aug. 12, 1814 { [See next chapter, A, 7.]
XI.   WILLIAM,⁷ }                  { [See next chapter, A, 8.]
XII.  JOHN,⁷ b. Jan. 6, 1817. [See next chapter, A, 9.]

A, 4.

## THE FAMILY OF WILLIAM⁶.

WILLIAM,⁶ son of Col. Frederick⁵ and Mary (Cole), b. Nov.
12, 1774; m. June 16, 1799, Sarah ["Sally"], dau. of John
and Sarah (Blake) Pierce. She was b. in Dorchester, Dec. 17,
1774. [See her pedigree in Appendix, under the title "Pierce
Ancestry."]

He passed his boyhood and early youth in Stoughton;
joined his brother Frederick⁶ in Dorchester, in the lumber
business, and they did good work in that direction. As they went
on, each developed qualities the counterpart of the other's:
Frederick, great push, nerve, fertility of resources; William, large patience, caution, foresight. Warmly attached to
each other, their wives, sisters, and the two families like one,
for many years they had an exceedingly delightful partnership
and success. The Machias branch of the business drew them
apart, unavoidably; other persons and interests occupied each,
so that there was not so peculiarly intimate a relation existing
between them as there had been; yet they loved as brothers to
the close of life.

WILLIAM⁶ continued in the business in Dorchester, having
most capable reinforcements in the persons of his sons, who
kept the old stand and trade in the family long years after he
had passed away.

He was an estimable man in all the relations of life; a strong
supporter of church and government; public-spirited, benevolent. His presence was dignified and courteous. A long
article might be written, describing interesting points in his
life.

He was elected a representative to the State legislature; was
repeatedly chosen a member of the parish committee. He
started the first Sunday school in connection with his church,
at a time when many excellent persons violently opposed such
a movement.

He was punctilious about fulfilling all his obligations, particularly to the poor and dependent. He died in Dorchester, May
20, 1860.

His wife was one of the most alert, vivacious, buoyant persons imaginable ; never tired of toil, till a task was done, nor of
talking, till her tale was told.  A beautiful singer, a member of
the choir long years, and ready to "substitute" for unfaithful
choir-members when needed.

The following item from "The Blake Family" must not be
left out of this book :

"Sunday, March 2, 1856, was a very stormy day ; there were so
few people at meeting,* that we met in the vestry.  There were but
eight of the choir of singers present, and Mrs. Pope, then in her
82ᵈ year stood up and sung with them through the day."

She survived her husband many years, attaining almost to the
full century.  She died Feb. 24, 1873, aged ninety-eight years,
two months and thirteen days.

### CHILDREN OF WILLIAM⁶ AND SARAH (PIERCE).

I.    HIRAM,⁷ b. March 13, 1800 ; d. April 20, 1802.

II.   CHARLES,⁷ b. April 13, 1801 ; d. Feb. 7, 1822.

III.  ANN,⁷ b. Oct. 5, 1803 ; m. Otis Shepard, Oct. 5, 1823.

IV.   RACHEL,⁷ b. Aug. 3, 1805 ; d. Aug. 12, 1822.

V.    SARAH,⁷ b. Jan. 4, 1807; m. Hiram Shepard, June 19,
      1826.

VI.   ALEXANDER,⁷ b. March 15, 1808. [See next chapter,
      A, 10.]

VII.  ADALINE,⁷ b. April 9, 1810 ; m. Julius A. Noble, May 15,
      1834.

VIII. ELIZABETH,⁷ b. March 3, 1812 ; m. John Ayres, Aug. 13,
      1835.

IX.   WILLIAM,⁷ b. Dec. 27, 1813. [See next chapter, A, 11.]

X.    LUCY,⁷ b. Dec. 3, 1815 ; m. Aug. 25, 1840, Jonathan
      Battles.

XI.   CATHARINE,⁷ b. Jan. 25, 1818 ; d. Feb. 11, 1840.

ANN,⁷ eldest daughter of William⁶ and Sarah (Pierce), b.
Oct. 5, 1803 ; m. Oct. 5, 1823, *Otis Shepard*, son of Ralph and
Nabby (Gay) Shepard, b. March 12, 1797, in Stoughton.  He

---

* This was the house of the First Parish Church, with which the Pope and Pierce families
have long been identified.

taught school in his early years ; he was engaged in the baking business in company with his brothers. Was much interested in town and public affairs and a very prominent citizen. He died Feb. 20, 1859.

Mrs. Ann (Pope) Shepard lived out a long and useful life. With a very large family of children, several of whom were quite young when the husband and father was removed, she was called upon to exercise a great deal of "faith and patience," and she responded to this "call" in a worthy manner. A woman of affairs, she kept stirring and striving, never at random, but always to some good purpose. As was said, after she had "fallen asleep" : " She possessed remarkable endurance ; up early, ever working through these many years in her home, in her garden, among her children, among her friends ; sorely tried and heavily burdened, yet very brave and strong through it all. She was constant in her fidelity to duty. She cared for the things of her household with a mother's love, going from room to room and from place to place to do whatever her hands could find to do, and doing it with her might. She was loyal to her church ; we know how glad she always was to join in its services, how well she was always supported by her faith in God and Christ, ready to do her part in building up the kingdom and doing the will." So spoke her pastor, Rev. S. J. Barrows, at the funeral. And her son-in-law, Rev. Thomas Hill, D. D., added this worthy exhortation and testimony to her worth :

"May this example of unobtrusive goodness show itself yet more and more effectively in the lives and characteristics of her children and children's children in the present and the coming generations, and in the lives of those who were bound to her by closer ties than those of mere neighborhood and acquaintance. May none of us forget the everlasting distinction between the laws of the outer and the inner world : that in the world within, our own choice and will have ultimately controlling power, and that in order to insure for ourselves the immortal blessedness of the saints, we must follow them in virtuous and godly living, — follow them in all things in which they followed Christ."

Mrs. Shepard's death took place Jan. 15, 1886.

CHILDREN OF OTIS AND ANN (POPE) SHEPARD.

1.  Otis *Shepard*, b. Sept. 27, 1824 ; d. Sept. 27, 1825.
2.  Katharine Amelia *Shepard*, b. Feb. 3, 1826.    Resides
    in Dorchester.    Has rendered a large amount of
    service with reference to this family record.
3.  Otis *Shepard*, jr., b. Sept. 27, 1827 ; m. May 4,
    1854, Emily Elizabeth, dau. of John Wheeler and
    Sarah Ann (Badger) Blanchard, of Dorchester.  He
    is a lumber dealer ; president of the Shepard &
    Morse Lumber Co., Boston ; resides in Dorchester.
    Children :

    (1.)  Horace Blanchard *Shepard*, b. April 12, 1855 ; m.
          Feb. 14, 1882, Florence Olivia, dau. of Samuel
          Newton and Susan Elliot (Dutton) Gaut, of
          Somerville.  *Children*, Ralph Atherton *Shepard*,
          b. Jan. 15, 1883 ; Newton Gaut *Shepard*, b. July
          18, 1884.  Is engaged in the lumber business
          with his father.    Resides in Brookline.
    (2.)  Otis Atherton *Shepard*, b. March 28, 1859 ; m.
          July 22, 1884, Susie Lesnow, dau. of Samuel
          Newton and Susan Elliot (Dutton) Gaut, a
          sister of the wife of his brother Horace.  Is in
          the lumber business in Boston.    Resides in
          Brookline.
    (3.)  Thomas Hill *Shepard*, b. Nov. 23, 1866.
    (4.)  Emily Blanchard *Shepard*, b. June 7, 1869.

4.  Charles Alexander *Shepard*, b. March 12, 1830 ; m.
    March 25, 1858, Ann Maria, dau. of William and
    Catharine (Robbins) Broomhead.    She died July
    18, 1887.  Children :

    (1.)  William Otis *Shepard*, b. Oct. 25, 1859.
    (2.)  Annie Clara *Shepard*, b. Aug. 26, 1861.
    (3.)  Charles Alexander *Shepard*, jr., b. Aug. 1, 1863.
    (4.)  Maud *Shepard*, b. June 11, 1866 ; d. Jan. 3,
          1867.
    (5.)  Addie Blanche *Shepard*, b. March 30, 1874.

Charles A. Shepard went to California in 1848, and remained there ten years. After his return he engaged in lumber business ; was in the firm of Mallock & Shepard. Was an active, persevering business man and a genial friend. He died Jan. 16, 1885.

5.   Horace Scudder *Shepard*, b. Dec. 13, 1832 ; m. Aug. 9, 1862, Hannah Bartlett, dau. of William and Lucy (Gibbs) Spooner. She died March 9, 1885, aged 45 years.   Children :

   (1.)   Lindsley Horace *Shepard*, b. March 27, 1864.
   (2.)   Lucy Lindsley *Shepard*, b. Oct. 27, 1866 ; d. Nov. 12, 1866.
   (3.)   Edward Spooner *Shepard*, b. Oct. 4, 1868.
   (4.)   Harry Bourne *Shepard*, b. March 7, 1870 ; d. March 13, 1870.

He m. (2d) Oct. 9, 1886, Anna Maria, dau. of George and Anna Maria Haines.

Mr. Horace S. Shepard is treasurer of the Shepard & Morse Lumber Co., Boston.   Resides in Sharon.

6.   Ann Adaline *Shepard*, b. May 4, 1835.   Graduated at Antioch College in its first class ; went to Europe, where she spent some time with the family of the celebrated Nathaniel Hawthorne ; preparing herself for the professorship of Modern Languages at her *Alma Mater*, which position she filled acceptably on her return.   Married, Aug. 30, 1859, Rev. Henry Clay Badger, son of Joseph and Eliza Mehitable (Sterling) Badger, at that time a professor in Antioch College ; now connected with the Library of Harvard University.   After her marriage she had a private school in Boston ; was one of the four ladies chosen on the school committee in the city, the first time women were elected to that office.   Her health broke down under the great pressure of cares and duties which her talents and capabilities drew upon her, in addition to home responsibilities.   She died Jan. 6, 1874.   Children :

(1.)   Theodore *Badger*, b. June 22, 1863.
(2.)   Frederic *Badger*, b. Dec. 27, 1865.
(3.)   Ernest *Badger*, b. July 8, 1869.
(4.)   Katharine *Badger*, b. Aug. 31, 1872.

7.   Lucy Elizabeth *Shepard*, b. Sept. 28, 1837.   Was
an exceedingly brilliant and attractive person.
Graduated from Dorchester High School and
Antioch College; taught at Eagleswood and in the
Cambridge High School.   Was peculiarly clear and
successful as a teacher of Greek and mathematics.
Fitted more than forty young men for college, giving
intellectual stimulus to all who came under her influence.   Lived a long and intense life within a third of a
century; m., July 23, 1866, Rev. Thomas Hill, D. D.,
son of Thomas and Henrietta (Barker) Hill.   Dr.
Hill was president of Harvard University many
years; is at present pastor of the First Parish
Church, Portland, Me.   He is widely known as a
profound scholar, a judicious writer and a devout
Christian teacher.   *Child:* Otis Shepard *Hill*, b.
Dec. 28, 1868.
   Mrs. Lucy Elizabeth (Shepard) Hill died Feb. 9,
1869.

8.   Eliza Frances *Shepard*, b. March 14, 1840; m. Oct.
20, 1869, Raphael Pumpelly, son of William and
Mary (Welles) Pumpelly, then a professor in
Harvard University.   Being an expert in Metallurgy
and mining engineering, he was sent to Arizona and
afterward to Japan on a tour of investigation and
inspection in those matters.   His book, "Across
America and Asia," describing these tours, is full of
entertainment and information.   He was the director of the trans-continental survey of the Northern
Pacific Railroad route.   He is connected with the
geological department of the United States government.   He resides at Newport, R. I.   Children:

(1.)   A son, b. April 23, 1871; d. same day.
(2.)   Margarita *Pumpelly*, b. Aug. 6, 1873.

(3) Caroline Eliza *Pumpelly*, b. May 14, 1875.

(4.) Anna Pauline *Pumpelly*, b. June 30, 1878.

(5.) Clarence King *Pumpelly*, b. May 12, 1879; d. Aug. 12, 1879.

(6.) Raphael Welles *Pumpelly*, b. May 23, 1881.

9.  Amasa Stetson *Shepard*, b. Sept. 27, 1842; d. Nov. 20, 1842.

10. Amasa Stetson *Shepard*, b. Jan. 21, 1844; d. March 30, 1844.

11. Rebecca Kettell *Shepard*, b. Jan. 21, 1844; m. July 7, 1869, George Haven Putnam, son of the celebrated publisher, George Palmer Putnam, and Victorine (Haven) Putnam, of New York City. Mr. George H. Putnam is at the head of the firm of George P. Putnam's Sons, who continue the business established by their father.  Children:

(1.) Bertha Haven *Putnam*, b. March 1, 1872.

(2.) Ethel Frothingham *Putnam*, b. Nov. 2, 1873.

(3.) Mary Corinna *Putnam*, b. Sept. 27, 1875.

(4.) Ellen Shepard *Putnam*, b. July 8, 1878; d. Aug. 2, 1880.

(5.) Dorothy *Putnam*, b. Oct. 10, 1882.

12. Rachel Pope *Shepard*, b. March 2, 1846.

13. Ellen Grace *Shepard*, b. May 17, 1849; m. Sept. 2, 1871, Henry Barker Hill, b. April 27, 1849, son of Rev. Thomas Hill, D. D., and Ann Foster (Bellows) Hill.  He is Professor of Chemistry in Harvard University.  *Child:* Edward Burlingame Hill, b. Sept. 9, 1872.

SARAH,[7] daughter of William[6] and Sarah (Pierce), born Jan. 4, 1811, was married, June 19, 1826, to Hiram Shepard, son of Ralph and Nabby (Gay) Shepard, born in Stoughton, Nov. 21, 1798. "His training under a ' school master ' was quite limited, for his father accumulated a fortune in the number of his children, not in the size of his exchequer : hence he was thrown early upon his own resources." He was a diligent business man, associated in the ownership and control of the bakery with his brother Otis, the husband of Ann[7] (Pope), sister of his wife. His tastes were quiet, and his habits domestic. He was a man of excellent repute. He died Sept. 10, 1869.

Mrs. Sarah (Pope) Shepard saw something of a mother's joys and sorrows. Five children came to her arms, but the eldest and the fourth failed to reach their first birthday. And when the rest were still of tender age, she was parted from them, May 18, 1839, to the great grief of her husband and little ones and a wide circle of loving friends and relatives. A third child died at the age of·eighteen, leaving only two to reach maturity.

Children, born in Dorchester :

1. Eliza *Shepard*, b. May 16, 1827; d. Jan. 25, 1828.
2. Hiram *Shepard*, b. Nov. 18, 1828; d. Dec. 17, 1846.
3. William Arthur *Shepard*, b. June 26, 1831; m. in Petersburg, Va., in January, 1864, Martha Emma, eldest daughter of William T. and Elizabeth Taylor Corbin (Beale) Davis, he of Gloucester County, she of Westmoreland County, Va., b. March 20, 1839. [See below.]
4. Edgar *Shepard*, b. Feb. 7, 1834; d. Sept. 23, 1835.
5. Sarah Pope *Shepard*, b. Nov. 14, 1836; m. May 3, 1865, Henry Augustus Warriner, son of Hezekiah and Hannah (Porter) Warriner. He died Nov. 16, 1871.

"William Arthur Shepard left at the age of fourteen, the school on · Meeting-house Hill' in Dorchester, which had at that time for its ' master,' Mr. Wm. S. Williams, a most efficient and faithful teacher, and became a member of the family of Mr. James B. Williams, druggist, of Manchester, Conn. He continued with him for more than four years, and then entered the Scientific School of Yale College, which was at that time officered by the younger Silliman and Prof. John P. Norton. It has since become the celebrated Sheffield School. He received the degree of Bachelor of Philosophy at the end of two years, in the first class that the school graduated, and was invited by Charles B. Stuart, Professor of Chemistry in Randolph Macon College, Boydton, Virginia, to open an Analytical Laboratory in connection with that College. The offer was accepted. He devoted one half of his time to Laboratory work and the other half to the prosecution of the academical course in the College, and received the Degree of Bachelor of Arts in 1857. He continued in connection with the College till 1861, at which time he entered the Southern Army as a private, where he remained until the surrender at Appomattox, having in the mean-time risen to the rank of Major. We clip from an editorial of a paper published twelve months after the war, the following :

"'We recollect a Massachusetts teacher who had been nine years South when the war broke out, who enlisted as a private in the 12th Virginia regiment, who fought most gallantly in twelve pitched bat-tles, never shirked a fight nor guarded the baggage, and was one of the few men in his company who went in at Sharpsburg. Massa-chusetts may well be proud of Major Shepard.' He was elected to the chair of Chemistry and Natural Philosophy of his Alma Mater in 1870, now located at Ashland, Virginia, and holds that position at the present time.

"Three years after the death of his first wife, Mr. Hiram Shep-ard married (2) Mary Swan Munroe, daughter of John Wiswell Mun-roe of Dorchester, by whom he had three children, one of whom is now living, Walter, Civil Engineer in the Boston and Albany Rail-road Company. He died in 1869 in the house which he had occu-pied for more than forty years, and where he had spent all of his married life, leaving his widow, three children, and a name that was above re-proach.

"Sarah (Pope) Shepard married before she was twenty years of age, but was not permitted to enjoy a long period in the society of her ever kind and gentle husband. Before the thirteenth anniversary of her marriage, her spirit had returned unto God who gave it. On her 32d birthday, as she was returning home through 'the lane ' from an afternoon's visit to her sister Ann, she observed that she spit blood. This so alarmed her that in a few days she took to her bed, and never left it again except for a brief period at a time. She, like her husband, was of a tender, gentle disposition, content rather to be at home surrounded by her family than to be mingling much in soci-ety. The author of this memorial, though not eight years old when she died, remembers distinctly the sweet melodies with which she would beguile him to sleep ; and now, after more than two score years, the 'Switzer's Song of Home,' ' The Maltese Boat Song,' and ' Two Orphan Boys of Switzerland ' are often heard in his own house-hold. He still recalls, as of yesterday, how she drew him to her bed-side, but a few days before her death, and in conversation and in an earnest prayer committed him and his brother and sister to the ten-der mercies of a covenant-keeping God. The following lines taken from the fly-leaf of the writer's Bible, the gift of his grandfather, when he was leaving home for life, show that his mother found time even in her childhood, to think of other than mere earthly things :

"'A present to William Arthur Shepard from his grandfather, hoping you will make this Book your daily friend and companion in all of your intercourse in life. . . . . Your mother's anxiety in her last sickness was not so much on her own account, as for her beloved children whom she was going to leave in this world of sin and trial. When she was fourteen years of age she could repeat all of the four Gospels.'"

ADALINE,[7] daughter of William[6] and Sarah (Pierce), m. May 15, 1834, Julius Augustus Noble. Mrs. Noble died at New Orleans, April 29, 1844. Children :

1. William Pope *Noble*, b. Dec. 30, 1835 ; m. Fannie Fullers. Children :

    (1.)  Adaline *Noble*.
    (2.)  William Pope *Noble*.

2. Lucy Ann *Noble*, b. March 15, 1841 ; m. July 14, 1861, Oliver Allen Peirce, of Medford, Mass., b. April 7, 1840. *Children*, born in New Orleans, La.:

    (1.)  May Adaline *Peirce*, b. May 9, 1862 ; m. March 30, 1884, William Louis Gottschalck, b. 1846.
    (2.)  Alice *Peirce*, b. Sept. 24, 1863, at Plaquemine, La.
    (3.)  Grace Allen *Peirce*, b. Oct. 10, 1865.
    (4.)  Lizzie Spencer *Peirce*, b. May 25, 1867.
    (5.)  Allan Noble *Peirce*, b. Oct. 23, 1869.
    (6.)  Oliver *Peirce*, b. June 21, 1871 ; d. July 3, 1872.
    (7.)  Oliver *Peirce*, b. May 22, 1873.
    (8.)  Lucy Ann Noble *Peirce*, b. Oct. 7, 1875. Mrs. Peirce died March 27, 1876.

ELIZABETH,[6] daughter of William[6] and Sarah (Pierce), m. Aug. 13, 1835, *John Ayres*, Truro, N. S., where he was born July 26, 1807. Children :

1. Helen Frances *Ayres*, b. July 3, 1836.
2. Alice Cleveland *Ayres*, b. May 17, 1838.
3. Elizabeth *Ayres*, b. May 26, 1840 ; d. June 22, 1875.
4. Mary Adeline *Ayres*, b. April 16, 1844. They reside in Dorchester.

LUCY,⁷ dau. of William⁶ and Sarah (Pierce), b. Dec. 3, 1815; was married August 25, 1840, to *Jonathan Battles*, son of Jonathan and Maria (Dickerman) Battles, of Stoughton, born Sept. 7, 1812. He was educated first in the common schools of his native town, then at the Academy in Milton. He entered upon the profession of teaching ; was engaged in the public schools of Dorchester and vicinity some twenty-five years, with good success. Resides in Dorchester. Children :

1. Catharine Pope *Battles*, b. May 23, 1841.
2. Edward Winslow *Battles*, b. June 29, 1844 ; d. Nov. 25, 1849.
3. Harriet Augusta *Battles*, b. April 23, 1856; d. Feb. 9, 1871.

---

A, 5.

## THE FAMILY OF ELIJAH⁶.

ELIJAH,⁶ son of Frederick⁵ and Mary (Cole), b. June 10, 1780; d. June 25, 1864; m. first, Joanna Tisdale, Aug. 17, 1802.

*Child of First Marriage.*

I. EBENEZER TISDALE,⁷ b. Dec., 1802 ; d. June 29, 1832.

Joanna (Tisdale) died Feb. 13, 1809, in Stoughton.
He married, second, July 2, 1809, Susanna, dau. of James and Zilpah (Cummings) Capen, also of Stoughton, b. Oct. 23, 1789.

*Children of Second Marriage*, born in Stoughton.

II. JOANNA TISDALE,⁷ b. May 14, 1810; d. Oct. 28, 1845.
III. HIRAM,⁷ b. June 29, 1811. [See next chapter, A, 12.]
IV. EMILY,⁷ b. Feb. 5, 1813 ; m. William Spear, of West Gardiner, Me. Resides in Gardiner. He died May 21, 1882.
V. FREDERIC,⁷ b. Nov. 12, 1814. [See next chapter, A, 13.]
VI. MARIETTA ANGELETTA,⁷ b. April 29, 1816; m. August, 1849, John Blaisdell, of Gardiner. She d. Dec. 22, 1851. *Child:* Frederic *Blaisdell*, b. May 25, 1851.

*Born in Gardiner, Me.*

VII. WILLIAM,⁷ b. Feb. 23, 1818 ; d. Sept. 17, 1841.

VIII. JOHN,⁷ b. March 2, 1820. [See next chapter, A, 14.]

IX. GEORGE,⁷ b. March 16, 1822 ; d. Sept. 4, 1839.

X. JAMES,⁷ b. May 10, 1824 ; d. May 10, 1848.

XI. FORTINA ADELAIDE,⁷ b. Oct. 12, 1826 ; m. June 27, 1852, Samuel Nash, of Gardiner, Me. She d. Feb. 16, 1858. *Child:* Clara L. *Nash*, b. Aug. 12, 1853 ; d. June 29, 1874.

XII. MARY ELIZABETH,⁷ b. June 8, 1831 ; m. September, 1850, John French, of Gardiner, Me. She died April 20, 1860. Children :

1. Elizabeth *French*, b. Nov. 14, 1851 ; d. Feb. 14, 1872.

2. Alberta *French*, b. Feb. 24, 1855 ; m. Sept. 25, 1879, *David Bradstreet*, of Gardiner, Me. Children :

   (1.) William Plummer *Bradstreet*, b. July 18, 1880.

   (2.) Carrol Pitkin *Bradstreet*, b. Sept. 24, 1881.

   (3.) Elizabeth *Bradstreet*, b. Jan. 27, 1885.

ELIJAH POPE⁶ lived in Stoughton, until 1816, when he sold his property there and removed to Gardiner, Maine. He bought a farm in the western part of the town, and conquered its forest and rock obstacles with great energy, assisted well by his cheerful, industrious, efficient helpmeet. He built, after a while, a fine brick house, the product of his toil *from the ground up*, and spent many happy years there with his growing family.

He was self-contained and capable, respected in the community which grew up around him. He died in West Gardiner, June 25, 1864.

Mrs. Susanna (Capen) Pope was a typical New England mother, who "looked well to the ways of her household," and was the reliance of her husband and children, as far as a human being can be. Strong religious convictions, high purpose for serving God and her generation, and vigorous common sense and energy combined with those spiritual elements.

Cataracts on her eyes rendered her blind for many years, yet not helpless.  On her 90th birthday the writer first saw her at the home of her son Hiram.  She had that day walked quite a distance up-hill and up-stairs to pay a call of comfort to a neighbor a year younger, who, though not crippled, was too feeble to leave the room.

"Aunt Susanna" had no difficulty in "placing" the stranger when informed he was "Frederick's grandchild"; and instantly gave the list of F.'s children in exact order; describing her visitor's father, James, in particular; "I remember," said she, "that his sisters thought he was a beautiful baby, because he had such long, brown eye-lashes."  Then she described Colonel Frederick, her husband's father, and told anecdotes of him; and even gave a bit of reminiscence of his mother, Rebecca (Stubbs), the widow of Dr. Ralph.

She was on the point, once, of visiting New York City at the request of her son John, to have the services of an eminent oculist in an operation for the restoration of her sight.  But she, at the last, declined positively, fearing that the operation might fail of removing her blindness, and leave her "a burden upon others."  She found ways of relieving the burden of others all her life, even to its closing days.  She died a few days before her 92[d] birthday, Aug. 29, 1881.

Four of the eleven children of the second marriage died single.  Three sons and four daughters lived to achieve something in life and leave successors.

---

## A, 6.

## THE FAMILY OF AZOR[6].

AZOR,[6] the oldest son of Captain James[5] and Sarah (Capen), who lived to maturity, dwelt on the old homestead in Stoughton.  He was a carpenter in early manhood.  He took an active part in the militia, and was full of interest in political matters.

Quick to think of a subject presented to him, he was good at repartee and trenchant and humorous in speech.  "President

Pope," a title given to him in sport, became his uniform "sobriquet." He was tall, large-framed, with dark hair.

When his children were grown he built a new house, near the old homestead, and lived there the rest of his life, giving his attention to the management of his farm. He kept full memoranda of family and general matters, and had many interesting documents, which perished in his "old chest," in one of those fearful "house-cleaning" periods which swept over the house after his departure. He died March 17, 1851.

He married, Dec. 6, 1807, Lucy, daughter of Isaac and Molly (French) Bird, of Stoughton, who bore him seven children. She died March 4, 1864, aged eighty-one years one month.

Neither of the daughters married. Sarah[7] died at the age of three years, Ada[7] at sixty-six, and Ruth[7] at fifty-four. One of the sons also, Asa Bird,[7] failed to enter wedlock, though he lived to the age of half a century.

James[7] married Sarah Holmes, of Stoughton, March 4, 1851. They had no children, but legally adopted his nephew, Charles Henry, son of Edmund and Abba Pope, of Stoughton, Dec. 14, 1861. He d. June 23, 1871. Was a farmer ; a man of medium height, dark hair, fair skin ; generous to the needy, though gruff in speech and unwilling to be thanked for his kindness.

Ada[7] and Ruth[7] built a cottage, and lived together many years after the death of their father. Ruth died of heart disease, while riding home from a visit, one winter's day.

Asa Bird[7] was a farmer ; never married ; was very fond of dumb animals, of excellent judgment about them ; had the full blue eye, high forehead, and light complexion characteristic of htat branch of the Pope family.

### CHILDREN OF AZOR[6] AND LUCY (BIRD).

I.   LUTHER,[7] b. April 29, 1808. [See next chapter, A, 15.]
II,  JAMES,[7] b. Dec. 26, 1809 ; m. March 4, 1851, Sarah Holmes ; d. June 23, 1871.
III. ADA,[7] b. Dec. 1, 1811 ; d. June 22, 1879.
IV.  RUTH,[7] b. June 13, 1814 ; d. Feb. 2, 1868.
V.   SARAH,[7] b. Sept. 12, 1816 ; d. Jan. 16, 1819.
VI.  ASA BIRD,[7] b. March 7, 1819 ; d. May 19, 1869.
VII. EDMUND,[7] b. Jan. 21, 1821. [See next chapter, A, 16.]

## A, 7.

## THE FAMILY OF WARD[6].

WARD,[6] son of Captain James[5] and Sarah (Capen) Pope, m. Nov. 30, 1809, Anna Gurney. He was a carpenter; lived in Stoughton. He died Nov. 2, 1836, aged 47. She died Jan. 20, 1828, aged 38.

Six children were born to them, four of whom died in child-hood, and a fifth merely reached womanhood to pass away from their grasp.

### CHILDREN OF WARD[6] AND ANNA (GURNEY).

I. MARY,[7] b. 1810; d. Oct. 15, 1822.

II. WILLIAM,[7] b. December, 1813; d. April 14, 1817.

III. WILLIAM,[7] b. Jan. 11, 1817. [See next chapter, A, 17.]

IV. } Twins,[7] b. Sept. 14, d. Sept. 24, 1819.
V. }

VI. SARAH,[7] b. Nov. 28, 1820; d. June 9, 1839.

I.

## JOHN[6] AND HIS FAMILY.

JOHN,[6] son of Micajah[6] and Sarah (Whitney), was born in Stoughton, baptized April 23, 1769, but removed to Braintree (now Quincy), with his mother and brother Asa, in the month of December, 1789. In 1792 he paid a tax, as the assessor's books show. He was a farmer and butcher.

His wife died Aug. 19, 1825.

He died at the advanced age of eighty, May 18, 1848.

His estate was administered upon, Aug. 26, following, by his eldest son, Norton Quincy[7]; his nephews, Samuel Brown[7] and Ozias Morse,[7] being appraisers.

### CHILDREN OF JOHN[6] AND HANNAH (PRATT).

I. A Child,[7] b. Aug. 22, 1799; d. Oct. 2, 1801.

II. Sally,[7] b. ——; m. John Elkins, removed to Illinois; d. ——.

III. Norton Quincy,[7] b. Jan. 28, 1804. [See next chapter, B, 1.]

IV. Evelina Derby,[7] b. ——; m. April 1, 1827, Harvey French; d. Jan. 25, 1872.

V. A Child,[7] b. December, 1806; d. Oct. 25, 1807.

VI. Sophia,[7] b. Nov. 9, 1809; m. June 2, 1833, Robert Hussey. Is still living in South Boston, fresh and vigorous in mind, erect and capable, though almost fourscore. Mr. Hussey is a carpenter in the Boston Water Works. Children:

1.  Eliza A. *Hussey.*
2.  Sophia M. *Hussey,* m. Aug. 11, 1857, Edward Dexter Wadleigh, son of Dexter and Louisa Wadleigh. He died ———. She resides in South Boston with her parents.
3.  Fannie W. *Hussey*; teaches in one of the city schools.

VII.  LUCY ANN,[7] b. ———; m. (1), Oct. 3, 1833, William Lowell of Boston.   Children :

1.  William F. *Lowell,* b. Sept. 20, 1834; m. 1856, Emeline Moulthrop. Resides in New Haven, Ct. Has children, William H. *Lowell,* Anna L. *Lowell,* and Mary B. *Lowell.*
2.  Charles C. *Lowell,* b. April 3, 1836; m. 1866, Kate Grondee of New Haven, Ct.; has children : Charles E. *Lowell,* John P. *Lowell,* George C. *Lowell,* and Daisy C. *Lowell.* Resides in New Haven, Ct.
•  3.  John P. *Lowell,* m. Ellen J. Morse, of Waterbury, Ct. Had children, Charles M. *Lowell* and Nellie E. *Lowell.* He was a captain in the 12th Connecticut Volunteer Infantry, and was killed at the battle of Cedar Creek, Oct. 17, 1864.

William *Lowell* d. Oct. 11, 1846.

Mrs. Lucy Ann[7] (Pope) Lowell m. (2d) Feb. 5, 1849, Henry L. Kettendorf, in Providence, R. I. Had a daughter, Henrietta *Kettendorf,* d. ———, and a daughter, Sarah B. *Kettendorf,* living.

Mr. and Mrs. Kettendorf reside in New Haven, Ct.

VIII.  ABNER B.[7] b. June 6, 1817 ; m. ———, 1842, Susan E. Jacobs.  [See next chapter, B, 2.]
IX.  JANE M.,[7] b. June 18, 1823 ; d. April 28, 1882.
X.  JOHN,[7] b. ———; d. in California.

---

B, 2.

## ASA[6] AND HIS FAMILY.

ASA,[6] second son of Micajah[6] and Sarah (Whitney), born in Stoughton, Oct. 28, 1775, went to that part of Braintree now Quincy, to reside, in 1789.

We find him appointed a member of a committee to purchase a lot for a town hall, July 8, 1816.

He was a Free Mason, a member of the "Rural Lodge," which was compelled to surrender its charter in the Anti-Masonic excitement of 1834, but re-opened in 1838, with "Asa Pope" as one of its officers. He lived to a good old age, passing away Dec. 20, 1858.

He married April 9, 1796, Susanna Ripley, who was born in Weymouth, Feb. 23, 1772, and who died in Quincy a little before her husband, Oct. 5, 1855.

But one child of this couple failed to grow up, a little one whose death is registered as having taken place " Sept. 1. 1803, aged 21 months."

The rest, three sons and three daughters, added to the list of the descendants of " Goodman Pope " of Dorchester, as we shall see.

CHILDREN OF ASA⁶ AND SUSANNA (RIPLEY).

I. Lucy,⁷ b. April 15, 1798 ; m. June 3, 1821, John Adams Newcomb of Quincy. He was born Oct. 26, 1798. He and sons have been engaged in the manufacture of boots. Their children are :

1. Henry Augustus *Newcomb*, b. April 1, 1823 ; who m. June 16, 1844, Ethelinda W., daughter of William Parker of ———, N. H. ; he enlisted July 29, 1862, in Co. D, 39th Mass. Vol. Inf. ; was made corporal ; was taken prisoner, carried to Salisbury (N. Carolina) prison, and *died there of starvation*, Dec. 23, 1864. His grave in Salisbury National Cemetery is numbered 2344. Children :

(1.) Lucy Frances *Newcomb*, b. April 8, 1846; m. Nov. 26, 1869, Jacob H. Hersey. In a millinery store in Boston. Have child, Alice *Hersey*, b. Aug. 29, 1870.

(2.) Charles Henry *Newcomb*, b. Nov. 6, 1847, died Oct. 21, 1860.

(3.) George Eugene *Newcomb*, b. Sept. 5, 1851; a jeweller in Quincy.

2. Francis Jeremiah *Newcomb*, b. March 17, 1826, m. Abbie C. Robie, of ———, N. H. ; d. July 5, 1857. She d. May 10, 1864.

3. John Adams *Newcomb*, b. June 30, 1830. Is a painter. Resides in Philadelphia, Penn. Is married.

4. George Washington *Newcomb*, b. Aug. 23, 1834. Boot-maker, resides in Quincy.

II. SAMUEL BROWN[7]. [See next chapter, B, 3.]
III. A CHILD,[7] b. Dec., 1801 ; d. Sept. 1, 1803.
IV. OZIAS MORSE,[7] b. June 18, 1804. [See next chapter, B, 4.]
V. JOANNA,[7] b. Jan. 19, 1807 ; m. June 6, 1826, George M. Briesler ; d. ———.
VI. ABIGAIL,[7] b. Oct. 23, 1809 ; m. April 13, 1828, Isaac Bass.
VII. GEORGE WASHINGTON,[7] b. March 30, 1812. [See next chapter, B, 5.]

---

## B, 3.

## THE FAMILY OF JOSEPH[d].

JOSEPH,[6] son of Ralph[5] and Hannah (Gay), b. Oct. 4, 1771 ; m. March 1, 1796, Betsey Tower, of Milton, b. March 5, 1775. She died and was buried at Quincy, Oct. 26, 1840. He died at Quincy, Jan. 12, 1845. Children :

I. NANCY,[7] b. July 28, 1796 ; m. May 24, 1829, Otis Bisbee, son of Benjamin and Milly (Vose) Bisbee. Children :

1. James Otis *Bisbee*, b. April 20, 1830 ; m. Jan., 1869, Laura Faunce, of Bridgewater. Children :

   (1.) Benjamin Stanton *Bisbee*, b. Sept. 20, 1869.
   (2.) Bertha Alma *Bisbee*, b. Sept. 7, 1870.
   (3.) Ellsworth Otis *Bisbee*, b. Oct. 22, 1878.　·

2. Benjamin *Bisbee*, b. April 10, 1832 ; m. Sept. 24, 1862, Susan Y. P. Monk, of Stoughton. He was a soldier in Co. B, 45th Mass. Vol. Inf., remaining through the whole period of the regiment's service. He resides in Stoughton.

3. Augusta *Bisbee*, b. July 16, 1834, was m. Oct. 25, 1854, to Caleb F. Kimball, of Charlestown. Child :

Alice Augusta *Kimball*, b. Aug. 13, 1855.

4. Eliza Ann *Bisbee*, b. Sept. 1, 1836, m. June, 1869, George *Mulliken*, of Somerville. Children :

(1.) Fannie Geraldine *Mulliken*, b. Dec. 2, 1870.
(2.) Walter Tower *Mulliken*, b. Aug. 29, 1876.
(3.) Albion Leslie *Mulliken*, b. July 22, 1879.

5. Joseph Pope *Bisbee*, b. June 26, 1839.    Enlisted in Co. I, 1st Mass. Vol. Cavalry, in the War of the Rebellion ; died at Hilton Head, So. Carolina, July 14, 1862.

II. ELIZA,[7] b. Dec. 21, 1798 ; unmarried.    Resides at Stoughton, Mass.

III. JAMES,[7] b. May 9, 1801 ; supposed to have died in S. America.

IV. JOSEPH,[7] b. Sept. 23, 1803. [See next chapter, B, 6.]

V. WILLIAM,[7] b. April 29, 1806 ; m. May 29, 1832, Mary Dill, of Hull. He was drowned at Hull.

VI. CLARISSA,[7] b. Dec. 20, 1809 ; m. William Howard, son of Samuel and Rhoda (Wellman) Packard. He d. Feb. 11, 1872. She d. July 24, 1875.    Children :

1. Elizabeth *Packard*, b. Oct. 25, d. Nov. 17, 1828.

2. William H. *Packard*, b. Nov. 17, 1834; d. Sept. 11, 1840.

3. Adaline E. *Packard*, b. July 9, 1836 ; m. Dec. 31, 1868, Capt. Edward Cole, of South Yarmouth, who died March 1, 1882.    Resides in South Yarmouth.

4. Henry T. *Packard*, b. May 9, 1839. Was a soldier in the War of the Rebellion, was captured and confined in a Southern prison, and d. Dec. 10, 1864, from disease he had there contracted.

VII. THOMAS,⁷ b. May 28, 1815; m. Feb. 16, 1837, Mary Ann Eldridge, of Hull. He died in Boston.

VIII. JOHN,⁷ b. July 12, 1819; unmarried. Was drowned at Boston.

---

## B, 4.

## THE FAMILY OF MICAJAH⁶.

MICAJAH,⁶ son of Ralph⁵ and Hannah (Gay), b. May 5, 1774, in Stoughton ; m. Mrs. Lucinda (Randall) Howard, of Easton, b. Jan. 16, 1784. She died in Quincy, May 31, 1874. He was a farmer, residing in Quincy. He died of palsy, Jan. 13, 1848. Children :

I. MICAJAH,⁷ jr., b. July 22, 1817. [See next chapter, B, 7.]

II. LUCINDA HOWARD,⁷ b. Oct. 24, 1820; m. ——, 1848, Lemuel Billings, son of John and Lydia (Faxon) Billings; d. —— ,1853. *Child*, Anna Caroline *Billings*, b. Sept. 11, 1851. Mr. Billings and his daughter reside at Wollaston, in the town of Quincy.

III. EDWARD RANDALL,⁷ b. March 26, 1823. [See next chapter, B, 8.]

IV. ANN BIRD,⁷ b. Oct. 11, 1825 ; d. May 7, 1840.

V. JOHN BIRD,⁷ b. Dec. 22, 1828 ; d. July 2, 1848.

---

## B, 5.

## THE FAMILY OF LEMUEL⁶.

LEMUEL,⁶ son of Ralph⁵ and Hannah (Gay), born Oct. 12, 1781; baptized Oct. 28, 1781; m. Jan. 31, 1803, Elizabeth (Betsey), daughter of James and Mary (Baxter) Clark, of Quincy, born March 7, 1778. He died at Quincy, Feb. 5, 1852. Lemuel Pope, of Quincy, makes a will Jan. 1, 1852 (proved March

6, 1852). Bequeaths to wife "Betsey, daughter Sarah C. Sanborn, and son Micajah C. Pope." She died at Quincy, March
10, 1866. Elizabeth Pope, of Quincy, widow, makes will April
5, 1853, bequeathing her property to her "son Micajah C. Pope,
and her daughter Sarah C. Sanborn, wife of Joseph W. Sanborn." Will filed March 22, 1866. Children :

I.  SARAH CLARK,⁷ b. July 3, 1803 ; m. Nov. 11, 1834, Joseph
    Woodman Sanborn, b. at New Hampton, N. H., March
    10, 1801. Spent some years in Benicia, Cal., having.
    his two sons with him, until their untimely deaths ; left
    a good name there, as well as at his Eastern home. He
    d. at Bridgewater, Aug. 9, 1868. She d. Dec. 27, 1882.
    Children :

    1.  Carlmira ["Mira"] Minot Glover *Sanborn*, b. Sept. 25,
        1835 ; m. April 11, 1866, Cary Mitchell Leonard,
        son of Samuel and Mehitable (Bennet) Leonard, of
        Bridgewater, a machinist.
    2.  Joseph Woodman *Sanborn*, jr., b. March 24, 1838 ; d. at
        Benicia, Cal., Nov. 10, 1860.
    3.  John Baird Pope *Sanborn*, b. Aug. 16, 1841 ; d. at
        Benicia, Cal., Sept. 9, 1860.

II. MICAJAH CLARK,⁷ b. Dec. 3, 1811. [See next chapter, B, 9.]

---

B, 6.

THE FAMILY OF LAZARUS⁶.

LAZARUS,⁶ son of Lazarus⁵ and Mary (Swan), b. April, 1782, in
Stoughton, m. in 1808, Elizabeth ("Betsy") Talbot, dau. of Isaac
and Susannah (Turner) Talbot of Stoughton.

For a few years he resided in Stoughton, then in Dorchester,
and afterward, for many years, in Marlboro, where he died Aug.,
1842. His wife died Nov. 24, 1856. He was a farmer; an
active, forehanded man ; brought up a large family. Children :

I.  RUFUS SPURR,⁷ b. in Stoughton, April 2, 1809. [See
    next chapter, B, 10.]
II. BETSEY,⁷ b. Oct., 1810; "d. Dec. 5, 1811, æ. 10 months."

III. ALEXANDER,[7] whose name was afterward changed to
Franklin Manser,[7] b. Oct. 16, 1814. [See next chapter, B, 11, under the latter name.]

IV. CAROLINE,[7] b. in Dorchester, March 11, 1816 ; m. Cyrus
Fay, of Westboro, Mass.; d. May 15, 1852.

*Born at Marlboro.*

V. ALMIRA,[7] b. March 6, 1818 ; d. April 24, 1876.

VI. SUSAN T.,[7] b. May 10, 1821 ; d. Oct. 2, 1830.

VII. SARAH M.[7] b. Aug. 7, 1823 ; resides in Marlboro.  (A
kind contributor of statistics for this work.)

VIII. PHILANDER,[7] } b. Oct. 20, 1825 ; { d. Aug., 1826.

IX. PHILINDIA,[7] } { m. to Solomon L. Met-
calf, of Lowell, Vt., Jan. 17, 1861 ; d. June 7, 1872.
*Child*, Luman Ellsworth *Metcalf*, b. May 4, 1865.
Mr. Metcalf died Oct., 1886.

---

B, 7.

THE FAMILY OF THOMAS[6].

THOMAS,[6] son of Lazarus[5] and Mary (Swan), b. ——, 1792;
m. Tyla, dau. of Mather and Silence (Fisher) Holmes, July 3, 1816.
He was a carpenter, and worked at the trade several years. After
his marriage kept the "Swan Hotel," in Stoughton. Lived
some time in Boston; then in Newton, where his wife died,
Nov. 19, 1837.  He died in Natick, but was buried beside his
wife at Watertown.  Children :

I. ANNA MARIA,[7] b. Dec. 11, 1817 ; m. Nov. 27, 1856,
Jesse Smith.  Living in Stoughton.  No children.
Has lent material assistance to the writer in gathering
details respecting this branch of the family.

II. THOMAS RICHARDSON,[7] b. Aug. 2, 1819.  [See following
chapter, B, 12.]

III. HARRIET DELIA[7], b. Sept. 11, 1825 ; m. (1) in May,
1843, in Boston, Aaron Littlefield, jr., of Randolph.
He died in East Stoughton.  Harriet Delia[7] (Pope)
Littlefield, m. (2) Sullivan Jones, of Randolph, where
they reside.  Children :

    1.  Aaron Walter *Littlefield*, b. June, 1849 ; d. ——, 1875.

    2.  George Wales Whitfield *Littlefield*, b. ——, 1851 ; m. Cora Burrell, of East Stoughton.

    3.  Franklin Hinkley *Littlefield*, b. —— , 1853 ; m. Lilla Burrell, of East Stoughton.  Both are dead.

IV.  LUCRETIA HAMMOND,[7] b. Nov. 7, 1826 ; m. Joseph Barnard of Canton, in 1861.  He died, 1865.  Children :

    1.  Charlotte *Barnard*, b. —— , 1862.

    2.  Edward Forest *Barnard*, b. March 16, 1865.

V.  ELIZA AUGUSTA,[7] b. in Dorchester, May 25, 1828 ; m. Nov., 1852, Levi Keith Drake, of Stoughton.  She died Aug. 28, 1885.  Children :

    1.  Irving Lawrence *Drake*, b. June 18, 1856.

    2.  Harriet A. *Drake*, b. Aug. 15, 1861 ; d. Dec. 14, 1862.

    3.  Milton Everett *Drake*, b. May 25, 1866; clerk in clothing store.

    4.  Eva Ellsworth *Drake*, b. Dec. 11, 1868.

------

### B, 8.

### THE FAMILY OF OTIS[5].

OTIS,[6] son of Lazarus[5] and Mary (Swan), b. October, 1795 ; m. Dec. 10, 1821, Mary Hutchins, b. in 1801, in Kennebunk, Me.  She d. Sept. 9, 1855.  Lived in Boston ; was a trader ; resided at 4 Decatur Street up to the time of his death, Aug. 30, 1868.  His disease was phthisis.  Children :

I.  ABIGAIL FROTHINGHAM,[7] b. Feb. 11, 1823 ; m. to Benjamin Franklin Baker, of Boston, b. Nov. 20, 1824 ; d. June, 1879.  Children :

    1.  Henry Franklin *Baker*, b. September, 1847.

    2.  William Frederick *Baker*, b. June 6, 1856.

    3.  Edward Francis *Baker*.

    4.  Richard Foster *Baker*.

    5.  Walter Frothingham *Baker*, b. Nov. 18, 1864.

II.  MARY ELIZABETH,[7] b. Sept. 2, 1825.

III.  SARAH JANE,[7] b. Dec. 16, 1828.

### THE SONS OF EDMUND[5].

———

I.

## THE FAMILY OF EBENEZER[6].

EBENEZER,[6] b. on the old place at Squantum, Aug. 5, 1808, m. April 5, 1832, *Hannah*, daughter of Stephen and Mary (Pierce) *Tolman*, of Dorchester, who was b. July 18, 1807. He lived in a part of the town of Milton called Railway Village, near East Milton.

He was of a stout build, with a pleasant, genial countenance, and a commanding presence. He was characterized by his general intelligence, sound judgment, accuracy and upright-ness in his business affairs. He was elected one of the Select-men in 1842, and held the office seven consecutive years, the last four as chairman of the board. He was public-spirited, and for several years previous to his death was one of the leading citizens in all public interests, and was looked and listened to for counsel and aid in all matters affecting the interests of the town. He was a strong anti-Freemason, and took an active part in the anti-Freemason campaign for governor of Massa-chusetts during the Morgan excitement. He was the first Treasurer of the Dorchester and Milton Samaritan Society, formed to clothe and feed fugitive slaves after they reached Canada from the South. He was also a warm friend of the temperance cause. He was one of the founders of the Congre-gational Church in East Milton, was a generous supporter of the gospel, and promoted all the good works to which the church lent her hand. He was a farmer, was much interested in agriculture, and a prominent member of the Norfolk Agricultural Society.   He was devoted to his family.   He d. March 24, 1853.

Mrs. Hannah (Tolman) Pope was tall and prepossessing in her personal appearance.   She had a fine mind, and was fond of intellectual occupations.   She was a sincere Christian, devoted to her church and family; a woman of zeal and activity, ready to aid every good work.   She entered into her rest in the full assurance of a blessed immortality through the pardoning grace of Christ, May 19, 1852.

CHILDREN OF EBENEZER[6] AND HANNAH (TOLMAN).

I.   SUSANNA,[7] b. March 31, 1833 ; d. Jan. 2, 1848.

II.   HANNAH HALL,[7] b. July 13, 1835, graduated at Maplewood Institute, Pittsfield; resides in Dorchester.

III.   EDENEZER,[7] jr., b. April 29, 1838 ; entered Amherst College in 1858, and almost reached the close of the course, taking very high rank as a scholar and a Christian· Was prostrated by sickness, and d. at his home, Oct. 3, 1861.   We append resolutions passed by his class.

*Whereas*, It has pleased Divine Providence in its mysterious dealings to remove by death our beloved class-mate, Ebenezer Pope,

*Therefore Resolved*, That in our present bereavement we recognize the hand of Him who doeth all things well, and bow in humble submission to His will.

*Resolved*, That we mourn the loss of a dear brother, whose scholarly attainments and consistent life won for him our esteem and confidence.

*Resolved*, That to his afflicted friends we extend our heart-felt sympathies, and desire for them the sweetest consolation of Heavenly Grace, confidently believing that this sad dispensation has brought to him eternal joy.

*Resolved*, That in token of respect to his memory, we wear the usual badge of mourning for thirty days.

*Resolved*, That a copy of these resolutions be sent to the friends of the deceased, and also be published in the *Amherst Express*, *Springfield Republic*, and *Boston Journal*.

In behalf of the Senior Class.

WILLIAM MCGLATHEY, &#125;
FRANK G. CLARK, &#125; Committee.
JOSEPH C. CLIFFORD, &#125;

IV.  ABIGAIL GLOVER,⁷ b. Oct. 1, 1840; m. Charles B. Whitney, June 5, 1867.

V.  JOHN TOLMAN,⁷ b. Aug. 25, 1844; m. Oct. 10, 1878, Lizzie C. Hammond. Resides at Neponset. Is in real estate business in Boston.

---

## C, 2.

## THE FAMILY OF EDMUND⁶.

EDMUND,⁶ son of Edmund⁵ and Susanna (Rawson), b. Sept. 3, 1813; m. April 2, 1835, Ann, daughter of John and Nancy (Harrington) Walker, of Weston, b. March 13, 1813. His life was spent on the ancestral lands, in the occupation of farming. He was a man of dignified appearance, of well-balanced faculties; a member of the school committee, and otherwise honored by his fellow-citizens. He d. June 1, 1885, of pleuro-pneumonia. Children :

I.  JOHN ALFRED,⁷ b. Nov. 13, 1836; m. June 30, 1887, Mrs. Rebecca (Luce) Stanton, of Vineyard Haven; resides at Atlantic, in the town of Quincy.

II.  EDMUND,⁷ b. April 11, 1839. Is clerk with T. F. Edmunds & Co., importers, 61 Kilby Street, Boston. Resides at Atlantic.

III.  ANNA FRANCES,⁷ b. April 1, 1841; m. Oct. 27, 1859, Thomas Jefferson Glover, son of James Madison and Harriet (Gibbs) Glover. Resides at Dorchester Lower Mills. Children:

    1.  Edmund Thomas *Glover*, b. July 25, 1860.

    2.  Herbert Gibbs *Glover*, b. April 23, 1864.

IV.  ELLA AUGUSTA,⁷ b. April 29, 1844; m. Dec. 1, 1868, Henry Ballard Martin, son of Dea. Nathan C. and Augusta (Allen) Martin, of Milton Lower Mills. He is a merchant, clerk of the town of Milton, etc. Children :

    1.  Waldo Allen *Martin*, b. March 7, 1870.

    2.  Ella Pope *Martin*, b. March 4, 1873.

V.  MARY LYDIA,[7] b. April 23, 1847; m. July 30, 1872,
     Elijah Glover Hall, son of Elijah and Joanna (Sevey)
     Hall, of East Machias, Me.  He is a cabinet-maker;
     his business is in Harrison Square, Dorchester.  Re-
     sides at Atlantic station, in Quincy.  Children :

     1.  Annie Pope *Hall*, b. May 7, 1873.
     2.  Gertrude White *Hall*, b. March 29, 1875.
     3.  Edmund Pope *Hall*, b. Jan. 21, 1877.
     4.  Laura *Hall*, b. Nov. 11, 1884.

VI.  SUSANNA JANE,[7] b. Aug. 8, 1851; m. July 7, 1881,
     William Creighton Nelson, son of Angus and Mary
     (Simpson) Nelson, of Boston, b. Aug. 25, 1852.  They
     reside at Atlantic, in Quincy.  Children :

     1.  William Pope *Nelson*, b. Nov. 29, 1882; d. Feb. 4,
         1884.
     2.  Eleanor May *Nelson*, b. Jan. 15, 1884.

---

## C, 3.

## THE FAMILY OF SAMUEL[6].

SAMUEL,[6] son of Edmund[5] and Susanna (Rawson), b. March
30, 1817; m. May 15, 1839, *Jane*, dau. of John and Lydia
(Harrington) *Beath*, b. in Boston, March 29, 1817.  John Beath
was b. in Boston, Sept. 27, 1776; Lydia Harrington was b. in
Croyden, N. H.  Samuel Pope settled in Milton, upon a farm.
He went to California in October, 1849, where he engaged in
gold mining for a short time, but died of bilious fever, Aug. 20,
1850, at Doten's Bar, on the North Fork of the American
river.

[Extracts from a letter written by an associate of Samuel
Pope in California, under date of "Sacramento, Aug. 29, 1850."
"The ship 'Richmond' arrived at Benicia on the 6th of April.
. . . . The rest of the company arrived in San Francisco on
the 6th of June, and reached Benicia on the 9th.  Mr. Pope
had been well up to this time, excepting a slight attack of diar-
rhœa, accompanied by some rush of blood to the head."  . . . .

After describing their adventures on the way to the mines, and their work there, the writer speaks of the continuation of Mr. Pope's illness, which ripened into bilious intermittent fever, of which he died, Aug. 20, 1850. Then follows a pathetic account of the burial. "The miners of the region collected together to the number of fifty, when the 90th Psalm was read, after which the procession was formed. It consisted first of the bearers with the corpse ; then followed Messrs. Harrington and Eaton [his partners], next those of his friends who had come out with him in the " Richmond," and afterward the other miners, two by two. They proceeded to the grave, which was dug near a large oak tree, where one other person had been previously buried. When the coffin had been lowered the 14th chapter of John was read, and the grave was covered."

It was a terrible shock, indeed, to the family in Quincy, when this letter reached them. The widow, however, met her trial with Christian fortitude, and brought up her daughters to womanhood. Children :

I.　ABIGAIL GLOVER,[7] b. Feb. 19, 1840, in Milton ; m. Sept. 15, 1870, Henry Edwards of Quincy. They reside in San Francisco, Cal. He is a wholesale boot and shoe dealer.

II.　EMMA JANE,[7] b. April 27, 1841, in Milton ; m. Nov. 3, 1864, Charles Thomas Reed, of Quincy, son of Thomas and Elizabeth (Hayward) Reed of Braintree. He resides in Quincy ; is organist of the Congregational church, is a salesman in Hunt & Russell's boot and shoe store, 124 Congress Street, Boston. She died Dec. 1, 1870.

III.　SAMUEL DANA,[7] b. July 28, 1846, in Quincy ; d. Nov. 28, 1847.

# CHAPTER X

# THE SEVENTH GENERATION.

## SECTION A.

DESCENDANTS OF DOCTOR RALPH.

### A, 1.

### THE FAMILY OF LUTHER WARREN[7].

LUTHER WARREN,[7] son of Ralph[6] and Abigail (Swan), was born in Stoughton in 1783. He m. Rebecca Edes, dau. of James and Rebecca (Edes) Avery, born in Boston, Feb. 11, 1785. Joined the church in Dorchester, Nov. 3, 1806, his daughter, "Rebecca Trescott," being baptized the same day. A second daughter, "Louisa Ann" [afterward called Louisa Atherton], was baptized Oct. 25, 1812, her mother joining the church at the same time. A third daughter, "Abigail Hammond," was baptized Feb. 25, 1816. Not far from that time he removed to Lubec, Me., having been for some time in the employ of his uncles, Frederick[6] and William[6]. His wife died in the year 1818. He m. (2) Nov. 10, 1821, Mary Walker of Lubec, born March 22, 1799. He died in the prime of life, Feb., 1823. His widow d. Aug. 8, 1879. Children :

I.  REBECCA TRESCOTT,[8] b. Sept., 1805, was married to William T. West, son of Eliakim and Mary (Hall) West, of East Machias, Me., b. Sept. 29, 1803.

She was a cheery, motherly woman, who had the secret of content-ment for herself and comfort for others. This in spite of much trouble which came to her; but she had strong faith and character. Mr. West died in Machias in 1842. She afterwar s resided in East Machias, where she died of apoplexy, Dec. 30, 1857. Children :

1. Mary Penniman *West*, b. June 2, 1827 ; m. Anson Wiswell of East Machias; d. ——.    Had no children.
2. Rebecca Avery *West*, b. Jan. 24, 1830 ; d. May 7, 1833.
3. Gideon O'Brien *West*, b. in Machias, Sept. 23, 1831 ; married, May, 1855, Almira Louisa Sevey, of East Machias.   No children.   She died, after a beautiful life, Aug., 1873.
4. Rebecca Edes *West*, b. Feb. 25, 1836 ; d. June 19, 1837.
5. James Edward *West*, b. in Machias, Sept. 2, 1838 ; m. Feb. 18, 1863, Georgianna Isabel, dau. of Gideon Elder and Abbie Sarah (Farnsworth) Morey, of Machias.   Children, born in Silver City, Idaho Territory : Carrie Vinton *West*, b. April 24, 1867.   George Edward *West*, b. Dec. 13, 1868.
6. Martha Emma *West*, b. May 3, 1842 ; d. Aug. 3, 1845.

II. JAMES EDES,[8] b. 1808 ; grew to manhood ; became mate of a brig.   His vessel sailed away from her port and never returned.   The fourth case among the descendants of Colonel Frederick[6].   He was unmarried.

III. HARRIET CARTER,[8] b. April 19, 1810, was married, Nov. 1, 1833, to Albert Penniman Cushing, son of Perez and Sarah (Billings) Cushing, b. in Boston Dec. 1, 1810. He was a blacksmith, worked at Machias some years, then at East M. many more.   Was a "well-set" man in body and mind, alive to all the questions of the day in town and nation ; was a critical listener in church and elsewhere, and a very intelligent talker ; a good neighbor and friend.

He d. April 30, 1884, after passing the golden anniversary of his wedding.   Mrs. Cushing resides in East Machias.

### *Children born in Machias.*

1. William Chauncy *Cushing*, b. Sept. 20, 1836 ; d. same day.
2. Edward Kent *Cushing*, b. May 18, d. May 28, 1839.
3. Sarah Rebecca *Cushing*, b. Jan. 30, 1843 ; d. Jan. 31, 1843.

*Born in East Machias.*

4.  George Henry *Cushing*, b. March 9, 1847 ; m. June 30,
    1870, Sarah Isabelle McGurk, b. in Eastport, Me., May
    19, 1849. He is a telegraph operator at Eastport, Me.
    She d. in Eastport, Nov. 8, 1882. Children :

    (1.)  Mary Pope *Cushing*, b. April 14, 1872.
    (2.)  Kate *Cushing*, b. July 3, 1873 ; d. Aug. 14, 1873.
    (3.)  Emily Wood *Cushing*, b. May 28, 1877.
    (4.)  Georgia Isabella *Cushing*, March 2, 1882.

5.  James Warren *Cushing*, b. Dec. 26, 1848. Resides at
    Eastport, Me. Furnished the principal part of the
    statistics of his grandfather's family for this book.

IV.  Louisa Atherton,[8] b. June 30, 1812, at Dorchester ;
     m. Feb. 25, 1830, at Lubec, Me., Josiah P. Davis, b.
     at Chichester, N. H., Oct. 29, 1804. She d. Nov. 13,
     1883. He d. Feb. 11, 1884 ; fell dead in the street.
     Children :

1.  Samuel Pope *Davis*, b. Nov. 27, 1830 ; m. May 3, 1862,
    Belinda S. Robinson, b. May 3, 1838, at Lubec, Me.
    Children :

    (1.)  Myrtie U. *Davis*, b. March 28, 1863.
    (2.)  Fannie L. *Davis*, b. April 27, 1871, at Strong's
          Prairie, Wisconsin.

2.  Thaddeus W. *Davis*, b. Aug. 4, 1832 ; d. April 2, 1867,
    at Hillsborough, N. H. ; m. Almira Robinson.

3.  Andrew Jackson *Davis*, b. Aug. 12, 1835 ; m. March 29,
    1863, Louisa Chaloner Fenwick, b. Jan. 16, 1843, at
    Lubec, Me. Capt. Andrew J. Davis d. at sea, two days
    out of Aspinwall, Nov. 2, 1878. His widow m. second,
    Dr. Harrison Richardson, of Portland, Me. Children :

    (1.)  Charles Starbird *Davis*, b. Dec. 13, 1864.
    (2.)  Henry Dewey *Davis*, b. Oct. 13, 1870, at Mil-
          bridge, Me.
    (3.)  Camilla Ursula *Davis*, b. Aug. 26, 1876, at Mil-
          bridge, Me.

4.  Harriet Maria *Davis*, b. Sept. 5, 1837 ; m. Nov. 16, 1856,
    Joseph W. Allan, b. in Lubec, May 14, 1834. Children :

    (1.)  Sophila F. *Allan*, b. Jan. 27, 1858, at Lubec, Me.;
m. March 7, 1877, at Necedah, Wisconsin, to
William M. Newlin, b. Sept. 14, 1850.

    (2.)  Ursula I. *Allan*, b. Dec. 9, 1859, at Lubec; m.
Feb. 6, 1884, at Necedah, Wisconsin, to Edwin
M. Lawrence, b. Aug. 9, 1857, at Lubec, Me.
*Child*, Glenn Allan *Lawrence*, b. Nov. 24,
1884.

    (3.)  Nellie A. *Allan*, b. Oct. 15, 1862; m. Feb. 6, 1884,
to Arthur L. Kingston, b. at Necedah, Wisconsin, February, 1861. *Child*, Arthur L. *Kingston*, jr., b. Feb. 9, 1885, at Warner, Dakota.

    (4.)  Frank W. *Allan*, b. Feb. 29, 1864, at Lubec, Me.

    (5.)  Rena B. *Allan*, b. Dec. 17, 1869, at Strong's
Prairie, Wisconsin.

    (6.)  Louisa A. *Allan*, b. Jan. 14, 1872, at Strong's
Prairie, Wis.; d. May 26, 1873, at Necedah,
Wis.

5.  Cyrus *Davis*,  } b. April 22, 1840; { drowned Jan. 1, 1861.
6.  Silas *Davis*,  }                        { d. Oct. 16, 1841.

7.  Ursula I. *Davis*, b. May 11, 1843; d. Aug. 25, 1854.

8.  Luther James *Davis*, b. Jan. 3, 1846; m. Dec. 16, 1869,
Ella Beyanson, of Lubec, Me., b. Aug. 2, 1850.

*Children, born in Boston.*

    (1.)  Ella Louisa *Davis*, b. Nov. 27, 1870; d. May 19,
1871.

    (2.)  Lillian Estelle *Davis*, b. Sept. 16, 1872.

    (3.)  Ernest Winfield *Davis*, b. March 19, 1881.

    (4.)  Alice *Davis*, b. Aug. 18, 1883.

9.  Orlando Chester *Davis*, b. Jan. 10, 1852.

10.  Omer Pasha *Davis*, b. Nov. 10, 1853; m. Dec. 25, 1880,
at Worcester, Mass., to Lizzie Caroline Bingham, b. at
Grafton, Mass., Sept. 24, 1861. *Child*: Myrton Omer
*Davis*, b. Dec. 8, 1883, at Worcester, Mass.

V.  ABIGAIL HAMMOND,[3] dau. of Luther Warren[7] and
Rebecca (Edes) Avery, b. 1815, was m. to Neal Pettigrove. Removed to a Western State. They had
children. She d. ———. No particulars received.

VI.  LEMUEL TRESCOTT,[8] b. in 1816; d. in infancy.

CHILD OF LUTHER WARREN[7] AND MARY C. (WALKER).

VII.  IRENE MATILDA,[8] b. Jan. 28, 1823, was married first,
      Nov. 25, 1847, to George McGregor, at Lubec.  They
      had no children.  He d. Oct. 2, 1851.

      She was m. second, Nov. 23, 1880, to Andrew
      Foster, son of Samuel and Comfort (Scott) Foster,
      and grandson of Col. Benjamin Foster, a distinguished
      pioneer of the Machias settlement.  He was for many
      years a jeweller at Machias.

      They reside in East Machias, Me.

---

### A, 2.

## THE FAMILY OF JAMES,[7] OF DORCHESTER.

JAMES,[7] second son of Ralph[6] and Abigail (Swan), was
born in Stoughton, Aug. 29, 1792.  His father dying, while yet
a young man, left him, at the age of five years, with his grandfather, Col. Frederic Pope, where he remained some years.  He
afterward went to live with an uncle near by, and when about
17 years of age went to Dorchester and learned the trade of a
carpenter.

As a master builder, he was highly esteemed for the excel-
lence and thoroughness of his work, as well as for his good
judgment, at a time when the builder was obliged to be his own
architect.  He had an amiable disposition, and was one of the
kindest and most affectionate of fathers.

Generous almost to a fault, no one who sought assistance was
ever refused, and in all charities, public as well as private, he
was willing to do more than his part.  His kindness of heart
was plainly shown in his face, and his greeting was especially
cordial.  He inherited a strong constitution, all four of his
grandparents living to an advanced age.  His mother lived to
be ninety years.  One sister lived to be eighty-two, and another
nearly ninety-two years.

He had a large family, six sons and three daughters, all of
whom, with the exception of two sons, are now living.

He was always constant at church, and for many years was Deacon of what is known as the "Third Religious Society" of Dorchester, holding that office at the time of his death, which occurred on July 17, 1866, of pleurisy fever.

On Jan. 30, 1814, he was married to Elizabeth Lake, by Rev. Dr. Harris, of Dorchester. She was born in Taunton, Somersetshire, England, May 15, 1792, and came to Boston when about three years old. When about ten years of age she moved to Dorchester, her mother dying shortly after. Refined and gentle in manner, through her whole life she was thoughtful of others; and, though caring lovingly for those in her own home, was ever a ready respondent to the frequent calls of the sick or of those in trouble, carrying peace and comfort to many an aching heart. Though very small, and never rugged, her unbounded faith, hopefulness, and cheerfulness continued through her long, useful, active life, busy almost to the last. She was considered a very remarkable woman, and her presence sought as much by the young as the old.

Mr. and Mrs. Pope lived together fifty-two years, with scarcely a break in their large family circle for half a century. Children and grandchildren, more than forty in number, gathered around them in the old homestead, at the Thanksgiving and birthday festivals, making the house ring with merriment, never to be forgotten by those who participated.

She survived her husband twenty years, and died of pneumonia, Feb. 28, 1886, at the age of 93 years 10 months, leaving a precious memory to all who knew her, to whom she seemed to be a very living embodiment of purity and goodness.

### Children, born in Dorchester.

I.   JAMES,[8] b. July 28, 1815.  [See next chapter, A, 1.]

II.  ALBERT,[8] b. Oct. 10, 1816.  [See next chapter, A, 2.]

III. SARAH ELIZABETH,[8] b. Jan. 12, 1819.  Resides in Dorchester.

IV.  HENRY,[8] b. Feb. 26, 1821.  [See next chapter, A, 3.]

V.   WILLIAM FRANCIS,[8] b. Aug. 5, 1823.  [See next chapter, A, 4.]

VI.  GEORGE,[8] b. May 18, 1825.  [See next chapter, A, 5.]

VII.  HARRIS WEEMAN,⁸ b. March 24, 1829. [See next chapter, A, 6.]

VIII.  MARY JANE,⁸ b. Oct. 25, 1831. Has been a teacher in the public schools of Dorchester for some years. Has assisted much in gathering materials for this work.

IX.  MARIA LOUISA,⁸ b. Jan. 20, 1833; m. in Dorchester, Dec. 25, 1860, Frank Seabury Hall, son of Timothy and Mary (Wentworth) Hall, of Portsmouth, where he was born, Feb. 2, 1835. He is manager of the New York branch of Baker's Chocolate Manufacturing Company. Resides at Glenridge, N. J. Children:

  1.  Frank Wentworth *Hall*, b. Sept., 1861; d. May 1, 1866.

  2.  Alice Louise *Hall*, b. July 21, 1863.

---

A, 3.

## THE FAMILY OF COLONEL WILLIAM⁷.

WILLIAM,⁷ son of Samuel Ward⁶ and Mary (Wood), b. March 30, 1787; was married in Boston, by Rev. Charles M. Lowell, D. D., Sept. 27, 1810, to Peggy Dawes, dau. of William and Lucy (Swan) Billings of Boston, b. March 6, 1788.

The following extracts are taken from the book entitled "Genealogy of a Portion of the Pope Family," published by Colonel William Pope in 1862.

"WILLIAM POPE, eldest son of Samuel Ward and Mary (Wood) Pope, was born in Charleston, S. C., March 30, 1787. . . .

His parents dying when he was quite young, he was brought up in the family of his grandfather until he arrived at the age of eighteen years. He then went to Dorchester to live with his uncles, Frederick and William Pope, who were engaged in the lumber business, and resided in Dorchester. He . . . went to Machias, in the District of Maine, and established himself in the same business in November, 1807.

. . . With his uncles in Dorchester, he had acquired a considerable knowledge of the lumber business, which was then the principal business of the District of Maine, and he fixed upon Machias as his future sphere of business operations. . . .

He took a vessel, and managed to convey his property to a lean market, and with the proceeds, small as they were, he bought a small farm, and, with others whom he found ready to join him, built a saw-mill, which, with the farm, made plenty of work, but small pay. He continued in the farming business several years. . . .

After having spent three years in Machias, he returned to Boston, in the year 1810, and was married to Peggy Dawes Billings, on the 27th day of September in that year. He returned to Machias again after his marriage. . . .

In the year 1821, when the Town of Machias was divided, Colonel Pope was elected one of the Board of Selectmen of East Machias, and continued to be elected to that office until he declined nomination. When Governor Kent was chosen Governor of Maine, Colonel Pope was elected as one of his Council, and also received the appointment of Justice of the Peace. He held several commissions in Maine and Massachusetts under the Governors of each State.

Colonel Pope held many offices in the militia of Maine, from a Lieutenant to a Colonel of a regiment, which office he at length resigned, and declined nomination as Brigadier General. . . .

Colonel Pope lived in Machias thirty-four years, and during the whole time he was actively engaged in business of some kind. In the war of 1812, he often joined with others in taking a vessel, and going out to sea for the purpose of capturing some of the British cruisers on our coast, which were lying in wait to seize on our merchant vessels; but without much success. The lumber business, however, was his principal pursuit, through all the changes and restrictions occasioned by the stringency of the times, furnishing dimension timber for large buildings, railroad bridges, factories, etc. He removed to Boston in April of 1841, with a part of his family, and resided at No. 2 Garland Street.

After his removal to Boston, he was elected to several offices of trust and honor. In the year 1844, he served one term in the Common Council; subsequently, four years in the Board of Aldermen; two years in the Massachusetts House of Representatives; and as Director in the Boylston Bank from its organization in 1845; was once elected president of the same bank, but declined the honor. When he removed to Boston, he took with him his wife and two daughters, and three youngest sons, viz.: Andrew J., Edwin and George W. Pope; and left in Machias his four eldest sons,— William Henry, Samuel W., John Adams and James Otis Pope, to carry on business there. The senior partner purchased a wharf on Harrison

Avenue, in Boston, which had been stocked by Wm. Pope & Sons previous to their removal to Boston, and conducted by Carter and Willard. The lumber business was also carried on in Maine, at East Machias, Machias and Whitneyville, by William H. Pope, Samuel W. and James Otis Pope, under the name and firm of S. W. Pope & Co.; and also by the same firm at Columbia on Pleasant River, Me., under the name of George Harris & Co., George Harris owning one third of the stock. On the 1st day of January, 1860, the three younger brothers were received into the firm of Wm. Pope & Sons; viz., James Otis, of East Machias, Edwin and George W. Pope, of Boston.

After the discovery of gold in California, the firm sent out a large quantity of lumber and other goods consigned to Macondray & Co., at San Francisco. Subsequently, in 1849, Andrew J. Pope went out there himself, and resumed the business in his own name, which was a fortunate movement. The business was then carried on in Boston under the name of Wm. Pope & Sons; in East Machias, Me., by S. W. Pope & Co.; and on the Pacific coast by A. J. Pope, for the company of Wm. Pope & Sons, as also at Puget Sound in Washington Territory. They have built more or less vessels every year at East Machias; some for coasting and West India trade, some sent to the Pacific Ocean, to be managed by A. J. Pope & Co. They have had several ships, barques, brigs, schooners, etc.; some in the coasting trade, some in foreign trade with China, the East Indies, the Sandwich Islands and Australia.

The lumber business was conducted by the company of Wm. Pope & Sons, for nearly thirty years, keeping no individual accounts between themselves and the company until January 1, 1860. On November 11, 1861, the senior partner, Colonel William Pope, of Boston, retired from the company.

Throughout his whole life, Colonel Pope has developed a firm and even character, built upon the sure foundation of honesty, truth and justice. Inheriting from his ancestors a mild and compassionate nature, — strict integrity, united with sound judgment, in all his acts he has shone forth in the same just and noble traits of character.

When he was in the Massachusetts Legislature, the question of abolishing capital punishment came up before the House; he voted for it, exposing himself to the censure of many of his friends.

In his religious views, Colonel Pope was always liberal and modest, and believed more in right doing than in much talking about a future world. When cast in society among those whose views differed from his own, he associated himself with them, and was never afraid to listen to the instructions of ministers who maintained more ardent and stringent sentiments. He invariably worshipped with religious denominations wherever his lot might be cast, and cheerfully contributed his share for their support from an inherent respect for the ministry and public worship, and for their uses in improving and advancing the condition of mankind ; and with the belief that it was better to educate a family under almost any religious society, than without the restraints of any, and also believing that no minister ever preached who did not lay down a better rule of action in life than man ever followed.

William Pope was married to Peggy Dawes Billings the 27th day of September, 1810, by Rev. Charles Lowell, D.D. She was the daughter of William Billings, of Boston, who was distinguished in his time for singing and the composition of music, musical teaching, etc. It is said of him that he was the first author and publisher of music in this country, and that none have ever come after him who excelled him in musical talent or artistic genius. He was the son of William Billings, of Dorchester and Stoughton, and Mary (Badlam) Billings, of Weymouth, who were married December 13, 1741-2, and settled in Stoughton; grandson of William and —— (Crehore) Billings, of Milton, who were married June 17, 1717, and settled in Stoughton ; and great grandson of Roger and Sarah Billings, of Dorchester. William Billings married, 1st, Mary Leonard, of Stoughton, and, 2d, Lucy Swan, daughter of Major Robert and Rachel (Draper) Swan, of Stoughton (formerly of Dedham), July 26, 1774, and removed to Boston. Their daughter, Peggy Dawes Billings, was born in Boston, March 6, 1788. Her parents dying when she was quite young, she went to live in Stoughton with her aunt Capen, the wife of Capt. William Capen, and resided there until she was eighteen years of age. She died in Boston, at No. 2 Garland Street, February 8, 1862, after a sickness of twenty years, aged 73 years and 11 months.

## OBITUARY NOTICE OF MRS. POPE.

Mrs. Pope was married early in life, and accompanied her husband to Machias, Me., where they lived thirty-four years, and had twelve children. They then removed to Boston, her native place. She was a woman of great energy and activity ; rearing her children and managing her large family with great care and industry. Her house might emphatically have been called her sphere of action, so constantly and

untiringly did she labor there, sacrificing her inclination to accompany
her husband on his business excursions, which were frequent and
which would have given her the opportunity of visiting her friends and
relatives, to her conscientious and unostentatious discharge of household duties. Nor was she neglectful of her neighbors. The sick
found her ever ready to contribute to their happiness by her counsel
and sympathy, while the poor ever found in her a bountiful benefac-
tress. Her doors were open to all, and her house might almost have
been called a hotel, so constantly was it filled by friends and even
strangers visiting that part of the country; and never will they forget
her cordial greeting and hospitable attentions. Possessing an affectionate disposition, great integrity of character, and a genial temperament, she was an agreeable companion and friend, until disease laid
his hand upon her, depriving her of all which could render life a bless-
ing to herself or her friends. Her sickness was painful and protracted;
taking from her, her speech, and the entire use of her limbs. Her
children lose in her one of the best of mothers, and her husband a
faithful wife."

### OBITUARY NOTICE OF COL. WILLIAM POPE.

"The death of Col. William Pope, which occurred on Sunday, Nov.
6, has already been noticed in several of the daily papers ; but a more
extended reference seems due at once to the man himself and to the
community. A life so honorably and successfully lived deserves the
tribute of praise ; while, for the good of society, as an eminent example of many worthy qualities, it were unjust to let it pass without some
special word to enforce its helpful lesson.

Col. Pope was noted for his modesty, having little faith in noise and
presumption; while, with this trait, he showed some of the best elements of character—strength, persistence, plainness, integrity, love of
country and all public interests, practical religion, sincere and endur-
ing friendship, and great domestic affection. In all these respects he
stood prominent. He had largeness of nature, with unusual symmetry
and proportion. None would fail to mark his presence and bearing,
while, at the same time, it would be difficult to say what was the particular trait of character that had arrested attention. His body was
well inspired by the presence and power of his higher life ; its athletic
amplitude was still full of beauty ; its ruggedness fitting it for hard work
and long endurance, was not gross and earthy, but eminently refined
and finished. Hence with equal fitness of presence, he could stand
in the midst of the lumber enterprise, at the head of a regiment of

stalwart Maine militia, or sit with Gov. Kent's Council, or with the
Board of Aldermen of our own city.

"Persistence was a ruling trait of his character. He insisted on
carrying his point, and wind and tide turned against him in vain. His
will had often to bend during the troublous times of 1812, when he
was commencing in life ; it never broke. It rose elastic and turned
disasters into victories. He out-rode many a commercial gale that
swept down and ruined the less firm in purpose.

"He was a man of great moral integrity, and confidence and trade
came naturally to his counting-room. He was plain and true. None
doubted his word. He disdained to make commerce a strategy, but
sought rather to base it on the high principles of industry and justice
—not a narrow and legal, but a broad and magnanimous justice.
Business was *life* with him, and a fit theatre for the exercise of the
noblest virtues. He gave to it his conscience and heart, and won a
name from the midst of traffic that stands untarnished by stain or
blot.

"He was an ardent patriot. He entered heartily into the spirit of
the late national campaign, and saw no honorable course to be pursued but to conquer rebellion and make liberty and equal rights uni-
versal, having nothing to do with concession and compromise. He
was equally friendly to all public interests, civil or social or religious,
and gave much time and money for their promotion. He loved his
race. He had a humanitarian heart. He never lost hope in even the
worst, but believed all would be, at some time, restored to God and
goodness. His theology was that of the liberal schools, and for many
years, even up to the Sunday preceding the one on which his death
occurred, he worshiped with the Universalist parish now occupying
the Shawmut church. Worship was ever a joy to him. He delighted
in religious conversation. The conference room he never failed to
visit while health and strength were spared to him. His piety was
simple, central, real. He was no sectarian, but of a catholic spirit,
and could offer his devotions at any altar, with any sincere people.

"At home he was full of peace and sunshine. He loved his family
with a constant and generous love, which was gladly and tenderly re-
quited. He has left them the treasure of a name that shall be
ever fragrant in their memories — an 'inheritance for his children's
children.' "

The writer counts it a high privilege to be able to place on
record his own testimony to the high worth and honorable life
of Colonel William Pope.

He was a man of fine face and form; his manners dignified and polite; his words well chosen and to the point. He possessed great sagacity in business and in public affairs. Had complete *poise* in holding and carrying out his views and plans, not troubled with questions or difficulties after he had once deliberately chosen a line of belief or a course of action.

Few men ever had an experience equal to his, holding together six sons with himself — all who lived to maturity — in co-operative business life; and the harmony of that co-operation was " not strained," but had the full naturalness of· a father with his " boys " and brothers with brothers. One of the results of this was accumulation of wealth quite remarkable for those times and the lines of business engaged in.

Probably much credit is due to the sons for great energy and willingness, as they grew up and cheerfully joined with their father in his business and in practical ways; but chief praise is doubtless due to the admirable training and harmonizing force of Colonel and Mrs. Pope.

They lived to enjoy a great deal in their children and grand-children, and in the comforts of life.

Yet they had sorrows, losing their first babe at two months old; another at about the same age; and a third at five and a half years. Still more heart-rending than even these bereavements was the loss of their son, JOHN ADAMS[8].

He was an excellent scholar, of high promise. Fitted for college at twelve years, but thought too young to enter, he cared less about study than other things, when a few years had passed; so he entered the firm, and alternated in residence between Machias and Boston, after his father removed to the latter place. Popular and attractive, he was elected Colonel of the same regiment of militia his father had before commanded.                                    •

He took passage from Machias in the brig " Martha Ann," one of the vessels of the firm, Dec. 5, 1843. In a heavy snow-storm which followed, the vessel was badly damaged, as was seen by other distressed vessels, but no help reached her, and she became a total wreck. No tidings ever came respecting any on board of her. It is supposed they all perished.

*Children born in Machias, Me.*

I. WILLIAM BILLINGS,⁸ b. July 11, 1811; d. Sept. 10, 1811.

II. WILLIAM HENRY,⁸ b. Sunday, March 14, 1813. [See next chapter, A, 7.]

III. SAMUEL WARD,⁸ b. Tuesday, March 7, 1815. [See next chapter, A, 8.]

IV. LUCY SWAN,⁸ b. Wednesday, Nov. 20, 1816; d. Jan. 27, 1817.

V. JOHN ADAMS,⁸ b. Monday, Jan. 19, 1818; d. Dec. 15, 1843 ; lost at sea.

VI. ANDREW JACKSON,⁸ b. Thursday, Jan. 6, 1820. [See next chapter, A, 9.]

VII. JAMES OTIS,⁸ b. Thursday, Feb. 17, 1822. [See next chapter, A, 10.]

VIII. ELIZA OTIS,⁸ b. Thursday, April 1, 1824 ; was married, June 9, 1850, in Boston, to Edward Faxon, son of Oren and Theodora (Billings) Faxon, b. in Waltham, Oct. 12, 1824 (twin brother, Edwin). Mr. Faxon was a whole-souled, energetic man. He was a member of the Boston Handel and Haydn Society, and foremost among its zealous promoters, while also a very fine tenor singer. He was a dealer in supplies for piano manufacture. He died Jan. 10, 1886. Mrs. Eliza Otis (Pope) Faxon died May 20, 1869. Children :

1. Ella Maria *Faxon*, b. June 26, 1851, was married June 23, 1875, to Donald McLeod Belcher. *Children*, Edward Faxon *Belcher*, b. April 7, 1877 ; Olive Mills *Belcher*, b. Feb. 2, 1879.

2. Gertrude Eliza *Faxon*, b. Oct. 22, 1853, was married, Oct. 16, 1875, to Clarence Ellery Hay, b. July 31, 1854. *Child*, Marion *Hay*, b. June 25, 1881.

3. Edward Pope *Faxon*, b. Dec. 30, 1855.

4. Florence Atherton *Faxon*, b. Sept. 10, 1859; was married Nov., 1885, to George Frederick Spaulding, b. April, 1859.

5. George Huntington *Faxon*, b. Nov. 28, 1864.

IX.   EDWIN,[8] b. Thursday, May 30, 1826. [See next chapter, A, 11.]

X.    JULIA,[6] b. Sunday, Oct. 5, 1828 ; d. April 27, 1833.

XI.   GEORGE WASHINGTON,[8] b. Jan. 30, 1832. [See next chapter, A, 12.]

XII.  HARRIET ELIZABETH,[8] b. Nov. 19, 1834; was married in Boston, May 9, 1872, by Rev. William A. Mandell, of Cambridge, to Richard Hopkins Young, son of Captain Joseph and Olive (Ames) Young of Camden, Me., born Sept. 27, 1841. Joseph was one of the nineteen children of Ebenezer Young, of Matinicus Island, Me.

Richard H. Young became a school-teacher. In 1862 entered the 26th Maine Vol. Inf., as Sergeant Major. After the close of its term of service, helped organize the eleventh Corps d'Afrique, and served as 1st Lieutenant and Adjutant of that regiment until 1864.

Was a phonographer, delivered lectures, etc., until difficulty of sight led to a change of occupation. Purchased an estate in Westboro, and keeps an extensive poultry breeding and poulterers' supply establishment, called " Lilac Hedge Poultry Farm."

*Children born in Boston.*

1.   William Henry *Young*, b. Sept. 26, 1874.
2.   Harriet Pope *Young*, b. Sept. 2, 1877.

---

A, 4.

## THE FAMILY OF FREDERICK,[7] JR.

FREDERICK,[7] jr., son of Frederick[6] and Mary (Pierce), born in Dorchester, March 28, 1806 ; married, May 29, 1829, Sally B. Phillips, born in Weymouth, Sept. 29, 1805.

He learned the carpenter's trade of Mr. Veazie, of Quincy. He carried on the business of house-building in Weymouth many years. Was elected captain of the militia.

Was a genial, friendly man, who gained a warm place in the hearts of many friends. He died Oct. 5, 1874. Children :

I.  SARAH ANN,[8] b. Aug. 7, 1830; m. May 1, 1852, Theodore
    E. Waters, of Cambridge, Mass. He was a sergeant
    in the 4th Mass. Vol. Inf.; d. in Cambridge, October,
    1863. Children :

    1.  Ella M. *Waters*, b. Oct. 22, 1853; d. November, 1864.
    2.  Theodore O. *Waters*, b. April 12; d. August, 1859.
    The mother died at Weymouth, May 25, 1859.

II. MARIA WESLEY,[8] b. July 12, 1833; m. April 18, 1851,
    Charles F. Pray, son of George and Octavia Pray, of
    Weymouth. He was captain of Co. E, 18th Mass., and
    fell June 3, 1864. Children :

    1.  Ada M. *Pray*, b. June 27, 1852; m. Jan. 1, 1874,
        George W. Jones, of Quincy. Children :

        (1.) Sadie M. *Jones*, b. Aug. 26, 1874. (2.) Alfred
        R. *Jones*, b. April 6, 1878. (3.) Pauline *Jones*, b.
        Dec. 7, 1879.

    2.  Elsie C. *Pray*, b. Aug. 2, 1854; m. Oct. 7, 1876,
        Henry A. Poe, of Boston. Children :

        (1.) Reine M. *Poe*, b. Nov. 15, 1877. (2.) Harry C.
        *Poe*, b. Nov. 30, 1879. (3.) Aubrey L. *Poe*, b. March
        8, 1882.

    3.  Antoinette *Pray*, b. March 14, 1857.

III. FREDERIC CLINTON,[8] b. March 15, 1835; m. March, 1870,
     Martha Gregory, of Boston. He served his country in
     the War of the Rebellion, being a member of Company
     A, 42d Mass. Vol. Inf. Resides at Weymouth.

IV.  WARREN WEBSTER,[8] b. March 5, 1838. [See next chapter,
     A, 13.]

-----

## A, 5.

## THE FAMILY OF SAMUEL[7].

SAMUEL,[7] son of Frederick[6] and Mary (Pierce), born in
Dorchester, Sept. 11, 1809; married, June 25, 1837, *Sarah Stet-
son*, daughter of Stephen and Roxalina (Eaton) *Mellish*, of
Walpole, N. H.

He was a large, fine-looking man ; had admirable business qualities; was a delightful companion in home and social circles ; had the courtly manners of a "gentleman of the old school."

Spent some of his early years in commercial life, at Worcester. Resided for a time in Roxbury, but for upwards of thirty years in Cambridge, his business being in Boston, or from that as a centre, extending somewhat into other States. He retired from active business in 1863. He died Feb. 26, 1886. Children :

I.   FREDERIC,[8] b. June 19, 1838; is an architect. Has planned and superintended the construction of a large number of buildings in Boston, several of the most extensive wholesale stores, blocks of offices, "Back Bay" residences, etc. Resides in Boston.

II.  SARAH EMMA,[8] b. Aug. 9, 1840. Resides with her mother in Cambridge.

III. ANGELA,[8] b. July 16, 1842 ; d. Sept. 10, 1843.

IV.  EUGENE ALEXANDER,[8] b. Aug. 3, 1846. [See next chapter, A, 14.]

---

## A, 6.

## THE FAMILY OF JAMES[7].

JAMES,[7] son of Frederick[6] and Mary (Pierce), b. in Dorchester, Nov. 23, 1811 ; m. in Methuen, Nov. 22, 1835, Eunice, daughter of Marshall and Susanna (Gardner) *Thaxter*, of Machias, Me., b. Jan. 10, 1810.

James[7] was taken by his father on one of his voyages to the lumber port of Machias, in 1820, and left, for a visit with his eldest sister, Mrs. Hill. He became so valuable a member of the household, and so happy in the family and town, that he remained permanently. He revisited Dorchester more than once, and spent two years at one time, but preferred the new State. He was a diligent helper on the farm, and afterward in the store of his brother-in-law. On reaching his majority, he became first a clerk and then a partner of Dea. William A. Crocker, in his store, and in the building and management of coasting vessels. He was a member of the Maine House of Representatives in 1841-2, and obtained the charter of the Franklin Railroad. Was much in town office, and county treasurer several terms. He became the accountant of the Whitneyville and Machiasport Mill and Land Company, in 1848 ; joined his East Machias cousins, S. W. Pope & Co., in purchasing a large share of that property, the whole business, timber-lands, mills, railroad and wharves being consolidated under the style of The Whitneyville Agency. He was chosen superintendent. He removed to Whitneyville, May 4, 1853, and still resides there.

He sold his interest in the business in 1866, and retired from it wholly in 1870. He engaged in trade in Machias for a few years ; later he invested in timber-lands and mills at Nictaux Falls, Nova Scotia. In 1880 and 1881 he served on the State Valuation Committee, at Augusta.

He married, Nov. 22, 1835, *Eunice*, daughter of Marshall and Susanna (Gardner) *Thaxter*, of Machias, born Jan. 10, 1810. She was educated at Machias and at Washington Academy, East Machias ; taught school successfully a number of terms ; kept her intellectual life active amid all the cares of motherhood, and was a very earnest Christian, at home and in the communities where she lived. She did much to stimulate her children and others in the study of all the true, the beautiful and the good. Through the loss of many children and other relatives, and in her own ill health, her faith grew riper and her hope stronger. She fell "asleep in Jesus," Sept. 27, 1861.

No language can express fitly the love and respect the writer feels toward her,— so much to him while living, so great a loss when dying, so hoped for in the coming Home !

> " Our eyes are weak,
>     The mists of earth have dimmed them.
>         Their chariots of fire
>     We see not,— but, to Him who hath redeemed them,
>         Our loved ones have gone higher."

### CHILDREN OF JAMES[7] AND EUNICE (THAXTER).

#### Born in Machias, Me.

I.   A SON,[8] b. and d. Oct. 22, 1836.

II.  JAMES OSCAR,[8] b. Sept. 2, 1837. Possessed great talent and had many winning qualities. Was assistant bookkeeper in the office of his father at Whitneyville, a while ; went to California as a sailor, but on arriving in San Francisco entered the employ of Andrew J. Pope and continued in the firm of Pope & Talbot several years. Embarking in business on

his own account at Carson, Nevada, he prospered
well ; but was taken ill of climatic difficulty, and died
in San Francisco, Cal., Jan. 4, 1862. He was
tenderly cared for by kind friends, especially members
of the Young Men's Christian Association, in which
he had been an active worker and officer.

III.   CHARLES FREDERIC,[6] b. Dec. 27, 1838 ; d. Nov. 27, 1840.
IV.   JULIA HELEN,[8] b. March 12, 1840 ; d. June 26, 1847.
V.    CHARLES HENRY,[8] b. Oct. 18, 1841. [See next chapter,
A, 15.]
VI.   SARAH HILL,[8] b. April 11, 1845 ; d. Feb. 16, 1847.
                        "Our Pond Lily."
VII.  WILLIAM HERBERT,[8] b. March 22, d. Oct. 26, 1847.
VIII. LUCY EMMA,[8] b. Oct. 5, 1848 ; a pupil for several terms
in the school of the Misses Springer, Brunswick, Me.;
married Joseph Allen Bacheller, son of Rev. Gilman
and Abigail (Thaxter) Bacheller, of Machiasport.
Resided in Whitneyville and in Jonesboro. She died
at Jonesboro, April 30, 1885. One of the most affectionate and confiding natures, strong in her attach-
ment to family and church. Mr. Bacheller is a bookkeeper. Has been in Houlton, Me., since the death
of his wife, until recently. Resides now in Minneapolis, Minn. Children :

1.  James Pope *Bacheller*, b. Jan. 24, 1867.
2.  Esselle *Bacheller*, b. April 8, 1869.
3.  Gilman *Bacheller*, b. May 27, 1872.
4.  Charles Henry *Bacheller*, b. Oct. 2, 1875.
5.  Susan Thaxter *Bacheller*, b. March 4, 1880.
6.  George Edgar *Bacheller*, b. Dec. 18, 1882.

IX.   HERBERT LESLIE,[8] b. Jan. 17, 1851 ; d. Sept. 24, 1852.
X.    EDGAR MARSHALL,[8] b. Feb. 4, 1853 ; d. March 6, 1860.
A rare boy, who made remarkable attainments in
learning, yet kept his childish simplicity. He died
of scarletina after but few days' illness.

JAMES[7] POPE married, second, Jan. 13, 1863, Lucy Randall,
daughter of John and Lucy (Randall) Knox, of Whitneyville,
born in East Machias, Me., June 21, 1833.

CHILDREN OF JAMES⁷ AND LUCY RANDALL (KNOX).
*Born in Whitneyville.*

XI.   ELLEN HAMMOND,⁸ b. June 21, 1866.
XII.  MARY KNOX,⁸ b. Jan. 30, 1871.

---

### A, 7.

## THE FAMILY OF CHARLES⁷.

CHARLES,⁷ son of Frederick⁶ and Mary (Pierce), born in Dorchester, Aug. 12, 1814, married Aug. 24, 1834, Elizabeth, daughter of Captain James and Parley (Nelson) Bogman, of Boston, born Oct. 20, 1812.

Captain Bogman was one of seven brothers, all but one shipmasters, natives of Providence, R. I. He pursued many successful voyages, but sailed at length out from the port of Norfolk, Va., only to meet one of the violent storms so characteristic of that coast; was "spoken" once, but never heard from again. His widow lived to a great age, a most worthy woman.

Mrs. Elizabeth (Bogman) Pope was very finely constituted, with strong mental qualities which made her gain wide knowledge and exercise vigorous judgment upon questions of public weal; and with practical self-denial which led her to the diligent performance of the manifold duties of a wife and mother. She infused great ambition and energy for all good into her children, and was a most sagacious and loving counsellor. Life brought her many trials, many tasks, but she neither flinched from those nor shirked these. Ill health came upon her, such as would have been sufficient ground for inactivity, — invalidism; but she always found some way of being useful.

She was spared to celebrate with her husband their Golden Wedding, in the autumn of 1884. It was a delightful occasion. Five of the bridegroom's brothers and sisters were present, the ages of the six aggregating 448 years, making an average of 74 years apiece. Many other relatives were present, beside a host of friends, old and young. All was joy and thankfulness.

But she had but a few more months to stay in "this earthly house." On the 10th of February, 1885, while suffering from acute bronchitis, she was seized with paralysis of the heart, and quickly "fell asleep."

Mr. Charles⁷ Pope was in the furniture and feather trade early in life. He afterwards engaged in the real estate business, in which he

continued many years.  He also attended to general business, such
as the settling of large estates.  Has been a justice of the peace
thirty-five years.  Resided in Brookline while his family were growing
up and receiving their education, but has had his home in the city of
Boston for a considerable period.  Children :

I. CHARLES ALLEN,[8] b. June 27, 1835.  [See following
   chapter, A, 16.]
II. ADELAIDE LEONORA,[8] b. Sept. 23, 1837.  Was a teacher
    in the public schools of Brookline several years.
III. MARY ELIZABETH,[8] b. Dec. 24, 1840 ; d. March 4, 1858.
IV. ALBERT AUGUSTUS,[8] b. May 20, 1843.  [See following
    chapter, A, 17.]
V. EMILY FRANCES,[3]     ⎱ b. Feb. 18, 1846.  Physicians.
VI. CAROLINE AUGUSTA,[8] ⎰ Graduated at the New England
    Female Medical College, Boston, in 1870.  Took
    additional studies in hospitals in Paris and London.
    Continued to study in Boston in the New England
    . Hospital for Women and Children until 1873, when
    they began practice in Boston.  Are attending physi-
    cians at the last-named hospital ;. members of the N.
    E. Hospital Medical Society, and of the Massachusetts
    Medical Society.
VII. ARTHUR WALLACE,[8] born March 9, 1850, married July
     22, 1869, Frances, dau. of William and Frances
     (Walker) Cook, of Brookline, b. Sept. 10, 1850.  Is
     head of the firm of A. W. Pope & Co., dealers in
     shoe manufacturers' supplies, in Boston.
VIII. LOUIS ATHERTON,[8] b. Oct. 6, 1852.  [See following
      chapter, A, 18.]

---

A, 8.

## THE FAMILY OF WILLIAM[7].

WILLIAM,[7] son of Frederick[6] and Mary (Pierce), born in
Dorchester, Aug. 12, 1814; married first, Aug. 12, 1840, Mary,
dau. of James and Parley (Nelson) Bogman of Boston.

She was a woman of strong, healthy impulses, sympathetic,
benevolent, affectionate.  Her home was a restful place.  Though
devoted to her family, she found time to carry practical help to

the sick or afflicted in other homes.  Delicate and sensitive in her feelings, she could summon great resolution and composure to meet trying emergencies.  She was a sister of Elizabeth, the wife of her husband's twin brother, Charles,[7] and they and their two families maintained the most unalloyed harmony.

While different in physique and mental qualities, the two sisters were much alike in the force and value of their characters ; and each mother contributed greatly to the development and happiness of the whole " double " family.

She died in the triumphs of Christian faith, Dec. 8, 1867.

### Children born in Boston.

I.   WILLIAM FRANCIS,[8] b. May 14, 1842 ; d. Sept. 14, 1842.
II.   GEORGE,[8] b. Jan. 9, 1844.  [See next chapter, A, 19.]
III.   EDWARD WALDRON,[8] b. Nov. 26, 1845.  [See next chapter, A, 20.]
IV.   MARY FRANCES,[8] b. Jan. 6, 1848 ; d. Dec. 30, 1851.

### Children born in Brookline.

V.   SARAH ELIZABETH,[8] b. Feb. 19, 1849 ; d. May 8, 1869.
VI.   WARREN HERBERT,[8] b. Sept. 22, 1851 ; d. June 8, 1852.
VII.   ANNIE,[8] b. June 5, 1853 ; d. Oct. 6, 1853.

WILLIAM[7] m. second, Feb. 15, 1871, Mary Jane, dau. of John and Hannah K. (Sanderson) Sweeten of Salem, Mass., born there March 28, 1826.  They had no children.  He died, July 27, 1876, at Watertown.  She resides in Lynn.

Mr. William[7] Pope was bred to the crockery business, and continued in it about forty-five years.  Was senior partner in the firm of Pope & Waldron for several years.  Had a long connection with the house of John Collamore & Co., a partner of the same concern, under the style of Curtis Collamore & Co., doing a very extensive wholesale and retail business.  After the dissolution of the firm, he was with Richard Briggs in the same line.

He was an ideal salesman, keeping himself informed as to the history of each quality and brand of goods, developing taste akin to that of a Palissy or a Wedgwood.

His habits were quiet, not disposed to long flights.  For years he followed the round of store, home, church, the house of his twin brother, and little else.  He loved books and art and nature.  In person he was below medium height, with pleasant, intellectual face and winning expression. His voice was gentle and peaceful. It was good to meet him, most delightful to be recognized by him as one of the inner circle. He was a member of the Baptist church, as were his brother Charles and their wives, and several of their children.

---

## A, 9.

## THE FAMILY OF JOHN[7].

JOHN,[7] son of Frederick[6] and Mary (Pierce), born Jan. 6, 1817; married, Sept. 4, 1845, Harriet Maria, daughter of Harvey and Clarissa (Mellish) Gilbert, b. at Brownington, Vt., Jan. 3, 1822.

He learned the trade of harness-maker and trimmer, in Weymouth. Later, learned the trade of stencil-cutting, with James Hall, at No. 8 Dock Square. Went into partnership with him in 1841, bought him out in 1860, and continued the business at the old stand. His son, Frank Gilbert,[8] learned and joined in the business. They have also dealt in brushes and inks for stencils. He died, Oct. 31, 1887.

He needs no eulogy for those who knew him, but deserves more than this pen is able to write. Bent by spinal disease in his youth, he was never robust, and was a great sufferer much of his life, yet, uncomplaining, a cheerer of others. Honest, pure, kind and true, he deserved in an unusual degree the title borne by our pioneer ancestor, — "Goodman Pope."

Retiring and domestic in his habits, he was not widely known, yet there are few who have come close to him, who will not feel deep regret at his loss, and hold him in loving and honorable memory, — with hope of joining him in his New Home some day.

CHILDREN OF JOHN[7] AND HARRIET MARIA (GILBERT).

I. FRANK GILBERT,[8] b. in Boston, July 7, 1846. [See next chapter, A, 21.]

II. CLARA MELLISH,[8] b. July 19, 1848; d. April 6, 1872. An earnest girl just ripening into beautiful womanhood, when called to a higher sphere.

III. MARY HELEN,[8] b. June 1, 1851; graduated from Cambridge High School, and has a position in Harvard University Library, in the cataloguing department.

IV. WALTER HARVEY,⁸ b. Oct. 29, 1853; m. July 25, 1877, Helen Maria, dau. of James Henry and Frances Theodora (Tenney) Beane, b. Aug. 23, 1856. He is a salesman in the wholesale boot and shoe store of the Winch Brothers, Boston. Resides at Cambridgeport.

V. ALICE ELIZA,⁸ b. July 25, 1856. Is in the cataloguing department of the library of Harvard University.

---

A, 10.

## THE FAMILY OF ALEXANDER⁷.

ALEXANDER,⁷ son of William⁶ and Sarah (Pierce), born March 15, 1808; married, first, Nov. 11, 1830, Elizabeth, dau. of John and Elizabeth (Soper) Foster of Dorchester. She died June 23, 1832.

He married second, April 27, 1837, Charlotte Caldwell, dau. of Jerome and Mary (Thaxter) Cushing, of Dorchester.

He was a man of brilliant qualities, enterprising, adventurous, efficient. After thorough training in the office of his father, he pursued the same business, dealing in lumber, for himself. He also erected a number of fine dwellings, on that "Pope's Hill" which had been so called from its ownership by our immigrant ancestor. He embarked in extensive operations at Ogdensburg, N. Y., in Eagleswood, N. J., and so on, achieving success except when general financial revulsions took place.

With generous, free impulses, he made hosts of friends everywhere. His latest years were spent in Dorchester, where he died of heart disease, June 16, 1878.

*Children of Alexander⁷ and Charlotte Caldwell (Cushing), born in Dorchester.*

I. CHARLOTTE CUSHING,⁸ b. April 6, 1838; d. Dec. 27, 1872.

II. ALEXANDER,⁸ JR., b. March 25, 1849. [See next chapter, A, 22.]

III. SIDNEY THAXTER,⁸ b. Dec. 25, 1858. Has a position in the office of the Chicago, Burlington & Quincy Railroad, at Chicago.

## A, 11.

## THE FAMILY OF WILLIAM,[7] JR.

WILLIAM,[7] jr., son of William[6] and Sarah (Pierce), born Dec. 27, 1813, married June 8, 1836, Sarah Ann, dau. of John and Elizabeth (Soper) Foster of Dorchester, born May 2, 1813.

She died Dec. 9, 1887, after only a week's illness. We quote the following memorial words :

"So rare and beautiful an individuality as that of the late Mrs. William Pope should not pass away without a word to emphasize the memory. Gifted with distinguished grace of person, and with musical and artistic talents, everything she did was touched with the subtle refinement of genius, and she instinctively sought, in all domestic and social surroundings, to express the pure perceptions of the beautiful, the picturesque and fitting. With all her appreciation of this life, of all the joy and value and grace of domestic affection, and the charms of every day's employments and duties, her inner life gave all a solidity of purpose and an elevation of aim. As she has passed on, the anguish of bereavement is transformed into a pæan of praise for the depth and richness of such a life. Although her taste centred in her home, where she was a most devoted wife and mother, her large heart was ever open to the cry of physical and mental suffering, and in her self-reliant nature and wisdom many weaker natures have found strength and comfort. There are those who have not forgotten the social gatherings in her pleasant home in Dorchester, with Ralph Waldo Emerson, Theodore Parker, Wendell Phillips, William Lloyd Garrison, Nathaniel Hall, Samuel Johnson, and others who have left us.

"For several years connected with the homœopathic hospital, as president of the Ladies' Aid Society, in her the hospital loses a kind and generous patron, and her co-workers a valued friend."

Mr. William[7] Pope, jr., received his education in the public schools of Dorchester, and his business training in the office of his father. He continued the lumber business at the old stand, for many years, and has always resided in his native town and parish. He was several years a member of the board of selectmen of Dorchester, and has been a member of the Common Council of Boston since the annexation. His influence has always been for worthy public improvements and against corrupt and injurious practices and traffics.

He was one of the incorporators and the president of the First National Bank of Dorchester.

Is associated with his son in the importing and mining business. Children :

I.   JOHN FOSTER,[8] b. Oct. 20, 1837.  [See next chapter, A, 23.]

II.  ELIZABETH FOSTER,[8] b. Oct. 21, 1840; was married, Nov. 18, 1863, to Conrad Wesselhoeft, M.D., of Boston, born in 1834, in Germany.  Widely known as one of the most learned and skilful physicians of the Homœopathic School of Medicine in the city of Boston.

He was a son of the late Dr. Robert and Mrs. Ferdinanda E. (Hecker) Wesselhoeft.

III. WILLIAM CARROLL,[8] b. May 8, 1847.  [See next chapter, A, 24.]

----

## A, 12.

## THE FAMILY OF HIRAM[7].

HIRAM,[7] son of Elijah[6] and Susanna (Capen), b. in Stoughton, June 29, 1811; m. Dec. 24, 1846, Dorcas A., dau. of William and Betsey Blanchard, of Gardiner, Me., b. Feb. 14, 1827 ; d. Nov. 7, 1884.

A cordial, sympathetic, hospitable woman, whose home life was faithful and her influence in the neighborhood helpful, in every social and moral matter; with her husband and his mother in the little church, — working dutifully in "the life that now is," and looking hopefully toward "the life that is to come."

Mr. Hiram[7] Pope was in the express business in Boston, with his brother Frederic,[7] several years.  Then he returned to Gardiner and became a farmer, whose fields, orchards, dairy and yards were well worth visiting.  Of great size and strength, unusually efficient in muscular toil, he was also a good thinker, an intelligent, independent, Christian patriot.  He went to his reunions and reward May 29, 1886.  Children:

I.   GEORGE HIRAM,[8] b. April 27, 1848.  [See next chapter, A, 25.]

II.  JOHN FREDERIC,[8] b. Oct. 4, 1850; m. July 3, 1887, Mrs. Ella J. (Ames) Davee.

## A, 13.

## THE FAMILY OF FREDERIC[7].

FREDERIC,[7] son of Elijah[6] and Susanna (Capen), b. Nov. 12, 1814, in Stoughton, m. in Boston, Oct. 19, 1837, Miriam Ball, dau. of George and Nancy (Ball) Bridges, b. in Marblehead, Jan. 1, 1818. Her father was b. in Marblehead Nov. 8, 1767, d. July 17, 1831. He owned and fitted out fishing vessels to the Grand Banks. · He m. Nancy Ball, who was born in Marblehead, Sept. 26, 1785; d. Dec. 9, 1855.

Mr. Frederic[7] Pope carried on an extensive piano-moving, express, and teaming business in the city of Boston. Like his brother, Hiram, he was large and strong, and developed excellent business qualities. Was much respected. Resided some time in Wayland. He d. Feb. 29, 1856.

*Children born in Boston.*

I.  ELLEN AUGUSTA,[8] b. Oct. 5, 1840; m. Oct. 31, 1858, Asa L. Gowell, of Richmond, Me. He is a piano-forte maker in Boston. Children :

    1.  Frederic William *Gowell*, b. Jan. 16, 1860; d. Feb. 24, 1860.
    2.  Frederic William *Gowell*, b. March 19, 1861; m. Nov. 1, 1885, Abby E. Erskine, of Wiscasset, Me., who was b. Nov. 11, 1860. One child, Nellie A. *Gowell*, was born to them Nov. 6, 1886, but the young mother survived only a few days; on the 25th of the same month she "fell asleep."
        Frederic W. Gowell is a piano-forte regulator; resides in Boston.

II.  MARY ELIZABETH,[8] b. March 9, 1843; m. Jan. 1, 1863, William N. Gowell, of Richmond, Me. He is a house builder in Boston, residing in Weston. She d. Dec. 2, 1885, of consumption.

    "A dutiful, affectionate daughter, a devoted wife and mother, she patiently bore her long illness. Was resigned to the will of God." Children :

    1.  Florence Ellen *Gowell*, b. March 31, 1864, in Boston.
    2.  Alberta Frances *Gowell*, b. Nov. 2, 1867, in Weston.
    3.  Louis *Gowell*, b. July 12, 1873, in Weston.

III. GEORGE WILLIAM,[8] b. April 28, 1845. [See next chapter, A, 26.]
IV. ANNIE LOUISA,[8] b. April 23, 1848 ; resides in Boston
with her mother.
V. EMILY FRANCES,[8] b. June 5, 1850 ; d. Feb. 8, 1851.

A, 14.

## THE FAMILY OF JOHN[7].

JOHN,[7] son of Elijah[6] and Susanna (Capen), b. March 2,
1820; m. (1), in the city of New York, Mary Strongarm, a
native of Germany. She gave birth to a child, but survived
only a few days, the child also passing quickly away.

He m. (2), June 20, 1869, Mary Loomis of New York, an
artist, and a teacher of painting. Children :

I. MINGA,[8] b. April 4, 1871.
II. JOHN RUSSELL,[8] b. April 24, 1872.

For many years his home has been in New York, and there
he died, Dec. 29, 1880.

"JOHN POPE, the artist," deserves more than a passing notice.
Trained to hard work on the farm, in his youth he did the part of a
helpful son, in humble toil. But he had great taste for the beautiful,
and desired to do something which would enter into the finer circle
of production. He set himself about learning how to draw and
paint, and such were his natural genius and his diligent application
that he painted portraits of members of the family and of some others
before he had received any considerable instruction; and his work
showed a quality which commanded respect and gave high promise.
He found employment and pursued his studies in Boston.

Then came the announcement that gold had been discovered in
California. Taking with him two practical men, he went to that
region, engaging with them in some agreement by which their labor
and his labor and venture were to be fairly paid. He toiled a few
years, settled with his associates, came back to Boston, and devoted
himself anew to art. He felt that he must see the works of Titian
and Rembrandt and the other old masters of portraiture. He must
go to Rome to study art. He must give himself up to the training of
some *modern painter*, and Paris must be the school where his eye
should learn to see and his hand to limn "the human face divine."

He went; he carried a boy's enthusiasm and a man's steady strength of application. When he returned, after several years, his relatives obtained commissions for him on the strength of their own standing. But one portrait in Boston made him a reputation, and henceforward he was *sought*. One of his grandest productions is the full-length portrait of the great orator, Daniel Webster, painted at the order of the city of Charlestown, representing Mr. Webster in the act of delivering his immortal oration on the completion of Bunker Hill Monument. It is in the city library at Charlestown.

During the years that followed, New York and New Orleans and other cities claimed our kinsman, and he took rank among the foremost American portrait painters. His works have the charm of naturalness; the beholder does not think, particularly, how well the artist has painted, but, rather, feels like speaking to the person portrayed. He has enriched many a home and gallery with his immortalizings of the loved and honored. He was a charming friend, remembered with ardent and admiring feelings by a large number of us, his relatives, who had the privilege of knowing him, and by a very wide circle of other friends.

The following obituary, from the Gardiner *Home Journal*, is of interest:

GARDINER, ME., Jan. 12, 1881.

Last Wednesday week John Pope, the artist, died at his residence on 337 Fourth Avenue, New York. He was born in this city, and developed his talents before he was sixteen. He went to Paris, and studied under Couture, and then went to Italy and studied the works of the old masters. He came from there to Boston, and devoted his attention to portrait painting. He went from Boston to New York about twenty-five years ago, and has done a profitable business in his profession.

He was elected an Associate of the National Academy, in 1857, and was one of the founders of the Artist's Fund Society. . . . A New York paper thus describes his last moments:

A man more thoroughly enraptured with his calling never lived. He painted while daylight lasted, and then spent the evening in producing the crayon drawings so much admired in the exhibitions at the Academy of Design. Though as a portrait painter he excelled, the dream of his life was to produce strong figure pictures, in which the background landscape would form as effective a part as the figures themselves. This was the ruling passion of his life, and as he neared the end the passion grew stronger.

On Wednesday evening, as he lay back on his pillows, very weak and ill with hemorrhage of the lungs, his wife, who, with their two children, was watching at his bed, was startled by his suddenly rising in bed and crying feverishly :

"Quick ! give me my palette and brush, I must paint.   Don't attempt to stop me now, for I have just discovered the art through the influence of visions of exquisitely graduated music.   It is plain as day at last."

His wife, alarmed at his excitement, made a weak attempt to dissuade him, but as opposition only increased his excitement and it was evident that his end was very near, she humored him.   His paints, brushes and canvas were brought to him, and his tearful relatives arranged the coverings of the bed so that they would look more like the drapery of his studio.   He began his work with a haste amounting almost to frenzy.

" At last, at last," he cried, " I have found the beauty which all my life and over all the world I have been struggling for."

He painted faster and faster, evidently believing that the canvas would show the beauty that he conceived, although it was but a sad realization of the conception.   It was late in the day when he began his deathbed picture.   It grew darker and darker as he went on, and his sorrowing family sat around him powerless to ease his last moments. At last it grew so dark that even he in his excitement noticed it.

" Let us go to the studio," he exclaimed.

"No, no ; not to-night.   Wait until to-morrow."

" We must go to the studio," he exclaimed, making an effort to rise to his feet.   The tax upon his strength was too great ; without another word he fell back on his pillows, dead.

May we not believe that his spirit has entered in that other life, where his genius shall find beauties of which it never dreamed, where freed from the clogs of earth it shall go on developing, and that he has really " at last found the beauty which all his life, and over all the world, he had been struggling for ? "

---

A, 15.

## THE FAMILY OF LUTHER[7].

LUTHER,[7] son of Azor[6] and Lucy (Bird), born April 29, 1808 ; married, Oct. 3, 1832, Eunice Maria Collyer, of Canton.

He was of rather more than medium height, sandy complexion and hair.   Had a position in Perkins' Iron Works, at Bridgewater, 30 years.   He died Aug. 28, 1886.   She died May 3, 1877, a. 65 years, 7 months, 11 days.   Children :

I.  LUCY MARIA,[8] b. in Raynham,  Feb. 7, 1834; m. Dec. 16,
     1849, Walter Pratt Deane, son of Francis William and
     Mary Deane, b. in Canton, June 4, 1830.  Mr. Francis
     W. Deane was town treasurer, cashier of Neponset
     Bank, etc., for many years, much respected.   He was a
     native of Mansfield, but died, as he had lived from
     early manhood, in Canton.   Walter P. Deane is a
     machinist and engineer; set up and ran engines in
     the mines in California, in 1854–5, and on sugar planta-
     tions in Cuba in 1861–2.   Resides in Brockton.   Chil-
     dren :

    1.  Mary Ella *Deane*, b. June 24, 1857.
    2.  Frances Waltena *Deane*, b. Nov. 2, 1859.
    3.  Frank William *Deane*, b. Oct. 24, 1863.
    4.  Henry Darwin *Deane*, b. March 7, 1865.
    5.  Ernest Walter *Deane*, b. May 27, 1866.
    6.  Lucy Maria *Deane*, b. Jan. 23, 1873.

II.  LUTHER EDMUND,[8] b. Oct. 7, 1836.  [See next chapter,
     A, 27.]
III.  SARAH KINGSLEY,[8] b. July 24, 1840; m. William Massena
      Drake, son of William and Ruth (Warren) Drake, of
      Stoughton.  He was a carpenter.  He died June 21,
      1876.  Mrs. Drake resides in Canton.  *Child:* Nellie
      Kingsley *Drake*, b. Aug. 31, 1863 ; m. Sept. 3, 1881,
      Frank Herbert Lane, of Stoughton.  *Child:* William
      Herbert *Lane*, b. June 16, 1882.
IV.  ADA FRANCES,[8] b. June 10, 1843 ; m. July 29, 1871, Lin-
     dol Jackson Sprague, son of Waterman and Betsey
     Lincoln (Sherman) Sprague.  Children :

    1.  Walter Collier *Sprague*, b. Sept. 9, 1872.
    2.  Roy Kinsley *Sprague*, b. Feb. 2, 1881.
        Residence, Brockton.

V.  MARY ELIZABETH,[8] b. Oct. 10, 1845; m. Dec. 6, 1863,
     Frederick West, b. May 5, 1840, in Derby, Derbyshire,
     England, son of Henry and Fannie Elizabeth (Palmer)
     West.  He was a carpenter; died at Cleveland, O.,
     Aug. 23, 1883.  Mrs. West resides in Brockton.

## A, 16.

## THE FAMILY OF EDMUND[7].

EDMUND,[7] son of Azor[6] and Lucy (Bird), b. Jan. 21,
1821 ; m. in North Easton, in 1843, Abby Ann, daughter of
Nathaniel and Abigail (Balcomb) Smith, of Norton.  He was a
shoemaker.  He d. July 26, 1851 ; his wife died October, 1859.
Children :

I.   CHARLES HENRY,[8] b. May 15, 1844.  [See next chapter,
     A, 27.]

II.  EDNA FLORELLA,[8] b. Sept. 15, 1846; was m. April 9,
     1864, to Loring Tilden, b. in Canton, July 28, 1838, son
     of Abner and Mary (Mansfield) Tilden, of Canton, and
     a descendant of Nathaniel Tilden, of Scituate.  He is
     a shoe-laster.  Resides at Elmwood.  *Child:* Albert
     Augustus *Tilden*, b. April 4, 1865 ; m. July 21, 1887,
     Alice Jeane Davis.  He is a druggist at Arlington, edu-
     cated at the Boston College of Pharmacy.  Mrs. Edna
     F. (Pope) Tilden has been a cheerful helper in gather-
     ing the statistics of her grandfather's family.

III. INA LUELLA,[8] b. Oct. 7, 1848 ; was m. March 11, 1866, to
     Alden Augustus Seeley, of Stoughton.  She d. Dec. 8,
     1869.  *Child:* Louis Edmond *Seeley*, b. March 16,
     1867.

IV.  ELVA ARMINELLA,[8] b. Feb. 11, 1852 ; was m. Nov. 29,
     1871, to George Edward Belcher, son of Sarda and
     Eveline (Leighton) Belcher, of Canton.  He is a maker
     of models for lasts ; was the inventor of a patent last-
     block fastener.  They reside in Stoughton.

---

## A, 17.

## THE FAMILY OF WILLIAM[7].

WILLIAM,[7] son of Ward[6] and Anna (Gurney), b. Jan. 11,
1817 ; m. Dec. 29, 1836, Hannah, daughter of Aaron and Nancy
(Wilmarth) Brown, of ———.  She was b. April 20, 1815.  He

was a baker.   He d. in Providence, R. I., Aug. 31, 1885.   Children :

 I.   LAURA MARIA,[8] b. Nov. 2, 1837; d. Jan. 19, 1838.
 II.   AUGUSTUS WILLIAM,[8] b. Dec. 17, 1839; d. June 21, 1841.
III.   AMANDA,[8] b. April 3, 1842 ; m. May 12, 1868, Julius Boyden, of Providence, R. I.; d. Sept. 28, 1868.
IV.   JOSEPHINE,[8] b. July 18, 1845 ; d. April 8, 1865.
 V.   WILLIAM,[8] b. March 13, 1856; d. Aug. 21, 1856.

DESCENDANTS OF LAZARUS[4].

I.

## THE FAMILY OF NORTON QUINCY[7].

NORTON QUINCY,[7] son of John[6] and Hannah (Pratt), b. Jan. 28, 1802; m. (1) Mehitable [Hitty] Jane Perry, b. in Portsmouth, N. H., in 1800; d. in Quincy, Sept. 29, 1852.

He m. (2), Nov. 17, 1853, Mehitable, daughter of Ebenezer and Betsey Leeman, of Wiscasset, Me., where she was born in 1805.

CHILDREN OF NORTON QUINCY[7] AND HITTY JANE (PERRY).

I.   JOHN QUINCY,[8] b. Oct. 25, 1824. [See next chapter, B, 1.]

II.   EBENEZER R.,[8] b. June, 1827; d. in California, 1885.

III.   ELIZA JANE,[8] b. in 1830; was m. April 24, 1853, to Charles P. Derby. She d. Dec. 31, 1866.

IV.   CHARLES EDWARD,[8] b. Nov. 13, 1834. [See next chapter, B, 2.]

V.   WALTER SCOTT,[8] b. July 30, 1840; d. Jan. 29, 1841.

VI.   JABEZ WALTER,[8] b. ———, 1841; d. Nov. 10, 1844.

VII.   ALEXANDER PERRY,[8] b. in 1842; enlisted in the 44th Massachusetts Volunteer Infantry, in the opening of the War of the Rebellion; participated in the battle of "Big Bethel" and other stirring engagements, but escaped mortal stroke, and lived to be honorably discharged, after three years' service.

Mr. Norton Quincy[7] Pope has been spared to a good old age. Upon his eightieth birthday a large number of his children and grandchildren, with other relatives and friends, assembled at his house to pay their respects to him.

He has always resided in Quincy.

---

### B, 2.

## THE FAMILY OF ABNER B[7].

ABNER B.,[7] son of John[6] and Hannah (Pratt), b. in Quincy, June 6, 1817 ; m. 1842, Susan E., daughter of John and Elizabeth Jacobs, of Frederick, Md.

He removed to Dayton, Ohio, in the year 1841-2, and has resided there ever since.   Children :

   I.  NORTON QUINCY,[8] was m. in Brooklyn, N. Y., June 6,
        1887, by Rev. Dr. Talmadge, to Abbie E. Hanscom, of
        Prattville, Mass.   Resides in Brooklyn ; a broker ; has
        operated at Chicago and New York, etc.
  II.  CARRIE E.[8]
 III.  JENNIE M.,[8] m. June 6, 1882, J. R. Sloan ; d. Feb. 4, 1885.
 IV.  ELLA M.[8]
  V.  MARY,[8] m. Nov. 1, 1877, L. J. Greulich, of Dayton, Ohio.

---

### B, 3.

## THE FAMILY OF SAMUEL BROWN[7].

SAMUEL BROWN,[7] son of Asa[6] and Susannah (Ripley), b. Dec. 26, 1799 ; m. first, Oct. 31, 1824, Eliza Everson, of Quincy, who was spared to him but a short time.   She d. June 8, 1826, and her ten months' old babe, Caroline M., followed her on the 20th.

He married, second, May 20, 1827, Mary Ann, daughter of John Capen, of Dorchester.

#### CHILDREN OF SAMUEL BROWN AND MARY ANN (CAPEN).

   1.  ELIZA ANN,[8] b. Feb. 28, 1828 ; m. Sept. 12, 1847,
       Nelson Mace, of Boston.
   2.  SUSAN CATHERINE,[8] b. Nov. 27, 1829.
   3.  SARAH ADELINE,[8] b. March 27, 1832.

4. MARY DOUGLASS,[8] b. June 20, 1834; m. Feb. 17, 1853, Henry G. Pratt, jr., son of Henry G. and Elizabeth Pratt, of Quincy.
5. LUCY FRANCES,[8] b. July 28, 1836; d. Oct. 21,[2]1842.
6. ASA AUGUSTUS,[8] b. July 20, 1838. [See next chapter, B, 3.]

Mr. Samuel Brown Pope died in Quincy, March 7, 1883. Mrs. Mary Ann (Capen) Pope d. March 18, 1884, aged 78 years 5 months, having lived with her husband fifty-six years in the house to which he took her as a bride. The daughters, Susan C. and Sarah A., reside on the old homestead on Elm Street, Quincy.

------

## B, 4.

## THE FAMILY OF OZIAS MORSE[7].

OZIAS MORSE,[7] son of Asa[6] and Susannah (Ripley), b. June 18, 1804; m. May 2, 1827, Maria Pray. Resided in Quincy. He d. at Taunton, July 11, 1870. .Children:

I. MARY HELEN,[8] b. ——, 1828; m. April 11, 1849, William L. Brackett, son of Joseph and Charlotte Brackett, b. 1828. Resides in San Francisco, Cal.

II. A CHILD, b. ——, 1829; d. Nov. 28, 1832.

III. EMILY M.,[8] b. 1831, m. July 4, 1850, Martin L. Cushing, son of Job and Elizabeth Cushing, b. in Cohasset, in 1827.

IV. SARAH O.[8]

V. NANCY M.,[8] b. ——, 1837; m. Dec. 30, 1860,.Charles E. Hall, son of Edward and Abigail S. Hall, b. ——, 1836. Resides in Hudson.

VI. LOUISA P.,[8] m. (1), Charles Brown; (2), Alonzo Howard. Resides in Quincy.

VII. WILLIAM O.,[8] b. ——, 1841; d. Jan. 22, 1864. He enlisted in the defence of our country against rebellion, in Company H, 4th Mass. Vol. Infantry. He took part, with his regiment, in the battle of " Big Bethel " in Virginia, June 10, 1861, and elsewhere in following campaigns. After three years' service, he met his death by drowning at Annapolis, Md., Jan. 22, 1864.

B, 5.

## THE FAMILY OF GEORGE WASHINGTON[7].

GEORGE WASHINGTON,[7] son of Asa[6] and Susanna (Ripley), b. March 30, 1812; m. Sarah Adeline Wiggin. Served three months in the army during the War of the Rebellion. Resided in Quincy until about 1872, when he removed to Malden. Health failing, he entered the Soldiers' Home, at Chelsea, where he d. March 20, 1887.   Child:

> ABBIE ANN,[8] b. in 1841; m. Jan. 20, 1864, George F. Pratt, b. in 1836, son of Henry G. and Elizabeth G. Pratt.   Resides in Malden.

---

B, 6.

## THE FAMILY OF JOSEPH[7].

JOSEPH,[7] JR., son of Joseph[6] and Betsey (Tower), b. Sept. 23, 1803; m. Feb. 26, 1832, Jane Lovell, b. Feb. 4, 1814. He d. May 29, 1887. Resided at Hull. He was appointed postmaster in January, 1850, and continued until his death, his daughter Bella being his deputy in recent years. She was commissioned as his successor Sept. 26, 1887. He was a justice of the peace, town clerk, assessor, etc., etc. For forty-eight years he was a telegraph operator, using the Semaphore signals from 1831 to 1852, then the Morse system. He signalled the first European steamer that ever came to Boston Harbor. Thus his life was most useful, a faithful service to the public good.

*Children born in Hull.*

I.   JOSEPH,[8] JR., b. Nov. 4, 1832; d. at San Francisco, Cal., March 3, 1853.

II.   JANE LOVELL,[8] b. March 12, 1835; was m. (1), April 15, 1858, to Nathan Henry Beal.   Children:

1.   Eliphalet Lovell *Beal*, b. Feb. 8, 1859.
2.   Joseph Ellsworth *Beal*, b. June 29, 1861.

3.  Mattie Clark *Beal*, b. Feb. 25, 1867.
4.  Arabella Grace *Beal*, b. Oct. 5, 1871.
    Mr. Nathan H. Beal d. Feb. 14, 1877. Mrs. Jane L.
    (Pope) Beal was m. (2) to Mr. Charles F. Wells, of
    Hingham Centre.

III. BENJAMIN FRANKLIN,[8] b. Sept. 23, 1837. [See next chapter, B, 4.]
IV. CALEB GOULD LOVELL,[8] b. July 16, 1841 ; m. Nov. 24, 1864, Martha Ann Gott Clark.   He is an experienced telegraph operator in the Western Union Company's office, in Boston.
V. RACHEL CUSHING LORING,[8] b. April 23, 1846; was m. Nov. 24, 1864, to Peter Loring, of Edge Hill.   Children :

1.  Webster Lovell *Loring*, b. March 21, 1867.
2.  Arthur Weston *Loring*, b. Oct. 6, 1869.
3.  Ernest Linwood *Loring*, b. June 19, 1874.

VI. ARABELLA CUSHING,[8] b. Jan. 8, 1853 ; resides at Hull; has been very much interested in gathering and contributing details of the history of this branch of the family.

----

B, 7.

## THE FAMILY OF MICAJAH[7].

MICAJAH,[7] JR., son of Micajah[6] and Lucinda (Randall) [Howard], b. July 22, 1817 ; m. Elizabeth Bradford, of South Boston.  He was a machinist ; made and set up engines and machinery in Cuba and elsewhere.  Became concerned in cotton manufacturing at Suncook, N. H., and was very successful. Child :

ANN ELIZABETH,[8] b. 1847 ; was m. in Boston, April 18, 1871, by Rev. W. H. Mills, to Irad Cochrane, of Oakland, Cal., b. 1831, in Pembroke, N. H., son of Norris and Sophia E. Cochrane.

B, 8.

## THE FAMILY OF EDWARD RANDALL[7].

EDWARD RANDALL,[7] son of Micajah[6] and Lucinda, b. March 26, 1823 ; m. (1) Almira C. Winslow, b. in Abington in 1827. She d. in Quincy, Nov. 16, 1852.

CHILD OF EDWARD RANDALL[7] AND ALMIRA C. (WINSLOW).

I.   ANN BIRD,[8] b. in Quincy, Aug. 23, 1852 ; d. of consumption, July 14, 1871.

He m. (2) Augusta Leavitt, of Bangor, Me.
He m. (3) Jane Maxwell, who was b. in Pictou, Nova Scotia. He d. Feb. 6, 1877.

CHILDREN OF EDWARD RANDALL[7] AND JANE (MAXWELL).

II.   EDWARD RANDALL,[8] JR.
III.   MARY JANE,[8] b. Nov. 21, 1874.
IV.   GEORGE ALBERT,[8] b. Dec. 4, 1876 ; d. Aug. 26, 1879, of cholera infantum.

---

B, 9.

## THE FAMILY OF MICAJAH CLARK[7].

MICAJAH CLARK,[7] son of Lemuel[6] and Elizabeth (Clark), b. Dec. 3, 1811 ; m. (1) Nancy P. Webster, b. in Rumney, N. H., in 1805, d. in Quincy, Aug. 7, 1844, having borne five children, three of whom survived her.

He m. (2) Mary Althea Lyon, b. in Augusta, Me., in 1827. She d. in Quincy, April 12, 1848.

He m. (3) Sept. 4, 1850, Hannah C., daughter of John and Mary (Prescott) Sanborn, b. in 1826, in Sanbornton, N. H. She had two children.

He resided on his father's former homestead in Quincy until 1870, when he sold it and bought a farm in Lynnfield Centre, to which he removed. There he passed the remainder of his days till he went " Beyond the sowing and the reaping," July 6, 1884.

*Children of Micajah Clark[7] and Nancy P. (Webster), born in Quincy.*

I.   AMOS WEBSTER,[8] b. Oct. 12, 1835; d. April 12, 1854.

II.  LEMUEL CLARK,[8] b. Nov. 21, 1836.  [See next chapter, B, 5.]

III. SILAS HALL,[8] b. March 24, 1838; d. July 15, 1873, at Lynnfield Centre.

IV.  DANIEL WEBSTER,[8] b. June 30, 1840; d. Jan. 30, 1841, at Quincy.

V.   ROBERT SHANKLAND,[8] b. Jan. 19, 1842; d. Sept. 19, 1843.

*Children of Micajah Clark[7] and Hannah C. (Sanborn), born in Quincy.*

VI.  ELTHEA LYONS,[8] b. Oct. 9, 1852.

VII. MARY ELIZABETH,[8] b. Feb. 27, 1854; d. Sept. 27, 1855, at Quincy.

Mrs. Hannah C. (Sanborn) Pope and her daughter, Elthe L., reside at Lynnfield Centre.

---

## B, 10.

## THE FAMILY OF RUFUS SPURR[7].

RUFUS SPURR,[7] son of Lazarus[6] and Elizabeth, or "Betsey" (Talbot), b. in Stoughton, April 2, 1809; m. Nov. 8, 1835, Sarah Brown Parkhurst.  She was the daughter of Capt. Silas B. and Lydia (Robbins) Parkhurst, of Milford, her mother being a daughter of Capt. Benjamin Robbins, b. Nov. 12, 1753, d. June 22, 1810, and Lydia (Hale), b. Feb. 3, 1755, d. April 15, 1830.

As the best memorial we can place on record here to the memory of this honorable kinsman, we reprint the following obituary notice of him, which was published by the *Barnstable Patriot* immediately after his death:

By the decease of Rev. Rufus S. Pope, the brief announcement of which was made in the *Patriot* last week, a long prominent figure has disappeared from our public life.  Nearly forty years ago he came to Cape Cod in the strength of vigorous manhood, and all these have been years of efficient labor. He was called here by a parish composed chiefly of clear-headed, energetic and enterprising men. They wanted a strong leader in religious thought and life, and they found what they sought in him. He was a man of clear perception, of positive conviction, of frank utterance, of honest action ; uncompromising in the advocacy of his own opinions, he was characterized by large charity for those differing from him, and by profound respect for honesty in faith and practice. He was an earnest and faithful preacher : did much useful labor in the community in which he dwelt, and far and near he went bearing messages of comfort to the afflicted.

The *Register*, in its obituary of Mr. Pope, well says :

" In his death, the Universalist denomination have lost one of their oldest and strongest champions — one who was not only a believer in its tenets, but whose sympathies embraced the whole human family, of whatever faith, condition or race. He was a writer of more than ordinary vigor and force ; his style was rather direct and forcible than polished and symmetrical, sense and judgment being his prominent characteristics. He unquestionably exercised a marked influence upon the thoughts and opinions of his contemporaries, and it is but justice to say that the tendency of his teachings has been to liberalize the feelings and enfranchise thought from the fetters of bigotry and superstition. As a neighbor, a citizen, a friend, he has left many among us who will ever cherish and respect his memory."

We feel that in the death of Mr. Pope we have sustained a personal loss. We have known him ever since we first entered this office, some thirty years ago, — and we always found in him a friend and an earnest co-worker. Ever since he first came upon the Cape, he has been a valued and always welcome contributor to the columns of the *Patriot*, and since we assumed its proprietorship but few numbers have appeared without his " HYANNIS BUDGET," which he always made so readable, and which will now be so greatly missed.

Of Mr. Pope's early life we know comparatively little. He was averse to recording its history, feeling that it was of little importance that those who came after him should know what seemed to him so unimportant. He was born in Stoughton, Mass., April 2, 1809, and was consequently, at the time of his death, 73 years, 2 months and 3 days old. In very early life his father removed to Dorchester and thence to Marlboro', where the young man spent his youthful days engaged in agricultural pursuits. He received his education in the common schools and in the Marlboro' Academy.

Naturally inclined to religious thought and inquiry he, at quite an early age, turned his attention to a candid consideration of the claims

of Christianity, and to the claims of the many dogmas presented for
his acceptance to be called Christian. He was drawn toward the
work of the ministry. His early love for it continued to the end.
He pursued a course of theological study with the late Rev. Sylvanus
Cobb, D. D., and early in 1833 entered into the work of his chosen
profession, preaching his first sermon at South Dedham that year. He
was settled over the following parishes: South Dedham (now Norwood),
Milford, Sterling and Hardwick. While settled in Milford he was
united in marriage with the faithful companion who has shared with him
all life's toils and its triumphs. These several pastorates covered a
period of ten years. Early in 1843 the Universalist Society in Hyannis
called him to its vacant pastorate. Here he labored faithfully thirty
years. Since closing his labors with the Hyannis parish he served the
church in Orleans three years, and briefly supplied some other parishes.
His health began to fail some eight or nine years since, and for some
time he has been unable to perform any ministerial labor.

Besides his ministerial labors, which have ever been faithfully and
acceptably performed and fruitful of good, Mr. Pope served Barnstable for years very efficiently upon the Board of School Committee, and
two years (1855 and 1856) as representative in the General Court, and
filled for a considerable time the office of Register of Probate for
Barnstable County, and was for several years Postmaster of Hyannis.

On the revival of Fraternal Lodge of Free and Accepted Masons,
nearly thirty-five years ago, Mr. Pope became an active working
member. His zeal never abated. He successively took all the
degrees of all the branches of that order within his reach, and was a
workman of whom his brothers and companions were not ashamed.
Much of the present prosperity of the Fraternity in this section of
the State is due to his persistent labor. He was elected Senior
Warden Jan. 3, 1851, and Worshipful Master Dec. 5, 1853, which
latter position he held until Dec., 1862, when he received the appointment of District Deputy Grand Master, which office he held for five
years. He was one of the Charter Members of Orient Chapter of
Royal Arch Masons in 1857, and served as M. E. High Priest from
1858 to 1866, and again in 1868 and 1869, in all ten years. He was
knighted in Boston Commandery in 1861, received the Ineffable '
Degrees up to the 32d in 1864 in Boston. Was Chaplain in the
Grand Chapter of Massachusetts in 1858, 1859, 1860, 1861 and 1862,
when he was elected R. E. Grand Scribe.

On Thursday afternoon, at 2 o'clock, prayer was offered at Mr.
Pope's late residence by Rev. C. A. Bradley of Brewster, when members of Fraternal Lodge and Orient Chapter of Hyannis, and James

Otis Lodge of Barnstable, escorted the remains to the Universalist Church, which was filled with citizens of Hyannis and neighboring villages. The funeral services were here held, conducted by Rev. Mr. Bradley, assisted by Rev. G. W. Fuller of the Baptist Church, who offered prayer; Rev. V. J. Hartshorne, formerly of the Hyannis Congregational Church, who made a few appropriate and feeling remarks touching upon his intimate and pleasant relations with the deceased ; and the venerable Baptist divine, Rev. Enoch Chase, who spoke with much feeling of the deceased, and of his pleasant relations with him during the long number of years he had resided in Hyannis. Mr. Bradley gave a very feeling and discriminating address, replete with pleasant reminiscences of the deceased, and words of sympathy to the family, the church, the fraternal brotherhood, and the community. Then followed the Masonic service, Bro. Robert Lambert, W. M. of Fraternal Lodge, officiating as Master, and Bro. V. J. Hartshorne as Chaplain.

The Masons took charge of the remains of their departed brother, and sent a delegation in company with the afflicted family to Wood Lawn Cemetery, near Boston, Friday morning. On arriving there, Rev. Dr. Miner made a few appropriate remarks and offered a prayer, when the remains were laid at rest beside those of his two sons, whose loss he so truly and tenderly mourned.

The sympathy of the church, of the fraternal brotherhood, and of the whole community is with the family, consisting of the companion of our late friend, two sons, two daughters, one grandson and one sister. The faith he so freely ministered is their consolation.

### CHILDREN :

I.   GEORGE HENRY,[8] b. at Sterling, Jan. 31, 1837 ; d. Oct. 12, 1837.

II.  ELLEN AUGUSTA,[8] b. Oct. 14, 1838.

III. CHARLES GREENWOOD,[8] b. Nov. 18, 1840, at Hardwick. [See next chapter, B, 6.]

IV.  MILTON GRANVILLE,[8] b. at Hyannis, July 15, 1845 ; was drowned at Campton, N. H., Aug. 22, 1868.

V.   RUFUS SPURR,[8] JR., b. Sept. 23, 1847 ; d. Feb. 12, 1868.

VI.  ELWYN HERBERT,[8] b. Oct. 13, 1849 ; m. Ada May Adsit. Resides at Traverse City, Mich.   One child.

VII. SARAH HALE,[8] b. Nov. 1, 1851 ; was m. June 27, 1876, to Francis A. Gorham, of Barnstable.

VIII. A SON,[8] b. April 4 ; d. April 8, 1858.

B, 11.

## THE FAMILY OF FRANKLIN MANSER[7].

FRANKLIN MANSER[7] (christened Alexander[7]), born Oct. 16, 1814, at Dorchester ; married, April, 1850, Emily Sherman.   Children :

I.  ELLA I.,[8] b. April, 1851 ; d. in 1853.
II.  FREDERIC AUSTIN,[8] b. May 4, 1853.  [See next chapter, B, 7.]
III.  CARRIE ESTELLE,[8] b. July 28, 1855.
IV.  NELLIE GERTRUDE,[8] b. Sept. 16, 1857.
V.  ADDIE LOUVISA,[8] b. Oct. 16, 1859.
VI.  LAVINIA HOWE,[8] b. Feb. 16, 1861 ; m. Nov. 30, 1880, Chester Frye of Marlboro.  *Child*, Ethel Bruce *Frye*, b. March 17, 1887.
VII.  EMILY LOUISE,[8] b. Oct. 2, 1864.
VIII.  WALTER CLIFTON,[8] b. Jan. 12, 1867.

Mrs. Emily (Sherman) Pope died in Nov., 1869 ; Mr. Franklin Manser[7] Pope died at Marlboro, May 12, 1881.

---

B, 12.

## THE FAMILY OF THOMAS RICHARDSON[7].

THOMAS RICHARDSON,[7] son of Thomas[6] and Tila (Holmes), b. Aug. 2, 1819 ; m. in Boston, Nov. 7, 1844, Nancy Ward, dau. of Samuel and Mary Ann (Ward) Leighton, of Columbia, Me., b. May 11, 1817 ; d. June 19, 1887. He resided in Newton, was a builder ; d. Feb. 10, 1861.  Children :

I.  CHARLES RICHARDSON,[8] b. Sept. 25, 1847 ; m. in Tyngsboro, Oct. 29, 1874, Mary Bridge, dau. of Augustus T. Pierce, M. D., and Mary P. (Bridge), born in Tyngsboro, May 15, 1852.  He is a commercial traveller, connected with a wholesale woolen cloth house in Boston ; resides in Boston.
II.  AUGUSTA MARIA,[8] b. June 10, 1849.
III.  ANNA LOUISA,[8] b. Nov. 14, 1852 ; m. in Newton, June 3, 1880, to Eben Smith, a merchant of Barnstable.

CHAPTER XI.

# THE EIGHTH GENERATION.

## SECTION A.

### DESCENDANTS OF DOCTOR RALPH[4].

I.

### THE FAMILY OF JAMES[8].

JAMES,[8] jr., son of James[7] and Elizabeth (Lake), b. July 28, 1814 ; m. Nov. 3, 1841, Sarah Louisa, daughter of Reuben and Ruth (Teele) Swan, of Dorchester, b. in Charlestown, Sept. 10, 1822.

He is a carpenter and builder, living in Dorchester Lower Mills. His wife died July, 1887. Children :

I. ALMIRA GARDNER,[9] b. Dec. 13, 1842 ; m. in Dorchester, Feb. 25, 1869, Edward Payson Hurd, son of Julius Curtis and Rebecca Ann (Payson) Hurd. He was born in Medway, Mass., June 28, 1841. Almira Gardner (Pope) Hurd died April 19, 1869.

II. JAMES FRANCIS,[9] b. May 28, 1845. [See next chapter, A, I.]

III. SARAH LOUISA,[9] b. Aug. 13, 1848 ; m. Edward Payson Hurd, son of Julius and Rebecca (Payson) Hurd (second wife). Mr. Hurd is superintendent of the McKay Manufacturing Company, Boston. Children :

1. Edward Lawrence *Hurd*, b. July 21, 1873.
2. Allie Louise *Hurd*, b. July 13, 1875.
3. William Robinson *Hurd*, b. Oct. 23, 1878.
4. Malcolm *Hurd*, b. Oct. 29, 1884.

IV.   HERBERT WEBSTER,[9] b. Oct. 2, 1852. [See next chapter, A, 2.]

V.   STEPHEN AUGUSTUS,[9] b. Dec. 6, 1855.   A carpenter and builder, Dorchester.

VI.   ABBOTT SWAN,[9] b. May 8, 1858.   On a cattle ranch, near Colorado Springs, Col.

VII.   KATHARINE TUCKER,[9] b. Nov. 10, 1863 ; d. June 14, 1865.

---

## A, 2.

## THE FAMILY OF ALBERT[8].

ALBERT,[8] son of James[7] and Elizabeth (Lake), was b. Oct. 10, 1816 ; m. Oct. 6, 1841, Harriet Williams, daughter of Spencer and Harriet (Williams) Johnson of Sharon, b. in Dorchester, June 27, 1820.   He is a builder.   Resides in Dorchester Lower Mills.   Children :

I.   CHARLES ALBERT,[9] b. July 29, 1842. [See next chapter, A, 3.]

II.   ARTHUR WARREN,[9] b. Nov. 30, 1846. [See next chapter, A, 4.]

III.   HARRIET LOUISA,[9] b. Feb. 26, 1854.

---

## A. 3.

## THE FAMILY OF HENRY[8].

HENRY,[8] third son of James[7] and Elizabeth (Lake), b Feb. 26, 1821, m. in Dorchester, October, 1853, Abigail, daughter of Thomas and Abigail (Tucker) French, of Canton, b. in Canton, Nov. 29, 1828.   He went to California in 1849, when quite a young man ; remained about eight years, when he returned to Dorchester.   Failing health caused him to give up active business, but after seven years he was appointed postmaster at Milton, Mass., which office he filled for twenty years.

To say that he filled it satisfactorily is not enough, for he
was called "the beloved postmaster," always cheerful and
bright, with a kind word and helping hand for all, taking an
active part in all good works, public and private.   His energy
went beyond his strength, and after an illness of one week he
died of typhoid fever, Feb. 8, 1880, mourned by the whole
community, for he was a "thorough Christian gentleman" in
every sense of the word.

He has left a precious memory to his family, and brothers
and sisters, for his life-long devotion to them.   His wife, a very
superior woman, survived him but a few years, dying June 28,
1883.   *Children, born in San Francisco, Cal.:*

I.   ANNIE FRENCH,[9] b. Aug. 28, 1854; m. Sept. 13, 1877,
     Herbert Shaw Carruth, son of Nathan and Sarah
     (Pratt) Carruth, b. in Dorchester, February, 1854.   He
     is a member of the firm of W. B. Clark & Carruth,
     booksellers and stationers, Boston.   Children :

     1.   Nathan *Carruth*, b. June 28, 1880.
     2.   Henry Pope *Carruth*, b. April 25, 1884.

II.  HENRY TEMPLE,[9] b. Dec. 13, 1864.   Student at Harvard
     University.

---

A, 4.

## THE FAMILY OF WILLIAM FRANCIS[8].

WILLIAM FRANCIS,[8] fourth son of James[7] and Elizabeth
(Lake), was born Aug. 5, 1823 ; married in Boston, Oct. 11,
1849, Sarah, daughter of Laban and Catharine (Johnson)
Adams, of Boston, b. in Boston, Nov. 5, 1824 ; d. in Dorchester,
Jan. 11, 1881.   He enlisted in the 22d Massachusetts Regiment in August, 1861 ; was wounded at the battle of Gaines
Mills, 1862, by a bullet passing through his hip.   This was his
first engagement with the enemy.   After lying all night on the
battlefield, with a companion dead at his side, he was taken as
a prisoner to Richmond, afterwards exchanged and sent to

Fortress Monroe, until able to join his regiment some months after, just before the battle of Fredericksburg; there he was killed, Dec. 13, 1863. A few months later his diary was sent to his family by a Michigan soldier, who found it on his body, with a letter stating that he was shot through the head. He left a wife and two young children. He was highly respected, a brave, tender and true man. Children : ·

I. CHARLES HENRY,[9] b. June 28, 1851; m. in Dorchester, Nov. 13, 1882, Mrs. Emma S. Vose, daughter of Alfred and Amanda Dearborn, b. in Tuftonboro, N. H., Nov. 8, 1854, widow of Mr. Irving Vose, of Quincy. [She has two sons. 1, Carlton Juan *Vose*, b. Nov. 29, 1874. 2, Clinton Dearborn *Vose*, b. Feb. 27, 1876.]

Mr. Charles Henry Pope[9] is in the real estate business in Boston. Resides in Charlestown.

II. WALTER FRANCIS,[9] b. March 12, 1855. Is a clerk with the Houston–Thompson Electric Company of Boston. Resides at Dorchester.

III. LIZZIE,[9] b. Nov. 15, 1857; d. Oct. 27, 1861.

---

### A, 5.

### THE FAMILY OF GEORGE[8].

GEORGE,[8] fifth son of James[7] and Elizabeth (Lake), b. May 18, 1826; m. Nov. 5, 1856, Emily Jane, youngest daughter of Reuben and Ruth (Teele) Swan, b. in Dorchester, Aug. 1, 1827. Reuben Swan, her father, was born in Charlestown, March 27, 1778, and Ruth (Teele) was born in Charlestown, July 30, 1786. He is a carpenter and builder; resides in Dorchester. Children :

I. GEORGE EDGAR,[9] b. Dec., 1857. In the same business as his father.

II. JENNIE SWAN,[9] b. Aug. 22, 1861.

III. WILLIAM HOWARD,[9] b. Feb. 6, 1865. Is a clerk in the First National Bank, Boston.

## A, 6.

## THE FAMILY OF HARRIS WEEMAN[8].

HARRIS WEEMAN,[8] sixth son of James[7] and Elizabeth (Lake), b. March 24, 1829; m. April 29, 1857, Julia Caroline, daughter of William and Jerusha (Arnold) Newcomb, of Quincy, born March 1, 1830.  She died Sept. 24, 1866.  He is a surveyor of lumber ; resides at Dorchester.  Children :

I.  FRED HARRIS,[9] b. Feb. 7, 1860.  [See next chapter, A, 5.]
II.  HENRY ARNOLD,[9] b. July 15, 1863.  Postmaster of Milton, where he resides.

---

## A, 7.

## THE FAMILY OF WILLIAM HENRY[8].

WILLIAM HENRY,[8] son of William[7] and Peggy Dawes (Billings), b. March 14, 1813, m. Aug. 16, 1837, Susan, daughter of Capt. John and Susan (Phinney) Keller, b. at Thomaston, Me., May 31, 1818.  He was a good son, husband, father and citizen.  He was of great assistance to his father during his youth.  He threw his whole strength into the business of the firm.  Cautious, scenting danger full early enough, conservative, yet untiring, persevering, strong, his judgment was excellent.  His qualities were exceedingly valuable in combination with the other partners, particularly his brother Samuel.  They were as unlike as a right hand and a left hand, and they *gathered well* together.  The obituary notice of that brother, given on following pages, is in great part applicable to William Henry, so far as it describes the business career of the family; and we say less at this point because that article had been printed in their father's book, while this son was still living.

He inherited from his mother's father a strong passion and high capacity for music.  Was leader of the village choir many years, and in this way did a good deal to help the social and religious life of the community.

He was an excellent neighbor, and had a very kind heart. His death, Dec. 13, 1876, was felt deeply by the entire community. His widow survives him, and has a home in Boston with her daughter.   Child :

I.   JULIA ANTOINETTE,[9] b. Oct. 19, 1838, was m. June 7, 1859, to Thomas Franklin Furber, son of Thomas and Sophia (Munroe) Furber, of Boston, Mass., b. July 25, 1830.

### *Children, born in Boston.*

1.   Henry Pope *Furber*, b. Dec. 31, 1860 ; m. in Boston, April 4, 1887, Grace Everett, daughter of Edward E. Tower, of Boston.

2.   Julia Monroe *Furber*, b. Feb. 7, 1863.

3.   Franklin Everett *Furber*, b. Sept. 6, 1865 ; d. Oct. 5, 1866.

4.   Everett Howard *Furber,* $\Big\}$ b. Nov. 24, 1868.
5.   Edwin Lemist *Furber,*
     They reside in Boston.

---

### A, 8.

## THE FAMILY OF SAMUEL WARD[8].

SAMUEL WARD,[8] son of William[7] and Peggy Dawes (Billings), b. March 7, 1815 ; m. Sept. 20, 1840, Betsey Jones, daughter of Micah Jones and Betsey (Rich) Talbot, of East Machias, Me., b. Nov. 16, 1816.  He died in East Machias, Feb. 1, 1862, of gastric fever, terminating with congestion of the lungs.

We make extracts from an obituary notice of this admirable man in the "Machias Republican" of Feb. 18, 1862, by George W. Talbot, Esq., of Machias ; quoted in full in "The Genealogy of a portion of the Pope Family."

"Putting to practical use a hasty academical education, he entered upon his father's business at a time when it was the highest mercantile ambition in the town where he lived, to own a quarter of a saw-mill and supply goods enough to pay for stocking it with logs and manufacturing the

All the then inestimable timber lands were held by non-residents, and their price rated per acre in cents rather than dollars; but the lumbermen were well enough satisfied if they could screen one half of the timber cut upon them from the eyes of the proprietor's agent, and thus escape a pitiful assessment of stumpage. While yet in his boyhood, his father's fortunes, up to that time fluctuating and marked with many reverses, felt the spell of his tireless activity. While other operators asserted that the timber was all cut off, Mr. Pope began quietly buying up the timber lands, first by sections and then by townships. When other men offered their mills for sale, Mr. Pope stood ready to buy them. It early occurred to his father and himself that to make the business remunerative, the selling as well as the manufacture of lumber must be systematized. Accordingly they applied to the principal sources of demand, studied out the wants of builders and contractors, and made bargains to supply upon orders the kinds and dimensions required for particular buildings, thereby diverting to themselves one profit paid to brokers, and selling their own lumber at enhanced prices. These special contracts not only employed their own mills, but were liberally distributed among other dealers who could pay them a commission, and at the same time secure better prices for their commodities than the general market afforded, and sometimes sales, in seasons when in the general market lumber failed to bring enough to pay what it had cost. This system was continued until a branch of the house, under the direction of Colonel William Pope, was established in Boston, through which the sale of the great quantities of lumber made at their various manufactories has been since principally managed.

Upon the removal of his father to Boston, Mr. Pope became the head of the firm, and entered at once upon a career of enlargement and expansion. About fifteen years ago he made his first purchase of Mill property at Machias and commenced operating here. Since then he has bought for himself and partners a share in the mills and railroad at Whitneyville, the Harwood mills and wharves at this place, and three entire townships and parts of four other townships of timber lands on this river. He joined Messrs. Talbot and Harris in the purchase of the fine water power at Columbia, and of two townships of land lying upon Pleasant River. . . .

There may be instances in this part of the State of more daring speculations than these, but none, we venture to say, in the whole State, where boldness of investment has been followed up by the same systematic administration, issuing in inevitable success. In the midst of commercial embarrassments, casual losses by fires and shipwreck, and in spite of the constant requirement of fresh capital for rapidly expanding enterprises, the paper of S. W. Pope & Co. has stood as the symbol of solvency and good faith.

Thoroughly trained in an apprenticeship not unfamiliar with the axe and the pickpole, Mr. Pope so carefully calculated the requirements of success in the employment in which he was engaged, that failure could only result from some extraordinary calamity.

The cares of large business were borne by Mr. Pope, with an ease that showed an almost unbounded capacity for the management of affairs. He was never perplexed or confused, but held his large business under an easy control. He never pleaded absorption in business as an excuse for being unsocial, unpatriotic or uncharitable. He had time enough to be a good citizen, a good neighbor, and a good Christian, to study all matters of national interest, to intervene actively for the promotion of sound politics, to devise means of helping the poor, to promote public improvement and moral reform, and to diffuse among the people the knowledge of the Christian faith. He recognized the demands his fellow men and his Master had upon his increased power of doing good. We cannot, in our regret that such a life has been so short, withhold our thankfulness that so short a life has accomplished so much."

To make this sketch more complete, we make extract from an appreciative notice of the deceased, furnished in the *Machias Union*, and from the appropriate remarks of the Rev. H. F. Harding on the occasion of the funeral.

"It was indeed a sad day in this community that recorded the death of a man so useful and so eminent, and by it a void has been made in society, that cannot well be filled, and that few now living will forget. We have other men distinguished in a single walk in life, but Mr. Pope stood pre-eminent in many. He turned the faculties God had given him, energy and sagacity, to a laudable purpose.

The poor he aided in the most Christian of all ways, by giving them employment and paying them. The sick and distressed he was ever ready to relieve by direct aid.

By his talents and through the medium of his business relations he had, and exerted, a large share of political influence. At first a Whig, then, when the Temperance issue controlled the politics of the State, he was on the side of Temperance; upon the formation of the Republican party, he became one of its most zealous supporters.

For many years he was an active member of the Congregational Church at East Machias, and Superintendent of the Sabbath School. He loved the church, not because he could gain distinction or profit from it, but because religion was congenial to his nature, and he found pleasure from laboring in his Master's cause. . . .

. . In his domestic relations, he was the pattern and model of a husband and father. When he crossed the threshold of his home, all the vexations, cares and irritation of the outer world and of daily life, he left behind him, and brought with him into the circle of his fireside and the bosom of his family only the heart of a true husband and father. With his children he became a child again, their friend, companion and equal. And it is a circumstance most pleasant to remember and speak of, that almost his last hours of health and strength were devoted to them, and were spent in sharing their amusements, and heightening their enjoyments.

He was a firm believer in Jesus Christ, the Saviour and Redeemer of mankind. Nor was his belief that vague and general acquiescence in the

Christian Religion, which all of us cherish, but a deep personal conviction and experience of its truth — that living faith which is unto salvation. And even in the pressure of weekly business, with all its harassing cares and fatigues, he found time for social worship and devotion.

And those who knew him best, knew well that he was not without the inner witness of the Spirit testifying with his spirit that he was born of God, and that indwelling of the Spirit which was the seal of his acceptance, and the earnest of his glorious inheritance, upon which he has now entered."

CHILDREN.

I.  WILLIAM JONES,[9] b. July 24, 1841.  [See next chapter, A, 6.]

II.  EMILY FRANCES,[9] b. Sept. 25, 1843 ; m. Dec. 15, 1868, Austin Harris, son of Peter Talbot and Deborah (Longfellow) Harris, of East Machias, Me.  He graduated from Amherst College, 1863 ; has represented his district in each of the branches of the Maine legislature.  Is engaged in the lumber business at East Machias, in partnership with J. O. Pope and others.  Children :

1.  Florence *Harris*, b. Aug. 14, 1869.
2.  Edna Pope *Harris*, b. June 19, 1871 ; d. May 7, 1873.
3.  Mabel Austin *Harris*, b. March 11, 1875.
4.  Samuel Pope *Harris*, b. Feb. 3, 1878.
5.  Philip Talbot *Harris*, b. Feb. 10, 1881.
6.  Emily *Harris*, b. May 2, 1882.

III.  BESSIE TALBOT,[9] b. May 2, 1845 ; was m. April 9, 1868, to William Henry Hawley, who was b. March 10, 1844, in Boston, the home of his parents, Truman Ripley and Harriet Augusta (Tobey) Hawley.

He served in the 44th Regiment Mass. Vol. Infantry in the War of the Rebellion.  Afterwards he raised and commanded a company of men.

Captain Hawley lived on a farm in Westboro some years ; now resides in Malden.  He is a salesman in the extensive clothing establishment of Macullar, Parker & Co., in Boston.  Children :

1.  Marion *Hawley*, b. Feb. 12, 1869.
2.  Augusta *Hawley*, b. Feb. 25, 1872.

 3. Mary Pope *Hawley*, b. Sept. 9, 1873.
 4. William Pope *Hawley*, b. Dec. 13, 1874.
 5. Truman Ripley *Hawley*, b. Oct. 17, 1876.
 6. Lillian *Hawley*, b. Oct. 12, 1883.

IV. EDNA,[9] b. Dec. 10, 1849; possessed a finely balanced nature, and gave promise of unusual attainments. While a pupil of a school in Lexington, she was seized with malignant typhoid fever, and died in Boston, Nov. 16, 1865.

V. MARY LORING,[9] b. Oct. 26, 1853; m. May 2, 1877, at Boston, George Allen Salmon, son of Dr. Ira Allen and Maria Whipple (Chaffee) Salmon, of Boston, Mass. *Child:* Bessie Talbot *Salmon*, b. Aug. 18, 1882, in Minneapolis, Minn.

VI. ALICE,[9] b. April 9, 1860. Resides in Boston with her mother.

---

## A, 9.

## THE FAMILY OF ANDREW JACKSON[8].

ANDREW JACKSON,[8] son of William[7] and Peggy Dawes (Billings), b. Jan. 6, 1820, m. in East Machias, Me., Sept. 6, 1852, Emily Foster, dau. of Dea. Peter and Eliza (Chaloner) Talbot, of East Machias. Mrs. Talbot was a daughter of the celebrated physician, Dr. William Chaloner, and his wife Mary Dillaway. Dea. Talbot was one of the most highly respected and beloved citizens of East Machias, and lived to a ripe old age.

### *Children born in San Francisco, Cal.*

I. FLORENCE TALBOT,[9] b. Sept. 20, 1857; m. Sept. 14, 1887, to Mr. Frederick A. Frank, of San Francisco, son of Augustus S. and Martha M. (Hopkins) Frank, all three natives of Granville, Washington Co., New York. He is a merchant.

II. CHARLES EDWARD,[9] b. July 27, 1859; d. Oct. 23, 1860.

III.  MARY ELLA,[9] b. Feb. 23, 1862.    Resides in San Francisco, with her mother.
IV.  GEORGE ANDREW,[9] b. April 26, 1864.  Is a member of
the firm organized by his father and uncle.

Mr. Andrew J. Pope was one of the most successful business
men to whom Maine has given a cradle or California a field.
Trained in boyhood to help his father in all departments of the
lumber business, he obtained thorough knowledge and experience
of practical details.  The "pickpole" and "quill" were alike
familiar tools ; and he could gauge a saw or estimate the price
of a cargo with equal facility.  With habits of honest, "square"
dealing ; with quiet determination which could tire out obstacles
from which others would retreat ; with calm confidence in men
he found trustworthy, but with complete indifference to the
cajolings of the unworthy, he made a steady march from his few
hundreds at his majority to his several millions at his death.

As the representative of the firms of William Pope & Sons of
Boston, and S. W. Pope & Co., of East Machias, he first went
to California, to dispose of shipments of lumber.  He sent back
large profits to father and brothers, and after a while began to
enter into business of his own.  He bought lands, which grew
to be immensely valuable.  He opened a store for the sale of
doors, sashes, and blinds, at the corner of Pine and Battery
Streets.  He took one of the piers in Stewart wharf, when that
was built, and afterwards moved to larger quarters.

He associated himself with his wife's brother, Captain William
C. Talbot, a man of remarkable vigor and enterprise, in the firm
of Pope & Talbot.  They, with others, purchased and erected mills
at Teekalet (Port Gamble), on Puget Sound, Washington Territory, and obtaining vessels from Maine and elsewhere, entered
upon the exportation of lumber, spars, etc., on a vast scale.  Not
only did they have wharves and store and office at San Francisco,
but sold many cargoes to other dealers, controlling that market,
and supplied the demand of many foreign and domestic ports.

Through all Mr. Pope remained temperate, upright, unostentatious, inclining to the habits of frugality which had helped
him to acquire wealth, and never becoming careless or wasteful.
He was a firm friend, fond of his family, regular at business, at

church and at home.   He was a good citizen, giving his voice
in private, and his vote and presence in public, and his contribu-
tions when needed, to help on good and humane causes.   Li-
braries, churches, benevolent societies, individuals, flooded him
with applications ; and many great gifts and many small ones
did he bestow.   The writer has been a witness of some of these
kind responses of his to the calls of the needy and claims of humanity and affection.

He died Dec. 18, 1878.   The following obituary appeared in
one of the journals of the city he had helped to build.   It is a
suitable memorial of our honored kinsman.

In accordance with the wishes of the family the funeral obsequies of the
late Andrew J. Pope were conducted as quietly and unostentatiously as possible, at the family residence on Folsom Street, yesterday afternoon, at two
o'clock.

This was in perfect accord with the habit and manner of the daily life of
the deceased.  Anything like ostentation or display was foreign to his nature, and at variance with his taste and disposition.  The funeral services
were conducted by Rev. A. L. Stone, pastor of the First Congregational
Church, to which Mr. Pope and his family were allied.  The pall bearers
were W. F. Whittier, W. F. Babcock, John Taylor, L. S. Adams, G. W.
Beaver, Jerome Lincoln, J. S. Bacon, and S. H. Harmon.  The remains
were interred in the family ground in Laurel Hill Cemetery.  From the
business community of San Francisco has dropped out one of its most
prominent and enterprising citizens.  His superior judgment, his tireless
energy, and his rare, extensive knowledge of the business to which his life
was devoted, will make his loss deeply felt not only by the firm of which he
was senior partner, but also by all the different branches of the business to
which this extensive firm is related in the State and on the Coast.

Mr. Pope has ever been known as a signally upright man, a man whose
word was as good as his bond, honest in his dealings, and faithful in all the
relations of life.  The relation between the partners in the firm, Messrs.
Pope and Talbot, has always been of the most harmonious character, and
for nearly a quarter of a century they have been building up their extensive
lumber business on this coast.  Their warm business relations were cemen-
ted still more strongly by intermarriages between the two families, Mrs.
Pope being a sister of W. C. Talbot.

In fact, we are informed that for more than a century these two families
have been interlinked by family ties.  In his home life Mr. Pope was
warmly beloved.  A kind husband, a tender father, and a faithful friend,
his loss will be sadly felt by those whose life was made glad by his love.
In the distribution of his charity as in everything else, Mr. Pope was
quiet and unostentatious, but a needy, deserving person never applied to
him in vain.

A, 10.

## THE FAMILY OF JAMES OTIS⁸.

JAMES OTIS,⁸ son of William⁷ and Peggy Dawes (Billings),
b. Feb. 17, 1822; m. June 9, 1857, Olive Frances, daughter of
Simeon and Louisa (Foster) Chase, of East Machias, Me., b.
June 9, 1835. He was a member of the firm of William Pope
& Sons, then of its successor in the Maine department of the
family's business, S. W. Pope & Co., afterward J. O. Pope &
Co., thus continuing in the business of lumber manufacturing
and shipping for his whole life, and in the place of his birth nearly
all of the time.   Children :

   I.  JOHN ADAMS,⁹ b. May 8, 1858.
  II.  WARREN FOSTER,⁹ b. March 30, 1861.
 III.  ARTHUR WARD,⁹ b. Sept. 13, 1864; d. Oct. 25, 1866.
 IV.  HELEN AUGUSTA,⁹ b. Jan. 6, 1868; d. Oct. 4, 1885, of
      consumption.   She was a very promising girl, exceed-
      ingly amiable, and many hearts were made sad by her
      untimely death.   She had advanced finely in her studies,
      and had chosen the Great Teacher for her Lord and
      Guide.   But the casket proved too frail, and the gem
      was lost to earth ; yet faith expects to find her where
      the Lord " makes up His jewels."
  V.  MACY STANTON,⁹ b. July 26, 1869.

---

A, 11.

## THE FAMILY OF EDWIN⁸.

EDWIN,⁸ son of William⁷ and Peggy Dawes (Billings), b.
May 30, 1826 ; was m. in Boston, Oct. 25, 1855, to Anna Rice,
daughter of Robert and Mary Billings (Thayer) Prescott, b. in
Boston, July 27, 1830.

Robert Prescott was b. in Carlisle, England, in 1803.   Mary
Billings Thayer was b. in Dorchester, Mass., Aug. 8, 1803.

Mr. Edwin Pope, though born in East Machias, Me., has spent nearly the whole of his life in Boston. He was associated with his father many years, and has continued in the lumber business to this time, enjoying the respect and esteem of a wide circle of business acquaintances and family friends.

### Children, born in Boston.

I. EDWIN HERBERT,[9] b. Dec. 28, 1857.

II. ARTHUR WARD,[9] b. Nov. 5, 1859; d. Nov. 12, 1863.

III. WALTER BURNSIDE,[9] b. Jan. 29, 1861.

IV. NELLIE BUCKINGHAM,[9] b. Dec. 29, 1862; was m. by Rev. M. J. Savage, Oct. 29, 1884, to Harry Wadley Cumner, of Boston, son of Nathaniel Wentworth and Harriet Elizabeth (Wadley) Cumner, b. in Manchester, N. H., July 18, 1860. *Child:* Marjorie *Cumner,* b. July 23, 1887.

V. WILLIAM,[9] b. Oct. 15, 1864; d. Oct. 29, 1864.

VI. EVERETT LINCOLN,[9] b. Nov. 27, 1865.

VII. MARTHA WASHINGTON,[9] b. May 23, 1868.

---

### A, 12.

## THE FAMILY OF GEORGE WASHINGTON[8].

GEORGE WASHINGTON,[8] son of William[7] and Peggy Dawes (Billings), b. Jan. 30, 1832, m. Nov. 17, 1867, Abigail Edwina, daughter of Lemuel Trescott and Zeresh N. (Hoyt) Avery, of East Machias, Me. She was great-granddaughter of James Avery, Esquire, Justice of the Peace, Town Clerk, etc., at Machias, in 1785 *et seq.* Children :

I. GRACE BILLINGS,[9] b. Aug. 1, 1869.

II. EDITH,[9] b. June 9, 1871.

III. GEORGIA WASHINGTON,[9] b. Feb. 21, 1873.

George Washington[8] was educated in Boston and trained in and into "the firm."

After the death of his brother, Samuel Ward,[8] the firm at East Machias found itself so burdened with cares, especially when trade was quickened by the war, that George W. was called from Boston to assist. He soon showed himself possessed of many of those business and social qualities which had distinguished his departed brother, and became a most valuable associate of his older brothers, popular with employees and neighbors, sagacious and strong in enterprise, affectionate and devoted to his family, and a public-spirited citizen. He was elected to the State Legislature, and proved a worthy successor of his father in public matters.

A serious rheumatic difficulty came upon him in the midst of his activities, and made his elastic spirit bend; but never did he lose his cheerfulness or his delight in others' pleasure.

Finding, however, that disease was breaking him down prematurely, he sought every hopeful means of recovery, and was *en route* for the famous Hot Springs of Arkansas when a violent attack arrested his progress at St. Louis, where, in spite of the best medical aid and the unwearied exertions of his fond wife and other ardent friends, he closed his eyes Dec. 9, 1875.

Thus, in the midst of his prime, with high hopes and expectations of a wide circle, was another of the "goodly boughs" of this "family tree" broken off.

But he lives in the love of many hearts, who yielded him up to the *Ever-living Father.*

---

A, 13.

## THE FAMILY OF WARREN WEBSTER[6].

WARREN WEBSTER,[8] son of Frederick,[7] jr., and Sally B. (Phillips), b. March 5, 1838; m. July 4, 1858, Marrilla Thayer of Braintree. He was a soldier in Co. H, 12th Mass. Vol. Infantry. Resides in Weymouth. Children:

    I.  SARAH E.,[9] b. June 30, 1859.
    II.  FREDERICK W.,[9] b. April 12, 1861.
    III.  FRANK H.,[9] b. Sept. 6, 1863.
    IV.  EDWIN L.,[9]   } b. Feb. 10, 1866; } 
    V.  ELLA F.,[9]    }                 } d. Dec. 10, 1868.

VI. HUBERT G.,[9] b. July 16, 1869.
VII. EDNA L.,[9] b. Sept. 1, 1871.
VIII. CHARLES W.,[9] b. June 9, 1874.
IX. HELEN L.,[9] b. May 30, 1875.
X. WALTER A.,[9] b. Aug. 26, 1877.
XI. LEO E.,[9] b. June 24, 1879.

---

## A, 14.

## THE FAMILY OF EUGENE ALEXANDER[8].

EUGENE ALEXANDER,[8] son of Samuel[7] and Sarah Stetson (Mellish), b. Aug. 3, 1846 ; m. April 13, 1876, Ella Malora, daughter of Charles M. and Zelida A. (Taft) Browne, b. July 7, 1851. Children :

I. FREDERIC,[9] b. Nov. 20, 1877.
II. GEORGE MELLISH,[9] b. Feb. 19, 1880.
III. MARY EMMA,[9] b. Nov. 1, 1881.
IV. BEATRICE ELIZABETH,[9] b. Oct. 23, 1886.

Eugene A. Pope has been connected with the real estate and business agency of Charles U. Cotting, Boston, for nearly twenty-five years. Resides at Cambridge.

---

## A, 15.

## THE FAMILY OF CHARLES HENRY[8].

CHARLES HENRY,[8] son of James[7] and Eunice (Thaxter), b. Oct. 18, 1841, was m. July 31, 1865, in East Machias, Me., at the home of the bride, to Elizabeth Leach, daughter of the late Niran Bates, M. D., and his first wife, Charlotte Lamson, daughter of Colonel John and Elizabeth (Lamson) Dennet, of Exeter, N. H. She was born in Oldtown, Me., March 16, 1837.

He fitted for college at Washington Academy ; graduated at Bowdoin College in 1862, and Bangor Theological Seminary in 1865. Was ordained, in company with five classmates, at

Bangor, Me., July 27, 1865, and went to California the following month, under the auspices of the American Home Missionary Society.   There he labored at Grass Valley, San Mateo, and Hydesville ; became pastor of the church at Benicia, May 11, 1869.   After three years he assumed the principalship of " The Young Ladies' Seminary, at Benicia," in which he and his wife wrought for three years.   In 1874 he resumed ministerial labors, taking the pastoral charge of the Second Congregational Church, Oakland.   In 1877 he returned to New England.   Was called to the pastorate of the church in Thomaston, Me., in December, and remained there until the autumn of 1882.   In February following, he accepted the call of the church at Farmington, Me., and removed thither.   Was installed June 5, 1883.   Offered his resignation in May, 1887 ; was given leave of absence for a journey to England ; was dismissed Aug. 9, 1887.   Child :

NIRAN BATES,[9] b. in Thomaston, Me., July 17, 1879.

---

A, 16.

## THE FAMILY OF CHARLES ALLEN[8].

CHARLES ALLEN,[8] son of · Charles[7] and Elizabeth (Bogman), b. June 27, 1835 ; m. April 3, 1860, Julia Anne, dau. of Henry and Sarah (Blackman) Mellish.

He passed several years of his youth and early manhood on the ocean, and visited a great many countries, observing men and things with fine discrimination.   Spent some time in Australia, gold hunting.   He settled down in Boston, declining the offer of good marine positions.   Engaged in a department of the hardware business.   His wife died Sept. 16, 1867.   He died Nov. 26, 1868.   The two surviving children were brought up in the family of their grandfather, Mr. Charles[7] Pope.   Children :

I.   HARRY MELVILLE,[9] b. Oct. 15, 1861.   [See next chapter, A, 7.]

II.   LUELLA FRANCES,[9] b. March 7, 1864.

III.   ADA EVELYN,[9] b. Jan. 23, 1866 ; d. Sept. 13, 1867.

## A, 17.

## THE FAMILY OF ALBERT AUGUSTUS⁸.

ALBERT AUGUSTUS,⁸ son of Charles⁷ and Elizabeth (Bogman), b. May 20, 1843 ; m. Sept. 20, 1871, Abby, daughter of George and Matilda (Smallwood) Linder, of Newton, Mass. Mr. Linder came to Boston from England, in his early manhood; was an importer, a well-known and much respected merchant.

Albert A. Pope was educated in the public schools of Brookline, and trained in the "leather findings" business in the store of Brooks & M'Cuen in Boston. Aug. 22, 1862, he entered the 35th Mass. Volunteer Infantry, and was appointed second lieutenant. In spite of his extreme youth he was promoted to first lieutenant, March 23, 1863, and was entrusted with a captain's commission, April 1, 1864. He was employed upon important detached services, and acted as commander of this regiment on many occasions, in the absence of its colonel. Organized a regiment of artillery for the defenses of Washington ; took part in the chief Virginia campaigns, and served under Burnside, in Tennessee. He was brevetted major "for gallant conduct at the battle of Fredericksburg, Va.," and lieutenant-colonel "for gallant conduct in the battles of Knoxville, Poplar Springs Church, and front of Petersburg," March 13, 1865.

After the war Colonel Pope returned quietly to his former employers, but before very long went into business for himself. He manufactured slipper decorations, and dealt in shoe manufacturers' supplies in general. He organized and became president of "The Pope Manufacturing Company," Boston, — in which he owns a controlling interest, — which made and sold several patented articles, but which finally became engrossed in the manufacture and sale of bicycles and tricycles. He has been justly termed "the founder of American bicycle industries." He is also president of the Municipal Signal Company, director in the Weed Sewing Machine Company, The Boston Cab Company, and several other corporations. He resides in Boston. Children :

 I. ALBERT LINDER,[9] b. July 14, 1872.
 II. MARY LINDER,[9] b. March 9; d. June 9, 1874.
III. MARGARET ROBERTS,[9] b. May 29, 1876.
IV. HAROLD LINDER,[9] b. Nov. 5, 1879.
 V. CHARLES LINDER,[9] b. Nov. 15, 1881.
VI. LINDER,[9] b. March 23, 1887.

---

A, 18.

## THE FAMILY OF LOUIS ATHERTON[8].

LOUIS ATHERTON,[8] son of Charles[7] and Elizabeth (Bogman), b. Oct. 6, 1852; m. Sept. 4, 1877, Imogene, daughter of James H. and Miranda (Peirce) Titus, born Dec. 30, 1850.

He graduated at Brown University, Providence, R. I., in the year 1874. He graduated at Newton Theological Seminary, 1877. Was ordained and installed pastor of the Baptist church at Mansfield, Aug. 30, 1877, and continued there until Nov., 1879. Became pastor at Phœnix, R. I., July 4, 1880, and closed his labors there March 1, 1884, when he accepted a call to Warren, R. I., where he is still settled.   Children :

 I. ROBERT ANDERSON,[9] b. Aug. 3, 1878.
 II. ATHERTON LEESON,[9] b. June 29, 1879; d. Aug. 29, 1883.
III. ARTHUR UPHAM,[9] b. Feb. 7, 1881.
IV. ELIZABETH BOGMAN,[9] b. July 8, 1885.

---

A, 19.

## THE FAMILY OF GEORGE[8].

GEORGE,[8] son of William[7] and Mary (Bogman), b. Jan. 9, 1844; m. Nov. 24, 1873, Annie Atwood, daughter of Lathley and Mary Baylies (Dean) Rich, of Watertown, b. in Winterport, Me., Oct. 24, 1849.

As a boy he entered the wholesale dry goods house of Wilson, Hamilton & Co., Boston, and rose from one position to another in the business. In the war of the Rebellion, he enlisted in the 44th Massachusetts Volunteer Infantry, and was in service with the regiment until discharged for promotion. He was commissioned captain, and placed in command of Company I, in the 54th Massachusetts, the first regiment of colored troops organized in the Northern States. He remained with it until the close of the war. Saw hard service,.was wounded ; was promoted major, Dec. 3, 1864, and lieutenant-colonel, July 11, 1865.

Since the war he has been in the lumber business for the most part ; for several years past has been the Montreal agent of The Export Lumber Company, shipping cargoes to many ports. He spends the winters in Boston.   Child :

MARION,[9] b. Dec. 18, 1874.

---

A, 20.

## THE FAMILY OF EDWARD WALDRON[8].

EDWARD WALDRON,[8] son of William[7] and Mary (Bogman), b. Nov. 26, 1845 ; m. Sept. 2, 1875, Florence Anna, daughter of Augustus Franklin and Hannah (Bright) Lemon, of Andover, b. April 28, 1846. Began business life as a clerk in the store of Frank Skinner & Co., dealers in woolens. In the fall of 1868 he made a change to out-of-door employment, and took a position in the lumber yard of Shepard, Hall & Co.

He was chosen secretary of the Pope Manufacturing Company at its organization, and has remained in the house until the present time, being now the treasurer of the corporation.

Resides in Newton.   Child :

MARY HANNAH,[9] b. Feb. 14, 1878.

---

A, 21.

## THE FAMILY OF FRANK GILBERT[8].

FRANK GILBERT,[8] son of John[7] and Harriet Maria (Gilbert), b. July 7, 1846 ; m. May 28, 1872, Mary Ella, daughter of Calvin P. and Lucy L. Elliot, of Boston, b. July 22, 1847.

He is a stencil-cutter, having learned the business with his father, and worked in partnership with him many years. Resides in Malden. Child :

MABEL ALICE,⁹ b. July 8, 1873.

---

A, 22.

## THE FAMILY OF ALEXANDER,⁸ JR.

ALEXANDER,⁸ JR., son of Alexander⁷ and Charlotte Caldwell (Cushing), b. March 25, 1849, m. Sept. 16, 1873, Alice D'Wolf, daughter of Samuel and Nancy Melville (D'Wolf) Downer, of Dorchester. He has attained considerable distinction as an artist, especially by his very clever paintings of animals.

Two books have issued from his studio : "Upland Game Birds and Waterfowl of the United States." Scribner & Co., N. Y., 1877. 20 pp., 20 plates. Letter press from Wilson's American Ornithology ; and "Celebrated Dogs of America, imported and native." S. E. Casino, Boston, 1880. His office and studio are in Boston ; his home in Dorchester. Children :

I.  SAMUEL DOWNER,⁹ b. Dec. 10, 1875.
II. CHARLOTTE D'WOLF,⁹ b. Nov. 19, 1878.

---

A, 23.

## THE FAMILY OF JOHN FOSTER⁸.

JOHN FOSTER,⁸ son of William⁷ and Sarah Ann (Foster), b. Oct. 20, 1837, was m. Nov. 10, 1868, by Rev. B. F. Barrett, to Odelia Louise, daughter of Constantine and Marianna Hering, b. in Philadelphia, March 28, 1840. Is connected with the house of W. C. Pope & Co., Boston. Resides in Dorchester.

The ancestors of Dr. Constantine Hering came from Moravia ; the family name was written Hrinka. Dr. Hering's father was Christian Gottlieb Karl Hering, b. Oct. 25, 1766, in Schandau, Saxony, d. Jan. 4, 1853, in Zittau ; m. in

1797, in Oschatz, to Christiane Friedericke Kreutzberg, b. June 26, 1777; d. Nov. 7, 1817, in Zittau, Saxony. Constantine Hering, b. Jan. 1, 1800, in Oschatz, Saxony, d. July 23, 1880, in Philadelphia; m. 1833, in Philadelphia, to Juliana Mariane Husmann, daughter of George Husmann, of Philadelphia, who was b. Jan. 16, 1814, at Bremen; d. 1840, in Philadelphia. Children:

I. WILLIAM CONSTANTINE,[9] b. June 29, 1869.
II. SARAH FOSTER,[9] b. July 4, 1875.

---

A, 24

## THE FAMILY OF WILLIAM CARROLL[8].

WILLIAM CARROLL,[8] b. May 8, 1847; m. Nov. 28, 1876, Mabel Richmond, daughter of Samuel and Nancy Melville (D'Wolf) Downer, of Dorchester, b. May 21, 1856.

Mr. Downer was extensively known as one of the earliest and most highly reputed manufacturers of refined kerosene oil. Another of his public benefactions was the development of that seaside resort which bears his name, at the entrance to Hingham Bay.

Mr. William Carroll[8] Pope is the head of the firm of W. C. Pope & Co., importers and jobbers of "East India products," principally copal and other gums, the basis of varnishes. In addition to this, the firm own and work a manganese mine, near Sussex, New Brunswick. He resides at Dorchester. Children:

I. ALLAN MELVILL,[9] b. Nov. 24, 1879.
II. BAYARD FOSTER,[9] b. Oct. 5, 1887.

---

A, 25.

## THE FAMILY OF GEORGE HIRAM[8].

GEORGE HIRAM,[8] son of Hiram[7] and Dorcas A. (Blanchard), b. April 27, 1848; m. Dec. 24, 1874, Abbie Isabel, daughter of Francis W. and Abigail Brann, of West Gardiner, Me.

He is an enterprising farmer, combining the industrious, thrifty, upright principles of his father with such "new-fangled notions" as are worth adopting. Resides on the place cleared and built up by his grandfather, Elijah⁶. Children :

    I.  HIRAM FRANKLIN,⁹ b. July 11, 1877.
    II.  CLARA BELL,⁹ b. March 5, 1879.
    III.  FOREST GEORGE,⁹ b. April 11, 1881.

---

## A, 26.

## THE ·FAMILY OF GEORGE WILLIAM⁸.

GEORGE WILLIAM,⁸ son of Frederic⁷ and Miriam Ball (Bridges), b. April 28, 1845 ; m. Nov. 26, 1883, Sarah E. Whitaker, of Boston, b. Jan. 19, 1865. He has been engaged in the express business in Boston. Child :

    MIRIAM ELIZABETH,⁹ b. March 21, 1885.

---

## A, 27.

## THE FAMILY OF LUTHER EDMUND⁸.

LUTHER EDMUND,⁸ son of Luther and Eunice Maria (Collyer), b. Oct. 7, 1836 ; m. Nov. 25, 1863, Lavina Emma, daughter of George Washington and Abigail (Rideout) Leavitt, of Richmond, Me. Child :

    ALICE EVELYN,⁹ was m. to Charles Wallace Whiting, of Brockton, who was b. Aug. 15, 1853. They had one child, Minnie Estelle *Whiting*, b. ——; d. Sept. 3, 1881. Mr. Whiting d. March 8, 1882, and Mrs. Alice Evelyn (Pope) Whiting d. May 3, 1884.

Luther E. Pope is a shoemaker, and resides in Brockton.

A, 28.

## THE FAMILY OF CHARLES HENRY⁸.

CHARLES HENRY,⁸ son of Edmund⁷ and Abby Ann (Smith), b. in Norton, May 15, 1844; m. in Stoughton, May 15, 1869, Alice, daughter of George and Martha (Tilden) Russell, b. in Stoughton, March 18, 1851.   Children :

     I.   ARTHUR C.,⁹ b. Jan. 19, 1870.
    II.   NETTIE F.,⁹ b. June 11, 1872 ; d. July 10, 1887.
   III.   EDITH F.,⁹ b. Jan. 23, 1874.
    IV.   MARY E.,⁹ b. Nov. 14, 1874.
     V.   CORA A.,⁹ b. Oct. 12, 1878.
    VI.   BERTHA T.,⁹ b. Aug. 2, 1880.
   VII.   WILLIAM F.,⁹ b. Sept. 1, 1882.
  VIII.   GEORGE E.,⁹ b. Dec. 1, 1885.

He is a boot and shoe maker in East Stoughton.   Served in the U. S. Navy and Army in the War of the Rebellion.

DESCENDANTS OF LAZARUS[4].

I.

## THE FAMILY OF JOHN QUINCY[8].

JOHN QUINCY,[8] b. in Roxbury, Oct. 25, 1824, eldest son of Norton Quincy[7] and Hitty Jane (Perry), m. (1), 1846, Dorcas Ann Bailey, of Wiscasset, Me. She d. April, 1850, aged twenty-three years. Child:

I.  JABEZ WALTER,[9] b. in Quincy, July 19, 1847. [See next chapter, B, 1.]

John Quincy[8] Pope married (2), Dec. 25, 1851, Elizabeth Todd, dau. of Capt. Benjamin and Elizabeth Todd (Currier) Stickney, of Salem. Child:

II.  HITTY JANE,[9] b. May 11, 1853 ; m. June 25, 1882, Charles H. Dodge, of Groton.

John Quincy[8] Pope served three years in a Massachusetts regiment in the war of the Rebellion. He has been one of the special policemen at the Boston and Albany Railroad Station, Boston, many years.

B, 2.

## THE FAMILY OF CHARLES EDWARD[8].

CHARLES EDWARD,[8] son of Norton Quincy[7] and Mehitable [Hitty] Jane (Perry), b. Nov. 14, 1834; m. Nov. 26, 1857, Sarah Eliza, dau. of Ezekiel C. and Phebe (Illsley) Benja-

min, b. Jan. 12, 1835. He served three years in the Federal
army during the War of the Rebellion. Is a painter ; resides
in Boston. Children :

   I.  FLORENCE ADELIA,⁹ b. Aug. 31, 1858 ; d. Feb. 25,
      1863.

  II.  CHARLES HENRY,⁹ b. June 20, 1860 ; d. March 11, 1863.

 III.  NORTON QUINCY,⁹ b. Oct. 13, 1865. Is a clerk in Boston.

 IV.  PHEBE GERTRUDE SOPHIA,⁹ b. Feb. 28, 1867 ; m. April 29,
      1886, to Charles Henry Blanchard.

  V.  FANNIE MAY,⁹ b. Nov. 4, 1870 ; d. Nov. 19, 1875.

 VI.  JANE MEAD ANTOINETTE,⁹ b. July 12, 1874 ; d. Nov. 19,
      1875.

---

### B, 3.

## THE FAMILY OF ASA AUGUSTUS⁸.

ASA AUGUSTUS,⁸ son of Samuel Brown⁷ and Mary Ann
(Capen), b. July 20, 1838 ; m. Oct. 19, 1867, Nettie F., dau.
of George and Mary E. Packard, b. July 13, 1846. She died
Dec. 28, 1880. He is a boot-maker ; resides in Quincy. Children :

   I.  GRACIE MABEL,⁹ b. May 21, 1878 ; d. of bronchitis, Dec.
      27, 1878.

  II.  NETTIE FLORENCE,⁹ b. Dec. 7, 1880.

---

### B, 4.

## THE FAMILY OF BENJAMIN FRANKLIN⁸.

BENJAMIN FRANKLIN,⁸ son of Joseph⁷ and Jane (Lovell),
b. Sept. 23, 1837 ; m. Jan. 30, 1860, Rosanna Dill James. He
is in the fishing business. Resides at Hull. Child :

    GEORGE FRANKLIN⁹, b. Aug. 24, 1860. [See next chapter,
    B, 2.]

B, 5.

## THE FAMILY OF LEMUEL CLARK[8].

LEMUEL CLARK,[8] son of Micajah Clark[7] and Nancy P. (Webster), b. Nov. 21, 1836 ; m. (1), June 15, 1865, Abbie Francis, dau. of Edwin B. and Sara A. (Hook) Bennette, of Dorchester. She d. Dec. 24, 1876. Child :

    I. LEWIS FRANCIS,[9] b. July 17, 1872.

He m. (2) Feb., 1878, Mrs. Sarah Noble (Plummer) Kenney, dau. of Alva and Olive (Littlefield) Plummer, and widow of Cornelius G. Kenney, of Dorchester, b. in Canaan, Me., June 22, 1845. She d. Aug. 14, 1884. Her daughter by former husband, Cornelia Golden Kenney, has been legally adopted by Mr. Pope, and is therefore to be registered as

    II. CORNELIA GOLDEN[9] POPE, b. June 14, 1871.

He m. (3), Ella Elizabeth, dau. of Wm. and Caroline Louisa (Ronimus) Littlefield, of Roxbury, born Jan. 3, 1859. Mr. Littlefield is a native of Kennebunk, Me., Mrs. L. of Havre, France.

Lemuel C. Pope was a soldier in the War of the Rebellion, a member of Co. B, 45th Mass. Vol. Infantry. Is a mounted policeman in the Field's Corner district of Dorchester.

---

B, 6.

## THE FAMILY OF CHARLES GREENWOOD[8].

CHARLES GREENWOOD,[8] son of Rev. Rufus Spurr[7] and Sarah Brown (Parkhurst), b. Nov. 18, 1840, at Hardwick ; m. Dec. 27, 1866, Josephine Harriet, dau. of Ephraim Erastus and Harriet Narcissa (Whitcomb) Cole, b. in Boston, Dec. 11, 1842. Mr. Cole was b. in Medfield, Feb. 5, 1815; d. in Somerville, July 4, 1878 ; Mrs. Cole was b. in Cavendish, Vt., Oct. 28, 1813.

Charles Greenwood[8] Pope graduated at Tufts College, in the class of 1862. Is a lawyer in Boston; resides in Somerville. Was a member of the Massachusetts House of Representatives, 1876, 1877.  Child :

TRACY COLE,[9] b. Dec. 18, 1869.

---

B, 7.

## THE FAMILY OF FREDERIC AUSTIN[8].

FREDERIC AUSTIN,[8] son of Franklin Manser[7] and Emily (Sherman), b. in Marlboro, May 4, 1853; m. June 6, 1873, Sarah Winch.  Resides in Marlboro.  Children :

I.   ELLA PHINETTE,[9] b. June 10, 1875.
II.  CLIFTON,[9] b. June 14, 1877.
III. GRACE ALMA,[9] b. June 10, 1879.
IV.  CHESTER FRANKLIN,[9] b. May 1, 1882.
V.   GEORGE PERCY,[9] b. Jan. 2, 1884.
VI.  LAURA GERTRUDE,[9] b. April 20, 1886.

# CHAPTER XII

# THE NINTH GENERATION.

## SECTION A.

### DESCENDANTS OF RALPH[4].

I.

## THE FAMILY OF JAMES FRANCIS[9].

JAMES FRANCIS,[9] eldest son of James[8] and Sarah
(Swan), born in Dorchester, Mass., May 28, 1845; married
Dec. 23, 1869, Harriet A., dau. of Benjamin and Mary J. (Day)
Gates, of Milton, b. in Dorchester, Sept. 20, 1845. She d.
March 27, 1883.

While a boy in the Dorchester high school, being then
only seventeen years of age, he, with others, was fired
with the prevailing spirit of patriotism, and wished to serve
his country. Much to the surprise of parents and friends
he was accepted, and joined the 13th Mass. Regiment. He
was taken prisoner at Gettysburg and sent to Belle Isle,
where he remained seven months. Fortunately release came
before it was too late, and he was granted a furlough for a
few months, during which time he visited his home, where he
regained his health. He afterward joined his regiment, remaining until the close of the war. He was some time cashier
of the Mattapan Bank, Dorchester. Is now in the ice business.
Child:

SARAH GATES,[10] born June 30, 1880.

## A, 2.

## THE FAMILY OF HERBERT WEBSTER[9].

HERBERT WEBSTER,[9] second son of James[8] and Sarah (Swan), born in Dorchester, Oct. 2, 1852; m. July 22, 1878, Julia Frances, dau. of George and Ruth (Cushing) Ellis, of Halifax, Nova Scotia.

He was a bank clerk; but his health failing he went to Colorado Springs, and engaged in the cattle business; died of consumption, Feb. 27, 1886. Children:

I. HERBERT ELLIS,[10] born July, 1879; d. Aug. 14, 1880.
II. RUTH CUSHING,[10] born at Colorado Springs, May 12, 1884.

---

## A, 3.

## THE FAMILY OF CHARLES ALBERT[9].

CHARLES ALBERT,[9] eldest son of Albert[8] and Harriet (Johnson), born in Dorchester, July 29, 1842; married in Flatbush, New York, May 17, 1866, Sarah Mary, daughter of George H. and Catharine (Langton) Bainbridge, b. in Lynn, Eng., Dec. 19, 1842. George H. Bainbridge was born in Chesterfield, and Catharine (Langton) was born in Cambridge, England.

Is bookkeeper for Walter Baker & Co., New York. Resides at Roselle, N. J.

*Children born in Brooklyn, N. Y.*

I. ALBERT ARTHUR,[10] b. June 3, 1867.
II. CHARLES BAINBRIDGE,[10] b. Aug. 4, 1869; d. Nov. 4, 1871.
III. GEORGE RICHARDS,[10] b. Feb. 12, 1872.
IV. ALICE MAY,[10] b. in Union, N. J., Sept. 8, 1881.

---

## A, 4.

## THE FAMILY OF ARTHUR WARREN[9].

ARTHUR WARREN,[9] son of Albert[8] and Harriet (Johnson), born in Dorchester, Nov. 30, 1846; married June 2, 1877, Fannie, dau. of John and Clara (Bussey) Kendrick of Dorchester, born in Dorchester, Aug. 13, 1851. He served three months during the War of the Rebellion; is an insurance agent with Cyrus Brewer & Co., Boston.   Resides in Dorchester.   Children :

I.   ARTHUR,[10] b. June 9, 1879.
II.  ELEANOR BUSSEY,[10] b. July 19, 1884 ; d. Nov. 20, 1885.

---

## A, 5.
## THE FAMILY OF FRED. HARRIS[9].

FRED. HARRIS,[9] son of Harris[8] and Julia Newcomb, born Feb. 7, 1860 ; married Sept. 11, 1884, in Montclair, N. J., Emelyn H., dau. of Josiah and Helen (Austin) Wilcox, born Nov., 1863. He is a salesman for D. C. Percival & Co., Boston, dealers in watches and jewelry.   Resides in Dorchester.   Child :

ARNOLD WATSON,[10] b. Sept. 25, 1887.

---

## A, 6.
## THE FAMILY OF WILLIAM JONES[9].

WILLIAM JONES,[9] son of Samuel Ward[8] and Betsey Jones (Talbot), b. in East Machias, Me., July 24, 1841 ; m. July 4, 1876, in Quebec, Canada, Janet, daughter of Robert and Isabella (Boa) Neil.   Robert Neil was born in Edinburgh, Scotland. Isabella Boa was born in Parish of St. Laurent, P. Q.

He was educated at Washington Academy, East Machias, and at Amherst College.   Spent several years in business in Boston. Is now in the lumber business in the city of Montreal, Canada.

*Children born in Quebec.*

I.   ETHEL NEIL,[10] b. Jan. 29, 1878.
II.  JANET,[10] b. July 18, 1880.

---

## A, 7.
## THE FAMILY OF HARRY MELVILLE[9].

HARRY MELVILLE,[9] son of Charles Allen[8] and Julia Anne (Mellish), b. Oct. 15, 1861 ; m. Sept. 19, 1883, Rosa, dau. of William and Ellen (Weston) O'Mara, of Cambridge ; she was born Feb. 7, 1858, in Kingston, Kent Co., N. B.

He graduated from the Massachusetts Institute of Technology in 1882, and entered upon the practical application of that course in the bicycle establishment of his uncle, Col. Albert A. Pope in Boston. He is now mechanical draughtsman at the Pope M'f'g Co's factory at Hartford, Conn.   Children :

I.   ALLEN,[10] b. June 22, 1884.
II.  JOSEPH,[10] b. June 20, 1886.
III. A DAUGHTER,[10] b. Jan. 18, 1888.

## SECTION B.

### THE DESCENDANTS OF LAZARUS[4].

### I.

## THE FAMILY OF JABEZ WALTER[9].

JABEZ WALTER,[9] son of John Quincy[8] and Dorcas Ann (Bailey), b. in Quincy, July 19, 1847 ; m. Dec., 1868, Sarah Elizabeth Hale. He served one year in the Federal army during the War of the Rebellion. He d. Sept. 23, 1872. The widow and children reside in St. Joseph, Mo.   Children :

I.  CLARA ESTELLE,[10] b. Dec., 1869.
II. JENNIE MAY,[10] b. Feb. 2, 1872.

### B, 2.

## THE FAMILY OF GEORGE FRANKLIN[9].

GEORGE FRANKLIN,[9] son of Benjamin[8] and Rosanna Dill (James), b. in Hull, Aug. 24, 1860 ; m. July 23, 1882, Josephine E. Galiano. He is in the fishing business.   Child :

JESSIE ALMA,[10] b. March 16, 1883.

# CHAPTER XIII.

THE records of Suffolk County Court contain brief notes of a suit brought, in the term opening July 31, 1683, by " *Watching Atherton*, son and heir to the estate of Major Humphrey Atherton late of Dorchester, deccsd," against " *John Pope, Senr.*," to obtain possession of a tract of four acres of land at Squantum's Neck, which he claimed belonged to his father. The jury decided that the land was Mr. Pope's. [See pp. 73, 76, 79.]

Another item on these records is this : " *John Pope* of Dorchester, upon certificate from Capt. John Capen, was discharged from attending Ordinary Traynings," April 20, 1684.

*Margaret Pope*, daughter of John[3] [see p. 84], made a deed of land in Lancaster, Oct. 13, 1715. *Beatrix*, widow of John,[8] sold to " her three brethren, John, Robert, and Jonathan Houghton, her share in the estate of their deceased mother, Beatrix Houghton, widow, April 14, 1725."

" Robert Morton and Hannah Pope " were " published " in Boston, Aug. 25, 1768. [See pp. 119 and 120.]

" *Ebenezer Pope* of Charlestown, husbandman," son of Lazarus[5] [see p. 142], made will, not dated, probated Aug. 21, 1811, bequeathing all his property to his sister, "Mary Pope of Stoughton"; refers also to brother, "Lazarus Pope of Dorchester." Thomas Pope, Otis Pope, and Ichabod Holbrook, jr., signed the citation.

## THE REVOLUTIONARY RECORD OF COL. FREDERICK[5] POPE.

*Additional to the particulars given on pp. 131-2.*

Two Muster Rolls of the company under command of Captain Frederick Pope, in Paul Dudley Sargent's regiment, are in Massachusetts archives, in the handwriting of the captain, one dated Aug.

1, and the other Oct. 6, 1775. The "time of enlistment" of the most of the company was June 23, 1775.

An interesting correspondence is on file, between Col. Sargent, the Massachusetts State officials, and Gen. Washington, the Commander-in-chief, as to the commissioning of Col. Sargent and the officers of his regiment in the Continental army; the objection being that the colonel and three companies of the regiment had come from New Hampshire, without commission from that State; but General Washington finally agreed, upon the recommendation of the Council, to commission them "the same as other officers of the army." They seem to have remained in service the following year.

The Massachusetts House of Representatives, May 7, 1777, balloted for "Field officers for two Battallions to be raised for the defence of the harbor of Boston"; and one of the six chosen was "Frederick Pope, major, of Stoughton." The Council concurred in the appointment the following day. [See certificate, p. 132.]

No particulars of the service rendered appear. But when the English were pressing Rhode Island sorely, the following summer, Massachusetts troops were at the front. The following letter occurs in the correspondence of Major General James Sullivan (file 2, No. 55), now in possession of his grand-nephew, Thomas C. Amory, Esq., of Boston, by whose courtesy we have been permitted to copy it.

"SWANSEY, 7th June, 1778.

*Hon'd Sir:* When your messenger came away from my Quarters, I had not received the full Information of the Occation of the Alarm we had last Evening; but since, I find by the intelligence my Sergeant gave me that went in the watch boat, he says he Discovered a Number of Boats supposed to be the Enemy, one of which was under sail, against Mount Hope, making towards Kikemuet river. He also says the firing began at Mount Hope, then at Howland's Ferry, so upon our shore by the sentries as well as the Field pieces, which gave us the alarm. Our watch-boat came in at Slade's Ferry, but I sent them back again immediately, who did not return till sunrise.

S^r the Small Number of men under my Command turned out on the shortest notice and waited for the enemy till light, but they did not appear, neither did they land anywhere as I have yet learned.

I would just acquaint the General a Number of the Militia turned out with spirit, and joined my Regiment.

FREDERICK POPE, Lt. Col.

MAJ. GEN. SULLIVAN."

In one of the "Orderly Books" reproduced by Wm. P. Upham, Esq., in Essex Institute Collections, Vol. V., there is a passage which neatly fits in here.

"HEADQUARTERS CAMP BEFORE NEWPORT, Aug. 20, 1778.

Major General for the day, tomorrow, Green.   Brigadier for the day, Lovell.   Field Officers, Col. Hawes, Lieutenant Col. Pope, Major Fenno, Brigade Major Niles," etc.

What after service he rendered, or when mustered out, does not yet appear.

### OTHER REVOLUTIONARY RECORDS.

*Captain William Pope*, brother of Col. Frederick, was one of the "officers of Militia who reinforced the American Army, joined Col. J. Ward's Regiment," Jan. 29, 1776.

*James Pope*, another brother, is mentioned among the members of the "Comp^y that marcht from Stoughton to the assistance of the Continental Troops when they fortified on the Heights of Dorchester under the Com^d of Capt. Simeon Leach in Col. Benj^a Gill's Regt. March 4th, 1776."

*Lazarus Pope*, a cousin, and a *Ralph Pope* were also in this company. Meantime, "in the first company of Col. Palmer's regt. under Capt. John Hall, jr.," another *Ralph Pope* was enrolled the same day. One of these was Ralph,[5] son of Lazarus,[4] the other Ralph,[6] son of Col. Frederick. And it is not possible for us to tell which of these it was who had served eight months in Capt. Frederick Pope's company at the siege of Boston, "May to December, 1775."

"*Sam. Ward Pope*" [see p. 152], who could not have been more than fifteen years old at the time, was mustered, July 26, 1777, as the roll shows, into Cole's company of Col. Robinson's regiment, of which his father Frederick[6] was major; and was afterward paid £2, 18s. for 2 months 27 days' service. He was also in Capt. Abner Crane's company of the same regiment, discharged Jan. 5, 1778, and received bounty, March 16, 1778. While the name "*Samuel Pope*," which stands on the "Pay Roll of Capt. Joseph Cole's company in Col. John Jacob's Regt. from the Massachusetts State Now in the service of the United States Engaged for one year from the 1st of Jany., 1778," seems to me to denote the same person; he served "12 months, 12 days."

"*John Pope of Dorchester*" was a corporal in Capt. Hopestill Hall's company, Samuel Robinson's regiment, from Jan. 29, 1776, 23 days; and a corporal in Capt. Clap's company, of Col. Pierce's regiment, March 1, to April 8, 1778.

"*John Pope, fifer*" of Capt. Joseph Palmer's company, in Col. John Cushing's regiment, Newport, Nov., 1776; sergeant in Capt. Seth Sumner's company, Col. Benj. Gill's regiment, "who marched for Rhode Island April 17, 1777.

"*John Pope*, Dorchester, pri., cor., ser., lieut., Mass. Militia," was on the Pension Roll of the U. S. Aug. 22, 1833, having begun to receive pension March 4, 1831.

# APPENDIX.

## SECTION A.

CONTAINING NOTES UPON VARIOUS PERSONS OF THE POPE NAME NOT
OF THE DORCHESTER FAMILY.

*Andrew Pope* was one of the witnesses to a power of attorney given
by William Williams, of Barbadoes, to Abraham Hagburne, of Boston, June 11, 1655, recorded in Suffolk Deeds.

*Anthony Pope*, who sailed from London in the "Falcon," Dec. 25,
1635, was an inhabitant of Charlestown. No evidence of family. He
died Feb. 1, 1712-13.

*Walter Pope*, also an inhabitant of Charlestown, on the list in 1630,
was one of the signers to the order creating a board of "select-men,"
passed Feb. 10, 1634-5. Had "only child," Mary, who married
Joseph Miller, both of whom signed a deed of land, inherited from
her father, Nov. 7, 1677.

*Ephraim Pope* was a watchman in Boston, Sept. 3, 1637. Was the
owner of a house and lot, noted in the Book of Possessions, in 1652.
Was a member of the First Church; his wife, Ann, joined June 3,
1657; his children, Ephraim, jr., and Elizabeth, and her son, "John
Bakon," were baptized at the same church, Oct. 18, same year. His
will, dated Jan. 24, 1676, gave all his property to Ephraim, jr., and
Elizabeth. The son was "sojourning" in Dedham, with Thomas
Paine, March 11, 1670; died, in Boston, soon after his father, and
bequeathed property to his mother and sister, with a legacy to the
First Church.

### INTENTIONS OF MARRIAGE, BOSTON.

"*Nicholas Pope* and Mary Hughes, of Boston," Oct. 27, 1738.

"*Lancit Pope* and Rebecca Hanagan, of Boston," Oct. 24, 1759.

"Charles Devons and *Sarah Pope*, of Boston," Nov. 28, 1765.

274

*John Pope, of Boston and Bristol.* April 2, 1640, the Boston Court disciplined one John Pope for improper behaviour and for insolence to his "master." He was evidently an apprentice, learning some trade or other. In 1677, a party of emigrants went from Boston to Bristol, then in Plymouth Colony, now in the State of Rhode Island. In 1683 the name of "John Pope" appears among those who "took the oath of fidelity" at Bristol. July 1, 1685, he sold land there. The Town Records state that "John Pope was buried April 2, 1686, being found dead on the beach near our ferry to Rhode Island." The Inventory of his estate gives, among other things, a full list of carpenter's tools, and incidental evidence that he had been at work upon the meeting-house, then in process of erection. There are no tokens that he was married, and no explanation as to who inherited his real and personal estate, which was appraised at forty-five pounds.

*Richard Pope,* "fisherman," bought land at Cape Elizabeth, Me., Nov. 12, 1685; sold the same in June, 1688, residing then with wife, Sarah, at Winter Harbor (Saco). Was a resident of Kittery in 1691, but died before Sept. 1, 1694. Another Richard Pope, of Kittery, probably son of the fisherman, member of Kittery Church in 1726, made will Dec. 27, 1760, admitted 1782, bequeathing property to wife Sarah,* sons David and Richard, daughters Sarah, Mary, and Dorcas Pope and Elizabeth Hammons [Hammond]. This third Richard died before the father. Sarah married "—— Pickernell." David died Dec. 13, 1798.

*William Pope,* of Kittery, "shipwright," residing there in 1715, was, perhaps, another son of Richard, sen. His wife, Joanna, daughter of Sylvanus and Margaret Tripe, owned the covenant, and their daughters, Mary and Margaret Pope, were baptized July 23, 1732. A Margaret Pope, probably William's second wife, had daughter Sarah, baptized Sept. 7, 1746. No other members of this Pope family have been found in Kittery or its vicinity, unless "*Jon⁰. Pope,*" a soldier at Newcastle, N. H., in 1708, be one.

"*William Pope, of Sudbury,* fourteen years old," requested the appointment of Joseph Browne as his guardian, April 12, 1753, "Sarah Pope" and William Muzzy witnesses. The mind naturally associates these two names with the Kittery family, in default of any other clew to their origin.

*William Pope,* of West Stockbridge, m. Lucy, daughter of Rev. John and Azeuba Mudge, b. in Sherburne, N. Y., 1783. Emigrated early to Ohio, and had William, Caroline, and several other children.

---

* Samuel Spinney, of Kittery, in will, March 10, 1737, bequeathes to his "daughter Sarah Pope."

"*Francis Pope, of Newport, in colony of Rhode Island, shop-keeper,*" brought suits in Suffolk County, Mass., May 11, 1700, against Charles Pope and Abraham Elton, of Bristol, and Mordecai Greene, of London, England, for moneys due him on accounts dating from 1696 onward, which are on file. Among the items are costs of building and equipping "the ship Charles," and despatching her "from Rhode Island to Virginia, and thence to London," and expenses connected with "the Dolphin Ketch." The bills are clearly drawn and signed by "Fran. Pope."

"Fra. Pope" is one of the persons who petitioned to Gov. Bellemont, Sept. 26, 1699, for leave to maintain worship at Newport according to the discipline of the Church of England. This was the origin of Trinity Church, Newport.

"Mr. Francis Pope, of Newport," was made freeman of the colony of Rhode Island and Providence Plantations, May 4, 1703.

"Capt'n Francis Pope" was chosen sheriff of Newport, May 5, 1703; re-elected May 3, 1704.

From Colony Records for July 5, 1715:

"Whereas Mr. Weston Clarke (late recorder) and Mr. Francis Pope (late sheriff, deceased) did, at their own cost and charge, build a small room in the colony house, for the use and service of the Colony, for the keeping of court rolls and other records necessary for said court; the which still remains for the colony's service: — Therefore, it is ordered by this Assembly that the said Weston Clarke and Col. John Cranston (for the use of the children of the said Francis Pope, deceased) be paid out of the general treasury, forty shillings each, for the charge of building said room, as is afore expressed."

At what time he had died we do not know. The following, from Newport records, has some color of being a clew to the date.

Baptized in Trinity Church, before 1709, "Sarah Pope, adult."

"Mrs. Sarah Pope married to Wm. ——, Barbadoes, Dec. 24, 1708."

This appears to be the widow of Francis Pope, senior, and suggests her removal to that West Indian isle, which, at that period, had such active commercial relations with both Old and New England, in which her former husband had evidently participated.

"Francis Pope and Freelove Easton were married Sept. 17, 1729," in Newport. And the following children of this couple are registered in N.:

Mary, b. Nov. 24, 1735.
Sarah, b. June 10, 1742.
Mary, b. March 8, 1748-9.

One of these, Sarah, was wedded May 19, 1757, to a son of another Newport family, William Ringwood, who was born June 1, 1734. They removed to Philadelphia, where they died, leaving no children, as the annalist of the Ringwoods states. [See Rhode Island Historical Magazine.]

"Francis Pope," whom we cannot err in pronouncing the son of the pioneer of that name, and the husband of Freelove Easton, was made a "freeman" of Rhode Island Colony, May 4, 1742. The "Newport Mercury," of July 8, 1760, contains an advertisement of a stock of dry-goods for sale in Newport by Francis Pope.

The court warrant of 1715, quoted above, mentioned "the children of Francis Pope, deceased"; considering Francis, junior, one of these, may we not count the following another?

"Susanna Pope was married to John Norris, May 5, 1723."

John Norris had a son John, presumably by this wife, and we find that,

Dec. 4, 1774, "John Norris" married "Eliz'th Freebody." He was a mariner.

The records do not show sons of this couple, but a daughter, Elizabeth, whose will mentions her nephews, "John Norris Allen and John N. Potter," June 13, 1831.

Abigail Norris, who married John Yeomans, June 5, 1755, *may* have been a daughter of John, senior, and Susanna (Pope).

There is a "Pope Street" in Newport, but in no other way does that ancient sheriff's name abide in the town he helped to found.

*Thomas Pope** was among the early settlers of Stamford, Conn., having land allotted to him Dec. 7, 1641. Many of the Stamford pioneers were from Wethersfield, which had been settled by a colony from Watertown and vicinity. In 1644 Thomas Pope went with his minister, Rev. Richard Denton, and others, to Hempstead, Long Island; thence he removed to Southampton, at the eastern end of the island. In 1666 he and his son, John, already a citizen of S., went to Elizabeth, New Jersey, where the family was perpetuated. He had died before 1676, when his widow, Mary, and son, John, sold land there. "Pope's Brook," flowing into Rahway River, marks the locality of one of the tracts of land allotted to John. He died before 1712.

Elizabeth Pope, widow, was m. to William Creed, yeoman, Jan. 19, 1759, at 1st or 2d Presb. Ch., New York City.

---

* These particulars were compiled from the several town histories and communicated by Mr. Frank L. Pope, Elizabeth, N. J.

## THE SOUTH CAROLINA POPES.

" Genealogy from the Camp at Port Royal." [Gen. Reg., 1862.] Nov. 12, 1861. "The house of William Pope, senior, was occupied by Gen. Drayton and his staff, and used as a hospital. It was the first house on which the U. S. flag was raised, and became the headquarters of Gen. Sherman and staff."

Noticing the above item, one day, in the autumn of 1885, I felt interested to make inquiry into the history of the family whose home had acquired such fame. Writing to " any descendant or relative of William Pope, senior," under cover to the Port Royal postmaster, I soon received a courteous reply from Mr. William John Verdier, a nephew of the late Mr. Pope, and through him a series of valuable letters from Hon. Joseph Daniel Pope, a prominent lawyer of Columbia, S. C. From him the following facts were obtained. George[1] Pope came, tradition says, " from Virginia," to St. John's parish, S. C., not far from 1700. He had sons, James[2] and George,[2] the latter born about 1716. James[2] had sons, James,[3] John,[3] William,[3] and Joseph,[3] young men in the Revolutionary period, who displayed great energy in those stormy days and the difficult times that followed. A large family thus grew up in that coast region, near Charleston ; planters on " sea-island-cotton " estates, with from 100 to 300 workmen apiece ; connected with the first families, representatives to legislature in several instances, etc. The owner of the Port Royal house, referred to in the Magazine paragraph above, was a son of William[3] just named. Joseph[3] had sons, Joseph[4] and John,[4] the former of whom had Joseph Daniel[5] and John W. R.,[5] now living in Columbia, S. C., while Joseph Daniel,[6] jr., and his son,[7] born in 1883, are among the numerous recent members of the clan. It must be noted that the numbers attached to these names give only the generations in South Carolina ; while George[1] was very likely in the second or third generation from the English ancestor of this line.

## AS TO VIRGINIA POPES.

The settlement at Jamestown having been made in 1607, the Pope family of the " Old Dominion " was somewhat earlier than either of those in New England. The very imperfect colonial records throw little light upon this matter in the first years. We find, however, in the reports made to the English government concerning " The Living in Virginia " and " The Dead " there, that " Elizabeth Pope, aged 8," came over " in the Abigail, 1621," and was reported as a member of the family of "William Gany, aged 33," who had come "in the George, 1616." Feb. 16, 1623, among those "Living in Jams iland," "*George Pope*" is registered. It may be *surmised* that he was the immigrant ancestor of the South Carolina line, in which his name appears. It is also *possible* that he was the progenitor of the family at Pope's Creek, Westmoreland County, Va., and ancestor of the first president of our republic.

John Washington married "Ann, sister of Thomas Pope, living in Virginia in 1675." [Rev. John G. Shea, D. D., Gen. Reg., 1863.] Their son, Lawrence Washington, was the father of Augustine Washington, and he the father of Gen. George Washington.

It will be exceedingly interesting for some faithful genealogist to trace out the history of these Virginia Popes,* thus intertwined with the family of "The Father of his Country."

A "Mr. Pope" was one of the very early residents of the city of Washington, D. C. Elsewhere in Virginia, Maryland, the Carolinas, Kentucky, and westward, our name occurs, the tradition of these families generally pointing back to the James River valley as the starting-point of their history in America.

*Maj.-Gen. John Pope*, U. S. A., is the son of Hon. Nathaniel Pope, who was born in Kentucky about 1780 ; removed to Kaskaskia, and was the first secretary of the Territory of Illinois, afterward judge of the United States Court for that district. His wife, Lucretia Backus, was a niece of Mrs. Ursula Walcott Griswold, of Connecticut. [See Hist. Mag., 1857 ; Gen. Reg., 1879.]

---

* The John Pope referred to on page 74 may be found to have settled in the South.

# SECTION B.

## GENEALOGY OF THOMAS POPE, OF PLYMOUTH.

BY FRANKLIN LEONARD POPE, ELIZABETH, N. J.

*Prepared for and Published in "The New England Historical and Genealogical Register," January, 1888. Reprinted here by the kind permission of the Author and the Editors of the Magazine.*

OF the life of Thomas Pope little is known beyond the brief entries which appear in the records of the town and colony of Plymouth, but these are sufficient to show that he was a man of positive character, and of some consideration in the community. His promptness in resenting a real or fancied injury, and his independent expressions of personal opinion, more than once caused him to be arraigned before the magistrates of New Plymouth, and no doubt ultimately led to his removal to Dartmouth, where he passed the last ten years of his life.

The records of the colony show that in the list of rates imposed by the Court, January 2, 1632–3, and again January 2, 1633–4, he was taxed 9s. October 6, 1636, he was granted five acres of land " at the fishing point next Slowly field, and said Thomas be allowed to build." June 7, 1637, we find his name among the list of persons who volunteered to go under " Mr. Prence " on an expedition against the Pequots. July 28, 1637, he was married by Gov. Winslow to Ann, daughter of Gabriel Fallowell. He sold his property at the fishing point to John Bonham, August 29, 1640, perhaps on account of the death of his wife, the precise date of which event is unknown.

November 2, 1640, he was granted " 5 acres of meadowing in South Meadows toward Gavans Colebrook meadows." His name appears in a list, August, 1634, entitled, "The names of all the males that are able to beare armes from XVI. years old to 60 years wth in the seuerall Towne Shipps." He was chosen constable June 4, 1645, and was on a jury August, 1645. In 1646 he is found in Yarmouth. May 29, 1646, he married at Plymouth, Sarah, daughter of John Jenney. In 1647, June 1, an action for slander was brought against him, confessed, authors and defendants were brought in equally

guilty, and damages paid.  He was chosen surveyor of highways
July, 1648, and again June 6, 1651.  In 1652, July 26, and in 1656,
he is "on an Enquest."  In "December, 1663, Thomas Pope and
Gyles Rickard, Seni'r" were arrested "for breaking the King's
peace by striking each other, and were fined each three shillings and
four pence;" and "said Pope, his striking of said Rickards' wife,
and for other turbulent carriages in word and deed, the Court have
centenanced him to find sureties for his good behavior."  But nevertheless his temper soon got the better of him again, for we find him,
February 7, 1664, and also May 2, 1665, quarrelling with one John
Barnes about that fruitful subject of dispute, a boundary.  He is
recorded as having taken the freeman's oath in 1668.  In 1670, June
7, he was again overhauled by the authorities, and as the record says,
"fined 10 shillings for vilifying the ministry."  Although he was
now over 60 years old, these troubles doubtless influenced him in the
determination to seek a new home, and accordingly we find him with
others, petitioning the Court in 1673 for a grant of land at Saconnett
(now Little Compton, R. I.).  For some reason not ascertained, this
project was unsuccessful, for it appears in the record that he is
"Granted leave since he and others cannot secure Saconnett neck
according to the grant, to look out some other place, undisposed of,
for their accommodation."  Acting upon this permission, he secured
a large tract on the east side of the Acushnet river at Dartmouth,
tradition says by direct purchase from the Indians.  This location,
however, must have been included within the prior purchase made by
Bradford, Standish and their associates, from the sachems
Wesamequen and Wamsutta, on November 29, 1652, which had been,
by order of the Court in June, 1664, erected into a separate township
to "be henceforth called and known by the name of Dartmouth."  At
a meeting of the proprietors of this purchase, held in Plymouth
March 7, 1652, the township was divided into thirty-four equal
shares, and hence it seems likely that Thomas Pope may have
acquired one of the shares.  A list made in 1652 shows that his
mother-in-law, "Mistris Jenney," was one of the Dartmouth proprietors, and two of her sons, Samuel and John Jenney, were among
the early settlers of D. in the immediate vicinity of the Popes.
Another original proprietor of Dartmouth was Robert Bartlett, whose
son Joseph married, about 1662, Hannah, daughter of Thomas Pope
by his first wife.  The date of the removal of Thomas Pope to
Dartmouth has not been ascertained, but it must have been about
1674.  The settlement at Dartmouth was a scattered one, and for
better security and defence against the Indians, who had already
begun to evince a hostile disposition, a fort or garrison house was
built on the east side of Acushnet River, about half a mile north of

the village of Oxford, the remains of which were visible until a recent date, on the lands of John M. Howland.

In the early part of July, 1675, his son John, a young man of 22, his daughter Susannah and her husband Ensign Jacob Mitchell, were killed by a party of Philip's Indians, "early in the morning as they were fleeing on horseback to the garrison, whither the Mitchell children had been sent the afternoon before" (REGISTER, XV. 266). This occurrence took place near the "frog pond" on the south side of Spring Street, between William and Walnut, Fairhaven. The settlement at Dartmouth being isolated, scattered, and difficult of defence, was shortly abandoned, and the deserted plantations were quickly laid waste and the buildings burned by the savages.

The following order of Court passed by the government at Plymouth, is of interest here :

[1675, 4th of October.] This Court, takeing into theire serious consideration the tremendus dispensations of God towards the people of Dartmouth, in suffering the barborus heathen to spoile and destroy most of theire habitations, the enemie being greatly advantaged therevnto by theire scattered way of liueing, doe therfore order, that in the rebuilding or resettleing therof, that they soe order it as to liue compact together, att least in each village, as they may be in a capassitie both to defend themselues from the assault of an enemie, and the better to attend the publicke worship of God, and minnestry of the word of God, whose carelesnes to obtaine and attend vnto, wee fear, may haue bine a prouocation of God thus to chastise theire contempt of his gospell, which wee earnestly desire the people of that place may seriously consider off, lay to hart, and be humbled for, with a sollisitus indeauor after a reformation thereof by a vigorous puting forth to obtaine an able, faithfull dispenser of the word of God amongst them, and to incurrage him therein, the neglect whereof this Court as they must not, and, God willing, they will not prmit for the future.*

No attempt appears to have been made for some three years to reoccupy the ruined settlement. Where Thomas Pope and his family found an asylum during this time, has not been ascertained. The following extract from the Plymouth records perhaps serves to throw a glimmer of light upon this question :

Wheras Phillip, late sachem of Paukanakett, and other sachems, his accomplises, haueing bin in confoaderation and plighted couenant with his ma^ties collonie of New Plymouth, haue lately broken couenant with the English, and they and theire people haue likewise broken out in open rebellion against our sou^r lord Kinge Charles, his crowne and dignitie, expressed by raising a crewell and vnlawfull warr, murdering his leich people, destroying and burning theire houses and estates, expressing great hostillitie, outrage, and crewellty against his said ma^ties subjects, wherby many of them were psonally slaine, and some bereaued of theire deare children and relations, among which said rebells an Indian named Popanooie is found to be one, who hath had a hand, and is found to be very actiue in the great crewelty and outrage acted upon seuerall of the inhabitants of the towne of Dartmouth, in the said his ma^ties collonie of New Ply-

---

* Book 5th, Court Orders, p. 102.

mouth, in p̄ticular it being manifest that hee was very active towards and about the destruction of seuerall of the children of Thomas Pope, late of Dartmouth aforsaid, and seuerall others of the said towne; in consideration wherof after due examination had of. the p̄mises, this Court doth hereby condemne and centance him, the said Popanooie, and his wife and children, to p̄petuall servitude, they likewise being found coep̄tenor with him in the said rebellion, and p̄ticularly that hee, the said Popanooie, is to be sold and sent out of the country. [July 13, 1677.]

It appears also that about a year previous to this (June 12, 1676), several Indians who had been captured and sent in by Bradford and Church were "convented before the councell" at Plymouth, being "such of them as were accused of working vnsufferable mischieffe upon some of ours."

One of these prisoners, named John-nom, being accused by his fellows, acknowledged, among other misdeeds, that he was concerned in the murder of "Jacob Mitchell and his wife and John Pope, and so centance of death was pronounced against them, which accordingly emediately was ekecuted."*

The following order of Court relating to the resettlement of Dartmouth explains itself.

To John Cooke, to be communicated to such of the former Inhabitants of Dartmouth as are concerned herein.

The councell being now assembled, considering the reason and necessitie of that order of the Generall Court made the 14ᵗⁿ October, 1675, respecting the rebuilding or resettleing the Towne of Dartmouth, a copy wheof is herewith sent, and considering withall that all the people of that place, by theire deserting it, haue left it to the posession of the enimie, which, through the good hand of God on the indeauors of this colonie is now recouered againe out of the enimies hand, do soe much the more look at it as a duty incombent on this councel to see the said order effectually attended, doe therfore hereby prohibite all and euery of the former inhabitants of the said towne of Dartmouth, or theire or any of theire assigns, to make any entrance on, building, or settleing in any p̄te of the said former townshipp of Dartmouth vntill satisfactory eccuritie be first given to the Court or councel by some of the principal p̄sons heretofore belonging to that place, that the said Court order shall in all respects be attended by them, as the transgressors of the prohibition will answare the contrary att theire pill.†

Of the subsequent history of Thomas Pope little is known beyond what may be gathered from his will, which is as follows:

1683. July the 9th. The last will and testament of Thomas Pope, being Aged and weak of body but yet in perfect understanding and memory wherein I have of my estate as followeth; I give unto my son Seth as an addition to what I have formerly given him ten shillings in money also I give unto my grandson Thomas Pope all that my twenty-five acres of up-

* Plymouth Col. Rec. Ms. v. 141-2.
† Book 5, Court Orders, p. 124.

land and two acres of meadow lying and being on the west side of Acush-
enett River be it more or less, and it is my desire that his father may take
the said land into his hands and make the best improvement of it that he
can for the good of my said grandson until he comes of age to make use of
it himself; also it is my mind that my son Seth shall in consideration of
the aforesaid land pay three pounds sterling unto my grandson Jacob
Mitchell when he comes to age of twenty one years.  Also I give unto
my daughter Deborah Pope five pound in money, and to each of my other
daughters five pound a peace in money ; also my meddow lying at the
south Meddowes in Plymouth or the value of it, I give to be equally divided amongst all my sons and daughters ; also I give and bequeath unto my
son Isack all my seate of land where I now dwell with all the meddowes
belonging thereunto and all the privilages thereunto belonging.  To him his
heirs and Assigns forever, but and if it should please god that he should
decease without an heir before he comes to the age of twenty and one
years, then my said seat of land shall belong unto the sons of my son Seth.
Also I give unto my son Isaack all my housing and household goods of all
sorts, also all my cattle and horse kine and swine ; Also all sorts of provisions, also cart and plowes with all the takeling belonging unto them.
Also I give unto my said son Isaack all my money except that which I have
given to my daughters, and I order my said son Isaack to pay all my just
debts and to receive all my debts that are due unto me also I order my
Indian Lydia to live with my son Isaack until he is one and twenty years
of age, and my Indian gerle I give to him during his life, also it is my
mind and will that my son Isaack shall make no bargain without the consent of his overseers until he be twenty years of age, I have made
choice of John Cook, and my son Seth and Thomas Taber to be for overseers to see this my will performed.        THOMAS POPE his J mark.

Signed and sealed in presence of
 John Cook
 and Thomas Tabor.

Isaac and Seth Pope took out letters of administration on the
estate November 2, 1683 ; which approximately fixes the date of
the death of Thomas.  They gave bonds in £400.

The homestead farm conveyed by the above will to Isaac Pope,
contained 172 acres, and comprised the larger portion of the thickly-
settled portion of the present town of Fairhaven.  Its north line
was a little south of the south line of the street leading east from
the bridge.

Before the Acushnet cemetery was laid out, which was during the
reign of Queen Anne, about 1711, an acre of the Taber farm, half
a mile or more north of the bridge, on a point of land projecting
into the river, had been set apart for a burial ground, and it is there
that Thomas Pope was probably buried.

In the following genealogy, in cases where the state is not given,
Massachusetts is to be understood.

1.

THOMAS[1] POPE, born in 1608 ; died in Dartmouth in October, 1683 ;
 married first, in Plymouth, Jan. 28, 1637, Ann, daughter of Gabriel
 and Catherine Fallowell, of Plymouth ; married second, in Ply-

mouth, May 19, 1646, Sarah, daughter of John and Sarah (Carey) Jenney, of Plymouth. Child of Thomas and Ann, b. in Plymouth :

   i.  HANNAH,[2] b.1639; d. March 12, 1710 :* m. Joseph Bartlett, of Plymouth (b. 1639, d. 1703). Seven children.

Children of Thomas and Sarah, born in Plymouth :

2.  ii.  SETH, b. Jan. 13, 1648 ; d. March 17, 1727.
  iii.  SUSANNAH, b. 1649 ; d. July, 1675 ; m. Nov. 7, 1666, Jacob Mitchell.† "Ensign." They were both slain by Philip's warriors, " early in the morning as they were going to the garrison, whither they had sent their children the afternoon before." This was in Dartmouth. Three children.
  iv.  THOMAS, b. March 25, 1651 ; probably died young.
   v.  SARAH, b. Feb. 11, 1652 ; m. first, Nov. 13, 1678, Samuel Hinckley ; m. second, Aug. 17, 1699, Thomas Huckins. Twelve children.
  vi.  JOHN, b. March 15, 1653 ; d. July, 1675. He was killed by Philip's warriors while fleeing to the Dartmouth garrison.
 vii.  JOANNA, d. about 1695 ; m. March 15, 1683, John Hathaway, of Dartmouth. Six children.
3. viii.  ISAAC, b. after 1663 ; d. 1733.

### Second Generation.

2.

SETH[2] POPE ( *Thomas*[1]), b. in Plymouth, Jan. 13, 1648 ; d. in Dartmouth, March 17, 1727. The records give no information concerning his early history. Tradition, in part confirmed by the records, says that about 1670 he appeared as a pedler in Sandwich, whereupon the constable, in pursuance of a regulation then in force, ordered him to depart, lest in future he might become a charge upon the town. He accordingly withdrew, taking occasion, however, to remark that he would yet come back and buy up the town. Procuring a boat at Monument, he followed the coast round to Acushnet, where he settled within the present limits of Fairhaven, and by his industry, energy and skilful business management ultimately became one of the most wealthy and influential citizens of the old colony. 1678-9, March 8, an allowance was ordered by the Court to be made him for expenses and time returning guns to the Indians after Philip's war ; 1685, June 2, was chosen selectman of Dartmouth ; 1686, March 4, took the oath of fidelity ; June 2, again chosen selectman ; June 4, commissioned lieutenant. He was chosen representative from Dartmouth to the General Court at Plymouth in 1689 and 1690 ; magistrate for Bristol County, July 7, 1691, and justice of the peace in Dartmouth, May 27, 1692. He is named as one of the fifty-six proprietors of Dartmouth in the confirmatory deed of Gov. Bradford in 1694. June 12, 1695, he appeared in Boston in behalf of his townsmen, to urge an abatement of taxes. He appears to have been for many years largely interested in the coastwise trade, and had a wharf and warehouse at Acushnet. In 1698 he was part owner of the sloop *Hopewell*, and in 1709 of the sloop *Joanna and Thankful*. In 1709, by way of fulfilment of his pro-

---

* The gravestones of Joseph and Hannah Bartlett are on Burial Hill in Plymouth.
† The so-called " Carver house," probably the oldest house now standing (1887) in Plymouth, was built in part by Jacob Mitchell, who was a carpenter, and in it he lived after his marriage until he removed to Dartmouth. It is on the west side of Sandwich Street about twenty rods south of the bridge.

mise made thirty years before to the Sandwich coustable, he purchased a large amount of realty in that village, including the grist-
mill, fulling-mill and weaving-shop, which was valued at the time
of his death at £3460. His estates in Dartmouth were extensive
and valuable, comprising several farms and dwelling houses, a saw
and grist-mill, a well-stocked store and warehouse, and other property, amounting in all to more than £15,000—a large sum for those
days.

He married first (date and place unknown), Déborah —— (born
1655, died Feb. 19, 1711), and second (date and place unknown),
Rebecca —— (born 1662, died Jan. 23, 1741). Children of Seth
and Deborah, born in Dartmouth except the first and perhaps the
second :

4. i.   JOHN,[3] b. Oct. 23, 1675 ; d. Nov. 18, 1725.
   ii.  THOMAS, b. Sept. 1, 1677.  Was a mariner, and was concerned with his
        father in the coastwise trade.  Was master in 1702 of sloop *Hopewell*,
        trading between Boston and Connecticut.  Married first (date and
        place unknown), Elizabeth Manser, of Charlestown (b. 1672), and
        second, July 16, 1702, Elizabeth Handley, of Boston (b. 1680, d. Jan.
        29, 1725–6).  He must have died some years prior to 1720, as in that
        year his widow is mentioned in his father's will as " my former
        daughter-in-law, now wife of Lt. John Chipman of Sandwich."
        Names of his children, if any, have not been ascertained.
   iii. SUSANNAH, b. July 31, 1681 ; d. Feb. 5, 1760 ; m. Dec. 31, 1701, Jona-
        than Hathaway, of Dartmouth.  Two children, perhaps others.
   iv.  SARAH, b. Feb. 16, 1683 ; d. Sept. 29, 1756 ; m. " Ensign " David Pea-
        body, of Boxford.  Eleven children.
   v.   MARY, b. Sept. 11, 1686 ; m. 1720, Charles Church, of Freetown.
5. vi.  SETH, b. April 5, 1689 ; d. Nov. 23, 1744.
   vii. HANNAH, b. Dec. 14, 1693(?) ; m. Rev. Samuel Hunt.  Five children.
6. viii. ELNATHAN, b. Aug. 15, 1694 ; d. Feb. 8, 1735–6.
7. ix.  LEMUEL, b. Feb. 21, 1696 ; d. May 23, 1771.

### 3.

ISAAC[2] POPE.  In his father's will Isaac is mentioned as being then
(July, 1683) under 20 years of age.  He lived with his father on the
homestead farm at Acushnet (Dartmouth), now covered by the
thickly-settled village of Fairhaven, south of the bridge.  He is
named as one of the Dartmouth proprietors in the confirmatory deed
of Gov. Bradford in 1694, having inherited the homestead after the
death of his father in 1683.  He had a wharf and warehouse at
Acushnet.  Married (date and place unknown) Alice Mind (died
1755).  Children, born in Dartmouth :

   i.   ABIGAIL,[3] b. Dec. 23, 1687 ; m. John Jenney, of Dartmouth.  Six ch.
   ii.  MARGARET, b. June 30, 1690 ; d. May 22, 1776 ; m. March 14, 1715–16,
        Elnathan Pope, Dartmouth.  (3. viii.)
   iii. DEBORAH, b. April 25, 1693 ; m. March 8, 1729, Samuel Spooner, of
        Dartmouth.  Three children.  She was his second wife.
   iv.  THOMAS, b. April 6, 1695 ; m. about 1720, Reliance, daughter of Rev.
        Nathaniel Stone (b. April 23, 1703).  Children recorded in Dart-
        mouth :
           1. *Joanna*,[4] b. April 5, 1721.
           2. *Amaziah*, b. Jan. 31, 1722–3 ; m. March 28, 1745, Sarah Mosher.
           3. *Abigail*, b. Jan. 15, 1725–6 ; m. Jan. 17, 1754, Peter Wash-
              burn, of Taunton.
           4. *Rachel*, b. Feb. 1, 1726–7.
   v.   ISAAC, b. Sept. 10, 1697 ; m. March 23, 1729, Lydia Mitchell, of Kings-
        ton (b. 1710).  Children recorded in Dartmouth :
           1. *Joanna*,[4] b. Nov. 8, 1731.

    2. *Susanna,* b. Jan 7, 1734-5.
    3. *Lydia,* b. March 3, 1736-7.
    4. *Thankful,* b. April 31, 1742.
    5. *Isaac,* b. July 3, 1744; d. June 21, 1820; m. in 1766, Olive (Jordan) Hovey, of So. Rochester. Eleven children. He joined Col. Cotton's Plymouth regiment, upon the "Lexington alarm" in 1775; was commissioned Lieut. May, 1775; Capt. in Shephard's 4th reg't, Jan. 1, 1777; Major 3d reg't, Oct. 12, 1782. Was on the staff of Brig. Gen. John Sullivan. Removed his family to Wells, Me., in 1779; purchased and lived in the "old garrison house." Many descendants are in Wells and Kennebunk, Me. Two of his sons, John Sullivan³ and Ivory.³ were mariners during the war of 1812. The latter was impressed by the British and never again heard from.
    6. *Betty,* b. Dec. 10, 1750.
  vi.  JOANNA, b. March 31, 1700.
8. vii.  ELNATHAN, b. Aug. 14, 1703; d. May 15, 1794.

### *Third Generation.*

4.

JOHN³ POPE (*Seth²*). He was born Oct. 23, 1675, after his parents were driven from Dartmouth by Philip's warriors, but where they found refuge has not been ascertained, perhaps at Plymouth or Sandwich, possibly in Rhode Island. Died Nov. 18, 1725, in Sandwich. His gravestone in Sandwich cemetery is probably the oldest one in America bearing the name of Pope. Married first, about 1699, Elizabeth, daughter of Mrs. Patience (Skiff) Bourne, of Sandwich (died April 15, 1715). Married second, Oct. 3, 1717, Experience (Hamblen) Jenkins, of Barnstable (born March 28, 1693). Children of John and Elizabeth, all, except perhaps the first, born in Sandwich:

9. i.  SETH,⁴ b. Jan. 3, 1700-1; d. 1769.
  ii.  DEBORAH, b. Jan. 6, 1702-3; m. —— Tobey.
  iii.  SARAH, b. March 25, 1705-6; m. Jan. 1, 1726-7, Zaccheus Tobey, of Sandwich.
  iv.  ELIZABETH, b. Jan. 3, 1706-7.
10. v.  THOMAS, b. 1709(?); d. March 25, 1784.
  vi.  MARY, b. Dec. 1713.

Children of John and Experience, born in Sandwich:

  vii.  EZRA, b. April 3, 1719; m. Aug. 18, 1748, Sarah Freeman, of Sandwich, and settled in Newport, R. I. Children: 1. *Experience,* b. Nov. 9, 1762; 2. *Sarah.* (?)
  viii.  JOANNA, b March 3, 1721-2.
  ix.  CHARLES, b. Feb. 28, 1724-5; d. after 1770; m. Dec. 3, 1749, Judith Smith, of Norwalk, Conn. (b. Aug. 21, 1728). Children, born in Norwalk:
    1. *Sarah,* b. May 21, 1751.
    2. *Joanna,* b. April 21, 1754.
    3. *Robert,* b. Feb. 15, 1756.
    4. *Charles,* b. March 22, 1758.
    5. *Judah,* b. Nov. 22, 1760.
    6. *Ezra,* b. Dec. 22, 1762; removed to Ohio about 1820.
    7. *John,* b. Jan. 15, 1764.
    8. *Lewis,* b. Oct. 7, 1766; m. 1st, Rebecca Jowell; m. 2d, Rhoda Hale; settled in Otsego Co., N. Y. Eleven children.
    9. *Edward,* b. Jan. 15, 1770; d. Jan. 23, 1857; m. 1st, Sarah Richards, of Norwalk (b. 1773, d. 1822); m. 2d, Mrs. Abigail Goodrich (sister of preceding); m. 3d, Lucinda Carter. Four children. Descendants in Otsego, N. Y.

**5.**

Seth[3] Pope (*Seth[2]*). Born in Dartmouth, April 5, 1689 ; died in Sandwich, Nov. 23, 1744. He probably settled in Sandwich as early as
1709, where his father owned a grist-mill, fulling-mill and weave-
shop, of which he was placed in charge. This property was given
him by his father's will, with the somewhat peculiar provision that,
in case he did not keep the works in proper repair, the executors
were from time to time, as found necessary, to take charge of and
repair them, and operate them until the expenditures had been re-
paid. Nevertheless, in October, 1734, we are told that "a committee waited upon the miller, Mr. Pope, to know if they could not
be better served in grinding their corn." Married first (date and
place unknown), Hannah, dau. of Mrs. Patience (Skiff) Bourne,
of Sandwich (born May 4, 1689, died March 18, 1744-5). Children, born in Sandwich :

  i.  Abigail,[4] b. Aug. 2, 1710 ; m. Isaac Parker.
  ii. Bathsheba, b. Dec. 2, 1713.
11. iii. John, b. Nov. 25, 1716 ; d. Feb. 8, 1762.
  iv. Mary, bapt. 1720.
  v.  Hannah, b. April 25, 1720.
  vi. Elisha, bapt. July 28, 1723 ; d. August, 1723.
  vii. Patience, b. Nov. 29, 1725 ; m. J. Wooster.
  viii. Elisha, b. July 28, 1729.

**6.**

Elnathan[3] Pope (*Seth[2]*). Born in Dartmouth, Aug. 15, 1694 ; died
same place, Feb. 8, 1735-6. He lived for a time on an estate belonging to his father in a locality called Springbrook, which came,
with other lands, into his possession upon the death of his father in
1727. Married March 14, 1715-16, his cousin Margaret, daughter
of Isaac Pope (3. ii.) (born June 30, 1690, died May 22, 1776)
Children, born in Dartmouth :

  i.  Sarah,[4] April 26, 1715 ; m. Nov. 27, 1753, Moses Washburn, Jr.
  ii. Joanna, b. Feb. 20, 1717-18.
  iii. Thomas, b. July 12, 1720 ; d. Nov. 19, 1732.
12. iv. Isaac, b. March 12, 1723 ; d. Dec. 9, 1793.
  v.  Deborah, b. March 26, 1726.
13. vi. Seth, b. April 15, 1729 ; pub. Feb. 3, 1752, to Sarah Winslow, of Roch-
    ester (b. 1732-3, d. 1775). Child, *Hannah,* b. March 8, 1756.
  vii. Hannah, b. May 20, 1732 ; d. July 24, 1802 ; m. Isaac Vincent, of Yar-
    mouth.
  viii. Margaret, b. June 13, 1735 ; d. Jan. 8, 1793 ; pub. Jan. 29, 1754, to
    Chillingsworth Foster, of Rochester. Eight children.

**7.**

Lemuel[3] Pope (*Seth[2]*), "Captain." Born in Dartmouth, Feb. 21,
1696 ; died same place, May 23, 1771. He inherited most of the
extensive estate of his father, lying within the present limits of Fairhaven ; was captain of militia and a prominent citizen. His will is
in Taunton probate records. Married Feb. 4, 1719, Elizabeth,
daughter of Ephraim Hunt, of D. (born 1697, died July 2, 1782).
Children, born in Dartmouth :

14. i.  Seth,[4] b. March 4, 1719-20 ; d. June 9, 1802.
  ii. Deborah, b. Dec. 9, 1721 ; m. Sept. 20, 1745. Nath'l Gilbert, of Berkley.
  iii. Ann, b. March 24, 1724 ; m. Sept. 20, 1745, Lemuel Williams, of
    Taunton
  iv. Rebekah, b. May 11, 1726 ; d. Dec. 8, 1726.

v.   Rebekah (again), b. Nov. 17, 1727 ; m. Sept. 0, 1750, Zaccheus Mayhew.
vi.  Mercy, b. Jan. 26, 1729–30 ; m. "Capt." —— Church.
vii. Lemuel, b. March 12, 1732 ; d. Dec. 13. 1796 ; m April 10, 1760, Mary
     Newcomb, of Sandwich (b. 1727, d. Dec 12, 1808). Children, b. in
     Dartmouth :
       1. *William,*[5] b. March 13, 1761.
       2. *Timothy,* b. Jan. 29, 1763 ; d. April 29, 1771.
       3. *Jonathan,* b. Feb. 10, 1765. Other children were *Eunice,* 1770,
         and *Sarah,* b. 1774, d. Oct. 27, 1777.
viii. Samuel, b. Dec. 17, 1734 ; d. Sept. 22, 1831 ; "Captain ;" published
     first, June 29, 1760, to Elizabeth Akin, of D. (b. Jun. 4,.1745, d. Nov.
     30, 1792) ; m. second, March 19, 1795, Patience Tobey. Children of
     Samuel and Elizabeth :
       1. *Abigail,*[5] b. June 14, 1764 ; d. April 19, 1804.
       2. *Elizabeth,* b. June 4, 1767 ; d. Nov. 1, 1850 ; m. Jan. 24, 1793,
         Benjamin Hammond.
       3. *Ebenezer Akin,* b. June 12, 1769 ; d. March 26, 1828 ; m. first,
         Hannah Kelly (b. 1777, d. May 12, 1803) ; m. second, Rebecca
         Allen (b. 1775. d. May 2, 1813).
       4. *Lemuel,* b. Sept. 27, 1771.
       5. *Ruth,* b. March 14, 1774.
       6. *Silvia,* b. Feb. 2, 1777.
       7. *Elihu,* b. May 27, 1779.
       8. *Lois,* b. June 28, 1781 ; d. May 6, 1848.
       9. *Silas,* b. Oct. 23, 1783 ; d. Feb. 21, 1862.
      10. *Loring,* b. Feb. 18. 1786 ; d. July 14, 1859 ; m. Sarah ——.
      11. *Lucy,* b. June 6, 1788.
      12. *Lenny* (?).
      13. *Patience.*
      14. *Reliance,* b. 1796 ; d. Dec. 28,1817.
ix.  Louin (Luen), b. May 8, 1737 ; d. about 1792 ; m. Mary West, of Dart-
     mouth; removed to New Braintree in 1778. Children :
       *Asa,*[5] *Louen, Thomas,* and others. Descendants in Burlington, Vt.,
       and Norwich, Ct.
x.   Elizabeth, b. May 20, 1739 ; m. Lemuel Newcomb, of Sandwich.
xi.  Joseph,  } b. May 15, 1742 ; { m. Hannah Pope (10, iii.).
xii. Richard, }             { d. May 27, 1742.

### 8.

Elnathan[3] Pope (*Isaac*[2]). Born in Dartmouth, Aug. 14, 1703 ; died
May 15, 1794. He lived in Dartmouth, and on the death of his
father in 1734, inherited the ancestral estate of his grandfather Tho-
mas Pope the emigrant, on the present site of Fairhaven. Married,
Nov. 12, 1727, Rebecca Mitchell, of Kingston (born 1705, died
Nov. 30, 1764). Children, all born in Dartmouth :

i.    Deborah,[4] b. Nov. 9, 1730 ; d. young.
ii.   Elnathan, b. Jan. 2, 1735.
iii.  Rebekah, b. Jan. 3, 1737.
iv.  Jacob, b. Jan. 12, 1738
v.    Ichabod, b. April 7, 1741 ; d. 1795 ; removed to S. Bridgewater ; m.
     widow Pope.
vi.  Freeman, b. April 5, 1744 ; m. Nov. 3, 1765, Phebe Spooner. Descend-
     ants in Enfield.
vii. Edmon, "Captain," b. Dec 9, 1718 ; d. Feb. 22, 1827 : m. Catherine
     —— . Children : *Rebekah,* b. 1782, d. May 10, 1806 ; *Elnathan, Free-
     man,* and probably others.

#### Fourth Generation.

##### 9.

Seth[4] Pope (*John,*[3] *Seth*[2]). Born in Sandwich; Jan. 3, 1701 ; died
1769. He was a respected citizen of that town, and was frequently

chosen to fill positions of public trust. Iu 1749 he removed to Lebanon, Conn., where he bought a farm at the north end of "Town
Street." Iu the spring of 1759 he sold this property and purchased
a large tract on the borders of Plainfield and Voluntown, Conn.,
where is now the village of Sterling Hill. In 1760 was rated £45
10s. among the tax-payers of the "old society" of Plainfield, Ct.
April 28, 1762, admitted inhabitant of Voluntown. March 1, 1762,
he conveyed his homestead to his sons Seth, Jr., and Gershom.
Married, June 22, 1719, Jerusha, daughter of Gershom and Mehetable (Fish) Tobey, of Sandwich (born March 23, 1697–8); Oct. 3,
1769, his son Seth was appointed administrator of his estate.
Children, all born in Sandwich :

i.   Ichabod,[3] b. Sept. 5, 1720 ; d. young.
ii.  Elizabeth, b. Oct. 3, 1721 ; m. Jan. 15, 1746–7, Joshua Phinney, of
      Plymouth.
iii. Deborah, b. Feb. 23, 1725 ; m. May 13, 1742, Israel Clark, of Plymouth.
iv.  John, b. April 24, 1727 ; m. Oct. 4, 1751, at Lebanon, Conn., Sarah
      Athearn of Martha's Vineyard.  Dec. 28, 1762, his father conveyed to
      him a farm in Plainfield and Voluntown, Conn., where he was rated
      £39 14s. in 1763.  Was at Coventry, R. I., Oct. 25, 1764.  Child :
      1. Betty,[6] b. May 15, 1755.
v.   Mehetable, b. May 27, 1729 ; m. Jan. 15, 1746–7, Benjamin Fish, of
      Sandwich.
15. vi.  Seth, b. April 19, 1731 ; d. 1774.
vii.  Gershom, b. Dec. 18, 1733 ; d. young.
viii. Elnathan, b. Aug. 16, 1735 ; m. Nov. 13, 1754, Hannah Tilden, of
       Lebanon, Conn.
ix.   Ichabod, b. Jan. 27, 1740.  Nov. 26, 1762, his father gave him a home-
       stead in that part of Voluntown which is now Sterling, probably about
       the time of his marriage to Freelove (Briggs ?), on which he was taxed
       £27 in 1763.  In 1772 he bought land in that part of Gt. Barrington
       afterwards set off to Alford, describing himself as of Plainfield, Conn.,
       and sold the same in 1793, being then of Saratoga, N. Y.  April 8, 1793,
       he was at Cooperstown, N. Y.  Oct. 27, 1794, he bought a farm on
       the west shore of Otsego Lake.  He was living there Jan. 7, 1810.
       Two of his children were Benjamin.[6] Polly.
x.    Gershom, b. Aug. 22, 1743 ; d. March 22, 1810.  "Captain."  March
       1, 1762, his father gave him half the homestead farm on the eastern
       edge of Plainfield, Conn.  About this date he married Hannah Smith
       (b. March 25, 1742, d. Feb. 9, 1830).  He served in the northern army
       under Arnold and Gates, and attained the rank of captain.  Feb. 3,
       1779, sold his property in Plainfield and removed to Vermont.  Sub-
       sequently, June 9, 1792, purchased a large tract in what is now Bur-
       lington, Otsego Co., N. Y., where he settled and remained until his
       death.  Was a man of strong character and unblemished integrity.
       Children :
       1. Phebe,[6] b. Oct. 22, 1762 ; d. July 19, 1843 ; m. Joseph Smith.
       2. Jedediah, b. Sept. 15, 1764 ; m. Lucy Angel.  Thirteen children.
       3. Deborah, b. Oct. 22, 1766 ; d. Jan. 16, 1816 ; m. William Monroe.
       4. John, b. Dec. 15, 1768 ; d. July 26, 1855 ; m. Alice Brooks.
       5. Timothy, b. Jan. 16, 1771.
       6. Squire, b. Jan. 16, 1773 ; m. Sally ——.
       7. Seth, b. Dec. 6, 1775 ; d. about 1857 ; m. first, Julia Angel ;
          second, Hannah May.  Twelve children.  Descendants in Cort-
          land, N. Y.
       8. Gates, b. March 5, 1778 ; d. in Columbus, Chenango Co., N. Y.,
          July 21, 1840 ; removed with his father to Vermont, and thence
          to Burlington, N. Y., in 1792.  Lived in Exeter, N. Y., 1808 to
          1814.  Afterwards removed to Columbus.  Married Dec. 25,
          1796, "Betsey" Brooks, of Burlington, N. Y. (b. Sept. 9,
          1777, d. Oct. 16, 1842).  Children, born in Burlington, Exeter
          and Columbus : 1. Alice Brooks,[7] b. Aug. 1, 1797.  2. John, b.

Dec. 29, 1798; d. Sept. 12, 1878, near Forestville, Chautauqua Co., N. Y.; m. July 19, 1818, Frances, daughter of Earl and Abigail Eaton, of Edmeston, N. Y. (b. June 22, 1798, d. June 4, 1885). Children: *Horatio Gates,* b. Sept. 5, 1819; *Chester,* b. Feb. 8, 1821; *Abigail,* b. Jan. 15, 1823; *Harrison,* b. Oct. 25, 1824; *Almona,* b. June 11, 1826; *Betsey,* b. March 31, 1828; *Leonora,* b. June 15, 1830; *Stephen Mather,* b. Nov. 15, 1831; *Daniel Eaton,* b. Aug. 5, 1833; *John William,* b. May 1, 1835; *Mary Ann,* b. April 22, 1837; *Sarah Ann,* b. Dec. 8, 1839. 3. Horatio Gates, b. Dec. 12, 1800; d. July 14, 1803. 4. Arnold, b. April 23, 1802. 5. Asa, b. Nov. 14, 1803. 6. Chester, b. Aug. 25, 1805; d. Sept. 12, 1806. 7. James, b. July 26, 1807. 8. Sidney, b. April 18, 1809. 9. Betsey, b. July 25, 1812. 10. Timothy, b. Aug. 15, 1814. 11. Gershom, b. Sept. 21, 1816. 12 and 13. Mary Ann and Sarah Ann, b. July 26, 1818. 14. Horatio Gates, b. Dec. 22, 1820. 15. Solomon, b. Dec. 22, 1822.

  9. *Arnold,* b. March 5, 1778.
  10. *Hannah,* b. May 19, 1780; m. Uriah Farmer.
  11. *Elizabeth,* b. Sept. 12, 1782; m. William Thomson.
  12. *Jerusha,* b. Jan. 6, 1787; d. March 9, 1788.

### 10.

THOMAS[4] POPE (*John,*[3] *Seth*[2]). Born in Sandwich, 1709; died March 25, 1784. Resided in Sandwich, and afterwards in Dartmouth near the junction of Acushnet Avenue and the Fairhaven road. His dwelling was the first building burned by the British troops after leaving the "head of the river" in their raid of 1778. Married first, Sept. 26, 1735, Thankful Dillingham, of Harwich (born 1718, died April 13, 1756); and second, Alice Jenney (born 1718, died Oct. 21, 1803). Children of Thomas and Thankful, first two born in Sandwich, others in Dartmouth :

i. LYDIA,[5] b. May 18, 1738; m. Joseph Ripley.
ii. EDWARD, b. Feb. 15, 1739–40; d. June 10, 1818; m. first, Elizabeth Bullard; second, Mrs. Elizabeth Greenleaf Eliot, of Boston. He was a leading citizen of New Bedford, and had a mansion at the corner of Main and North Sixth Streets. He was Judge of the Court of Common Pleas for Bristol County, and subsequently for many years collector of the port of New Bedford. Children :
    1. *Edward,*[6] b. July 18, 1787; d. Feb. 15, 1812; m. Charlotte Ingraham.
    2. *Thomas,* b. April 7, 1789; d. March 3, 1872; m. Emily Brown.
    3. *Juliana,* b. Oct. 10, 1791; d. Oct. 5, 1792.
iii. HANNAH, b. Nov. 29, 1743; m. Joseph Pope (7. xi.).
iv. JOANNA, b. Oct. 30, 1748; d. Sept. 25, 1813; m. Nov. 17, 1769, Simeon Nash.
v. SARAH, d. Dec. 25, 1750 :[d. Dec. 17, 1782; m. Feb. 9, 1775, Paul Swift.
vi. THANKFUL, b. May 29, 1753; d. Nov. 22, 1769, unm.
vii. ELIZABETH, b. April 8, 1756; d. Dec. 20, 1835; m. (about 1777) Lemuel Tobey.

Child of Thomas and Alice :

viii. NABBY, b. Nov. 11, 1761; d. Nov. 16, 1831; m. Jan. 4, 1791, Capt. William Gordon, an officer of the Revolution. She was his second wife.

* Daniel Eaton[4] Pope, to whom the writer is indebted for much valuable assistance in this work, is a graduate of Madison University, 1859; a lawyer, and prominent citizen of Cornwall-on-Hudson, N. Y. He married in Cornwall, Aug. 18, 1862, Anna Silliman, daughter of William V. and Mary (Jessup) Dusinberre (b. Oct. 4, 1839). Children : 1. *William Harold,* b. Jan. 9, 1864. 2. *Francis G. Eaton,* b. July 8, 1865. 3. *Mary Jessup,* b. April 30, 1869. 4. *Daniel Webster,* b. Oct. 3, 1871; d. Dec. 3, 1866. 5. *Leonora,* b. Dec. 22, 1873. 6. *Philip Sidney,* b. Dec. 29, 1876. 7. *John Augustus,* b. May 8, 1879. 8. *Benjamin Franklin Victor,* b. March 6, 1881.

**11.**

John[4] Pope (*Seth,[3] Seth[2]*). Born in Sandwich, Nov. 25, 1716; died
same place, Feb. 8, 1762. Married Oct. 25, 1734, Mercy Swift
(born 1719, died 1815). Children, born in Sandwich:

i.   Lois,[3] b. May 25, 1738; m. Cornelius Tobey.
ii.  Elisha, b. Nov. 1, 1740; d. Feb. 1, 1809; m. Feb. 15, 1761, Joanna
     Tobey.  Children :
       1. *John,[4]* b. July 8, 1762; d. in Maine, March 4, 1829; m. Mary
          Freeman, of Sandwich.
       2. *Warren.*
       3. *William,* b. 1769; d. March 2, 1845.
       4. *Elisha,* b. 1781; d. March 8, 1860.
       5. *Lewin,* m. Temperance Parker.
iii. Lemuel, b. April 23, 1743; d. April 9, 1827; m. Oct. 25, 1764, Mary
     Butler, of Sandwich (b. March 19, 1745, d. May 11, 1839).  Children :
       1. *Daniel,[4]* b. April 10, 1766; d. Oct. 24, 1772.
       2. *Elizabeth,* b. Oct. 1, 1768; d. Sept. 27, 1773.
       3. *Thomas,* b. Dec. 17, 1771; d. Feb. 1, 1841: m. May 21, 1795,
          Lucy Bourne (b. Sept. 26, 1778, d. Nov. 1, 1845).  Ten child'n.
       4. *Daniel Butler,* b. Feb. 15, 1773; d. May 1, 1773.
       5. *Abigail,* b. Jun. 23, 1775; d. Oct. 16, 1848; m. Ansel Bourne.
       6. *Lemuel,* b. Jan. 30, 1777; d. Aug. 3, 1851; m. Sarah Belknap
          Russell.
       7. *Mary,* b. March 31, 1780; d. March 6, 1803, unm.
       8. *Joseph Henry,* b. May 22, 1782; d Sept. 27, 1860.
       9. *Mercy,* b. Aug. 12, 1784; d. Sept. 29, 1826.
       10. *Seth,* b. May 29, 1786; d. March 13, 1863; m. Hannah Crocker.
iv.  Hannah, b. May 28, 1745.
v.   Abigail, b. July 28, 1749.

**12.**

Isaac[4] Pope (*Elnathan,[3] Seth[2]*). Born March 12, 1723; died Dec. 9,
1798.  Very little has been learned of his history.  He is thought
to have lived at or near Dartmouth.  Married Sarah —— (born
1726, died March 2, 1795).  They are buried in Acushnet cemetery.  Of their ten children, the names of but two have been ascertained, as follows.  (The remaining eight were daughters.)

ix.  Jonathan.[5]  Removed to Ohio in 1819.  Many of his descendants live
     in Strongsville in that state.  Children :
       *Thankful,* m. —— Nash; *Margaret,* m. first, Elijah Lyman,
       second, Peter D. Wellman; *Ansel Jenne,* m. Lucinda Brittan.
x.   Worth.  "Captain."  Children :
       1. *Sally,* m. Sylvester Ames; d. 1875 at Door Creek, Wis.;  2.
       *Isaac;*  3. *Reliance;*  4. *Charles;*  5. *John;*  6. *Mary Ann.*

**13.**

Seth[4] Pope (*Elnathan,[3] Seth[2]*).  Born April 15, 1729.  He lived perhaps in Rochester.  Published Feb. 3, 1752, to Sarah Winslow, of
R. (born March 23, 1732-3, died Aug. 20, 1775).  His name appears in the muster roll of the company of Capt. Abial Pierce, in
Col. Nicholas Dyke's regiment, which served in the continental
army, having enlisted from Rochester.  Two of his children were :

i.   Hannah,[5] b. July 2, 1753; d. Aug. 9, 1753.
ii.  Hannah (again), b. March 8, 1756.

**14.**

Seth[4] Pope (*Lemuel,[3] Seth[2]*), "Col."  Born March 4, 1719–20; died
June 9, 1802.  He lived in Dartmouth; was one of the leading men
in the colony, both in civil and military affairs, during the revolu-

tionary period, and held a commission as colonel.  July 18, 1774, he was chosen on a committee by his townsmen to report what action ought to be taken respecting British taxation.  The committee's report, earnestly recommending non-importation of goods from the mother country and the raising of funds in aid of the Congress, was adopted by the town and ordered to be published.  In consequence of his activity as a patriot leader, his dwelling at Acushnet was burned by British troops in 1778, having been pointed out to them by a tory neighbor.  Married July 30, 1741, Abigail Church (born 1719, died May 8, 1778).  They are buried in Acushnet cemetery.   Children:

i.   Richard,[5] b. Dec. 22, 1742; d. Nov. 21, 1808.  Mariner and shoemaker. Lived in Fairhaven; removed in 1770 to Plainfield, Conn., and in 1803 to Middlefield, Otsego Co., N. Y.  Married about 1765, Innocent Head, of Little Compton.  He died while on a visit to New Bedford.  Chil'n:
    1.  Benjamin,[6] b. 1766 in Dartmouth; d. Jan. 4, 1854, in Hartford, Washington Co. N. Y.; m. 1793, Margaret Foster.
    2.  Job, m. Feb. 3, 1792, Sarah Dennison, of Voluntown, Conn.; was of Cherry Valley, N. Y., 1813, Middlefield, N. Y., 1816, and was living in 1828.
    3.  Lemuel, was of Middlefield,'N. Y., 1810 and 1838.
    4.  Caleb.
    5.  Seth, b. Dec. 5, 1783; d. Feb. 21, 1869; m. (date unknown) Rebecca Delano, of New Bedford (b. May 25, 1786, d. Feb. 21, 1869).  He was of Middlefield, N. Y.  Ten children.
    6.  Deborah, m. Joseph Nichols.
    7.  Mercy.
    8.  Lydia.
    9.  Ruth, m. first, Constant Wetmore; second, James Hazard.
    10.  Nathaniel.
ii.   Alice, b. Jan. 18, 1744; d. May 7, 1778; m. Feb. 9, 1764, Ebenezer Hathaway.
iii.   Nathaniel, b. June 22, 1747; d. July 17, 1817.  Lived in Fairhaven; was lieutenant in command of a volunteer naval expedition, which on May 14, 1775, recaptured two provincial vessels from the British sloop-of-war Falcon.  This occurred in Buzzard's Bay, and was the first naval action of the Revolution.  (Ricketson's Hist. N. Bedford, 291.) Married Oct. 14, 1790, Mary Barstow, of Mattapoisett (b. Nov. 15, 1762, d. May 12, 1851).  Children:
    1.  Nathaniel,[6] b. July 29, 1791; d. May 19, 1822.
    2.  Wilson, b. Sept. 14, 1793; d. Jan. 8, 1879; m. Sept. 8, 1824, Sarah Eldridge.
    3.  Gideon, b. Jan. 1, 1796; m. July 26, 1831, Jane D. Cunningham.
    4.  Joshua Loring, b. July 19, 1798; d. March 17, 1863; m. Oct. 17, 1831, Anna Sophia Barstow.
    5.  Alice, b. May 9, 1802; d. April 23, 1863.
    6.  Lucy Barstow, b. March 9, 1805; m. Sept. 27, 1832, Rowland Fish, of Fairhaven.  Both living in 1867.
iv.   Innocent, b. Dec. 8, 1749.
v.   Ephraim, b. July 20, 1752.
vi.   Yet Seth, b. April 15, 1755; d. Oct. 17, 1820; m. first, Thankful Foster (b. March 27, 1761, d. Oct. 31, 1792); m. second, Mrs. Margaret —— (b. Aug. 13, 1762, d. April 12, 1848).  Children of Seth and Thankful:
    1.  Child,[6] b. and d. Sept. 6, 1785.
    2.  Abigail, b. Oct. 21, 1788.
    3.  Enos, b. July 5, 1795; m. first, July 16, 1823, Lois Alden (d. Dec. 2, 1823); m. second, Abigail Haskell (d. Feb. 23, 1836); m. third, Jane R. Heustis.
    4.  Thankful, b. Jan. 3, 1797; m. Thomas Shaw.
    5.  Sarah, b. July 31, 1798.
    6.  Orpha, b. April 7, 1800; d. May 10, 1838.

7. *Margaret*, b. Jan. 8, 1802.
8. *Seth*, b. Oct. 16, 1803 ; m. Mary Henwood.
9. *Ephraim*, b. Aug. 8, 1807 ; d. May 31, 1874.

*Fifth, Sixth, Seventh and Eighth Generations.*

15.

SETH³ POPE (*Seth*,⁴ *John*,³ *Seth*²). He removed with his father to Lebanon, Conn., in 1749; married about 1750, Martha, daughter of
Ebenezer and Lydia (Lothrop) Bacon, of L. (born Nov. 6, 1734).
March 1, 1762, his father conveyed to him the homestead in Voluntown, now Sterling Hill, Conn. He was killed by being run
over by a cart, in September, 1774. Children :

i. ANSEL,⁶ b. 1751(?) ; m. Anne,——. Took oath of allegiance. Voluntown, April 19, 1781. Removed from thence in spring of 1783 and
settled in Exeter, N. Y. Descendants in New Berlin, N. Y., and Jackson, Pa. Child :
    1. *Hannah*,⁷ b. April 7, 1780. Other children were *Ansel, Allen S.,
Abraham, William, Thomas* and *Seth*.

ii. LOTHROP, b. 1753 ; d. 1841, in Keeseville, N. Y. About 1790 he removed to Saratoga, now Northumberland, N. Y., and in 1831 to Keeseville. Married about 1791 Abigail Newell, of Washington Co., N. Y.
Children :
    1. *Abigail*,⁷ b. Nov. 19, 1792.
    2. *Seth*, d. unm. about 1831, Northumberland, N. Y.
    3. *Martha*, d. unm.
    4. *Martin*, was living in 1830, Northumberland, N. Y.
    5. *Susan*.
    6. *Elizabeth*, m. Richard H. Peabody, of Yonkers, N. Y.
    7. *Mary*, b. May 5, 1809 ; m. Samuel Ball, of Rahway, N. J.
    8. *Lothrop*, b. Feb. 28, 1813 ; d. at Keeseville, N. Y. ; m. Mary
Bushee.

iii. HANNAH, b. 1757 ; d. April 12, 1814 ; m. Zechariah Fairchild,* of Great
Barrington, Mass. Nine children. One of these children was *Fran-
ces*,⁷ b. March 27, 1797, who m. Jan. 11, 1821, at Great Barrington,
William Cullen Bryant, poet and journalist.

iv. SETH, d. August, 1802, in Georgetown, S. C., unm. He was a master
mariner.

v. WILLIAM, b. 1763(?) ; d. Nov. 1799, in St. Albans, Vt. He went from
Voluntown, Ct., to Sheffield, probably about 1781, appearing in the
tax-list of S. in 1784. He removed to Great Barrington in 1789, and
to Hubbardston, and finally to St. Albans, Vt., where he died. Married April 13, 1784, Rhoda Dewey, of Sheffield, who after his death
returned to S. and m. April 26, 1801, Zebulon Spaulding, of the same
place. Children :
    1. *Calvin J.*, d. 1835 ; m. Abigail Kellogg.
    2. *Julia Maria*,⁷ m. Martin Callender.
    3. *Mira*, m. Sarah ——.
    4. *Almira*, b. Oct. 15, 1791 ; d. March 8, 1872 ; m. Dec. 1808, Har-
ry Day Austin.
    5. *Stephen Dewey*, b. April 17, 1794 ; d. Nov. 27, 1873 ; m. Mary
Fitch.
    6. *William*, b. April 23, 1800 ; d. Sept. 27, 1882 ; m. first, Anna
Maria Fassett ; second, Sarah Ann Parmenter. Eleven child'n.

vi. ESTHER, m. Philo Hamlin, of Bloomfield, N. Y.
vii. LYDIA, b. Feb. 29, 1767 ; d. Nov. 26, 1839 ; m. Aug. 17, 1789, Elijah
Hamlin, of Bloomfield, N. Y.
viii. MARTHA, m. first, John Fairchild ; second, Tyrranus Collins.

16. ix. EBENEZER, b. April 3, 1772 ; d. March 8, 1841.

---

* In the will of her brother Seth, dated August 9, 1802, she is called " Hannah Stilles,"
which may indicate that she had been previously married.

16.

Ebenezer[4] Pope (Seth,[5] Seth,[4] John,[2] Seth[3]), "Captain." He was reared from childhood and lived until 1784 in the family of his maternal grandfather, Ebenezer Bacon, of Lebanon, Conn. From 1795 to 1809 he lived in Alford and carried on a small iron works. In 1809 he removed to Great Barrington, where he was for many years a leading citizen and a prominent mason. Was several times chosen selectman in Alford and G. B., and three times elected to the state legislature. In 1827, meeting with financial reverses, he removed to Verona, N. Y., but in 1831 returned to Massachusetts and settled in West Stockbridge, where he died, March 8, 1841. Married first, Dec. 17, 1800, Keziah, daughter of Simon[4] (Simon.[3] John.[2] Simon.[1] of Kent, England, born 1605) and Anne Willard (born 1776, died Feb. 6, 1804)'; married second, Rhoda Willard (sister of preceding, born 1782, died Jan. 13, 1813) ; married third, Mrs. Zady (Prindle) Tobey (born April 5, 1777, d. Feb. 5, 1864). Children, born in Alford, of Ebenezer and Keziah :

17. i. Ebenezer,[7] b. Oct. 22, 1801 ; d. Dec. 12, 1878.
ii. Keziah, b. Feb. 6, 1803 ; d. Aug. 29, 1868 ; m. July 6, 1826, "Capt." Levi Kilbourne, of Great Barrington. Three children.

Children of Ebenezer and Rhoda, born in Alford and Gt. Barrington :

iii. Abby, b. Aug. 20, 1805 : d. July 31, 1886, in Rochester, N. Y. ; m. Benjamin Ford, of Clyde, N. Y. Three children.
iv. Amanda, b. Nov. 4, 1806 ; lives (1887) in St. Paul, Minn. ; m. Henry Acker, of Clyde, N. Y. Nine children.
v. William, b. July 21, 1808 ; d. Jan. 15, 1884, in Quincy, Mich., unm. Was an extensive contractor and stock-raiser.
vi. Martha, b. June 30, 1810 ; d. July 4, 1882, in Chicago, Ill. ; m. George Sedgwick, of Stockbridge. No issue.
vii. John Willard, b. Oct. 1, 1812 ; d. Feb. 16, 1813.

Children of Ebenezer and Zady, born in Great Barrington :

viii. John, b. Aug. 2, 1814 ; d. in Maquoketa, Iowa ; m. ——. Children :
    1. William.[8]
    2. Delphina.
    3. Adrian D.
    4. Augusta.
ix. Harriet, b. July 21, 1817 ; m. in Pittsfield, Nov. 3, 1887, Thomas Pettijohn, of St. Peter, Minn.
x. Seth Griswold, b. Dec. 14, 1819. Builder and contractor. Lived first in Great Barrington; removed in 1850 to Ogdensburgh, N. Y. ; was several times chosen president of that borough, and member of New York State Assembly. Resides (1887), at Alexandria Bay, N. Y. Married first, Isabella M. Carter, of Whitesboro', N. Y. (d. April 6, 1857) ; m. second, Mrs. Harriet (Haskell) Chapin, of New Haven, Conn. (d. July 9, 1878). Child of Seth and Isabella, b. in Ogdensburgh :
    1. Frances Elizabeth,[8] b. Dec. 3, 1851 ; m. Dr. Weston, of N. York.
    Children of Seth and Harriet, b. in Ogdensburgh :
    2. Harriet Isabella, b. Sept. 13, 1864.
    3. Deodatus Haskell, b. June 28, 1868.

17.

Ebenezer[7] Pope (Ebenezer,[6] Seth,[5] Seth,[4] John,[2] Seth[3]). Born in Alford, Oct. 22, 1801 ; died in Union township, N. J., Dec. 12, 1878. Blacksmith and farmer. Removed with his father to Great Barrington in 1809, and to Verona, N. Y., in 1827 ; returned to West Stockbridge in 1831. He afterwards lived in Great Barrington until 1867, when he went to Union township, N. J., with his sons.

Married at G. B. Jan. 27, 1840, Electa Leonard, daughter of William and Mary (Leonard) Wainwright (born Dec. 19, 1803, died in Elizabeth, N. J., Feb. 27, 1878).  Children, born in Great Barrington:

18. i.   FRANKLIN LEONARD,[8] b. Dec. 2, 1840.
    ii.  WILLIAM, b. and d. Nov. 27, 1842.
    iii. RALPH WAINWRIGHT, b. Aug. 16, 1844, Union township, N. J.; m. first, in South Lee, Nov. 25, 1868, Alice Ellen Judson (b. Sept. 4, 1849, d. Oct. 31, 1880); m. second, at Great Barrington, Feb. 6, 1884, Ruth Emma Whiting   Children of Ralph and Alice:
             1. *Ellen Lowry*,[9] b. May 27, 1870.
             2. *Frank Judson*, b. July 27, 1873.
             3. *Gertrude Castle*, b. Sept. 28, 1876.
    iv.  HENRY WILLIAM, b. Nov. 2, 1848, Elizabeth, N. J.; m. in Pittsfield, May 10, 1870, Lucy Delia Porter, of P. (b. April 23, 1851). Child'n :
             1. *Grace Electa*,[9] b. June, 11, 1871.
             2. *William Henry*, b. Aug. 20, 1873.
             3. *Irving Wainwright*, b. Sept. 29, 1875.

### 18.

FRANKLIN LEONARD[8] POPE (*Ebenezer*,[7] *Ebenezer*,[6] *Seth*,[5] *Seth*,[4] *John*,[3] *Seth*[2]).  Born in Great Barrington, Dec. 2, 1840.  Was telegraph operator in G. B., Springfield and Providence, R. I., from 1857 to 1862; assistant engineer of American Telegraph Co. in New York until 1864 ; assistant engineer of Russo-American telegraph from Washington Territory to Siberia and Behring's Straits (partially completed and abandoned in 1867), in which capacity he made the first exploration of the region lying about the sources of the Skeena, Stickeen and Yukon rivers in British Columbia and Alaska.  In 1867 settled in Union township, near Elizabeth, N. J., where he now (1887) resides.  Is an electrical engineer and author, place of business in New York.  Married in Amherst, August 6, 1873, Sarah Amelia, daughter of " Captain " Marquis Fayette and Hannah (Williams) Dickinson (born Oct. 8, 1848).  Children, born in Union, N. J.:

    i.   SON,[9] b. and d. 1874.
    ii.  HANNAH DICKINSON, b. May 3, 1876.
    iii. AMY MARGARETTA, b. Aug. 9, 1879.
    iv.  FRANKLIN LEONARD WAINWRIGHT, b. July 29, 1880.
    v.   SETH WILLARD, b. Oct. 23, 1883 ; d. Nov. 13, 1883.

# SECTION C.

## JOSEPH POPE, OF SALEM.

"THE Last will and Testiment of Joseph Pope of Salem being weake of body but of perfect memory.

Imp<sup>r</sup>. I doe appoynt my Loveing wife Gartrude Pope to be Executrix of this my Last will and testament.

Itt<sup>m</sup>. I give unto my two Eldest sonns Joseph and Benjamen Pope: all that Land and medo which I bought of goodman ffareington of Linne tto them and there heirs forever : they to injoy the said land whe thay cum to age.

It<sup>m</sup>. I give unto the abovesaid Joseph and Benjamen Pope the House which I now dwell in together with the Land or farme on which it standeth with all the apurtenances thereto belonging to them and to there heirs forever thay to injoy the same after ther mother deseas : provided and it is my will that they shall pay to my two yongest sonns Enos and Samuell Pope tenn pounds apeece within two years after they shall injoy the same, the house and Land above said to stand as security for the payment of the said Legase to my two yonger sonns.

It<sup>m</sup>. I give unto my two yongest sonns Enos and Samuell Pope tenn pounds apeece to be payde when thay cum to age.

It<sup>m</sup>. I give unto my Daughter Damaris Buffum tenne pounds beside what she have alredy had to hir and to hir heirs.

It<sup>m</sup>. I give unto my Dafter Hanah pope twenty pounde to hir and hir heirs.

the rest of my Estate I doe give to my wife during hir Life and to be disposed of by hir will at hir decease, provided it be to my Children.

It<sup>m</sup>. I doe desier my brothers George and Richard and Joseph Gardner and Cos Samuell Shatok the elder to be overseers of this my Last will testament.

the marke of

JOSEPH P POPE.

September the : 11<sup>th</sup> : 1666.
Test Joseph Gardner.

[Memorandum on the back of the paper.]

the within writing being presented to this Court held at Salem by Garthred the wife of the said Joseph Pope deceased, & there being noe witnes p'sent: the Court being informed by Leif¹ George Gardner that it was the mind of yᵉ deceased to his knowledge, the Court doe appoynt the said Garthred Administratrix and doe order that the Estate be disposed of according to the within writing. duᵣ the 27 : 4ᵐᵒ 1667. in Court.

Attestes HILLYARD VEREN Clericus."

As George, Richard and Joseph Gardner are here called "brothers" by Joseph Pope, we must connect him in some way with their father, Mr. Thomas Gardner, who was sent over from England (probably from Dorsetshire) in 1623–4 by the Dorchester Company, to be· overseer of the farming at Cape Ann, as Roger Conant was of the fisheries connected with that colony. In 1626 he removed to Salem, where he continued, a much honored citizen, until his death, Dec. 9, 1674. His surviving wife was widow Damaris Shattuck, whose son, "Samuel Shatok the elder," is called "cos." [cousin] by Joseph Pope. Thomas Gardner's will specifies wife Damaris, daughters Sarah Balch, Seeth Grafton, Miriam Hill's two daughters, Miriam and Susanna; sons Thomas, George, John, Samuel, Joseph and Richard Some of these were children of a former wife, said by the Shattuck Memorial to have been Margaret Frier: and either she or an earlier wife may have been a widow Pope, the mother of Joseph Pope. Or Gertrude Pope, Joseph's wife, may have been a daughter of Thomas G., sen., and her mother a sister of Damaris Shattuck. The relation· ship of the Pope and Gardner and Shattuck families is certain; the mode not yet plain.

Joseph Pope and his wife and many of their descendants were members of the Society of Friends, commonly mis-called Quakers. That body of people would never have been persecuted, had all its members been as law-abiding, courteous and *friendly* as the Salem Pope family have been.

[By the great kindness of Dr. Wheatland, we are permitted to reprint the following article. The notes within the columns are his; those across the foot of the pages are ours.]

# NOTICE OF SOME OF THE DESCENDANTS OF JOSEPH POPE, OF SALEM.

### BY HENRY WHEATLAND.

*Published in Essex Institute Collections of June, 1866. (Vol. viii.)*

THIS account is only a compilation of a few facts that have been gathered from various sources, without any extended research, and should be considered merely as *materials for a history of this family*, which, I trust, some future antiquary will, ere long, be induced to prepare. The compiler desires notice of any error or omission.

JOSEPH POPE, the progenitor of the various families of the name now residing in this vicinity, is said[1] to be the son of Robert Pope, of Yorkshire, England. He came to this country in the "Mary and John," of London,[2] in 1634, was recorded a Church Member before 1636, made a Freeman in 1637, had lands granted in 1637 and at other times in that portion of Salem now known as West Danvers, and some of it bordering on Ipswich River. He and his wife Gertrude were before the court in 1658 for attending Quaker Meetings, and in 1662 were excommunicated for their adherence to the opinions of that sect. He died about 1667. His will, dated Sept. 10, 1666, mentions wife Gertrude executrix. In court, 27. 4, 1667.

The following children are recorded among the baptisms of the First Church, in Salem:—

2. Damaris,[2] bap. 1643, 22. 2; m. Joshua Buffum.

3. Hannah,[2] bap. 1645, 20. 5.

4. Hannah,[2] bap. 1648, 26. 1; m. Caleb Buffum, 26 March, 1672; had son Caleb, b. 14th May, 1673; Robert, b. 1. 10, 1675.

5. George,[2] bap. 1649, 8. 5.

6. Joseph,[2] bap. 1650, 27. 8. (*Vide infra.*)

7. Benjamin,[2] bap. 1653, 17. 2. (*Vide infra.*)

8. Samuel,[2] bap. 1656, 18. 3. (*Vide infra.*)

9. Enos,[2] mentioned in his father's will, not recorded among the baptisms.

### II. GENERATION.

#### (6)

JOSEPH POPE,[2] bap. 1650, 27. 8, a farmer, lived at "The Village;" m. Bethseda[3] Folger, daughter of Peter Folger,[*] of Nantucket, one of the first settlers on that island, and in

[*] See an account of the Folger family in N. E. Hist. and Gen. Reg. vol. 16, p. 269.

---

[1] Family Tradition only.

[2] The "26th day of March," the second day of the new year, his name was entered on the list.

[3] Joseph,[2] in his will, calls wife and daughter "Bethshua."

consequence of his valuable services at that period, his name has always been held in high esteem. Abiah, the sister of Bethseda, m. Josiah Franklin, and was the mother of Dr. Benjamin Franklin, a name that stands high in the annals of science.

Joseph Pope died in 1712, having had the following children:—

10. Joseph,[3] b.        ; d. young.
11. Bethseda,[3] b. Ap. 9, 1683; d. unm.

12. Gertrude,[3] b. Aug. 27, 1685; m. Ebenezer, third son of Thomas Flint, a farmer, lived in North Reading, born April 6, 1683, and died 1767; had six children, Nathaniel, Ebenezer, Lois, Nathan, Amos, Eunice. See "Flint's Genealogy," p. 13.

13. Joseph,[3] b. June 16, 1687. (*Vide infra.*)

14. Enos,[3] b. June 6, 1690. (*Vide infra.*)

15. Eleazer,[3] b. Dec. 4, 1693. (*Vide infra.*)

16. Jerusha,[3] b. April 1, 1695; m. July 9, 1713, George Flint, son of George and Elizabeth (Putnam) Flint, b. April 1, 1686; she died June 29, 1781; had seven children, namely,

Susanna, Jerusha, Elizabeth, Abigail, George, Eliezer, Hannah. See "Flint Genealogy," p. 15.

17. Nathaniel,[3] b. Nov. 20, 1679. (*Vide infra.*)

(7)

BENJAMIN POPE,[2] bap. 1653, 17. 2, a farmer; m. Damaris, dau. of Samuel and Hannah Shattuck,* of Salem, b. Nov. 11, 1653; administration on estate granted to his son Benjamin April 13, 1702; children,—

18. Benjamin.[3] (*Vide infra.*)
19. Samuel,[3] husbandman, lived in "The Village." Inventory of estate returned Sept. 26, 1753, nephew John Pope, administrator. Probably no issue.

20. Ebenezer,[3] died without issue in 1717; administration on his estate to his brother, July 12, 1718.

21. Jerome,[3] mentioned in 1718, having been absent a long time at sea, and supposed to be lost.

(8)

SAMUEL POPE,[2] bap. 1656, 18. 3, a mariner; m. Jan. 28, 1685, Exercise Smith, dau. of John and Margaret Smith,† of Salem. Children,—

---

* Samuel Shattuck, son of widow Damaris, was born in England about 1620. He was a hatter in Salem, where he died June 6, 1689. He was one of those who suffered persecution for being called a Quaker. For an account of his connection with this persecution, see "Bessie's Collection of the Sufferings of the People called Quakers," "Bishop's New England Judged," "Fox's Journal," and elsewhere. Shattuck went to England and presented the subject of the suffering to the notice of Charles II., and by the assistance of Edward Burroughs obtained, Sept. 19, 1661, "a mandamus," commanding the magistrates and ministers in New England "to forbear to proceed any farther" against the people called Quakers,—and he was appointed agent to carry this mandamus to New England. The

General Court, Nov. 27, 1661, accordingly passed an order suspending the laws against the Quakers, and the jailers were directed to release those who were in custody. Thus, principally through his instrumentality, terminated one of the most extraordinary persecutions that this country ever witnessed. Afterwards he was permitted to live in Salem undisturbed. He seems to have been a man independent in his opinions, and unwilling to submit to oppression.— See "Shattuck Memorials," by L. Shattuck, p. 361.

† John and Margaret Smith were among those who were persecuted for their adherence to the opinions of the Quakers. Bishop's "New England Judged" contains an account of these persecutions, also letters addressed to Governor John Endecott, one signed by John

22. Damaris,⁴ b. Feb., 1686-7; d. 1½ years after.

23. Samuel,³ b. June 11, 1689.

24. Margaret,³ b. Oct. 21, 1691.

25. Enos,³ b. Feb. 1, 1694-5.

26. Hannah,³ b. Feb. 17, 1696-7; m. Nov. 25, 1714, Isaac Hacker, and had Hannah, b. Oct. 24, 1715; Sarah, b. Aug. 29, 1717; Eunice, b. Jan. 24, 1719; Isaac, b. July 2, 1722; Jeremiah, b. May 27, 1725;* Isaac, b. Nov. 28, 1727; Hannah, b. May 16, 1729; Isaac, b. March 4, 1730.

27. Elizabeth,⁸ b. May 23, 1698.

28. Eunice,⁸ b. Aug. 12, 1700; m. Nov. 14, 1728, Joseph Cook,—had Eunice, b. Sept. 6, 1729; Hannah, b. June 19, 1732; John, b. July 22, 1735.

29. Ruth,³ b. March 11, 1705; d. July 6, 1705.

This is without doubt the Samuel Pope who married, in 1709, Martha, the widow of William Beane, jr., and dau. of Samuel and Martha (Hawkins) Robinson, b. 1673, 11. 20. She m. Joseph Winslow, and by him had Joseph, b. Feb. 21, 1695-6; m. secondly, Oct. 29, 1702, William Beane, and had William, b. July 2, 1703, Caleb, b. Feb. 22, 1704-5; m. thirdly, Samuel Pope, and had the following, who were baptized at First Church, Salem.

30. Martha,⁸ bap. May 20, 1711.

31. Mary,³ bap. Aug. 30, 1713.

32. Susanna,⁸ bap. June 30, 1717.

33. Abigail,⁸ bap. Dec. 31, 1727, adult.

Samuel Pope died before 1735.

III. GENERATION.

(13)

JOSEPH POPE,⁸ b. June 16, 1687, a farmer, resided at "The Village"; m. Feb. 7, 1715-16, Mehitable Putnam, dau. of John and Hannah Putnam, b. July 20, 1695. Will signed March 25, 1755, mentions wife Mehitable, and appoints sons Ebenezer and Eleazer executors. In Court, Oct. 13, 1755. Children,—

34. ¹Joseph,⁴ bap. Sept. 1, 1717; m. Hannah Shaw, of Salem, Oct. 7, 1743; was living at Pomfret, Conn., in 1755.

---

* Smith and delivered to him shortly after the death of Mary Dyer in 1660; another signed by Mary Trask and Margaret Smith, dated, "From your House of Correction, where we have been unjustly restrained from our Children and Habitations; one of us above ten months, and the other about eight, and where we are yet continued by you. Oppressors that know no shame. *Boston*, the 21st of the 20th month, 1660." Margaret Smith died at Salem, 11. 11, 1677. Inventory of estate of John Smith, deceased, was appraised 16th April, 1680.

* Isaac Hacker, known as Master Hacker, was a son of this Jeremiah, and a native of Salem. He died very suddenly in September, 1818, aged sixty-eight. He was a much respected member of the Society of Friends and an instructor of youth for about forty years. He was the master of the "West School" in Salem, now known as "Hacker School," from its institution in 1785, till within two or three years of his decease. This long continuance in the situation is the strongest testimony of the public approbation and respect.

---

1 Joseph Pope,⁶ jr., b. in Pomfret, Conn., Sept. 28, 1746; grad. Harv. Univ. 1770, ord. Cong. minister 1773; preached long at Spencer, Mass.; d. March 8, 1826; m. Oct. 9, 1777, Anna, dau. of Col. Benj. and Sarah (Brown) Hammond, of Newton, who d. July 14, 1859, aet. 104 yrs., 7 mos. *Children:* Joseph,⁶ Charles,⁶ William,⁶ Anna⁶; Joseph⁶ lived in Portland, m. (3) Harriet, dau. of Roland and Mary (Godson) Jones, still living: dau., Caroline Eliza, m. Hon. Thomas Houghton Weston, of Portland. William⁶ has son, Joseph⁷, and dau., Mrs. Lucretia⁷ H. Upham, at Spencer. Rev. Charles W. Park, of New Haven, Conn., is a grandson of Rev. Joseph³ Pope.

35. Mehitable,[4] bap. May 3, 1719; m. April 18, 1741, Joseph Gardner, son of Abel and Sarah (Porter) Gardner, and had Joseph, Mehitable, Nathaniel, Eunice.

36. Hannah,[4] bap. Sept. 3, 1721; m. June 30, 1739, Israel Putnam, son of Joseph and Elizabeth (Porter) Putnam, b. Jan. 7, 1717-18; d. May 19, 1790. In 1739, removed from Salem to Pomfret, Conn.; having purchased a tract of land, he applied himself successfully to agriculture. He died May 19, 1790, widely known as a celebrated major-general in the Continental Army during the American Revolution. She died in 1764.

37. Nathaniel,[4] bap. May 17, 1724, (*Vide infra*.)

38. Eunice,[4] bap. April 30, 1727; m. October, 1745, Col. John Baker, of Ipswich. She died at Ipswich, January, 1821, aged ninety-four. A contemporary says, "She was a remarkable woman, and retained her faculties to the last. She was a connection of the late General Putnam, and was full of the same ardor that possessed him."

39. Mary,[4] bap. May 31, 1730; m. Nov. 28, 1748, Samuel Williams, of Pomfret, Conn.

40. Ebenezer,[4] bap. June 9, 1734. (*Vide infra*.)

41. Eleazer,[4] bap. Nov. 14, 1736. (*Vide infra*.)

42. Elizabeth,[4] bap. October 14, 1739.

## (14)

ENOS POPE,[3] b. June 6, 1690, a clothier; lived near the Fowler house on Boston Street. In 1718, he built the house now occupied by Mr. John C. Wilkins, 92 Boston Street, where he, his son Enos, and grandson Enos carried on the same business for up-

wards of a century; m. 1715, 1 mo. 17, Margaret Smith, b. March 18, 1691, a daughter of George and Hannah Smith, of Salem, who was the son of John and Margaret Smith. (See No. 8.) He died Feb. 24, 1765; administration granted to Enos Pope, his son, Oct. 25, 1766; had,—

43. Enos,[4] b. 9.mo. 18, 1721. (*Vide infra*.)

44. Margaret,[4] b. 6. 7, 1723; d. 25th of same month.

45. Joseph,[4] b. 5. 29, 1724; d. 23d of yᵉ 12mo. following.

46. Benjamin,[4] b. 10. 3, 1725; d. 2d of yᵉ 11 mo. following.

47. Joseph,[4] b. 4. 5, 1728; d. 14. 6 mo. following.

48. Seth,[4] b. 11. 23, 1730; d. 5 of 8 mo. following.

49. John,[4] b. 9. 17, 1732; d. 18 of yᵉ 5 mo. following.

50. Hannah,[4] b. 4. 19, 1734; d. 27 of yᵉ 5 mo. following.

## (15)

ELEAZER POPE,[3] b. Dec. 4, 1693, cordwainer, m. April 3, 1718, Hannah Buffington. He died 2. 5 mo. 1734. Inventory of his estate taken Oct. 15, 1734, including dwelling-house, land, and shop (near the Elm tree on Boston Street, Salem), Hannah Pope, his widow, administratrix.

51. Stephen.[4] (*Vide infra*.)

## (17)

NATHANIEL POPE,[3] b. Nov. 20, 1679, a blacksmith, of Salem; mar. Dec. 17, 1703, Prisca Chatwell, dau. of Nicholas and Sara Chatwell. b. 22. 2, 1679; died . The widow, April 14, 1711, m. John Meachum, of Enfield, Hampshire county, and removed to that place. Children,— ,

52. Mary,⁴ b. Feb. 27, 1704-5; m. Nathaniel Parsons, of Enfield, husbandman.

53. Sarah,⁴ b.        ; m. Nathaniel Meachum, of Enfield, husbandman.

(18)

BENJAMIN POPE,³ husbandman, m. June 24, 1710, Sarah Smith, of Cape Ann. Inventory of estate returned Nov. 29, 1769, son John Pope, administrator.

54. Mary,⁴ b. January, 1711-12; died Sept. 8, 1712.

55. John,⁴ b. March 16, 1713-14. (*Vide infra.*)

(23)

SAMUEL POPE,³ b. at Salem, 1689, 4. 11; d. 1769, 9. 21; m. Sarah Estes, of Lynn, November 20, 1714; born at Salem, 1693, 3. 5; d. 1773, 1. 10. Children,—

56. Elizabeth,⁴ b. 1716, 4. 16; d. 1716, 5. 5.

57. Robert,⁴ b. 1717, 6. 9. (*Vide infra.*)

58. Ebenezer,⁴ b. 1719-20. 1. 23. (*Vide infra.*)

59. Estes,⁴ b. 1721-2, 12. 18; d. 1725-6, 11. 16.

60. Philadelphia,⁴ b. 1723-4, 12. 26; d. 1750, 8. 3.

61. Sarah,⁴ b. 1726, 5. 2; d. 1768, 4 4.

62. Ruth,⁴ b. 1728-9, 1. 6; d. 1764, 1. 30.

63. Samuel,⁴ b. 1731, 7. 27.

64. Henry,⁴ b. 1733, 6. 14; died the same night.

65. Hannah,⁴ b. 1734, 7. 20.

IV. GENERATION.

(37)

NATHANIEL POPE,⁴ farmer, resided at "The Village." Baptized May 17, 1724; m. Mary, dau. of Jasper Swin-

nerton, b. 1728; d. Dec. 20, 1773. He m., secondly, Dec. 23, 1784, Sarah, dau. of Rev. Peter and Deborah (Hobart) Clark, of Danvers. She was born Dec. 18, 1738; d. Feb. 12, 1802. He died in Nov., 1800, and administration on estate granted to Amos and Elijah Pope, March 2, 1801. Children,—

66. Mary,⁵ b. Dec. 12, 1748; m. June 4, 1777, Aaron Gilbert.

67. Eunice,⁵ b. Feb. 19, 1751; m. Sept. 16, 1773, James Putnam.

68. Nathaniel,⁵ b. March 22, 1753; d. unmarried, Feb. 10, 1778.

69. Rebecca,⁵ b. April 16, 1755; m. Jan. 27, 1784, Jonathan Proctor, of Dunstable.

70. Hannah,⁵ b. Aug. 21, 1757; d. at the age of twenty-one years.

71. Jasper,⁵ b. Oct. 10, 1759; d. at the age of nineteen years and two months.

72. Ruth,⁵ born Nov. 7, 1761; d. at the age of two years.

73. Zephaniah,⁵ b. May 6, 1764; d. unmarried, aged thirty-two.

74. Elijah,⁵ born Jan. 28, 1766. (*Vide infra.*)

75. Mehitable,⁵ b. April 3, 1768; d. June 2, 1837; m. Caleb Oakes, of Danvers. Was the mother of William Oakes, of Ipswich, a very distinguished botanist, who was born in Danvers July 1, 1799; graduated at Harvard College in 1820; died July 31, 1848. See an obituary notice in American Journal of Science and Arts, vol. 7 (Second Series), p. 138.

76. Amos,⁵ b. Feb. 20, 1772. (*Vide infra.*)

(40)

EBENEZER POPE,⁴ bap. June 9, 1734; d. Nov. 4, 1802; m. October, 1754, Sarah, dau. of John and Mary (Eaton) Pope. See No. 113. She died in

South Reading October 12, 1832, aged 94 years. Children, —

77. Lucretia,[5] m.      Poole, of South Reading.

78. John[5]. (*Vide infra.*)

79. Eben[5]. (*Vide infra.*)

80. Lucy[5].

81. Oliver[5]. (*Vide infra.*)

82. Mary,[5] m. Ananiah Parker, of South Reading.

83. Elizabeth,[5] m. Thomas Swan, of South Reading.

84. Jane[5].

85. Abraham Gould[5]. Removed to Maine, married and died there.

### (41)

ELEAZER POPE,[4] bap. Nov. 14, 1736; m. Nanny Putnam, July 7, 1757.

86. Eleazer,[5] b. Feb. 4, 1758; m. April, 1780, Mary Gardner.

87. Rebecca,[5] b. Dec. 31, 1759; m. Nov. 28, 1781, Thomas Gardner.

88. Molly,[5] bap. April 16, 1762.

89. Joseph,[5] b. June 28, 1764; m. Susanna Marsh, March 20, 1789.

90. Mehitable,[5] bap. Nov. 8, 1767.

91. Nanna,[5] bap. July 24, 1769; m. Jesse Leavenworth, of Danville, Feb. 20, 1791.

92. Allen,[5] bap. July 12, 1772.

93. Huldah,[5] bap. Dec. 5, 1773.

94. Perley Putnam,[5] bap. July 9, 1775; m. Jan. 13, 1799, Rebecca, dau. of Hezekiah and Esther (Coose) Flint, of North Reading; removed to Danville, Vermont.

95. Betsey,[5] b. Aug. 13, 1777; m. Sept. 25, 1795, Deacon Simeon Flint, who was born in North Reading June 24, 1775; removed to Danville, Vt., 1797, and thence in 1810 to Shipton, Canada East, where he died July 3, 1877, having had nine children. (See "Flint Genealogy," p. 161)

96. Jasper,[5] b. Jan. 1, 1780. (*Vide infra.*)

97. William Walton,[5] bap. Oct. 31, 1784; d. unm., at Salem, aged twenty-one.

The members of this family removed principally to Vermont.

### (43)

ENOS POPE,[4] b. at Salem, 1721, 9. 18; d. March 12, 1813, — the oldest man in the town of Salem, a clothier by occupation, and lived in the same house which his father built. He married Lydia, dau. of Joshua and      Buffum, of Salem; b. Oct. 10, 1726; d. Oct. 15, 1781. Children,—

98. Lydia,[5] b. 1750, 1. 28.

99. Margaret,[5] b. 1752, 6. 5.

100. Eunice,[5] b. 1755, 5. 2; d. Sept., 1819, unmarried.

101. Hannah,[5] b. 1757, 4. 2; d. at Salem, 1836, 9. 16.

102. Enos,[5] b. 1759, 4. 27, a clothier; lived in the house built and occupied by his grandfather Enos, also by his father Enos; died unmarried Nov. 24, 1838.

103. Damaris,[5] b. 1761, 8. 11.

### (51)

STEPHEN POPE,[4] b.      ; d. Oct. 9, 1765, cordwainer; resided in Salem, near the Elm Tree on Boston Street; m. Mary, dau. of Joshua and      Buffum, b. July 8, 1723; d. July, 1788. Children, —

104. Hannah,[5] b. May 31, 1746; d. May 20, 1840, æt. ninety-three; m. Thomas Nichols, of Somersworth, N. H., and Salem, son of David and Hannah (Gaskell) Nichols; died at Salem December, 1805, aged sixty years.

105. Mary,[5] b. March 24, 1748; d. young.

106. Eleazer,⁶ b. March 21, 1751.
(*Vide infra.*)

107. Gertrude,⁵ b. Oct. 19, 1753;
d. 1833, 9. 24.

108. Folger,⁵ b. Feb. 14, 1756.
(*Vide infra.*)

109. Stephen,⁶ b. June 6, 1759; d.
young.

110. Sarah,⁵ b. Aug. 20, 1761; d.
1841, 10. 18; m. David Nichols,
brother of Thomas, and lived at Ber-
wick, Me.

111. Joshua,⁵ b. Nov. 24, 1763.
(*Vide infra.*)

112. James,⁵ b. Dec. 16, 1765.
(*Vide infra.*)

(55)

JOHN POPE,⁴ b. March 16, 1713–14;
m. April 22, 1736, Mary Eaton, of
Lynn; a yeoman; lived in Danvers.¹
His will was dated March 20, 1756.
In court, June 5, 1756, Mary Pope,
the widow, was appointed executrix.
This is probably the widow Mary
Pope, who m. Jacob Sawyer, of Read-
ing, April, 1758. Children, —

113. Eben,⁵ probably died young.

114. Sarah,⁵ d. 1832; m. Eben
Pope. (See No. 40.)

115. Mary,⁵ m. William Deadman,
jr., of Salem, in 1758.

116. Elizabeth,⁵ m. Isaac Needham,
of Salem, Jan. 9, 1769.

117. Lydia,⁵ m. Sept. 16, 1762,
Thomas Flint, who was born in North
Reading Oct. 8, 1733, and died about
1800; a physician; removed to Maine
in 1770, and settled in Nobleborough,
on the Damariscotta River; she died
in 1784, having had ten children. (See
" Flint Genealogy," p. 32.)

(57)

²ROBERT POPE,⁴ b. 1717, 6. 9; d. at
Falmouth, Casco Bay, 1776, 2. 22; m.
Phebe. She was b. 1716, 11. 8.

118. John,⁶ b. at Boston, 1740, 10.
19. (*Vide infra.*)

119. Robert,⁵ b. at Boston, 1741,
10. 14; d. 1742, 6. 9.

120. ³*Elijah*,⁶ *b. at Boston*, 1742,
12. 23.

121. Abigail,⁶ b. at Boston, 1743,
12. 9.

122. Phebe,⁵ b. at Boston, 1745, 8.
7; d. 1745, 8. 20.

123. Phebe,⁶ b. at Boston, 1746, 8.
5; d. 1747, 11. 9.

124. Robert Brown,⁶ b. 1748, 2. 5;
d. 1748, 6. 4.

125. Joseph,⁶ b. 1748, 11. 19.

126. Elizabeth,⁵ b. 1750, 2. 20.

---

¹ Baptized at the Episcopal Church, Salem, " 21 Sept., 1746, John Pope, 30, from Lynn End."

² Called in deeds, " Robert Pope of Boston, blacksmith " and " scythemaker."

³ M., at Falmouth, Me., 5. 19, 1768, Phœbe Winslow (b. 2. — 1753). Had twelve children, of whom *Samuel*,⁵ b. 12. 30, 1773, m., 10. 28, 1802, Mary Wing. b. 6. 1, 1783; had twelve children. One of these, *John*,⁷ b. ———, m., ———, Lydia Taber, b. ———. They had two children, Alton⁹ and Jacob⁸. *Jacob*,⁶ b. Dec. 23, 1811, m., May 25, 1836, Lavina Morrill Stackpole, b. Jan. 3, 1812. Resides at Manchester, Me. Children: L. Maria,⁹ Irana Lang,⁹ Elmira Lang,⁹ *Charles Stackpole*,⁹ b. Sept. 13, 1842, m. Elizabeth Carpenter. Has *Edward Carpenter*,¹⁰ b. Oct. 23, '80, and Edith Flagler,¹⁰ b. Aug. 17, '82. Another descendant of (120) is *Charles Henry* Pope, of St. Louis, son of *Samuel*,⁷ son of *Samuel*,⁶ son of *Elijah*⁵ (120). *Alton*⁶ has sons, *Edward Cobb*,⁹ *John Lang*,⁹ and Alfred A⁹. Live at Cleveland, O. Irana Lang⁹ and Elmira Lang⁹ are teachers in Oakwood Seminary, at Union Springs, N. Y. Other children of Elijah⁶ are: Robert,⁶ descendants in Pownal; Samuel,⁶ descendants in Wheatland, N. Y., and Rochester (*Elmer*⁷); Nathan,⁶ Windham, lived on his father Elijah⁶'s old place progeny numerous in vicinity; Ebenezer⁶ has descendants in Vassalboro, and Elijah⁶ in Vassalboro and Hallowell.

127.  Phebe,[5] b. 1751, 7.
128.  Robert,[5] b. 1754, 9. 3.

(58)

EBENEZER POPE,[4] b. 1719-20, 1. 23;
m. Elizabeth, b. 1717-18, 12. 5.

129.  Elizabeth,[5] b. 1745, 7. 6; d.
1745, 7. 22.
130.  Robert,[5] b. 1746, 7. 1; d. 1767,
8. 11.
131.  Ebenezer,[5] b. 1748-9, 11. 4;
d. 1749, 2. 16.
132.  Fourth child born dead, 1750,
4. 4.
133.  Estes,[5] b. 1757, 10. 2.

### V. GENERATION.

(74)

ELIJAH POPE,[5] b. Jan. 28, 1766;
d. Feb. 16, 1846; m. June 20, 1791,
Hannah Putnam.  She died Sept. 10,
1844; lived in Danvers.  Children, —
134.  Nathaniel,[6] b. Aug. 2, 1792.
(*Vide infra.*)
135.  Hannah,[6] b. Sept. 29, 1794;
m. Francis Fletcher, of Dunstable,
and had three daughters, — Rachel,
Hannah, and Mary.
136.  Betsey,[6] b. Feb. 18, 1797; m.
Samuel Putnam, son of Eleazer Putnam, and removed to Brooklyn, N. Y.
137.  Mary,[6] b. April 19, 1799; d.
June 25, 1823, unmarried.
138.  Jasper,[6] b. July 14, 1802. (*Vide
infra.*)
139.  Phebe,[6] b. Nov. 8, 1807; d.
Aug. 25, 1830.
140.  Elijah,[6] b. July 13, 1809. (*Vide
infra.*)

(76)

[1]AMOS POPE,[5] born at Danvers, Feb.
20, 1772; d. at Danvers, Jan. 26,
1837; m. at Danvers, Jan. 16, 1806,
Sarah Goodale, b. April 19, 1773; d.
Sept. 7, 1832.  Children, —
141.  Zephaniah,[6] b. Dec. 15, 1807.
142.  Eunice,[6] b. May 30, 1810; d.
Oct. 20, 1834.

(78)

JOHN POPE,[5] d. at Salem, December, 1820, æt. sixty-three, a baker by
trade, also a soldier of the Revolution.  His wife, Ruth Newhall, born
at Lynnfield, died at Salem, December, 1810, æt. forty-nine.  He married, secondly, Lydia M. Tunnison.
Children, —
143.  Sally,[6] d. March, 1808, æt.
twenty-seven.
144.  Ruth,[6] m. Archelaus Fuller,
May 30, 1802.
145.  John,[6] d. abroad.
146.  George,[6] d. at Salem, Aug.
31, 1832.
147.  Sophia,[6] m. Oliver Parker.
148.  Thomas S.,[6] d. Nov. 29, 1844,
aged forty, at Salem; m. Rebecca
Spencer of Beverly.  Children living in Salem.
149.  Eben,[6] d. Sept., 1811, æt.
eighteen.
150.  Sarah,[6] m.            Deland.

(79)

EBEN POPE,[5] of Salem, baker, b.
in Danvers, July 7, 1759; d. in Salem, Feb. 14, 1821, æt. sixty-two.
He married August, 1779, Mehitable
Carroll, dau. of Capt. Samuel and

---

[1] Amos[6] studied hard, though furnished with few books and indifferent instruction.  Became
a very accurate scholar.  Prepared an almanac amid great difficulties, and published it in 1791 for
the coming year, 1792.  He also issued almanacs for three years following, and prepared one
for 1796, but did not publish it.  These were replete with choice literary selections and notes
on current events, as well as calendar matter.  Quite an extended notice of the man and his
works is given by Mr. Stickney, of Salem, in the Essex Institute Collections, June, 1866.

Mehitable (Williams) Carroll. She died in 1784. He m. secondly, January 31, 1790, Lydia, widow of James Hayes, of Salem, and dau. of William Darling, of Cambridge. She died Feb. 16, 1816, aged sixty-two.

151. ¹Samuel C.⁶ (*Vide infra.*)

(81)

OLIVER POPE,⁵ resided some time in South Reading, afterwards moved to Salem, and resided on Dean Street; d. Oct. 23, 1825, æt. sixty; m. 1st : secondly, Jan. 26, 1819, widow Mary Holman, dau. of James and Sarah Fabens. She died at Salem, Jan. 26, 1854, æt. 73½ years. Children,—

152. Oliver,⁶ resides in one of the Western States.ᵈ

153. Lois.⁶

154. Lucretia.⁶

155. Samuel,⁶ m. Nov. 2, 1823, Betsey Newhall.

156. John,⁶ resides in South Reading; m. Sept. 11, 1820, Harriet Holman.

(96)

JASPER POPE,⁵ a tailor, resided in Salem and sometimes in Danvers; born in Danvers, Jan. 1, 1780; died March 2, 1850; m. Dec. 14, 1804, at Salem, Abigail Lander (b. June 11, 1782, in Salem; d. Jan. 12, 1837). Children,—

157. Abigail Lander, b. at Salem, June 14, 1805; d. at Worcester, July 10, 1861.

158. William Allen, b. April 30, 1808, at Salem; d. 1817.

159. Ann Putnam, b. March 29, 1810, at Salem; d. at Danvers, April 12, 1837.

160. Caroline, b. Nov. 3, 1811, at Salem; d. July 22, 1845, at Danvers.

161. Matilda, b. July 18, 1814, at Salem.

162. Horatio Gates, b. at Salem, Dec. 7, 1815; engaged in business in Boston, resides in Malden.

(106)

' ELEAZER POPE,⁵ resided in Salem, yeoman, b. March 21, 1751; d. 1818, 2. 5; m. Esther, dau. of Jonathan Buxton, b. 1760, 12.9; d. 1818, 10. 17.

163. Mary,⁶ b. 1788, 7. 16; m. Joshua Buxton, of Danvers, who was born July 17, 1785, and had Joshua, b. Oct. 14, 1817; Mary Jane, b. Oct. 20, 1821, and Henry Varney, b. July 23, 1824.

164. Esther,⁶ b. 1790, 10. 27; m. Henry Grant, of Salem.

165. Eleazer,⁶ b. 1793, 3. 14. (*Vide infra.*)

166. Stephen,⁶ b. 1796, 3. 11: m. March 13, 1821, Abigail, dau. of Daniel Shehane, of Salem. She d. Aug. 6, 1844, æt. forty-one. He d. at Liverpool, Eng., Jan. 25, 1837.

167. Gertrude,⁶ b. 1799, 8. 14; m. Dec. 26, 1822, Jona. Barrett, b. at Salem, Dec. 11, 1790, and d. April 18, 1829; had Eleazer Pope, b. Sept. 29, 1824; Martha Osborn, b. July 9, 1827.

(108)

FOLGER POPE,⁵ b. at Salem, 1756, 2. 14, a saddler, shop on Washington Street, opposite City Hall; m. Theodate, who was born at Salem, 1759, 1. 1. Children, —

168. Folger,⁶ b. 1782, 9. 18, at Salem.

---

¹ " Bap. at Tabernacle Church, Salem, April 30, 1780, Samuel, son of Ebenezer and Mehitable Pope."

² Son Alexander at Jonesville, Mich.

169.  Stephen,[6] b. 1784, 1. 11, at Salem.  (*Vide infra*.)

170.  Lydia,[6] b. 1785, 10. 31, at Salem.

171.  Daniel,[6] b. 1787, 11. 11, at Salem.

172.  Hannah,[6] b. 1789, 12. 28.

(111)

JOSHUA POPE,[5] b. 1763, 11. 24; d. 1842, 2. 25; a tanner in Salem; first, m. Bethiah, dau. of          Dean. She was born 1764, d. 1817, 2. 14; m. secondly, Lucretia, the widow of I. Johnson, and dau. of Zach. and Lucretia Collins, of Lynn. She was born at Lynn, and died at Salem, July 21, 1856, aged eighty-one.

173.  Jonathan Dean,[6] b. 1792, 8. 8.; d. 1846.

174.  Gertrude,[6] b. 1794, 9. 6; d. 1796, 10.

175.  James,[6] b. 1797, 3. 12; d. June 6, 1852; a tanner, lived in Salem, m. Lucy M., dau. of Capt. Daniel Lord, of Ipswich. She died Nov. 29, 1823, æt. twenty-one.

176.  Peter,[6] b. 1799, 6. 25; d. 1803, 7. 5.

177.  Lot,[6] b. 1803, 4. 27; d. at Salem, April 8, 1859, tanner. His wife, Maria, d. at Salem, June 9, 1842, aged twenty-nine.

(112)

JAMES POPE,[5] b. Dec. 16, 1765; d. 1830, 8. 7; saddler, place of business on Federal street, near Baptist Meeting-House; m.          Lydia, dau. of Daniel and Hannah Newhall. She was b. at Lynn, 1775, 3. 16; d. at Salem, 1830, 12. 8.

178.  James,[6] b. 1795, 3. 6; d. 1796, 3. 11.

179.  Hannah,[6] b. 1797, 2. 15; d. 1843, 1. 18.

180.  James,[6] b. 1799, 7. 21; d. 1800, 12. 24.

181.  [1]Daniel,[6] b. 1801, 11. 30; d. at Milwaukee, Aug. 10, 1852.

182.  Mary Ann,[6] d. May 13, 1852, aged forty-four.

183.  Lydia,[6] b. 1808, 2. 27.

184.  James,[6] b. 1810, 7. 25; d. 1834, 7. 9, at Tobasco, Mexico.

185.  Elizabeth Hacker,[6] b. 1813, 3. 17.

186.  Joseph,[5] b. 1816, 8. 22; d. 1820, 9. 22.

187.  Sarah Nichols,[6] b. 1821, 6. 2.

(118)

[2]JOHN POPE,[5] of Boston, b. 1740, 10. 29; m. Hannah, dau. of James and Sarah Raymar, of Boston; b. 1743 – 4, 12. 16.

188.  John,[6] b. at Boston, 1769, 4. 8.

189.  James,[6] b. at Boston, 1770, 12. 25.

190.  Hannah,[6] b. at Boston, 1772, 8. 13.

191.  Benjamin,[6] b. at Boston, 1774, 6. 11; d. 1774, 8. 24.

192.  Sarah,[6] b. at Boston, 1775, 8. 25.

193.  Ruth,[6] b. at Boston, 1777, 9. 30.

194.  Susanna,[6] b. at Boston, 1779, 10. 13.

195.  Samuel,[6] b. at Boston, 1781, 9. 15.

196.  Benjamin,[6] b. at Boston, 1783, 3. 3.

197.  Betsey,[6] b. at Boston, 1786, 2. 7.

---

[1] *Daniel Newhall Pope;* dau. m. Dr. M. D. Mann, now of Buffalo, N. Y.

[2] Was a physician; d. 1796.

VI. GENERATION.

(134)

NATHANIEL POPE,[6] yeoman, of Danvers, b. Aug. 2, 1792; m. Aug. 8, 1815, Abi Preston, b. Feb. 13, 1791; d. March 1, 1841; m. secondly, March 9, 1848, Charlotte, dau. of Elijah and Elizabeth (Putnam) Flint, of South Danvers. She was born May 12, 1801. Children, —

198. Elizabeth Putnam,[7] b. Feb. 12, 1816; m. Andrew M. Putnam, of Danvers.

199. Harriet Adeline,[7] b. Sept. 8, 1817; m. Henry F. Putnam, of Danvers.

200. Mary Putnam,[7] b. July 26, 1819; m. Calvin Putnam, of Danvers.

201. Aseneth Preston,[7] b. Sept. 19, 1821; m. Nathan Tapley, of Danvers.

202. Ira Preston,[7] b. Sept. 11, 1823; m. Eliza C. Batchelder.

203. Daniel Putnam,[7] b. March 8, 1826; m. Lydia N. Dempsey.

204. Hannah Putnam,[7] b. June 2, 1828; m. Dr. B. Breed, of Lynn.

205. Phebe Mansfield,[7] b. May 12, 1830; d. Aug. 29, 1830.

206. Jasper Felton,[7] b. April 4, 1832; m. Sophia J. Richards, of Townsend.

(138)

JASPER POPE,[6] b. July 14, 1802; m. Dec. 13, 1830, Harriet Felton. She was born Sept. 19, 1803; d. Nov. 24, 1843. He m. secondly, Feb. 9, 1846, Sarah Felton. She was born Jan. 4, 1807, had —

207. Jasper Elijah,[7] b. Feb. 12, 1847.

(140)

ELIJAH POPE,[6] b. July 13, 1809; m. December, 1831, Eunice Prince. She was born May 19, 1811.

208. Francis Elijah,[7] b. May 29, 1832.

209. Nathaniel A.,[7] b. Dec. 24, 1837.

210. Samuel Putnam,[7] b. Dec. 16, 1844.

211. Mary Elizabeth,[7] b. June 14, 1847.

212. James Arthur,[7] b. July 29, 1817; d. Jan. 9, 1852.

(141)

ZEPHANIAH POPE,[6] yeoman, of Danvers, b. Dec. 15, 1807; m. April 9, 1835, Nancy Mudge; b. at Danvers, June 9, 1816. Children, —

213. Amos Alden,[7] b. at Danvers, Feb. 16, 1838; d. at Danvers, Sept. 15, 1864.

214. Sarah Ann,[7] b. at Danvers, May 5, 1842.

215. Caroline Eunice,[7] b. at Danvers, Feb. 2, 1847. ~~ Frank Marsh

151
(161)

SAMUEL CARROLL POPE,[6] b. at Salem, Nov. 25, 1783; d. at Salem, Jan 2, 1821; m. at Londonderry, Dec. 23, 1806, Frances Dinsmore, of Londonderry, dau. of Capt. Thomas Dinsmore. She was born in Boston, Sept. 28, 1785; d. in South Danvers, March 25, 1858.

He was a baker by trade. In 1807 was elected the first commander of the Salem Mechanic Light Infantry, but declined the position. In 1808, he was a Lieutenant in the Salem Artillery Company. Soon after the commencement of the war of 1812, he entered the U. S. service, and was 1st Lieutenant in the 40th Regiment of Infantry, and was stationed at Fort Gurnet, Plymouth. (See Vol. III. of these Collections, p. 181.) Children, —

216. Ann Hall,[7] b. Nov. 13, 1807 at Salem; d. Nov. 3, 1831, at Salem, unm.

217. Samuel Lysander," b. Jan. 20, 1809; d. July 29, 1829, at sea, off the coast of Timor, on board of ship Zephyr.

218. Orlando Ebenezer,[7] b. March 17, 1810, at Salem, now resident of South Danvers; m. June, 1832, Rebecca S. Fairfield, dau. of Moses and Elizabeth Fairfield, of Salem. She was born April 10, 1810. Children born at Danvers,—Francis P., b. Dec. 19, 1832; Orlando Lysander, b. Dec. 10, 1834; d. Oct. 11, 1839; George Stephen, b. July 29, 1836; d. Sept. 6, 1839; Elizabeth Mehitable, b. Sept. 11, 1838; Orlando George, b. July 29, 1840; d. Dec. 6, 1840; George O. H., b. Oct. 5, 1844; Ellen M., b. Sept. 4, 1848.

219. Frances Dinsmore,[7] b. Dec. 25, 1811; m. Stephen Palmer, of Lynn, Aug. 25, 1833. He died.

She and her son, William L. Palmer, reside now in Salem. He served the country with honor during the recent rebellion. At the first call for troops, he went as a private in the Salem Light Infantry, April 18, 1861, and served three months in that capacity. At the organization of the 19th Reg. Mass. Vol. in August, 1861, he received the appointment of 2d Lieut.; 1st Lieut., June 18, 1862; April 16, 1863, Capt.; April 8, 1865, Major; March 13, 1865, Brevet Lieut. Colonel.

220. Mehitable Carroll,[7] b. Dec. 2, 1815.

(165)

ELEAZER POPE,[6] b. at Salem, 1793, 3. 14. Tanner, m., May 24, 1818, Mary Nimblet, dau. of Robert Nim-

blet, of Salem. She died May, 1822; he m. secondly, April 27, 1823, Esther Reith, dau. of Capt. John Reith, of Salem. Children,—

221. Henry E.,[7] b. Feb. 16, 1819; during the recent war was an assistant surgeon in the 6th Reg. Indiana Vols.; now resides in Salem; m. May 18, 1856, Catherine M., dau. of Munroe W. and Mary (Dole) Lee. She was b. at Madison, Ind., and d. at Salem, April 24, 1866, æt. thirty, having had William H., b. Feb. 22, 1857, and Charles S., b. Sept. 1, 1858.

222. William A.,[7] a tanner of Salem, b. April 18, 1820; m. Elizabeth, dau. of Alexander and Jane McCloy, Oct. 31, 1844; she d. June 6, 1847, aged twenty-three; he m. secondly, Mary D. Symonds, Sept. 25, 1852. Children,—William H., b. May 26, 1845, d. Aug. 8, 1845; William H., b. April 14, 1847; Mary E., b. March 7, 1853; George, b. Jan. 7, 1855; Frank A., b. March 27, 1857, d. Jan. 2, 1861.

223. Mary,[7] b. April, 1822; m. Lorenus Warner, of South Danvers; she died October, 1852, having had Mary E., b. April 8, 1852.

224. John R.,[7] a tanner, of Salem, b. Sept. 4, 1825; m. Mary J. Brown. Children, — Esther, b. Sept. 11, 1849; John H., b. Jan. 30, 1852; Mary Jane, b. July 21, 1854; Stephen F., b. Feb. 14, 1858. He died Nov 22, 1861.

225. Esther,[7] b. Nov. 28, 1826; m. Jan. 1, 1854, Andrew Mace; she died June, 1855.

226. Stephen,[7] b. Nov. 28, 1828.

227. James,[7] b. 1830; d. 1831.

228. James,[7] b. March 29, 1839. July 6, 1861, he was commissioned 1st Lieut. 1st Reg. Heavy Artillery,

Mass. Vols.; Capt., June 10, 1862, discharged Oct. 18, 1864; resides in Salem.

229. Frank,[7] b. Jan. 18, 1841; m. Sarah Morison, Nov. 30, 1865; he was commissioned 2d Lieut., 1st Reg. Heavy Artillery, Mass. Vols., Feb. 15, 1862; 1st Lieut., March 19, 1863, discharged on expiration of service, Oct. 7, 1864; Capt., March 17, 1865. He died Dec. 28, 1866.

( 169 )

STEPHEN POPE,[6] b. 1784, 1. 11; m. Sally ____ ; b. 1788, 8. 7. Children,—

230. Daniel,[7] b. 1808, 11. 4.
231. Sarah,[7] b. 1811, 1. 11.
232. Mary,[7] b. 1813, 7. 21.
233. Seba,[7] b. 1816, 3. 9.
234. Abel H.,[7] b. 1825, 4. 13.
235. George F.,[7] b. 1827, 3. 23; d. 1828, 2. 8.

---

Married in Boston, "Feb. 21, 1736, Stephen Driver and Susanna Pope"; and "July 2, 1743, John Swinnerton and Elizabeth Pope." These seem to be (32) and (27), daughters of (8).

( 118 )

Mr. Joseph[5] Pope, son of Robert[4] (57), became a clock and watch maker and repairer in Boston. He constructed the first Planetarium or Orrery ever made in America, in the period from 1776 to 1786. In the great fire of 1787 it was saved by Dr. Waterhouse and others, at the instance of Gov. Bowdoin, and taken to the governor's house. It was afterwards bought by Harvard College, with the proceeds of a lottery, and is still in its possession. He went to England in 1788, and was highly honored by Sir Joseph Banks and others; made many studies and inventions in mechanics, though he received little pecuniary profit from them. A clock of his manufacture, with compound metallic pendulum and calendar attachments, was for a long time the standard time-piece for the whole city of Boston. He died at Hallowell, Me., at the residence of his son, and was buried there.

These facts are taken from a letter of his daughter, Mrs. Elizabeth (Pope) Ware, of Medfield, read (with additional particulars) by Mr. Ephraim G. Ware, before the New England Hist.-Gen. Society, Boston, Dec. 2, 1857, from which we are kindly allowed to draw.

One suggestive saying of Mr. Joseph Pope was quoted by Mr. Ware. On one occasion, speaking of his labors on the orrery, he stopped, and, after a moment's pause, said, "Mr. Ware, *God* is a great Mechanic."

In the administration of the estate of "John Pope, of Boston, physician," June 14, 1796, "Joseph Pope," the maker of the orrery, and "Joseph Balch," a son-in-law, were bondsmen of the widow "Hannah." Married in Boston, "Oct". 5, 1794, Joseph Balch, Jr., and Hannah Pope" (190).

Among the "marriage intentions" filed in Boston are those of "Joseph Pope and Ruthy Thayer, Feb. 4, 1773"; "Robert Pope and Susannah Holland, Aug. 15, 1775"; and "Robert Pope and Polly Stoneman, Jan. 15, 1778." Braintree records note that "Mrs. Ruth Pope, wife of Mr. Joseph Pope, of Boston, died at Ebenezer Thayer's, jun., in Braintree, Aug. 22, 1775, aged 20 years & 6 months."

## FURTHER REVOLUTIONARY NOTES.

"*Samuel Pope*" was in Capt. Joseph Richards' company, in Col. Gill's regiment, "in the detachment of four hundred men that went from the State of Massachusetts Bay to do duty in the State of Rhode Island, agreable to an order of Council of Aug. 10, 1779." The same name enrolled in Capt. Samuel Holden's company, Col. Eben Thayer's regiment, three months' troops, discharged Oct. 30, 1780 ; also, in "Capt. Ralph Thompson's co. Lt. Col. Commandant Webbs Reg$^{nt}$, fr. Aug. 26, 1781." These latter records undoubtedly refer to Captain Samuel Pope of Dartmouth. [See Plymouth Pope Family, No. 7, viii.]

"*John Pope*, 18 yrs. old, 5 ft. 6 inches high, light complexion, from Watertown, Middlesex," was one of the " Fourth Division of six months' men raised to reinforce the Continental Army, who marched from Springfield under the command of Capt. Frothingham of the Artillery, July 5, 1780."

*William Pope*, in Capt. Henry James' company, "for service done in Marching to Rhodisland agreable to a Resolve of the General Court passed the 28th of February, 1781." " A Pay Roll of Lieut. *Nathaniel Pope's* company (when on the Late Alarm at Rhode Island : but now under the Command of Lieut. Joseph Damon) in the second Regment in County Bristol : commanded by Col. John Hathaway Esq. in Pay of the State of Massachusetts Bay New England, in Service : by order of Council ; in ye State of Rhode Island." *Will$^m$ Pope, Edmund Pope, Jona$^n$ Pope* are among the soldiers. The pay-roll bears this memorandum : " N. B. The Original sworn to before *M$^r$. Justice Pope*. [See Ply. P., 8, VII, 12, IX, and 14, III.]

" *Ansel Pope, corporal*," and " *Elnathan Pope, private*," in " Capt. Mighill's co. in Col. Baldwin's Regt for the year 1776. Ansel engaged again." [See 15, I, 9, VIII, 8, II.]

*Elnathan Pope*, of Rochester, was a member of Capt. Isaac Wood's company, in Col. Thomas Carpenter's regiment of militia, in service in Rhode Island, from July 20, to Aug. 27, 1777.

" *Gideon Pope, piper*," is entered on " A pay Roll of Capt. Samuel Warner's co, in Col. John Brown's regt. of Militia from the co. of Berkshire " ; he was discharged Oct. 23, 1780, after 3 months and 13 days' service.

" *Edward Pope, Esq.*, of Bristol co., Col$^o$. 2d Regt., Feb. 8, 1776." Was elected by the legislature naval officer of the port of Dartmouth in 1781. [See 10, II.]

"*Thomas Pope, of Bridgewater,*" was in Capt. Calvin Curtis' company, of Col. Jacob's regiment, "6 m. 15 d." from Jan. 1, 1778.

*Seth Pope* was in Capt. Barnabas Doty's company, of the 4th Regiment, in the county of Plymouth, Col. White, in service by order of the Council in the State of Rhode Island in pay of the United States. *Ephm. Pope* and *Seth Pope* were in the company of Capt. Henry Jenne, in the 2d Regiment Bristol county, Col. John Hathaway, "in pay of the State of Massachusetts Bay in service by order of Council in the State of Rhodisland," Dartmouth, Jan. 5, 1781.

*Seth Pope* enlisted from Rochester, in the company of Capt. Abial Pierce, in Col. Nicholas Dyke's regiment. [See 13, and 284, 14, VI.]

*Asa Pope's* name is on the roll of Capt. Joseph Elliot's company, in Col. William Turner's regiment, on Rhode Island, Camp Batte's Hill, Dec. 1, 1781.—9 days. [See 7. IX.]

*Ichabod Pope* was in Capt. Abram Washburn's company, Col. John Cushing's regiment at Newport, Nov. 28, 1776. Also a corporal in Joseph Keith's company, in Col. Cotton's regiment, "in the secret expedition to Tivertown, from the 25th Sept. to the 30th October, 1777." [See 8, V.]

*Jacob Pope,* in Capt. John King's company, Col. John Brown's regiment of militia, from the county of Berkshire, State of Massachusetts Bay, "for services Don under Leonard Skyler, from the 29 day of June, 1777, untill the 21 day of July next following." [See 8, IV, 3.]

*Ebenezer Pope* served 2 months, 1 day in Miles Greenwood's company, Col. Jacob Gerrish's regiment.

"*Henry Pope,* Marblehead, 30 years old, 5 feet 6 inches high, light complexion," was one of the men of the ship "Junius Brutus," Capt. John Leach, at Salem, June 15, 1780.

"*Jno. Pope,* Salem, 23 years, 5½ feet high, light complexion," was a seaman on the brig "Addition," June 17, 1780.

"*Ebenezer Pope,* light complexion, 22 years old, 4 feet 2 inches high" [must be an error for 5 ft. 2, I think], was a mariner on the brig "Lexington," Oct. 2, 1780.

*Robert Pope,* commissary for government troops at Springfield, 1787, during "Shay's Rebellion." See his reports, Mass. Arch., vol. 189, pp. 85, 89, 168.

*William Pope,* "of Sheffield," private in Lieut. David Barton's Co., Col. John Ashley's regiment, enlisted Feb. 27, 1787, among the forces that suppressed the rebellion just mentioned.

POPES IN MASSACHUSETTS LEGISLATURE.

*Col. Edward*, Dartmouth, House, 1780-3, Senate, 1809-10.   See pp. 291, 312, of this book.

*Col. Frederick*, Stoughton, House, 1787-1796 ; p. 131.

*Col. Seth*, New Bedford, House, 1787 ; p. 292.

*Hon. Elisha*, Sandwich, House, 1810-11, 1823-4, 1832 ; Senate, 1828-30 ; Constitutional Convention, 1820 ; p. 292.

*Jonathan*, New Bedford, House, 1810-11 ; pp. 289, 292.

*William*, Dorchester, House, 1812-14 ; p. 165.

*Capt. Ebenezer*, Great Barrington, House, 1824-5 ; p. 295.

*William*, Spencer, House, 1827 ; p. 301.

*Ebenezer*, Sterling, House, 1828, cousin of preceding, son of Ebenezer[3], of Joseph[1] ; p. 301.

*Stephen*, Marlboro, Senate, 1836, 1837 ; p. 311.

*Ichabod*, Enfield, House, 1840, 1841 ; b. 1796, Bridgewater, son of Freeman[4] and Hannah (Thayer) ; p. 289.

*Capt. Henry*, Halifax, House, 1840, 1841.

*Col. William*, Boston, House, 1851, 1852 ; p. 200.

*Rev. Rufus Spurr*, Barnstable, House, 1855 ; p. 233.

*Ezra T.*, Sandwich, House, 1864, 1865, Messenger do. since 1875.

*Richard*, Boston, House, 1874, 1875 ; b. Feb. 28, 1843, South Boston.

*Charles Greenwood*, Somerville, House, 1876-7 ; p. 264.

---

# SECTION D.

NOTES UPON SOME OF THE INTERMARRYING FAMILIES.

---

## THE MELLISH FAMILY.

[See pp. 163, 209, 216, 253, 254, 268.]

AMONG the Revolutionary soldiers of Dorchester we find the name of John Mellish. His son, Stephen, born Oct. 22, 1772, married Roxalina, dau. of Nathaniel and Sarah Eaton, of Mansfield, Conn., a sister of General William Eaton, who was U. S. Consul to Tripoli, Algiers, and commander of the American forces there during the war betwen that country and ours.

Stephen Mellish was married May 10, 1796, in Greenwich, Conn., and started the same day for Walpole, New Hampshire, which was to be his home.  One horse carried bride and groom!  He was an ingenious cabinet-maker, a person of fine appearance and gentlemanly manners, and an esteemed citizen.

Of his twelve children, four contributed to our Pope "tree."  William Eaton Mellish married Hannah[7] Pope.  Clarissa Mellish, born March 13, 1798, married Harvey Gilbert, of Brownington, Vt.  Their dau. Harriet Maria married John[7] Pope.  Henry Mellish (whose dau., Julia Ann, m. Charles Allen[8] Pope), b. March 30, 1804, m. April 29, 1829, Sarah Blackman of Dorchester; possessed great mechanical ingenuity, having a number of inventions patented; was representative to General Court in 1856-7; practiced medicine somewhat; d. Oct. 20, 1878.  Sarah Mellish, b. April 4, 1807, married Samuel Pope.

## THE TALBOT FAMILY.

Peter Talbot was an early resident of Dorchester, where he married Mary Wadell, Jan. 12, 1677.  His son George[2] married Mary Turel, and lived in Stoughton, a part of the original Dorchester.  His son, Peter,[3] was the Revolutionary captain mentioned on page 130, whose wife was Abigail Wheeler.  Peter,[4] jr., b. Nov. 5, 1745, married Lucy Hammond, of Brookline; removed to Machias, Me.  His son, Micah Jones,[5] was the father of Betsey Jones,[6] who married Samuel Ward[6] Pope, of East Machias.  Peter[6] was the father of Emily Foster,[6] who married Andrew Jackson[8] Pope.  Another descendant of Peter[1] of Dorchester, was Isaac, of Stoughton, whose daughter Elizabeth married Lazarus[6] (see page 186).

## PUMPELLY.

*Raphael Pumpelly* [p. 170] was born at Owego, Tioga County, N. Y., Sept. 8, 1837.  Was educated in Europe, studied his profession at the Berg Academie Freihe of Saxony.  In 1860-5 made a scientific journey around the northern hemisphere; entered successively the services of the Japanese and Chinese Imperial governments as geologist.  On returning, was appointed professor of mining engineering in Harvard University.  Had charge of the State geological surveys of Michigan and Missouri, and of the department of mining industries in the census of the United States.  He organized the Northern Transcontinental Survey.  Was elected a member of the National Academy of Sciences in 1872.  Published "Geological Researches in China, Mongolia, and Japan," and "Across America and Asia," besides several State and National geological survey reports, etc.

## PIERCE ANCESTRY.

Two hundred and twenty-one of the persons enumerated in the foregoing genealogy descended from the two Pope brothers and two Pierce sisters, alluded to on page 159, etc. The following notes on the *Dorchester Pierce Family* will be particularly interesting to such of them as are now living, and to their descendants.

Persons of the name of Pierce have been numerous in America. At Boston, Watertown, Malden, Plymouth, Rehoboth and elsewhere, there were families in colonial days, some of whom may have been related. Genealogies of several of these have been published. A prevalent pronunciation of the name in Dorchester has been *purse*; the spelling in all has been various. It may have been derived from the French form of the name Peter (Pierre), or from the verb *pierce* (anciently pronounced purse). Here are three entries in the records of St. Andrew's parish, Plymouth, Eng., which may be of service in inquiries after the origin of this family.

"Robert Peers and Nicoll Lamb, married Aug. 11, 1599." "Robert, son of Robert Peers, baptized Oct. 8, 1600." "Thomas Pierce and Jane his wife married March 21, 1586." "Robert, son of Thomas Pearse, baptized April 18, 1605."

### THE DORCHESTER PIERCE FAMILY.

"It is ordered that *Robert Pierce* shall be a commoner."— Dorchester Town Records, Oct. 31, 1639. This language, used in no other case, refers to a vote passed Jan. 18, 1635: "All the hoame lotts within Dorchester Plantation which have been granted before this present day shall have right to the Commons, and no other lotts that are graunted hereafter, to be commoners." It is certain, then, that Robert Pierce did not own a home lot in D. until after Jan. 18, 1635. He may have been here earlier, but there is no mention of his name before. The tradition that he came in the "Mary and John" may point to one of her later voyages (she brought passengers in 1634, we know). "Decimo 9mo : 1639," he was admitted to the church. In 1644 a road was laid out to "Robert Pears house on the pyne necke"; about 30 rods N. E. of Neponset R. R. station there is a well to which credible tradition points as the very "watering-place" of that early dwelling of the pioneer. Near by lived his father-in-law, "*John Grenaway*, millwright," one of the original members of the Dorchester church-colony, [see article by W. B. Trask in Gen. Register, Jan., 1878,] who is mentioned in D. town records in the oldest clause extant, dated "Jan. 21" [1631 or 1632]. He was one of the first persons made "freemen," applying Oct. 19, 1630, and

admitted May 18, 1631; stood high in town and church.   Had
several daughters, but no son known.   He d. about 1651, his wife,
Mary d. Jan. 23, 1658.   The following English note may refer to
this man and his marriage to a former wife; or may be the record of
another person of the name.

"John Greeneway and Elinora Braylie of Ashregnie" were
licensed to marry by the bishop of Exeter, Jan. 15, 1615.

John Grenaway, of Dorchester, deeded lands in Pine Neck, to
"my son-in-law Robert Pearse, and Ann Pearse my daughter, now
wife of the said Robt. Pearse."   "*Now wife*" may imply that either
Robert or Ann had been previously married.

"Robert Pearse" was chosen a fence-viewer for the great lots in
1651 *et seq.*, and was paid five shillings for mending a gate there in
1657.   The church record says: "Robert Pearse of the great lots
died 5th was buried 7th 11 mo., 1664."   In his will he left to his son
and daughter this noble charge:

> "And now my dear child a ffather's blessing I bequeath unto you both
> & yours, bee tender & loving to your mother Loving and kind unto one
> another.   Stand up in your places for God and for his ordinances while you
> live.   Then hee will bee for you & Blesse you."

A stone in the old burying-ground told of the extraordinary age to
which the "goodwife" lived.

Here Lyes ye
Body of Ann
ye wife of
Robert Pearce
Aged about 104 year.
Died December
ye 31 1695.

*Thomas,*[1] only son of the above, b. 1635, built and lived in the
"Pierce House," on Adams Street, where bread, left from the
pioneers' voyage from England, is still shown.   He m. Oct. 3,
1661, Mary, daughter of William Fry, b. in Weymouth Jan. 9, 1641,
d. in Dorchester March 22, 1704.   He d. Oct. 26, 1706.   [See article
by William B. Trask in Gen. Register, July, 1885.]

*William Fry* was in Weymouth before 1636.   He d. Oct. 26,
1643, bequeathing his property to his wife, his "two daughters,
Elizabeth and Mary," and "Thomas Harris, Thomas Rawlens and
John Meggs, his three sisters youngest children."   Part of the land
was to be his widow's for her life, then to revert to the daughters.   The town records show that she afterward married "Thomas
Doget."

Our English note-book contains the following, which may afford some clue to the origin of this family :

"William, son of William ffry of Stonehouse," was baptized at St. Andrew's Church, Plymouth, Devon, Oct. 6, 1594.

"William ffry, armiger, and Mary Younge of Membury, daughter of John Younge of Culliton Yew," were licensed to marry, by the bishop of Exeter, April 19, 1610.

*John*,[3] b. "27.8.68," m. Jan. 25, 1693, Abigail, dau. of Dea. Samuel Tompson, of Braintrèe.

*John*,[4] *jr.*, b. April 5, 1707 ; m. Nov. 10, 1741, Elizabeth, daughter of Thomas and Abigail (Locke) Fessenden, b. in Lexington, March 18, 1721. Her father was son of the pioneer, *Nicholas Fessenden*, and Margaret, daughter of Thomas and Jane (Atkinson) Cheney. Thomas was a son of *William Cheney*, one of the founders of Roxbury. The parentage of Jane Atkinson is not known to us. *William Locke*, as a boy of six, came to New England in the "Planter," May 22, 1634, with his cousin, Nicholas Davis. He m. Dec. 27, 1665, Mary, daughter of William and Margery *Clarke*, of Woburn ; lived a long and reputable life, and d. June 16, 1720. His son, Joseph, and Mary, had dau. Abigail, who m. Thomas Fessenden. [See Locke Book.]

"*William Clarke*, weaver, aged 27, and wife, Margaret, aged 21," came to Watertown in 1635, in "The Plaine Joan." Their dau. Mary b. Dec. 10, 1640.

One of the fourteen children of John[4] Pierce and Elizabeth Fessenden was *John*,[5] b. Sept. 22, 1742 ; m. June 9, 1772, Sarah, daughter of Samuel and Patience (White) Blake, b. Sept. 21, 1754, the second of his four wives, and the mother of all his ten children. He was forty years leader of the choir, as his sire and grandsire had been ; president of the first local Temperance Society from its organization, in 1829 ; full of earnestness in religion ; interested in remembering and telling historical and genealogical matters ; accurate and conscientious, to a proverb. His eldest son, Rev. John[6] Pierce, D. D., a graduate and long a trustee of Harvard College, fifty years pastor of the Unitarian Church in Brookline, was very eminent and much beloved ; his monument bears this motto, chosen by himself, — "Christ is my hope." The second son, Samuel Blake,[6] lived on the old homestead. The third, Jonas,[6] made his home at East Machias, Me. The youngest, Lemuel,[6] settled at West Farms, N. Y. The six daughters, two of whom wedded Popes, [see pp. 156, 175,] married in Dorchester, and enjoyed delightful fellowship for years. One of these was Patience,[6] wife of William Trask, mother of the genealogist, William Blake Trask.

## BLAKE.
### [See pp. 67, 70, etc.]

*William*[1] is first mentioned in the town records Jan. 2, 1637–8, but the reference to his previous ownership of a home lot shows that he had already been there some time. If he had been a "first-comer," it is strange his great-grandson, James,[4] did not say so in his "Annals of Dorchester," when naming several who were. He seems to have been a very discreet, trustworthy man, much in town affairs, and devoted to the church. Mr. Samuel Blake in his admirable "Blake Family" gave a pedigree, obtained from England by John H. Blake, Esq., of Roxbury, tracing the family back to "John Blake of Little Baddow, Essex, gent. :" but Mr. W. H. Whitmore, publishing notes of the late G. A. Somerby, Esq., in "A Record of the Blakes of Somersetshire," etc., Boston, 1881, proposes another hypothesis, *viz.*, that the Dorchester family is a branch of the Somerset house.

This is the evidence on which this second theory rests : Eleanor Blake, baptized at Aisholt, Somerset, Feb. 27, 1602–3 ; m. James Clark. In her will, dated at Over Stowey, June 19, 1647, she mentions her late husband, and bequeaths to her daughter Eleanor, a house and lands, "formerly in possession of her brother, now in New England." One of her brothers, whose baptism is recorded at Over Stowey, is *William*, bapt. June 5, 1594. Robert, John, Humphrey and Hugh are the other recorded brothers, the burials of Robert and John being recorded in 1602 and 1613. William Blake, of Dorchester, is said by the Annalist to have died "the 25th of the 8th month, 1663, in the 69th year of his age," which seems to identify him with the Somerset man; yet the case is not proven, however strong a *presumption* there may be in its favor.

In St. Andrew's Church, Plymouth, Eng., we noted the following, which may help further investigation of the origin of this family. "William Blake and Julyure Halse [Julia Halsey] were married June 25, 1594." "William Blake and Pacience Parkins were married Feb. 22, 1595." "Willm, son of Wilm Blake, was baptized Jan. 12, 1598." "Joan, daughter of Wm. Blake, of Stonehouse, was baptized July 7, 1604." In Exeter probate office, we found indexed the wills of Wm. Blake, Plymouth, 1614 ; Wm. Blake, Plympton, 1615 [Totness]; John Blake, of St. Breock, 1628 [Consistory]. At Bristol, Nicholas Blake was sheriff in 1576, warden of St. Thomas' Church in 1564, 1571, 1578, 1586. Married in St. T., "Mr. Nicholas Blake and Joane ffrowde yᵉ 17 day March 1577." "John Blake, the son of Nicholas Blake baptized Maie 17, 1584." "William Blake yᵉ sonn of Nicholas Blake, baptized October 23, 1587." "John Blake, yᵉ sonn of

Augustine Blake, baptized March 4, 1586." "Joane Blake, the daughter of Willm Blake, baptized Jan. 13, 1604."

The second son of William[1] Blake, of Dorchester, and his wife Agnes (who died July 22, 1678) was *James*,[2] b. in England about 1623; married Elizabeth, dau. of Dea. Edward and Prudence (Clap) Clap, born 1633, d. Jan. 16, 1694. He was a deacon, and afterward ruling elder of the church, and was much in town offices. He built and lived in what is still known as the "Blake House," just off of Cottage Street. His son, *James*[3] *jr.*, b. Aug. 15, 1652, d. October 22, 1732; m. (second) July 8, 1684, Ruth, dau. of Nathaniel and Deborah (Smith) Bacheller, of Hampton, N. H., b. May 9, 1662, d. Jan. 11, 1752. Miss Agnes Blake Poor, of Brookline, a gr. dau. of Rev. John Pierce, D. D., has brought to our attention the facts concerning "Mother Ruth's" parentage. Nov. 1, 1755, "Increase Blake, of Boston, tin-plate worker;" "James Blake, joiner," "Patience Blake, relict widow of Samuel Blake," and "John Spur, yeoman," all of Dorchester; and "Roger McKnight, of Boston, and Ruth, his wife;" the first specified as a son, the rest as grandchildren of "Ruth Blake, late of Dorchester, who was daughter of Nathaniel Bachelder, late of Hampton, yeoman, deceased," deeded their right to her share in her father's estate to her brothers and others.

*James*,[4] *jr.*, b. April 30, 1688, d. Dec. 4, 1750, was a celebrated surveyor and accountant. Was clerk of the town many years; compiled its first history, "Annals of the Town of Dorchester," which was recognized as an authority even while in manuscript, and was published, almost a century after his death, by the Antiquarian and Historical Society of Dorchester [Boston, David Clapp, jr., 1846. See foregoing pp. 10, 46, etc.]. He m. Wait, daughter of Jonathan and Wait (Clap) Simpson, b. in Boston in 1684, d. in Dorchester, May 22, 1753.

*Samuel*,[5] b. Sept. 6, 1715, m. June 5, 1740, Patience, dau. of Edward and Patience (Bird) White, b. Dec. 22, 1714, d. Dec. 19, 1786. He was a surveyor; died May 1, 1754. Their dau., *Sarah*,[6] became the wife of John[5] Pierce. [See previous pp.]

## SIMPSON.

*John Simpson*, with Susanna, his wife, lived in Watertown in 1634. Their daughter Sarah was b. there Aug. 10, 1634; son Jonathan b. Dec. 17, 1640. "Susan Simson, widdow," deeded lands to William Page Nov. 9, 1643. The inventory of her husband's estate was filed April 24, 1645. She afterward married George Parkhurst and removed to Boston. Jonathan[2] m. April 3, 1673, Wait, daughter of Capt. Roger and Johanna (Ford) Clap, b. March 17, 1649, d. May 3,

1717. Blake says of her: "She was a godly woman, following the good example of her parents. She often spake of that charge which her father left his children, viz.: *Never to spend any time in idleness ;* and practised accordingly in a very observable manner."

## WHITE.

[FROM HOTTEN'S ORIGINAL LISTS.]

"xxii June, 1635. In the Abigail de Lond Hackwell, vers New England p'r Cert. frō minister of Craiebroke in Kent.

Edw: White *husbm :* 42
Martha White *his wife* 39
Martha White } 10
Mary White } *children* "

This *Edward* [1] *White** had an allotment of twelve acres of land at Squantum, June 27, 1636, and afterward several tracts in the village.

*James,* [2] b. Jan. 1, 1637; m. (1) Feb. 22, 1664, Sarah, daughter of Richard and Faith (Withington) Baker, the mother of all his children; she d. Oct. 13, 1688 ; he m. (2) Elizabeth Withington. He d. Nov. 11, 1713.

*Edward,* [3] b. Aug. 4, 1683; d. Oct. 17, 1716 ; m. Patience, daughter of Thomas Bird, jr., and Thankful, daughter of Maj.-Gen. Humphrey Atherton, b. Nov. 27, 1683, d. Dec. 11, 1757. Their daughter, Patience, became the wife of Samuel [5] Blake.

## BIRD.

*Thomas Bird,* sen., joined the Dorchester church in 1642 ; was a tanner, a useful, honorable citizen. Left a good posterity. He d. June 8, 1667; his wife, Ann, Aug. 21, 1673. Thomas, jr., was b. May 3, 1640; m. Feb. 2, 1665; d. Jan. 30, 1709—10.

## BAKER.

*Richard Baker* was a member of the Dorchester church in 1639, and a freeman of the colony in 1642 ; a man of good standing in the community. He married Faith, daughter of Henry Withington, who bore him a good number of children, one of whom, Sarah, mentioned above, became the wife of James White. Faith died Feb. 3, and Richard followed her, Oct. 25, 1689. His will is in Suffolk files. A descendant of his, Dr. James Baker, made himself, his family, and his town famous, by the manufacture of chocolate, from 1780 onward. The following jottings in England may not come amiss to the future historian of this family. The index to wills, at Taunton, Somerset-

---

* "Craiebroke" is the modern Cranbrook. Probably this "husbandman's" forty-two years had been spent in that parish. It is believed that Martha's maiden name was King.

shire, gives, " Richard Baker, Wayford, 1609." Among Totness wills
at Exeter, Devon (indexed, but missing), " Richard Baker, Dartmouth,
1559," " Richard Baker, Broadwood Kelly, 1595." Parish register of
Winwick, Lancashire, chronicles, " Richard Baker, buried Aug. 23,
1630," " Richard Baker, buried Oct. 2, 1633."

## WITHINGTON.

*Henry Withington*, believed to have come in the Mather party,
was a man of prominence, ruling elder of the church twenty-nine
years; member of the board of selectmen at important times; one of
the " Seven Pillars " who signed the second covenant of the church.
[See p. 48.] His first wife, Elizabeth, left four children, certainly:
Richard; Mary (m. Thos. Danforth); Ann (m. James Bates, jr.), and
Faith (m. Richard Baker). He m. a second wife, Margerie, who
survived him. He d. Feb. 2, 1666, aged 79.

## ATHERTON.

*Humphrey Atherton*, first mentioned in town records, March 18,
1637, made "freeman" May 2, 1638, following. He may have come
with his brother-in law, Nathaniel Wales, in the "James," along with
Rev. Richard Mather, in 1635. [See pp. 14 and 46.] He became a
leading citizen of Dorchester; was selectman, etc., officer in the town
militia; captain of the Ancient and Honorable Artillery from 1650 to
1658; became known to the colonial authorities as a man of great
bravery and sagacity, and rose to the rank of Major-General.
Though a terror to *warlike* Indians, yet he was the trusted friend of
all who were well disposed, helping on their education and Chris-
tianization, and guarding their rights, so that he had immense personal influence with them, and was a successful treaty-maker. In 1645
the N. E. Colonies met by representatives to consult upon the Indian
problem, and appointed a Council of War; Capt. Miles Standish, of
Plymouth, was chairman. Mason of Connecticut, Leverett and Atherton of Massachusetts, were the other councillors. He was some-
time deputy governor, representative to the General Court; long
a justice of the peace, and solemnized many marriages. Was killed
by a fall from his horse on his way home from Boston, the night following Sept. 16, 1661. The following epitaph is expressive :

> " Here lyes our Captaine & Major of Suffolk was withal ;
>  A Godly Majistrate was he, and Major Generall,
>  Two Troops of Hors with him heare came, such love his worth did crave.
>  Ten Companyes of Foot, also mourning marcht to his grave.
>  Let all who Read be sure to keep the Faith as he has don.
>  With Christ he lives now crown'd, His name was Humpry Atherton."

Mary Atherton, widow of Humphrey, died in 1672; her will was admitted Oct. 3.

Mr. J. C. J. Brown, in Gen. Reg. Vol. X., p. 31, gives a list of the children of Maj.-Gen. Atherton, viz: Jonathan; Isabel (m. Nathaniel Wales, jr.); Elizabeth (m. Timothy Mather); Consider; Mary (m. Joseph Weeks); Margaret (m. James Trowbridge); Rest, bapt. May 26, 1639 (m. Obadiah Swift); Increase; Thankful, bapt. April 28, 1644 (m. Thomas Bird, jr.); Watching; Patience (m. Isaac Humphrey). W. B. Trask, in Gen. Reg. XXXII., p. 197, also gives important facts relative to this family.

The name Atherton is an ancient and honorable one in Lancashire, England. There is a village of the name in the county. "William de Aderton" was a witness to a document, "Friday, the feast of St. Mary Magdalene, in the twenty-eighth year of the reign of King Edward," July 22, 1300. [See collections of Warrington public library.] The will of

"Humphrey Atherton of Norley in Pemberton in the county of Lancaster, gentleman," is on file at Chester, dated March 3, 1525. Requests to be buried "in my ancient buriall-place" at the parish church of Wigan. Bequeaths the "titles to his estate" to his late father, James Atherton. Makes bequests to his daughters Elizabeth, Margaret, and Ellen Atherton; to the children of James Winstanley, his son-in-law; to his wife Elizabeth, whom he makes co-executor with Richard Leigh of Holland, gentleman;" mentions a debt he owes to Jane Atherton. Peter Atherton is one of the witnesses. This may have been an ancestor of our pioneer.

At Winwick, the native parish of Rev. R. Mather, we note the following baptisms recorded:

"Anne, dau'. of Humfrey Atherton, June 26, 1609." "Elizab., dau. of Humphrey Atherton, Sept. 28, 1628;" "John, son of Hum. Atherton, Dec. 26, 1629;" "Isabel, dau. of Humfrey Atherton, Jan. 23, 1630."

We may conjecture that two families are referred to here; "Anne" being the child of one, the other three of another. But Elizabeth and Isabel correspond well with two of the children of the Dorchester pioneer. Further investigation may prove their identity, and lead to a full exploration of the history and pedigree of our honored ancestor.

## THE CLAP FAMILY.

Osgod Clapa was a famous Danish noble who was a favorite of the English king, Harthacanute. This may indicate a Norse origin of the name Clap. There is a German name, Klapp, which may be a cog-

nate form of some ancient Gothic word. The Salcombe family spelled
the name with one p; notaries and other writers often doubled that
letter. In Exeter probate files (Dean and Chapter) we took notes of
two wills, which we are glad to offer as *addenda* to that fine book,
"The Clap Family in America."

"William Clapp, of Salcombe, yeoman (the sonne of William Clapp,
the elder)," made will Sept. 6, 1636. Bequeathed property to his
father ; to his wife, Dorothy; "to my brother Edward now living in
New England my best wedding suit ; to my brother Roger my second suit of Azell ;" to his brothers, Robert and John; "to my sister
Jane and my sister Sarah, each of them a plaine hand kierchiefe ;"
"to my sisters son Thomas Weekes a bible;" another bequest of four
pounds to his brother Edward ; to his sons, William and Elizeus.
"William Clap the elder," and "Robert Clap" signed as witnesses.

"The Will of William Clapp thelder of Salcombe," dated "March
1st, 1640," probated "March 25, 1641," bequeathed twenty shillings
to each of his sons, Edward, Roger, Robert and John ; something to
his daughters, Jane and Sarah; to John, Hester, James and Elizeus
Clapp, and "William Clapp the younger," his grandchildren ; Dorothy
Clapp, his daughter-in-law ; "Robert and John, my son Robert's sons ;"
to "Elizᵃ. Tuck my godchild"; to the poor of Salcombe,* etc. Robert
and John were named executors. Signed in a clear hand, "William
Clap."

*Edward* and *Roger Clap* each contributed to the Blake branch of
the Pierce ancestry, the former through his daughter Elizabeth, the
latter through his granddaughter, Wait Simpson. It is also stated
that Edward's wife Prudence was his cousin, daughter of his father's
brother.

Thus the Clap strain is one of the most important elements in the
Pierce-Pope stock.

*Roger*, b. in Salcombe, Devon, England, April 6, 1609, d. in
Boston, Feb. 2, 1690, was a member of the colony which came in the
"Mary and John," in the spring of 1630, and entered into the toils
and cares of the Dorchester plantation with great earnestness and
efficiency, having the confidence and respect of his fellow-citizens, in
spite of being one of the youngest of the "proprietors." He was a
good soldier, and was in command of Castle Island many years.
The closing part of his life he resided in Boston, and his dust reposes in King's Chapel burying-ground, with that of his wife and

---

*This is Salcombe Regis, a lovely hamlet, just east of Sidmouth. Its registers for the first
half of the seventeenth century have vanished, but the quaint old church still endures.

daughter Wait. His funeral was a notable one, "the Military Officers going before the Corps; and next to the Relations, the Governour and the whole General Court following after: and the Guns firing at the Castle at the same time." [Blake.]

He left, in manuscript, an account of his life and instructions to his children, which has been published under the title of "Memoirs of Roger Clap" [Boston, David Clapp, 1844]. This book stands alone as a history of the Dorchester Colony's gathering and coming; its straightforward, graphic story has been verified in many points, already, and will never cease to gain the admiration of all who love the manly devoutness of the genuine Puritan character. When a young man he found employment near Exeter, and became a parishioner of Rev. John Warham in the city, into which he removed for religious privileges. He "heard of many godly persons that were going to New England, and that Mr. Warham was to go also," and was personally solicited by Rev. John Maverick, to whom his father yielded him. After coming over he persuaded his brother Edward and the husbands of his two sisters to follow.

Nov. 6, 1633, he m. "Johanna, dau. of *Mr. Thomas Ford* of Dorchester in England, when she was but in the 17th year of her age; who with her parents came over in the same ship with himself, and settled also here in Dorchester;" she was b. June 8, 1617, and d. June, 1695. Mr. Ford was one of the first freemen of the colony; he removed to Windsor, Conn., and was a man of note there.

Roger and Johanna had fourteen children, several of whom died young. The names of some of these are tokens of Bible piety: Samuel, Elizabeth, Preserved, Hopestill, Wait, Desire, Unite, Supply. At the baptism of one of these, "24, 1 mo. 50," "Leuitenant Clap declared the Reason why he called his child (Wait) was because he did suppose the fall of antichrist was not Farre off."   .

*Edward Clap*, older than Roger, came at an unknown date, after his brother, and spent his life in Dorchester. He was one of the owners of a mill, "near the bend of the creek." The following memorial, placed on the church records after his decease, gives a good account of the man:

"The 8th day of the 11th mo., 1664, being the Sabbath day, Deacon Edward Clap departed this life and now resteth with the Lord, there to spend an eternal Sabbath with God and Christ in Heaven, after that he had faithfully served in the office of a Deacon for the space of about five or six and twenty years, and being the first Church officer that was taken away since the first joining together in covenant, which is now 28 years 4 mo. and odd days."

It is stated in the "Clap Family" that his first wife, Prudence, was a daughter of Richard Clap of Dorchester, England, and a sister of Thomas of Hingham and Nicholas of Dorchester ; on what evidence I cannot learn.  Elizabeth, dau. of this first marriage, became the wife of Elder James Blake.

*Rev. Stephen Bachiller* sailed from London in the "William and Francis," March 9, 1632 ; Mr. Winslow, of Plymouth, was a fellow-passenger.  Gov. Winthrop notes their arrival, June 5, following, "with about sixty passengers, whereof Mr. Welde and old Mr. Batchelor (being aged about 71) were, with their families and many other honest men."  He was pastor of the church at Lynn ; was not allowed by the magistrates to organize a church at Saugus, as he desired.  Was one of the originators of the settlement at Hampton, N. H., to which he gave the name, and where his son Nathaniel settled (whose daughter Ruth m. James[3] Blake).  (*John Smith*, whose daughter Deborah m. Nathaniel Bacheller, was also a Hampton man.)  "Stephen Bachiller " [so signed] "late of Hampton in y[e] county of Norfolk in New England & now of Strabery bank " deeded to " John, Stephen and William Sanborn and Nathaniel Batchiller, all now or lately of Hampton aforesaid " certain property, providing that his dwelling-house and land in Hampton should "be estated upon " John Sanborn, under certain conditions ; the "8th of 7th Month : 1647." [Rockingham Co. Deeds ; lib. 13, p. 221.]  After several brief ministries and many sharp trials, he returned to England.  He was a very energetic and serviceable pioneer, but made some enemies by his wilful manners and disregard for colonial authority.  He was unjustly treated sometimes, perhaps at fault in a few instances.  He d. in Hackney in 1660, at a great age.  He had sons Stephen and Francis, a brother-in-law Francis Mercer, and a nephew Paul Pryaulx.  The coat-of-arms of the family is said to be " Vert, a plough in fesse, and in base the sun rising *or*." [See Gen. Reg., vol. xxvii, p. 364.]

"*Rev. William Tompson*," says Savage, " was born in 1599, in Lancashire.  He was matriculated at Brazen Nose College, Oxford, 23 Jan., 1620, but his graduation is not on record ; preached in Winwick, Lancashire.*  Afterward — in 1637 — came to New Eng-

---

* Investigations at Winwick failed to disclose evidence that he preached there.  From 1626 to 1639, Rev. Charles Herle, M. A., was rector.  The parish registers are signed from time to time by curates who kept them ; and in other ways the names of these assistants are recorded ; but in no way is any *minister* named Tompson alluded to.  However, we find that " 21 October, 1635, Eliezar sonn of Wm. Tompson " was baptized ; which may point to our man, and indicate that his *home* was in that neighborhood.  There was a "John Tompson," who had daughter "Anne," baptized May 28, 1626.  This peculiar spelling of the name seems to have been especially common in Lancashire.

land; was engaged first at Kittery or York ; but after the church was instituted at Braintree, Sept. 17, 1639, he was ordained in company with Rev. Henry Flint, Nov. 19th of that year. He was made a freeman May 13, 1640. He brought with him from England his wife Abigail, his sons, Samuel and William (the latter graduated at Harvard in 1653), and perhaps daughters Mary and Elinor ; had here, Joseph, b. May 1, 1640 ; Benjamin, b. July 14, 1642 (H. C. 1662). His wife died Jan. 1, 1643, while he was on a mission to Virginia with Rev. John Knowles and Thomas James, begun in the previous October. He d. Dec. 10, 1666." He was highly respected.

An account of this "mission" is given in Minutes Nat. Cong. Council, 1883, p. 118. In 1642 Philip Bennet of Nansemond, Va., came to Boston, asking for ministers of the Congregational order for three parishes in his vicinity. After a day of fasting and prayer, the Boston officials selected Messrs. Knowles of Watertown, Tompson of Braintree, and James of New Haven, to undertake the transplanting of New England ideas into "Old Dominion" soil. But the Virginia assembly enacted a law, banishing all non-conformists to the Church of England; so, they soon returned to their parishes in New England. *Samuel* Tompson, b. Feb. 16, 1630, deacon of Braintree Church, m. April 25, 1656, Sarah, daughter of *Edward* and *Violet Shepard*, b. 1636, their daughter Abigail, b. Nov. 10, 1667, m. John² Pierce. Edward Shepard, mariner, bought land in Cambridge about 1639; was made freeman May 10, 1643. His wife, Violet, d. Jan. 9, 1648–9. His will was proved Aug. 20, 1680.

THE PILGRIM ANCESTORS *of the Pierce family may be thus summed up, — twenty-one pioneer families definitely known* :

Robert and Ann (Grenaway) Pierce, John and Mary Grenaway, William and Mary Fry, Nicholas and Margaret (Cheney) Fessenden, William and —— Cheney, William and Mary (Clarke) Locke, William and Margery Clarke, William and Agnes Blake, John and Susanna Simpson, Edward* and Martha White, Thomas and Ann Bird, Richard and Faith (Withington) Baker, Henry and —— Withington, Humphrey and Mary Atherton, Edward and Prudence (Clap) Clap, Roger and Johanna (Ford) Clap, Thomas and —— Ford, Rev. Stephen and —— Bachiller, John and Deborah Smith, Rev. William and Abigail Tompson, Edward and Violet Shepard.

---

* Rev. John White, of Dorchester, Eng. [see p. 10], was b. at Staunton, St. John's, Oxford, 1575; grad. New College 1606; was rector of All Saints' Church, Dorchester, till his death, July 21, 1648. Was buried in the porch of Trinity Church. Deserves honor from all descendants of the Puritans. We do not know of any relationship between this "patriarch" and Edward White above.

# THAXTER.

[See pp. 160, 210, and 217.]

*Deacon Thomas*[1] *Thaxter* (ancestor of all of the name in America, we believe), with wife Elizabeth, son John and daughter Elizabeth, came from England to Hingham, Mass., in 1638 ; was made freeman May 18, 1642 ; d. Feb. 4. 1654 ; his wife d. July 18, 1660.   Their son, Captain *John*[2], m. Dec. 4, 1648, Elizabeth, daughter of *Nicholas Jacob*, who, " with his wife and 2 children and their cosen Thomas Lincoln, weaver, came from old Hingham in 1633." [Cushing's Record.] Captain John's tombstone may be seen at Hingham ; he d. March 14, 1686–7.

*Hon. Samuel*[3], b. Aug. 6, 1665 ; d. Nov. 3, 1740 ; m. Dec. 29, 1691, Hannah, daughter of Tremble Gridley, granddaughter of the pioneers Richard and Grace Gridley, of Boston.   Was a man of much note, captain of a company in the Ancient and Honorable Artillery, one of the commissioners to lay out the boundary between Plymouth and Massachusetts Bay Colonies.   *Samuel*,[4] jr., b. Oct. 8, 1695 ; graduated at Harvard College, 1714 ; d. Dec. 4, 1732.   " Samuel Thaxter of Hingham and Sarah Marshall,[*] of Boston, were joyned in marriage at Dorchester the 3d day of January 1721–22 by the worshipfull Samuel Thaxter Esq."   She was b. April 5, 1700, d. July 26, 1727, and he m. (2) March 5, 1730, Mary Hawke, who outlived him and became the wife of Rev. John Hancock of Braintree, and the mother of John Hancock, Esq., the Revolutionary leader.   *Major Samuel*,[4] son of Samuel[3] and Sarah (Marshall), b. Nov. 15, 1723 ; graduated Harvard 1743 ; m. Aug. 18, 1743, Abigail Smith, of Sandwich, b. Dec. 16, 1722.   He was a very efficient officer at Fort William Henry, etc., in the French and Indian War.   He d. Aug. 6, 1771, his widow in 1807.   Several of his sons became physicians.   *Marshall*,[5] b. May 14, 1760, learned the trade of tanner and currier, and went to Machias, Me., about 1683 ; m. (1) Lucy Drew ; (2) Mrs. Susannah Sevey, daughter of Ebenezer and Damaris (Merrill) Gardner, b. Oct. 15, 1770, d. April 10, 1843.   Ebenezer Gardner was a descendant of Mr. Thomas Gardner, superintendent of Cape Ann Colony in 1623-4, afterward of Salem [see p. 298].   Damaris was daughter of Nathan and Susannah Merrill, of Haverhill, bapt. Sept. 6, 1747.

---

* *John Marshall* came in " Hopewell " from London in 1635, aged 14; admitted inhabitant of Boston Feb. 24, 1639–40; m. Sarah ———.   Will proved March 20, 1715–16. Sarah d. Sept. 28, 1680, aged 66.   One of his sons, *Samuel*,[2] b. about 1646, m. Ruth, daughter of Thomas Rawlins, who came in the fleet with Gov. Winthrop, in 1630, bringing wife Mary and five children.   He lived first at Roxbury, then at Scituate, where Mary d. about 1696.   [Roxbury Church Records.]   *John Marshall*, son of Samuel[2] and Ruth (R.), b. March 19, 1678; m. May 26, 1699, Sarah, daughter of Joseph and Grace Webb, b. Oct. 14, 1673.   Joseph was a son of the immigrant Richard Webb, of Weymouth and Boston.

# CHRISTIAN NAMES

OF

# POPES MENTIONED IN THIS BOOK,

## POPES OF PLYMOUTH.

# POPES OF SALEM.

# GENERAL INDEX OF NAMES.

## TABLE OF ERRATA.

*Page* 141. — Ralph[8] is *not* written in the "next chapter." He m. Ruth Tower April 11, 1805. Nothing further has been gleaned respecting him.

*Page* 191, *eighth line under Edmund[6].* — For " 1885 " read " 1875."

*Page* 198, *first line.* — " C." is an error.

*Page* 259. — The names of the parents of A, 24, are omitted. They are stated on the previous page, in connection with his brother, A, 23.

*Be so kind as to notify the publisher of any other error or omission you may discover, stating the page where it occurs, and giving your authority for the proposed amendment. Kindly inform us also, from time to time, of important family events, with dates and names in full.*

# SUBSCRIBERS.

Col. Albert A. Pope, 79 Franklin St., Boston.
Mr. M. C. Warren, 8 Dock Sq., „
  „ Ivory h. Pope, Custom House, „
  „ Charles G. Pope, 209 Washington St., „
Mrs. Miriam B. Pope,
  cor. Washington and Newcomb Sts., „
Mr. George W. Pope. 19 Newcomb St., „
  „ Edwin Pope, 5 Pelham St., „
  „ Horace S. Shepard, Mason Building, „
  „ Samuel Atherton, Equitable Building „
  „ Eugene A Pope, 9 Tremont St., „
  „ Oscar Mellish, 20 Charlestown St., „
  „ Edward W. Pope, 79 Franklin St, „
  „ Fred. W. Gowell. 2777 Wash. St., „
  „ Fred. Pope. 209 Washington St, „
Miss Carrie Hill, 50 Montgomery St., „
Col. George Pope. 7 Durham St., „
Hon. Newton Talbot, Hotel Guildford, „
Mrs. B. J. Pope, Hotel Vendome, „
Mr. Charles R. Pope, 24 Hancock St, „
Mrs. Susan K. Pope, 224 Warren St., „
  „ Julia A. Furber, Warren St., „
Mr. Walter H. Pope, 130 Federal St., „
  „ Henry D. Pope, 91 Federal St., „
  „ Arthur W. Pope, 45 High St., „
  „ David Clapp, 33 Bedford St., „
  „ Otis Shepard, Mason Building, „
The Boston Public Library, Boylston St., „
Joel Munsell's Sons, Albany, N. Y.
Mr. Daniel E. Pope, Cornwall on Hudson, N. Y.
Dr. M. D. Mann, 610 Main St., Buffalo, N. Y.
  „ Abner E. Pope, Dayton, O.
Mechanics Library, Lewiston, Me.
Mr. Warren W. Pope, Weymouth.
  „ Frank H. Pope, „
Mrs. Sarah H. Gorham, Hyannis.
Mr. George Mulliken, Somerville.
Prof. W. A. Shepard, Ashland, Va.
Dea. Thomas Pope, Quincy, Ill.
  „ Warren Hill, Machias, Me.
  „ Gilbert Longfellow, Machias, Me.
Mrs. J. F. O'Brien, Machias, Me.
Mr. J. O. Pope, East Machias, Me.
J. Warren Cushing, Eastport, Me.
Mr. Frank W. Thaxter, Kansas City, Mo.
  „ Luther E. Pope, Brockton.
Prof. Raphael Pumpelly, Newport, R. I.
F. M. Ray, Esq., Portland, Me.
Hon. Thos. H. Weston, 17 Deering St., Portland, Me.
  „ Joseph D. Pope, Columbia, S. C.
Rev. G. Stanley Pope, Grand View, Tenn.

Mrs. Solomon Hall, 45 Adams St., Dorchester.
  „ Hannah P. Mellish, 6 Hamlet St. „
  „ Olivia M. Bird, Hamlet St., „
Miss Kate A. Shepard, Meeting House Hill.
Mr. William Pope, 269 Commercial St., „
  „ J. Foster Pope. Centre Avenue, „
  „ William C. Pope, DeWolf St., „
  „ Alexander Pope, DeWolf St., „
Mr. Henry A. Pope, 861 Adams St., „
Miss Mary J. Pope, 861 Adams St., „
Mr. James Pope, Adams, near Dor. Ave., „
  „ George Pope, 1137 Adams St., „
  „ Henry T. Pope, Beaumont St., „
  „ Richard C. Humphreys,
          Humphreys St., „
Miss Mary Beals, Humphreys St., „
Mrs. Amelia B. Hemmenway, Hump's St., „
Mr. Lemuel C. Pope, 13 Charles St., „
  „ J. Frank Pope, Milton.
Miss Agnes B. Poor, Brookline.
Mr. John T. Pope, Neponset.
Mrs. Abigail Glover, Atlantic.
Mr. Edmund Pope,
  „ Lemuel Billings, Mt. Wollaston.
Miss M. Helen Pope, 45 Cottage, Cambridge.
Library, Harvard University, Cambridge.
Mr. J. Otis Bisbee, Stoughton.
Mrs. Elva A. Belcher, „
Mr. Lemuel Pope, Jamaica Plain.
Mrs. Hannah C. Pope, Lynnfield Centre.
  „ Harriet E. Young, Westboro.
  „ Emily P. Spear, Gardiner, Me.
Mr. George H. Pope, „
  „ John F. Pope, „ „
Mrs. Nancy P. Bisbee, North Stoughton.
  „ Ada F. Sprague, Crescent St., Brockton.
  „ C. W. Sumner, 42 Allen St., „
  „ W. M. Drake, Canton.
Mr. Charles A. Pope, 207 Fulton St., New York.
  „ Ralph W. Pope, 16 Dey St., „
  „ Frank D. Pope, Elizabeth, New Jersey.
Mrs. Frank S. Hall, Glen Ridge, „
Mr. Edward C. Pope, 11 Wade Building, Cleveland, Ohio.
  „ Chas. E. Pope, Esq., 132 La Salle St. Chicago, Ill.
  „ O. C. Pope, 310 Pine St., S'n Francisco, Cal.
  „ Dorville Libby, 3 Sansome St., „
Miss Mary E. Pope, 1601 Van Ness Ave., „
Mrs. Florence Pope, Frank Avenue, „
  „ Henry Edwards, 418 Eddy St., „
Rev. C. M. Blake' 427 Geary St., „
Mr. T. Henry Beals, Sequoia, Cal.

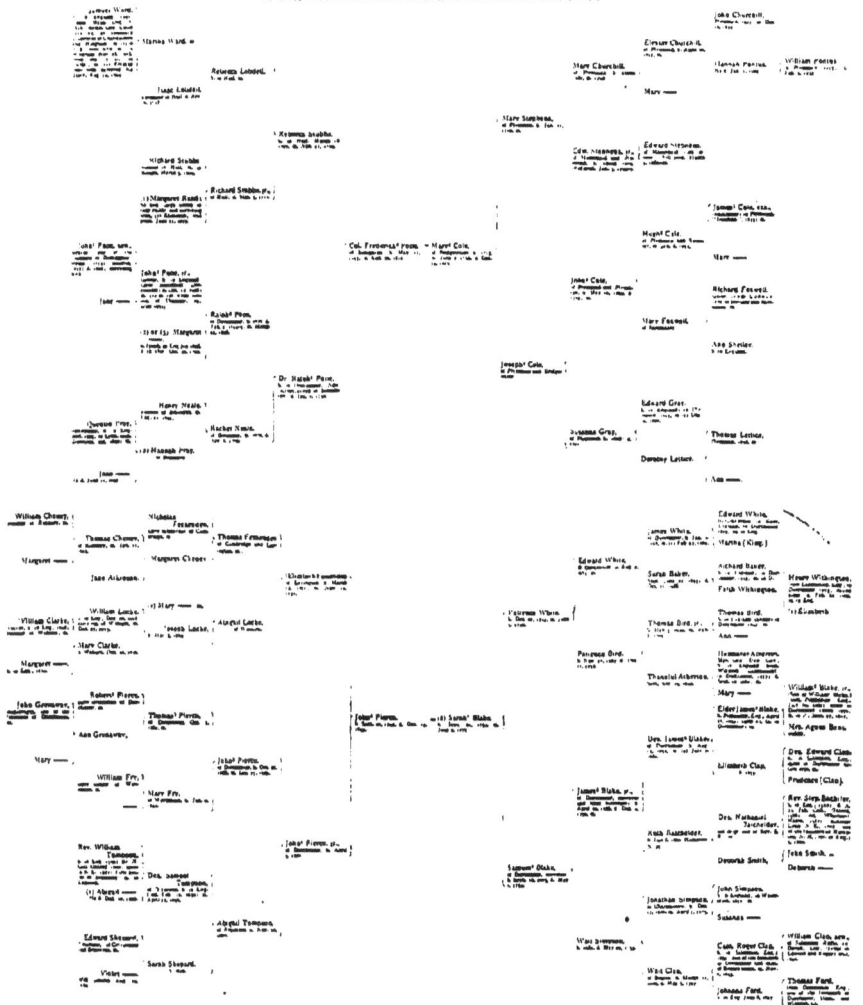

# THE POPE—PIERCE PEDIGREE.

# ADDENDA.

May, 1892, to be bound in with final lot of copies of "The Dorchester Pope Family." Not indexed.

## [*Additional to pp. 66 and 74.*]

In the Town Records of Salem there is a list of land grants, not dated, but believed by experts to have certainly been made prior to 1638, giving the names of proprietors and their number of acres. One line runs thus :

"Jo: Pope . . . . . . . . . . . . . . . . . . . . . . . . . 2 "

Joseph Pope, who came to Salem in 1634, and remained there through his long life (see page 297, etc.), was recorded as "Jos :" or "Joseph"; but "Jo:" was the common abbreviation for *John*, and the Salem clerk so used it often. It seems to be clear that *some John Pope* was here enrolled. Was it our John[2] of Dorchester ?

## [*Additional to page 98.*]

THE NEW HAMPSHIRE BRANCH of the Dorchester Pope Family can be now (May, 1892) fairly well described.

THOMAS[4], son of Thomas[3] and Elizabeth (Merrifield), b. in Dorchester, Nov. 26, 1670, m. (1) in Boston, Jan. 2, 1705, Margaret Downing, and (2), in Ipswich, filed intention of marriage with Mercy Lufkin, Oct. 21, 1727. He resided afterward in Gloucester, later in Haverhill, then in Plaistow, N. H. His son, THOMAS[5], m. Hannah Austin, Oct. 14, 1742, and was one of the founders of Goffstown and Henniker, N. H. [See pp. 95–98.] His son, DAVID[6], resided in H.; m. —— Clark; had three sons who had families, viz. Thomas[7], David[7] and William[7].

[See additions published soon after issue of book.] We present below particulars of the descendants of Thomas[7].

THOMAS[7] POPE, m. Sally Jones, and the most of their life was passed at Washington, Vt. He d. in 1850, she in 1857.

Of their children, Elisha Brown[8] m. but had no issue. Ralph[8] [see below]. Hannah[8] m. —— Noyes; Lucinda[8] m. B. K. Freeman; Maria[8] m. J. D. Hall; Sally[8] m. J. S. Hall. All had good families. All d. before 1889.

RALPH[8] POPE, b. May 14, 1802, at Washington, Vt.; resided there till 1860, when he rem. to Beaver, Minn.; there he d. April 12, 1874. He m. in 1829, Mary Richardson, b. December 6, 1805, at Orange, Vt.; she d. at Beaver, Minn., March 3, 1873.

CHILDREN OF RALPH[8] AND MARY (RICHARDSON) POPE.

I.   IRA B.,[9] b. Sept. 21, 1831, d. at Neillsville, Wis., in 1880, without issue; was clerk of courts of Jackson and Clark counties.

II.  SARAH R.,[9] b. Dec. 16, 1832, m. D. B. Messer, June 6, 1858. *Children:* (1) Nevada Messer, b. Aug. 4, 1862; (2) Edna Messer, b. April 12, 1866, m. Murray Marshall, June 1, 1887; all reside at Plainview, Minn.

III. CARL C.,[9] b. July 22, 1834, m. Ellen M. Hitchcock, Aug. 10, 1859, at Black River Falls, Wis. *Children:* (1) Eugenia M:,[10] b. July 20, 1861, m. E. A. Le Clair, Sept. 26, 1883, d. Nov. 21, 1885, leaving an infant son, Hugh Pope Le Clair, b. Oct. 21, 1885; (2) Ralph C., Jr.,[10] b. March 16, 1867.

*Hon. Carl C.*[9] *Pope* was educated at Woodstock Academy, read law with Hon. J. P. Kidder, W. Randolph, and was adm. to the bar at Chelsea, Vt., in 1856. Has resided at Black River Falls, Wis. Has been district attorney, county judge, member of the State assembly and senate, variously from 1862 onward. Was chairman of com. on Federal relations in 1863, and of judiciary com. in 1865 and 1877. Member of convention which nominated Lincoln and Johnson, in 1864. Meantime has had a large and successful law practice.

IV.  JOHN F.,[10] b. March 7, 1837, m. Sarah L. Welch, Dec. 11, 1864. *Children:* (1) Clayton F.,[10] b. Nov. 11, 1865, d. Dec. 22, 1870; (2) Frank Edgar,[10] b. March 6, 1880; lawyer, Plainview, Minn.; has been county clerk.

V. JAMES R.,[9] b. March 21, 1839, m. Amanda Allen in
1873. *Children:* (1) Ira,[10] b. 1875, and (2) Lucy,[10]
b. 1879. Lives at Lac Qui Parle, Minn.

VI. WILLIAM H. H.,[9] b. March 18, 1841, m. Dec. 13, 1868,
Eliza J. Boatman, who d. Feb. 5, 1887. *Children:*
(1) Carl C.,[10] b. Oct. 20, 1872; (2) Raleigh M.,[10] b.
June 20, 1874; (3) Eliza M.,[10] b. Oct. 8, 1878. Res.
Plainview, Minn.

VII. MARY LEMIRA,[9] b. May 27, 1843, m. William More,
Sept. , 1877. *Children:* (1.) Warner Ralph More,
b. Aug. 21, 1878, and (2) Irma Ellen More, b. Feb. 12,
1881. Res. Beaver, Minn.

VIII. ELLEN B.,[9] b. June 10, 1845, m. James Jacobus, May,
1866, d. at Lincoln, Neb., Feb. 3, 1887. *Child,* Cora
Ellen Jacobus, b. March 2, 1868.

IX. JACOB C.,[9] b. March 12, 1849, at Washington, Vt., m.
Elva Struble, June 29, 1882. He has been attorney
successively of Lac Qui Parle and Kenabac counties;
now real estate dealer, Mora, Minn.

[*Additional to Page* 119.]

JOHN[5] POPE (Elijah,[4] Ralph,[3] John,[2] John,[1]), after serving in
the Revolutionary Army, m. Frances Willard, and soon after
removed to the "townships" of Canada. He d. May 7, 1853,
a. 90, leaving the impress of a stately gentleman. Mrs. Pope
d. Feb. 12, 1843, a. 80.
CHILDREN:

I. ELIJAH,[6] b. Lunenburg, Mass., Sept. 3, 1784; farmer,
Clifton, Que.; d. Feb. 22, 1843.

II. WILLARD,[6] a lawyer, rem. to Kentucky.

III. JOHN,[6] res. Cookshire, Compton Co., Que.

IV. BETSEY,[6] m. David Hotten; d. in Charleston, N. H.

V. NANCY,[6] m. J. Labaree.

VI. LEMUEL.[6]

VII. HARRIET,[6] d. in 1816 at Sawyersville, Que.

VIII. FANNY,[6] m. in Eaton, Que.

IX. WILLIAM.[6]

X. POLLY," m. in Eaton, Que.

JOHN[6] had son JOHN HENRY[7] who has left a most noteworthy record.

Hon. John Henry Pope, b. 1824, was elected to the Canadian Parliament in 1857, and served at various times until 1887. He was in the Queen's Privy Council for the dominion as minister of education, etc., but became most widely and favorably known in the department of railways and canals. He died, honored and lamented, in April, 1889. His son, WARREN HENRY,[8] has been elected to the seat in Parliament he had filled, and is regarded as a worthy son of so distinguished a sire.

LEMUEL[6] left a son *Lemuel*,[7] *jr*., who is postmaster at Robinson, co. Compton, Que., and has very courteously supplied most of the facts in this article; *Colonel Frederick M.*,[8] son of Lemuel, jr., b. 1848, is prominent in militia; was efficient at the time of the Fenian raid in 1866. Other sons of Lemuel[6] reside in Winchendon, Mass.

RACHEL,[5] b. in Dorchester, accompanied her brother John[5] to Canada, and m. Rev. John Doty, of Three Rivers, b. 1745, d. Nov. 23, 1841. She d. after 1807, and Rev. Mr. Doty m. Rachel Jeffery July 28, 1819.

I judge this to have been a niece of Rachel[5].

*[Additional to page* 130.]

JAMES[1] COLE, innkeeper, came from England to Plymouth before 1633, and established the celebrated tavern mentioned by Sewall and other historians. He owned "Cole's Hill"; gave his business to son James, jr.

HUGH[2] COLE, enrolled among the men above sixteen years old in August, 1643, together with his father and brother James, must have been born in England. He m. Jan. 8, 1654, Mary, dau. of Richard and Ann (Shelley) Foxwell, of Barnstable. His children were recorded at Plymouth where he spent some years; but the latter part of his busy life he resided in Swansey. He owned extensive tracts of land, had good relations with King Philip before the war. His son *John*,[3] b. May 16, 1660, became a resident of that portion of Plymouth afterwards incorporated as Plympton. He m. Susanna, dau. of Edward and Dorothy (Lettice) Gray. He d. in 1724, leaving his large estate to his wife; she a little later left it to their children. One of these, *Joseph*,[4] lived in Plympton many years, but rem. to North

Bridgewater. He m. Mary Stephens (see below). Their dau.
Mary m. Col. Frederick⁵Pope, of Stoughton.

RICHARD FOXWELL, taylor, was a member of that Puritan
church in London, whose pastor, Lothrop, with many members,
were imprisoned for meeting to worship in simple, Christian
ways. He came to Boston in 1630; was one of the earliest freemen of the colony; joined his former pastor and associates in
the colony and church at Scituate in 1634, and removed with
them to found Barnstable, 1639. Left a good name. Ann
Shelley, his second wife, came to Roxbury in 1632, was a member of that church, and later of the 1st church, Boston, until her
marriage in 1634. Their dau. Mary was b. Aug. 17, 1635.

EDWARD STEPHENS is first referred to in the town records of
Marshfield, Aug. 2, 1669. His lands are referred to May 30,
1677. His will, dated Nov. 2, 1689, prob. March 3, 1689-90,
makes his son William chief heir and executor; leaves 10£ to
his son Edward, at 21 years of age or marriage; to daughter
Elizabeth, at 18 or marriage, 8£ and some sheep and half of his
pewter; to daughter Patience, 8£ and the other half of his
pewter; commits his two youngest children to the care of
his "loving brother, John Sherman," and his son William, and
makes John Sherman the overseer of his will.

The inventory, amounting to 85£ 5s. 2d. (debts of 4£ 4s.),
included house, barn, land, farming outfit, household effects,
pewter, books, a gold ring, etc., and a "Loome and weavers'
Tackling."

William, son of Edward Stephens, is recorded as b. Dec. 18,
1666. "A son," whom some one has designated in a later hand
as *Edward*, is recorded b. Jan. 1, 1677-8.

Edward, jr., removed to Plymouth, m. Mary, dau. of Eleazer
and Mary Churchill, b. about 1788.

Their eldest daughter, Mary, was b. June 21, 1710, and m.
Joseph⁴ Cole, of Plympton. Edward, jr., in will July 14, 1756,
(prob. Jan. 3, 1656-7), names his wife Mary, daughters Mary
Cole, Hannah Bartlett, Sarah Sherman, and Elizabeth Harlow,
and sons Edward and Eleazer.

JOHN¹ CHURCHILL came to Plymouth in 1643, and m. Dec. 18,
1644, Hannah dau. of William Pontus. He bought land Aug.
18, 1645, was made freeman June 5, 1651; d. Jan. 1, 1662. His

widow had confirmed to her May 3, 1664, land which had been her father's.

Eleazer[2] Churchill, son of John and Hannah (Pontus) Churchill, b. April 20, 1652, m. Mary ——, and had a good number of children, of whom the seventh was Mary, b. 1688 or 9, who m. Edward[2] Stephens, jr.

WILLIAM PONTUS, in Plymouth in 1633, a freeman of the colony, and proprietor of considerable estate; he died Feb. 9, 1652.

THOMAS LETTICE (or *Lettis*) ·had lands assigned to him in Plymouth, Dec. 2, 1639 and May 5, 1640, and bought a tract of Thomas Cushman, March 24, 1641. He was admitted a freeman of Plymouth in 1643.

He was one of the six Plymouth men in the "jury to lay out the road from Joanes river to the Massachusetts path through John Rogers ground," June 10, 1650.

EDWARD GRAY came as a boy of fourteen to Plymouth, and made his way to a position of respectability and influence. He m. Dorothy, dau. of Thomas and Ann Lettice, Dec. 12, 1665. Their dau. Susanna became the wife of John Cole.

*[Additional to page 327.]*

The Pilgrim Ancestors of the Pope-Pierce line have been traced further since the writing of this paragraph, and can be seen in the pedigree chart which is attached to the books bound in 1892. So far as known, they are : (a) Pope, Ward, Lobdell, Stubbs, Pray, Neale; (b) Cole, Stephens, Churchill, Pontus, Foxwell, Gray, Lettice ; (c) Pierce, Cheney, Fessenden, Locke, Clarke, Grenaway, Fry, Tompson, Shepard ; (d) Blake, White, Bird, Simpson, Baker, Withington, Atherton, Clap (3 lines), Bachiler, Smith, Ford,—33 families.

*[Additional to page 327, foot-note.]*

Rev. John White is buried at *St. Peter's*, Dorchester.

[Page 199.]

ELIZABETH LAKE, b. May 13, 1792.

---

[Page 240.]

II.   HENRY TEMPLE[9] was b. in Dorchester.

---

[Page 242.]

II.   HENRY ARNOLD,[9] b. July 15, 1862.

---

[Additional to page 251.]

III.   WALTER BURNSIDE,[9] was m., by Rev. M. J. Savage, March 29, 1886, to Eva Margaret, dau. of James Strawbridge and Mary Agnes (Vetter) Maffitt, of Boston, b. in Pittsburg, Pa., July 23, 1860.   Child :

   1.   Gladys,[10] b. Aug. 27, d. Aug. 29, 1887.

---

[Page 256.]

VI.   RALPH LINDER[9].

---

[Page 208.]

   I.   ARTHUR KENDRICK,[10] b. June 9, 1879.
  II.   ELANOR BUSSEY,[10] b. July 19, 1884 ; d. Nov. 20, 1885.
 III.   KENNETH BUSSEY,[10] b. Nov. 30, 1885.

### A, 5.

   m. Emelyn Hardenburg, dau. of Josiah and Helen (Watson) Wilcox, b. Nov. 2, 1861.

[Additional to page 228.]

## NORTON QUINCY[3] POPE.

Born in Dayton, O., Jan. 7, 1844. At sixteen years of age became a commercial traveller. At twenty located in Louisville, Ky, in the real estate business. In 1873 moved to Chicago, Ill., where he entered into the grain business with Mr. John Hanscom and others. Was never connected in any way with the Board of Trade. Retired, after a successful career, in the spring of 1885, and removed to Brooklyn, N. Y., where he now resides.

Mr. John Hanscom, b. in Danville, Me., July 4, 1833. Went to Boston, Mass., in his boyhood, and remained there in business until 1872, when he removed to Chicago, Ill. He m. Miss Charlotte E. Pratt, dau. of Hon. Alpheus Pratt, of Raynham (Prattville). Their dau., Abby Ellen, b. in Raynham, May 13, 1858, was m. to Norton Quincy[8] Pope (above) June 8, 1887.

Norton Reed Sloan, son of J. R. and Jennie Mead[8] (Pope) Sloan, was b. in Dayton, O., Jan. 14, 1885.

---

[Page 208.]

Mr. Thomas Gardner came, in 1623, "to oversee the planting," and with him came Mr. John Tilley, "to oversee the fishing." Two years later Mr. Roger Conant was appointed to govern the colony, as the successor of Mr. Gardner. A year later the fisheries were abandoned altogether, and the "Western Adventurers," as the proprietors were called, dissolved partnership. Rev. John White and others of them joined the Massachusetts Bay Company, and continued to foster and mould the affairs of the colony thus begun. Mrs. Damaris Gardner, mentioned in her husband's will, dated Dec. 7, 1668, d. Nov. 28 before his decease, Dec. 29, 1674. Seeth Grafton's first husband was Joshua, son of Roger Conant.